and the ~~neat~~ ~~freight~~ effeant

glint in the [to]

his face jams ~~howard~~ ~~betta~~ ~~unkindly~~ ~~block~~

to the wrenched ~~it~~ away tin hat

blind ~~this way~~ this way that ~~this way~~.

nor ~~it~~ no ventaille ~~ventaille~~ to the ~~to~~ so

clambt ~~down & hard on~~ ~~but~~ dark inn . cross the morning

then stretch. still where weeds ~~rattens~~

~~the~~ chalk predella..

& Jy Quilt. takes over ~~Quilt~~

~~stilt him~~ ~~unkindly~~ ~~toatha~~ unkindly

~~toatha~~ ~~this~~ ~~away~~ ~~unkindly~~ to the

~~to tha~~ ~~airs tala~~ ~~this~~ ~~unkindly~~

wrenched over ~~tin away~~ tin-hat ~~the list~~.

~~they ata~~ fingering

blind ~~this way that~~ ~~this~~ ~~away~~ ~~fixing~~

~~this is na~~ ventaille ~~this~~. to the ~~to so~~

but ~~hard~~ ~~dark~~ cross the morning
                                    quite
then stretch ∧ still where weeds

chalk predella;

and by T. Quilt takes over.

David Jones

Engraver, Soldier, Painter, Poet

The Liturgical Parenthesis of David Jones
The Shape of Meaning in the Poetry of David Jones
Reading David Jones
David Jones in the Great War
Here Away (poetry)

David Jones, *Inner Necessities: the Letters of David Jones to Desmond Chute*
David Jones, *Wedding Poems*
S. T. Coleridge, *The Rime of the Ancient Mariner*, illustrated by David Jones
with Susan Holbrook, *The Letters of Gertrude Stein and Virgil Thomson*

DAVID JONES

Engraver, Soldier, Painter, Poet

Thomas Dilworth

JONATHAN CAPE

LONDON

1 3 5 7 9 10 8 6 4 2

Jonathan Cape, an imprint of Vintage,
20 Vauxhall Bridge Road,
London SW1V 2SA

Jonathan Cape is part of the Penguin Random House group of companies
whose addresses can be found at global.penguinrandomhouse.com

 Penguin
Random House
UK

First published by Jonathan Cape in 2017

penguin.co.uk/vintage

A CIP catalogue record for this book is available from the British Library

ISBN 9780224044608

Typset in India by Integra Software Services Pvt. Ltd, Pondicherry

Printed and bound in India by Replika Press Pvt. Ltd

for Alison, Molly, Christine, Zachary, Zoey

It is about how everything turns into something else & how you can never tell when a bonza is cropping up ... & how everything is a balls-up & a kind of 'Praise' at the same time.

David Jones

Contents

Preface

A latter-day British original, David Jones is *sui generis*. This and aversion to self-promotion limited his recognition as one of the foremost figures of modernism. If Beckett was the last great modernist, Jones was the lost great modernist. In scope of achievement, he resembles William Blake – both in the first rank of engravers, both eminent painters, both important poets, though Jones is the better painter and, arguably, a far greater poet. He wrote two of the best epic-length poems in English – *In Parenthesis* (1937) and *The Anathemata* (1952). Yet he has been omitted from academic discussions of modern poetry – even, in 1986, from a book on the modern long poem. This neglect was owing largely to his poetry being unusual. Ignoring lyric conventions (verse, metre, regular stanzas, brevity), it often even went unrecognised as poetry.* And it is generally regarded as difficult, vast in vocabulary and range of reference, requiring rereading. T. S. Eliot, W. H. Auden, Basil Bunting, and Hugh MacDiarmid considered it, as does W. S. Merwin, among the best writing of the twentieth century. Most of Jones's paintings are subtle and complex, impossible to appreciate at a glance, but Kenneth Clark thought him the best modern painter.¹ Few have read his essays on aesthetics and culture, yet they have been recognised by Kenneth Clark, Harold Rosenberg, W. H. Auden, and Guy Davenport as important to understanding modern culture and civilisation.

Here is a little of what some have said or written of Jones and his work. Eric Gill placed him 'in the first rank of modern artists'. Kenneth Clark thought him 'absolutely unique, a remarkable genius'. T. S. Eliot called *In Parenthesis* 'a work of genius'. W. H. Auden considered it 'the greatest book about the First World War'. The military historian Michael Howard called it 'the most remarkable work of literature to emerge from either world war'. The novelist and poet Adam Thorpe wrote, 'It towers above any other prose or verse memorial of . . . any war'. Graham Greene ranked it as 'one of the great poems of the century', Herbert Read called it 'one of the most remarkable literary achievements of our time'. Of *The Anathemata*, Auden wrote, it is 'very probably the finest long poem written in English in this century'. Seamus Heaney described Jones's *The Sleeping Lord* (1974) as 'enrich[ing] not only the language but people's consciousness of who they have been and consequently are'. T. S. Eliot considered Jones 'of major importance', 'one of the most distinguished writers of my generation'. Igor

---

* Poetry is language used to its fullest potential, whether or not written in short verse lines.

Stravinsky thought him 'a writer of genius'. Dylan Thomas said, 'I would like to have done anything as good as David Jones has done'. Hugh MacDiarmid publicly pronounced Jones 'the greatest native British poet of the century'. W. S. Merwin considers him 'one of the greatest twentieth century poets in English'. About Jones's essays on culture, Harold Rosenberg wrote, 'He formulated the axiomatic precondition for understanding contemporary creation.' And Guy Davenport wrote, 'He realised for us the new configuration, which only our time can see, into which culture seems to be shaped, and the historical processes that shaped it.'[2]

PART ONE

BEGINNINGS

At 8.54 on the cold, foggy evening of 1 November 1895, he was born into an argument. His Welsh father, Jim Jones, wanted to name him after his own dead younger brother, David. His English mother, Alice, wanted to name him 'Dorian', after the protagonist of Oscar Wilde's novel. Jim protested against any association with Wilde, whose trials in the spring had been a public scandal. She said, 'I do not care what was said about Wilde. *The Importance of Being Earnest* is the most brilliant and certainly the most amusing play ever written. I dislike the name Oscar, and, therefore, Dorian *it shall be*!' Jim nevertheless persisted, and eventually she conceded that 'Dorian' might be unwise. But she then insisted on 'Walter', probably (since not a family name) in homage to recently deceased Walter Pater. 'David' could be his middle name.[1] The child would later insist on being called David, and that is what I will call him, though for most of his childhood he was Walter.

His father was thirty-five years old, a printer's overseer for the *Christian Herald*, the son of a North Welsh plasterer and builder, John, and Sarah (née Jones), both descendants of North Welsh stonemasons and farmers. Jim's natal family was Anglican, anglophile, monarchist, and Conservative. His parents spoke only Welsh to each other, allowing their eight children to speak Welsh or English as they liked, except for Jim, their eldest son, who, to ensure worldly success, was allowed to speak only English. Consequently, he was not fluent in Welsh. Usually calm and with 'inward strength', Jim was gentle, generous, humble, and affectionate but had a fiery temper. He smiled easily and often, had a ready sense of humour, and laughed uproariously. An open-air speaker for the parish of St James, Hatcham, he spoke publicly with ease in any circumstance. Soon after moving to London from Holywell in 1884, he had begun teaching Sunday school in Rotherhithe, where he met tiny, auburn-haired Alice Ann Bradshaw, with dark brown eyes. She was six years older.[2] On 20 September 1888, they married.

Alice was descended from carpenters and shipwrights. Her father, Ebenezer Bradshaw, had been a master mast-and-block maker during the height of Victorian Thames-side prosperity. He was handsome and his wife, Ann Elizabeth, beautiful. She was the daughter of a boatbuilder, Joseph Mockford, and a Piedmontese beauty maiden-named Vergado. Eb's workshop was east of Cherry Garden Stairs in Rotherhithe, its yard running down to the river. He was a devout Anglican – for forty years parish clerk of St Mary, Rotherhithe – but, his daughter Alice said, 'very Protestant'. He nicknamed her 'Hard Nails'. As a girl she took her own boat onto the Thames and later boasted, 'I could row better than any man.' Fully grown, she was 4 feet 5 inches tall, replying tartly to comments on her size, 'Little and good, like Zacchaeus!' Nervously energetic, with quick intelligence and wit, she conversed well but was anxious, prickly, impatient with those she considered fools and liable to flay them with her tongue. According to her grandson, Tony Hyne, she was 'quite a Tartar'. Emotionally undemonstrative, she was embarrassed by any show of affection. She had been a teacher for twelve years at the School of Industry in Rotherhithe, instructing older children in all subjects, including drawing, at which she excelled. Then, in 1878, she trained in Oxford to be a governess. Under the influence of the Oxford Movement, she became theologically High Church, 'bowing and scraping', a nephew, Maurice Bradshaw, recalled, until her evangelical family 'knocked that nonsense out of her'. She became headmistress of Christ Church School and helped with Sunday school. In her fifth year as headmistress, Jim Jones courted her, frequently visiting the Bradshaw home with his brother David, who loved Alice's sister Dolly. David and Dolly intended to marry, but he died in 1887 of typhoid fever while teaching on the Isle of Wight. Alice would retain her High Church doctrinal convictions but in practice deferred to Jim's evangelicalism. She admired his lack of worldly ambition but, caring about social distinctions, disliked his addressing meetings of Nonconformists because 'those people have not Holy Orders – and anyway half of them are grocers'.[3]

Jim and Alice began married life in her father's house at 11 Princess Street, in a row of the grandest Georgian houses in Rotherhithe. Here their first son was born in 1889, Harold Thomas Peart, and, two years later, a daughter, Alice Mary, called Cissy. Eb Bradshaw died in Jim's arms of a heart attack in 1891, and the Joneses moved with his sixty-eight-year-old widow into a terraced house at number 1 Arabin Road (fig. 1) in Brockley, south-east of London. Four years later, upstairs in the master bedroom, their third and last child was born and contentiously named. When he was three, they moved west along Arabin Road to number 67.

The family was artisan lower-middle-class. Housemaids in black dresses, white caps, and aprons came to do the housework. Alice suffered from indigestion and ate very little

1. Arabin Road

and only bland food – boiled chicken, fish, rice, stewed fruit – which is what the family also ate.[4]

Jim and Alice gave their children a strict upbringing. She enforced discipline with a thin bamboo cane called the 'tickley-toe', whacking the hand of a child resting elbows on the table or improperly holding a fork. She was, her daughter remembered, 'a tyrant' in the house. Seeing David take a halfpenny from a chest of drawers, she gravely warned, 'That way lies the gallows', words he never forgot. He was spanked but rarely by his father, who was mild, gentler than Alice, and, unlike her, quick to show affection. The children called him 'Dad', her 'Mother'.[5]

She was less strict with David. He was her favourite and, Cissy later said, 'spoiled'. When he was indulged, his brother, Harold, muttered, 'It's always little Benjamin's mess', alluding to Genesis 43:34, in which 'Benjamin's mess [portion] was five times' that of any of his brothers. The rebuke stung.[6]

Harold and Cissy resented him. He was, she said, 'a nuisance … always crying and grizzling'. Ordered to take him in a pushchair to the Hilly Fields, a nearby park, they sat him in the wet grass hoping he would catch cold and be kept indoors. A few years later, they put a firework down his jumper, burning his neck and back. April Fools tricks were, David would remember, 'cruel and violent'. And there were accidents. Re-enacting the escape of St Paul from Damascus (Acts 9:25), Harold and Cissy lowered him from an upstairs window in a laundry basket. The bottom gave way but close enough to the ground to prevent serious injury to the apostle to the Gentiles.[7]

The children called Alice's mother Granny Brad.* She sat in a chair in the corner, wearing a buttoned black Dickensian dress. In mid-July when 'Lavender: Who'll buy my sweet lavender?' was sung in the streets, she would say, 'Winter is not far off.' After Christmas, she said, 'As the light lengthens, so the cold strengthens.' David later thought that her 'gloomy forebodings' contributed to his own 'apprehensive psychology'. She became senile, acting oddly at meals and wandering the house at night. He found her behaviour unnerving. Twice he was caught shaking his fist at her – the first time he was warned; the second, he received 'a real whacking'. She died at the age of 78 in the autumn of 1907, when he was twelve.[8]

On Sundays, they visited or were visited by Alice's relatives, including her aunts and uncles, who were, he later said, 'absolutely pure "Dickensian"'. The language of nautical commerce suffused their conversation and would emerge decades later in his poetry. He knew best his Great-uncle Jack Mockford, a maritime engineer who had made the family proud and himself

---

* She is mistakenly identified as an aunt by W. Blissett, *Long*, p. 123, and J. Miles and D. Shiel, *Maker Unmade*, p. 269.

wealthy by inventing a device to improve steam-navigation which was exhibited in the South Kensington Museum. Once or twice David visited his riverside workshop. His Dickensian elders were also Dickensians, speaking of Dickens characters as though living acquaintances. Their chief poet was Robert Browning.[9]

David's language had its deepest roots in nursery rhymes, songs, and stories. 'Three Blind Mice' was the first song his mother sang to him – it would surface in his poetry (*A* 60) – another was 'Johnny's so long at the Fair' (*IP* 43, 49). She told stories of the Norman kings including Henry I, whose elder brother died in a hunting accident and who, after his son perished in the foundering of the *White Ship*, never smiled again. (Deaths of brothers and sons would soon have special meaning for David.)[10]

His first vivid memory was of being awakened from a nap in his cot beside his parents' bed by noise in the road. Slipping to the floor and lifting a slat of the venetian blinds, he saw cavalry riding in column in a cloud of dust and heard, above the clatter of hooves, bugles. It was January 1900. The Boer War had begun, and the City Imperial Volunteers were on recruitment parade. His mother arrived and lifted him back into his cot. 'Who are they?' he asked. She said, 'You'll know soon enough.' Persisting, he asked whether they were guardian angels. (He had heard a friend of hers mention guardian angels and his father say there was no warrant for them in scripture.) Before falling asleep, the distant bugles convinced him that the riders were indeed angels. He now wanted someday to ride a horse.*

His second vivid memory was of being awakened on the night of 16 May 1900 by a frightening noise and explosive light – a motor car, the first of his experience, come to take his father to insert news of the relief of Mafeking on the front page of the morning paper.[11]

That summer he would sit in the garden beneath a pear tree on a small log of lignum vitae from his grandfather's workshop. At the bottom of the garden was a wall he liked. From its top and through a hole in the brickwork, he enjoyed watching a fruiter's horses stabled on the other side.[12]

At the age of five, he was moved into his brother's bedroom, where, on a wall map of the Transvaal, Harold pinned tiny Union Jacks to mark places captured by the British. David became aware of the strain between his father, who opposed the war, and other relatives – one of them his mother's brother Ebenezer, who, pounding the table, declared, 'Jim, you're a Little Englander!' David saw pictures of the war and the far reaches of the empire in newspapers and magazines that inundated the house. His father brought

* While reading *The Mabinogion* in adolescence, he would be struck by the similarity between his early experience and that of young Peredur (Percival), who sees knights ride by and asks his mother what they are. Not wanting him to leave home to be a knight, she says, 'They are angels', and he says, 'I will go and become an angel with them.'

these home each weekend from the printing office. David's was, he later said, a 'Kipling-conditioned world'.[13]

His parents subscribed to the Books for Bairns series of monthly volumes, of which his favourite was *King Arthur and the Knights of the Round Table* (September 1899). Of its stories, he liked best 'Prince Geraint and Fair Enid', in which Geraint avenges Guinevere by defeating a knight who is a bully and a thief. David's mother read them aloud to him, and he paid his sister a penny an hour to read them.[14]

After teaching him the alphabet with difficulty, his mother sent him to a series of children's schools in nearby houses. In one of these, he fell in love with a young teacher, from whom he began learning to read and write and add. Subtraction eluded him. Wearing her hair in two long plaits, she asked whether if she wore her hair in a bun that would be 'a plus or a minus in plaits'. Failing to understand, he wept, but she was kind. The school soon closed, and then he 'vaguely understood what was meant by "minus two plaits"'.[15]

*   *   *

Shops delivered groceries. In the street passed church parades, organ-grinders with dancing monkeys, a man with a donkey offering children a ride for a penny, and a man with a bear dancing at the end of a leash – for David, 'a horrible' sight. Peddlers filled the air with cries. The 'heavenly' singsong, 'Lavender: Who'll buy my sweet lavender?' held him spellbound – it would bracket the central monologue of his long poem *The Anathemata* (125, 168). Until he was five or six, a dancing Jack o' the Green appeared on May Day at the door, frightening him – the green man would later emerge in his poetry (*IP* 168; *SL* 68). David bowled an iron hoop, which his mother considered a 'regrettable . . . low class habit' and allowed only in the garden. Stilts were in vogue – he found them difficult. Bicycles were popular, and he learned to ride one.[16]

Not yet part of greater London, Brockley was an unfinished housing development. Near Crofton Park station were remnants of a farm, including stiles on which he climbed to improve his view. Behind the pub across from Brockley Hall were open fields and a scattering of houses under construction. To the south were fields of wheat; to the north open space, with a brickfield between Brockley and Wickham Roads and a blacksmith's shop, where he took his hoop to be soldered and watched the smith shoe horses. Farther north, New Cross was open country. At the east end of Arabin Road was a yard with chickens; across the road, a builder's yard. On Easter and Whitsun his father hired an open carriage to take the family into the country. David was impressed by how near the country was. A short walk south along Brockley Road and east along Adelaide Avenue, the Hilly Fields was a green area nearly a half-mile square rising high above the roofs of bordering houses.

As a schoolboy and later, he would go there alone and with friends. From its height he could look south to the bare green hills of Kent and south-east to the towers of the Crystal Palace and, at night, the weekly fireworks display there. To the north-east, he could see Blackheath and the southern slope of the hill of Greenwich Park, and far to the north-west the dome of St Paul's.[17] This was his native hill, the height of his earliest imagining, the familiar prototype of the ancient hills with maternal guardian spirits celebrated later in his poetry (*A* 55–8; *SL* 59–69). Only in 1910 with the felling of the elms lining Brockley Road to accommodate tramlines would Brockley lose its feeling of being in the country. The matrix of his spatial imagination was this semi-rural zone of metamorphosis.

* * *

His mother took him into London. He loved the Thames and its shipping. In 1903 she introduced him to the British Museum. His father took him to visit his office in Tudor Street, off Fleet Street, where he talked with the Cockney compositors. He visited the office of his Uncle Ebenezer, who manufactured paper in Great St Thomas Apostle Street near the river, an area David later remembered as having 'the atmosphere of Dickensian London'.[18]

Apart from excursions into the city, his mother disliked 'going places'. When Jim received an offer of a better job in the United States and wanted to emigrate, she refused. (David later wondered what he would have been like as an American.) Jim wanted to travel during his two-week holidays, but she preferred staying home, so they did, sometimes taking short trips to the seaside.[19]

When David was four or five, the family visited Deal, where he first saw, at the far end of a narrow street, the taut blue horizon of the sea. It stirred in him 'a distinct emotion' he never forgot. Astride a cannon in the ruins of Sandown Castle north of town, he gazed at the Channel and, when weather and the tide were right, the wrecks on the Goodwin Sands, to which he would refer in his poetry (*A* 110). The family travelled to Herne Bay, Tankerton, and, in the summer of 1899, Littlehampton, where they had a family photograph taken (fig. 2), the grouping suggesting the closeness between David and his mother.[20]

* * *

David was brought up on the Authorised Version of the Bible and the Book of Common Prayer. He heard scripture read in Sunday school, at church, and at home, where his father read favourite passages 'in his best manner'. (On Sunday evenings, Jim also read aloud from *The Pilgrim's Progress*, which impressed David 'a good bit', and, on Christmas mornings, Milton's 'Hymn

2. Jim, Harold, Cissy, David, Alice Ann Jones, 1899

on the Morning of Christ's Nativity'.)²¹ His father made lists of scriptural passages for family members to read prayerfully each day. David would know scripture better than any other important modern writer, being able to quote it from memory easily and at length.

He liked looking at Keble's *Christian Year*, illustrated by Johann Friedrich Overbeck.²² He paged through the weekly tabloid his father worked on, the *Christian Herald and Signs of our Times* – an ecumenical paper except for marked antipathy to 'Romish and Ritualistic influence'.

Evangelising kept his father busy. For a time he travelled, selling Bibles. With a *hwyll* (the high-pitched monotone of Welsh preachers), he preached on weekends to small audiences on Clapham Common and Peckham Rye, where the family sometimes accompanied him and picnicked. (David heard him call people to Jesus in the field where young William Blake had seen a tree spangled with angels.) Four evenings a week, his father took part in mission meetings – in Church of England Mission Halls, Deptford lodging houses, and Nonconformist halls – for which he acted in turn as speaker, leader, secretary, and organiser.

Jim brought five- or six-year-old David to a meeting, sat him on a chair at the back of the speaker's platform, told him to stay put, and commenced preaching. Unnoticed by his father, David, wriggling, got his head stuck in the double loop of the chair-back. Attendants removed the chair-and-boy and, unable to separate them, one said, 'We'll have to get a saw.' Horrified, David thought they were going to cut off his head. The man returned and, without explaining what he was doing, sawed through the top of the chair-back, freeing him. (His father had to pay for the chair.)[23]

On Good Friday afternoon when David was six or seven, playing alone in the garden, he tore up two wooden slats bordering a flower bed and (after accidently breaking pots in the garden shed) nailed them together to form a cross. Holding it aloft, he was carrying it round the garden when his father came upon him. Pale with rage, he lectured David about doing such damage 'on this most solemn day of the Christian year' and, with patient fury, explained that parading round holding up a cross was the sort of thing 'people called Catholics' do 'but true Christians do not'. For punishment David was sent to bed, broken-hearted at his father's failure to appreciate his intention. Afterwards, Jim asked his wife, 'Where did the boy pick up such a papistical and Puseyite idea?'[24]*

For David, Jesus would always be 'our Lord'. Religion contributed to his formation in many positive ways, as when he overheard his mother ask the family doctor, a Yorkshire Quaker, why Quakers have no sacraments. And the doctor replied, 'But Mrs. Jones, surely the whole of life is a sacrament.' David remembered his words and, as an adult agreed with them. But religion also encouraged psychologically toxic guilt feelings. At home the family sang a hymn including the words, 'I wake I sin, I sleep I sin, I sin in every breath.'[25]

* * *

With his mother's encouragement and example (some of her framed red-crayon drawings hung in the house), he began drawing, drew well, and was praised for it. By the age of five, he was making pictures obsessively. After aunts took him to a Royal Academy summer exhibition of animal drawings, he began drawing animals. Seeing that he was good at it, his mother took him to Regent's Park Zoo to draw mainly the big cats, antelope, and deer.[26] In 1901 he made a large picture (18 by 18 inches) of a truncated leopard backing away from a tiger (fig. 3), an astonishing achievement for a five-year-old, and the media – ink, wash, and white body paint – surprisingly sophisticated. At the age of seven he quickly sketched from the front window a bear dancing at the end of a leash, finishing the drawing from memory (fig. 4). (To get the fence slats straight, he borrowed a ruler from his sister, who said, 'No real artist would use a ruler.' He thought, 'blow what a real artist would do', and ignored her.) The drawing is large (20

---

* 'Puseyite', derogatory term for an idea or member of the Oxford Movement, after one of its leading tractarians, Edward Pusey.

3. *Tiger and Leopard*, 1901

4. *The Bear*, 1903

by 11 inches), the work of a prodigy. In 1958, he would hang it over his mantel and write to a friend, 'It's much the best drawing I've ever done, which shows how, in the arts, there ain't no such thing as getting better as you get older!'[27]

Adding enthusiasm to his mother's encouragement and providing large sheets of paper, his father thought that David's drawing might lead to a career in journalistic art. In 1902, he enrolled him in the Cork International Exhibition and the Royal Drawing Society's Revival of Youthful Art League, which commended him for a drawing. In 1903, *The Bear* and a drawing of a roaring lion were 'Highly Commended', and the *Morning Advertiser* singled him out as noteworthy for his 'series of wild animals'.[28] In the autumn of 1903, after visiting the zoo, he drew from memory a lion, a rhinoceros, and an elephant – drawings that his father sent to the *Daily News*, where they were engraved and published in the 'Children's Corner' (fig. 5).

He made a painting for the family Christmas card for 1904 which his father had photographically reproduced in pale green (fig. 6), its lettering and floriate border erratically alive.*

When David was eleven or twelve, the quality of his drawing declined, owing to the appeal of realism (the nemesis of all children's art) and the influence of the publications that flooded the home

* Other impressive early work is reproduced in J. Miles and D. Shiel, *Maker Unmade*, p. 15.

5. Sketches, *Daily News*, 19 October 1903

6. Christmas card, 1904

with perfunctory, lifeless illustrations. Equally baleful was the influence of old Royal Academy catalogues and tasteless praise by relatives and teachers. As he later said, his artistic ability was 'practically destroyed'. Such a fall from grace happens to most children who draw. Spontaneity gives way to imitation as eagerly, proudly, inevitably they exit aesthetic Eden. Still drawing continually, he produced little of merit. Among his last impressive childhood works, done in 1906, is a painting of a wolf in

7. *Wolf in Snow*, 1906

a snowy mountainous setting (fig. 7). His mother hung it along with *The Bear* in the sitting room.[29]

Alice did not share her husband's optimism about David having a career as a journalistic illustrator. During trips into the city, whenever she and David passed a pavement artist, she invariably dropped a coin into the artist's cup or extended hand. David asked, 'Why do you give to all regardless of the quality of their work?' She said, 'That is my business, and anyway we are obliged to give to the poor.' Years later she confessed to fearing that if he continued drawing he, too, would end up in the gutter.[30] For his sake she was giving alms in the spirit of sympathetic magic.

* * *

At the age of seven, David began attending Brockley Road School, half a mile south of the family home. He joined an unruly class of nearly sixty junior boys and was, he later said, 'appallingly bad' at lessons. In compensation he drew and painted more. He could not read with ease until he was nine and would remain a slow reader – at the age of 69 saying about reading, 'it takes . . . time for things to sink in'.[31]

At school and at home he read history. He learned about the Roman conquest of Britain and was made to memorise Cowper's poem about Boudicca, the 'British warrior-queen/Bleeding from the Roman rods'.* He probably read in *Stories from Ancient Rome* (Books for Bairns, May 1901) about the fall of Troy, the founding twins, the attack on Rome by Gauls – all strands woven into *The Anathemata* and later poems. He read Kipling's *Puck of Pook's Hill* (1906), which influenced him deeply – its phrases and episodes echo in his poetry† – and its sequel *Rewards and Fairies*. All this history and historical imagining deeply impressed him, partly because he had been to Deal, where Caesar had landed, and partly because London was originally a Roman town. As half British-Celt, three-eighths English, and one-eighth Italian, he embodied the genetic imprint of his nation's history.[32]

Chauvinism distorted the history he learned. He was taught, for example, that the British fought the Hundred Years War against 'the tyrant's

---

* When, in 1961, *The Times* published an article praising Boudicca for giving 'the Anglo-Saxons something to boast about at an extremely thin time in their history', he sent a letter asking what 'this Celtic queen' had to do with Anglo-Saxons and hoping that, in Hilaire Belloc's words, 'the truth might be allowed to prevail a bit'.

† These echoes include the beer 'metheglin' (*SL* 55), 'Vecta Insula' (*A* 110), Phoenicians sailing to Britain to procure tin (*A* 97–108), and Romans serving on Hadrian's Wall (*RQ* 64–83).

yoke' and won it on the strength of victories at Crécy and Agincourt but not that the French subsequently reconquered. He imbibed Victorian admiration of the Romans as forerunners of the imperial British in spreading enlightened civilisation. On Empire day, he and his schoolmates sang Kipling's 'Recessional', about imperialism being virtuous if humble and contrite. He read the patriotic stories in the Union Jack Library. A naval commander addressed the student body on 'the Bull-dog breed' and 'the Union Flag in very hot, and very cold places' and 'how the sea was free'. History lessons stressed 'the Inquisition and the habitual cruelty of foreign nations'.[33]

By the age of eight, David was devoted to Nelson, whose death was the most poignant historical moment in popular imagination – emphasised by the centenary celebrations of Trafalgar in 1905. In the upper Painted Hall of the Royal Naval College at Greenwich, he repeatedly saw the objects handled by the admiral and the uniform in which he had died. To view these relics, David several times walked from Brockley across Blackheath – with its, to him, 'heavenly deer' – a distance of two and a half miles. (He enjoyed walking.) In his hero-worshipping he was torn between Nelson, later criticised and commemorated in his poetry (*WP* 38; *A* 114), and Owen Glendower.[34]

At school David was unable to memorise multiplication tables. When his teacher brusquely challenged him with 'Seven sevens', he ventured a guess and covered his head because she hit him when he was wrong, as he usually was. (No wonder, as an adult, he could not easily count by tens.) Neither did he learn to spell well. This was a special irritant at home. His proofreading father spelled perfectly, and his mother – 'very hot on spelling', David later remembered – was particularly 'horrified' at his misspelling common words. Anxious about this fault, she tutored him, and, with the help of Butter's *Etymological Spelling Book and Expositor* (1878), he made progress but still tended to spell phonetically. His adult writing contains 'desease', 'desasterous', 'devision', 'devine', 'rediculous', 'ribbonds', 'peninsular' (the noun), and 'aspedister' (the plant) – 'Passchendaele' defeated him. He would always regard his faulty spelling as 'an awful curse', exclaiming near the end of his life, 'Great God, *how* I wish I could spell.'[35]

He was academically inept for the same reason he was artistically gifted: the right hemisphere of the brain, which thinks and imagines spatially, was dominant rather than the left hemisphere, which thinks and imagines temporally. Left-brain people are proficient at mathematics, enjoy music, read early, quickly, and easily, are highly articulate, spell well, but are (usually without realising) visually imperceptive. Jones was the opposite. His speech would always be hesitant, groping. Apart from his father's singing in Welsh and a madrigal called 'Livia's Frock', he did not, as a child, care for music.[36]

'Physically feeble', he 'loathed' and avoided organised games. But he may have joined in dancing round the schoolyard maypole draped with ribbons which dancers interwove, unwove, and rewove round the pole – imagery that emerges in his poetry (*A* 243; *SL* 61) and suggests a paradigm for its interwoven texture.[37]

He had loved 'Here we go round the mulberry bush'. Now he participated in a circle-chant that began slowly and accelerated until the reciters became breathless or confused: 'It was a dark and stormy night, the brigands sat round their camp fire, the chief said to Antonio, "Antonio, tell us a tale", and the tale ran thus: "It was a dark & stormy night, the brigands sat round their camp fire . . ."'[38]

Encouraged by teachers to visit historical sites, with a class-six school friend David went to the Tower of London and Westminster Abbey, where, at the age of twelve (careful that no one was looking), he spat on the tomb of Edward I, conqueror of Wales.[39]

By the age of seven, David had felt strong affinity with Wales. At a boarding-house table during a seaside holiday, his father had spoken about failing to get a job requiring fluency in Welsh because *Taid* (grandfather) had forbidden him to speak it. David announced, '*Taid* was a bloody old bastard.' His father whisked him away and told him that, though he did not know the meaning of those awful words, picked up from older boys, he had to be punished 'for offending against man and God' – he told the story of Elisha who, jeered at by boys, prayed to Jehovah, who sent two bears to devour them (2 Kings 2:23–5). David said, '*Taid* was a bloody old bastard and Jehovah isn't any better.' A spanking ensued.[40]

David's Uncle Ebenezer and four cousins, who lived nearby in Wickham Road, were aware of his attachment to Wales and, when playing a children's version of rugby in the garden, infuriated him by taunting, 'Don't you try any of your Welsh tricks.'[41]

In one respect at least, his affinity was political. He was, like his father, a Lloyd George enthusiastic and sent him a fan letter, to which the Chancellor replied on 23 December 1910, thanking 'Mr. W. David Jones for his good wishes'. One of his teachers would remember him as 'a worshipper of Lloyd George'.[42]

*   *   *

His mother was not entirely happy in her marriage. Jim suffered by comparison to her handsome and capable father, with whom she remained enamoured. And her brother earned more and lived in a bigger house. Regarding the English as superior, she spoke of the Welsh scornfully as 'country people', joked about 'Welsh heathens', and would say, 'That's your father, born half way up a mountain with the back door open.' In later years when Jim was late for tea, she would, in the presence of grandchildren, call him an 'old fat head'. Moreover, she was devoid of domestic interests and frustrated at not working outside the home. (No middle-class wives then did.) Having delayed marriage, she had become used to independence and responsibility. Now, watching children on their way to and from school, she wished she was their teacher.

For her, David's company made the house less a prison. At the slightest sign or attestation of illness, she allowed him to stay home from school. He liked her attention. Sickness got it, and that conditioned him to be ill and malinger. Later in life, he would stay in bed for weeks with colds that would keep few from going out to work.[43]

Her concern for his health was genuine. He was thin, small, and prone to respiratory ailments; and she feared tuberculosis, which had killed her sister Dolly, and afflicted her brother. So when her younger son had a cold, she put him to bed and pumped steam at him. Her habitual response to illness was, 'Be *sure* and stay in bed – & be still for a while.' As a consequence, he spent much of his childhood in bed drawing and reading – whereas, ill or not, Cissy was sent to school and resented it. Even in 1908 when the family moved to 128 Howson Road, shortening the walk to school to a few hundred yards, he stayed home as often as possible. He missed so much school that he could later say with some truth, 'I had no education.'[44]

In their long conversations, Alice recreated her Thames-side childhood in Rotherhithe, which, when David was eight, 'seemed an almost mythological world'. She spoke of the technical details of shipbuilding and enacted her father and uncles speaking of sight-drafts, brokerage, bonded goods, and harbour dues. (Years later the phrase 'C.i.f. London documents: at sight' in *The Waste Land*, line 211, would instantly evoke for him the world of the Pool of London as his mother had spoken of it.) She regaled him with family anecdotes in which her father figured large and her mother hardly at all. She praised her father's integrity as a workman and related an argument about repairs to a ship bearing sulphur from Sicily that would inform the 'Redriff' section of *The Anathemata* (118–21). She spoke of the churches and wards of the city, as would 'the Lady of the Pool' at the centre of that poem (124–68).[45] Her description of family prosperity declining as metal steamships replaced wooden sailing vessels made him aware for the first time of momentous technological changes transforming the world.

David's parents were both, he later said, 'very wonderful people … absolutely marvellous'. His relationship to them enriched him imaginatively. He drew and painted largely to please his mother. This may be reflected in his 'always' finding 'so moving' the medieval story of the tumbler who, lacking other gifts, performed acrobatics before the Blessed Mother.[46] His father also valued his artistic gift and modelled love of language. David would psychologically negotiate his relationship with his parents through his visual art and, later, his writing – in which he would revere maternal figures and find complementary value in male saviour-figures, though never with comparable lyricism.

*   *   *

During his first eight years, the family did not visit Wales. His mother got on badly with her in-laws. When they visited, she would leave the sitting room and bustle about the kitchen, banging saucepans and slamming doors. There may also have been moral disapproval of Jim's father cohabiting (since 1891) with his dead wife's sister Eleanor without benefit of marriage. Eleanor died in 1903, and in 1904 the Jones family visited North Wales.[47]

David first saw Wales at the end of an all-night train journey, waking to his father saying, 'Well, here you are now.' To his right, the coastal flats of the estuary of the Dee extended to the sea horizon; to his left rose hills and, beyond, mountains appearing and disappearing in the mist. It was a life-changing moment, for which he was well prepared. Among his earliest memories were his father beautifully singing – *Ar Hyd y Nos* ('All Through the Night'), *Aderyn Pur* ('The Pure Bird'), *Dafydd y Garreg Wen* ('David of the White Rock'), and the national anthem, *Mae Hen Wlad Fy Nhadau* ('Land of

8. David Jones reclining; behind him Effie Tozer and parents; back right, Harold and Cissy, c. 1910

My Fathers') – filling David with pride and 'awe'. Jim had no close Welsh friend and belonged to no society of London Welshmen but was proud of being Welsh. He told his children stories of his native Gwynedd (Flintshire), and conveyed a sense of place in which his identity was rooted. David found that the 'otherness' of this place, seen for the first time, left 'an indelible mark on the soul'.[48]

The family stayed at Llandrillo-yn-Rhos, later called Rhos-on-Sea, on the western point of Colwyn Bay, with Jim's older sister, Elizabeth, and her husband, James Tozer, a pawnbroker (see fig. 8). (Alice said he could speak English and Welsh out of the two sides of his mouth simultaneously.) The Tozers' two daughters, Effie and Gladys, were determined to be as English as possible. Close to David in age, Effie told him that his interest in Welsh history and language was 'crazy'.[49]

He and Effie played by the sea, often squeezing into St Trillo's Chapel there (fig. 9), a sixteenth-century building on the site of a sixth-century oratory. In its dank, cobwebbed darkness was a shallow, gravel-bottomed 'holy well' filled with cool fresh water. He thought it 'marvellous' that the spring at the edge of the sea should be free of the taste of salt. Just offshore was a fishing weir, 630 yards long and 9 feet high, constructed in the twelfth century by Cistercian monks and still in use. David loved its rough wattling.[50]

Behind Rhos on *Bryn Euryn* (Hill of Gold), the Joneses and Tozers picnicked in the overgrown ruins of *Llys Euryn* (Golden Court), originally the thirteenth-century fortified manor house of the chief minister of Llywelyn the Great (fig. 10). Eight-year-old David sat in these vine-covered ruins

9. St Trillo's Chapel, c. 1900

10. Ruined manor house on *Bryn Euryn*

thinking 'a lot' about Llywelyn and his minister.[51] At the top of the hill, from a circular Stone Age fort, David could view Rhos, the immensity of Colwyn Bay, Conwy Valley, and the craggy summits of Snowdonia.

He met his Welsh grandfather, tall, now bent and using a cane. As they sat together on a bench near St Trillo's Chapel, David's resentment against *Taid* evaporated. The chapel, its holy well, the fishing weir, the ruins of *Llys Euryn*, and his Welsh-speaking grandfather combined powerfully to link him with an ancient past. A few years later he would associate the weir with Gwyddno's weir in the Taliesin story and his grandfather with King Maelgwyn the Tall, whose principal seat had been nearby, and with Llywarch Hen, who uses a walking stick in Middle Welsh poetry.[52] His grandfather died in 1909 before they could meet again. Rhos was, for David, an enchanted place.

Back in Brockley, while listening to his father sing, he felt a 'passionate conviction' that he belonged to his father's people without understanding why. Cissy showed some interest in Wales, Harold none. When David was nine or ten, he read his brother's copy of J. F. Hodgetts' *Harold the Boy-Earl* (undated, *c.* 1890) and wrote 'furiously all over it in uninformed, passionate disagreement' with its Germanophile bias for Anglo-Saxons and against Celts. Did his fury reflect rivalry with his brother, who felt entirely English and shared the boy-earl's name? Coinciding with nine-year-old David's determination to be an artist, his identification with Wales seems partly to have been compensation to his father for attachment to his mother, which underlay drawing. Indicating this was his renouncing at the age of nine the name 'Walter' – the choice, he knew, of his mother – because it was Saxon. Now he answered only to 'David'. By his eleventh year, the name

'Walter' shrank to the initial 'W', which would vanish in his early twenties. Becoming David was also a way of abrogating his nickname since infancy, which was 'Toady' (as he spelled it) and originated, he was convinced, in Harold insisting that as an infant David resembled a toad.[53] Being 'David' was Oedipal compensation and a minor victory in sibling rivalry.

On visits to North Wales, David was encouraged in his enthusiasm for Wales by the vicar of St George's Church, Thomas Evans Timothy, a classicist and Welsh patriot, avidly interested in the antiquities of his parish. He urged David to learn Welsh and read the Welsh poets. In 1910 Timothy was transferred to Raegs-y-cae, a hamlet near Holywell. David and his father visited him there, and Timothy spoke to David of local fighting in 1149 to win back for Wales what had been part of English Mercia for centuries. At the wall of the vicarage garden, Timothy pointed out hills that David's father had often mentioned as landmarks of his boyhood: *Moel Famau* (Hill of the Mothers), *Foel-y-Crio* (Hill of the Cry), and *Moel Arthur*. He also identified *Moel Ffagnallt*, which he said meant Hill of Dereliction.[54] They impressed David as a kind of poem in place. By the time he commemorated them in *The Anathemata* (233), they would partake in an association between Calvary, Arthur-as-Christ-figure, the history of Wales, and the universal experience of decline and loss for all people and cultures.

With his father he visited Ysceifiog, the birthplace of his Welsh grandparents. Near it Offa's Dyke is presumed to have run, and David began associating his grandfather with the eighth-century earthwork. At what had been his grandfather's workshop outside Holywell, Jim stressed that both David's grandfathers had been builders and taught him the Welsh word *saer* (carpenter), which would gain in significance when he learned that, for the Welsh, poetry is 'carpentry of song'. They visited Gwenfrewi/Winifred's Well, and he met the large ex-Chief Constable of the town, Ben Caesar Jones, whose name epitomised for David the historical Welsh-Roman connection and who looked to him like a fifth-century centurion left behind by the departing legions. In 1911, his father took him to Caernarfon for the investiture of the Prince of Wales. On that trip, David hoped to see Mt Snowdon but it was 'too misty' – he never would see it. Always their base was Rhos, where, playing on the shore one day, he came upon the corpses of two drowned men, a gruesome experience underlying references in his poetry to sailors lost at sea (*A* 104, 106, 141).[55]

* * *

David had a small bow-shaped mouth, large ears, ginger hair, like his father's – it would darken with age to brown like his mother's – and deep brown eyes, inherited, his mother told him, from his Italian great-grandmother. In manner he was sweet natured and gentle like his father but with his high-strung, anxious mother's inner disposition. He would later say, 'I've always been deeply depressed inside' like her 'though she had great fortitude in tribulation'.[56]

Since early childhood he had masturbated and felt guilty about it. In 1910, with acute embarrassment, he confided to his parents that his erections were painful. He suffered from tightness of the foreskin. The only cure is circumcision. His mother took him to a surgery, where a nurse chloroformed him for the operation. Recovery was slow and painful, acutely so after an erection broke the stitches. The initial problem, the operation, the pain, the involvement of his mother and the nurse, and his being fourteen: these are enough to make even a non-Freudian wince. Thirty years later the experience would give him nightmares.[57]

A fter primary school, David wanted to go to art school. His
parents and other relatives wanted him to attend nearby Hilly
Fields College, but he was stubborn and, after months of
argument, he got his way. The nearest art school was three miles away,
the London County Council School of Arts and Crafts in Camberwell on
Peckham Road. It was red-brick Victorian Baroque, had three storeys,
and high-ceilinged studios with immense north-facing windows. On 20
September 1909, wearing an Eton collar and knickerbockers, he joined
the beginning class. Small for his age and years younger than the other
students, upon arrival he was deposited by them in a wastepaper basket.
Among his schoolmates, seventeen-year-old Harold Weaver Hawkins and
eighteen-year-old Frank Medworth became his best friends. David went
to school (classes began at 10 a.m.) by horse-drawn bus, in winter with
hot potatoes in his coat pockets to warm his hands. The trip shortened in
1910 when the family moved a mile north to 31 Vesta Road near the top
of Telegraph Hill. He continued going to school by bus but liked walking
home, avoiding main roads, keeping as much as possible to open fields.[1]

During his first year, he enrolled in 'unclassified' still-life drawing and
'Drawing the Figure', which began with 'doing antique' – drawing plaster
casts mostly of Classical and Renaissance statues. After a few weeks, the
other students went on to sexually segregated Life Drawing classes. At
thirteen he was considered too young for nude models and continued
drawing casts of statues. Among his subjects were: Michelangelo's *David*,
which 'bored' him; Donatello's *St George*, whose shield he liked; Myron's
The Disk-thrower, which he found 'angular in a boring sort of way'; and
the *Venus de Milo*, his favourite, which he later called 'a marvel of serene
beauty', 'the Academic at its best'. Drawing her, he experienced an
'immense stillness'. He also loved *The Dying Gaul*, especially liking his
neck-torque. Prolonged 'doing antique' was arduous training for the eye
and an extensive lesson in distortion – its informing principles, then
unknown to him, made capturing their 'subtleties' 'surprisingly difficult'.
After two months, he joined the life class and found live models far easier
to draw.[2]*

* * *

* J. Miles and D. Shiel are mistaken in writing that at Camberwell he studied for 'years'
before drawing Life (*Maker Unmade*, p. 18).

In the autumn of 1910, his brother, Harold, age 21, entered the advanced stages of tuberculosis. Afraid of infection, his parents withdrew David from school and sent him to stay in Brighton with his wealthy Great-uncle Tom Pethybridge and his unmarried daughters. Semi-retired from the paper business and a former justice of the peace, Pethybridge was a Gladstonian Liberal, who celebrated the Glorious Revolution of 1688, and a Germanophile. He recited for David a poem he had written about 'Our Saxon fathers'. David protested, 'I *am not* a Saxon.'

Pethybridge insisted that David spend time in his library reading certain books, about which he questioned him each evening. David read J. R. Green's *Short History of the English People*, William Stubbs on constitutional law, J. A. Froude's *Caesar*, and Macaulay's *Lays of Ancient Rome*, memorising parts of 'Horatius' and the whole of 'The Battle of Lake Regillus'. It was 'doggerel', he later said, 'but it got to me' and left 'an indelible mark' – 'one never gets rid of these Roman things'. For his birthday the following year, Pethybridge would give him Evans's translation of Geoffrey of Monmouth, inscribed to a 'Champion of the Ancient Welsh from a converted Saxon'. David would say of his great-uncle, 'I owe him ... quite a lot.'[3]

David's stay ended on 20 November, when his brother died at home. Afterwards, his parents never spoke of Harold in the presence of David or Cissy – it was as though he had never existed. David, too, in later life never mentioned him even to close friends, one of whom felt it was a subject he wanted to avoid.[4] All children sometimes wish siblings dead. Many say so. For him the wish came true. Illness, his best weapon in rivalry with Harold, had been turned against him. Survival was a pyrrhic victory – so great the cost in guilt, which he would pay for the rest of his life. In 1966 he would write in an essay that 'The Death of Harold' marks the end of Anglo-Saxon rule. The title also marks a rupture in his personal history. From now on, he would be free of residual sibling rivalry. Avoiding quarrels and disinclined to speak ill of others, he was careful not to repeat the mistake he had made unavoidably, because largely unconsciously, with his brother.

That Christmas was not merry. As usual, the extended family assembled at the home of Alice's brother Ebenezer, now at 30 Dalrymple Road, on Boxing Day. After supper for about twenty-five people, the children put on a concert, complete with printed programme. Cissy played the piano. 'Master W. Jones' recited 'selections from *Henry V* and the whole of "Griffith's Answer to Harold"', a Welsh refusal to surrender to Harold Godwinson in 1063. The children processed in costume carrying sparklers – Cissy dressed as Britannia and David as 'Cadwal (a Briton)'. Their father concluded the evening by singing *Mae Hen Wlad Fy Nhadau*, tears streaming down his face. For him, for all of them, the festivities were haunted. The previous year, too ill to join the entertainers, Harold had lain on a couch, calling, after each performance, 'Encore!'[5] David had never liked Christmas but from now on, because it celebrated family and stirred conflicting feelings, he would dislike it with Scroogian intensity.

Arriving at school on 19 January 1911, he stepped off the rear of an electric tramcar, began crossing the street behind it, and was struck by a tram passing in the opposite direction. He was helped from the street with 'a nasty cut on his head' and an injured eye, bandaged, taken home by taxi, and immediately taken to a doctor by his mother. He nearly lost the sight in his eye and had to wear an eyepatch for weeks.[6] Some psychologists believe that the victims of such accidents are unconsciously motivated by guilt.

*   *   *

Having decided to specialise in 'Book Illustration, Composition and Drawing from Life', Jones enrolled repeatedly in 'Drawing and Design for Book Illustration and Composition', taught separately by Reginald Savage and A. S. Hartrick, and in Hartrick's 'Drawing and Painting the Draped Figure'.[7]

For Savage's course, he drew objects and animals – the school kept a small menagerie, and Savage sent the pupils to the zoo. There Jones drew two lions, a male and a female, later adding watercolour and a natural setting (fig. 1). He learned composition, including the convention of placing a dark patch in the foreground of a picture. A man of the '90s, Savage (nicknamed 'Solly') had known Charles Ricketts, Charles Shannon, and Sturge Moore. Savage had, Jones later said, 'a civilising influence'. He showed his class work by the great nineteenth-century illustrators – George Pinwell, Frederick Sandys, Aubrey Beardsley, and Louis-Maurice Boutet de Monvel – and taught the history of art as culminating in the Pre-Raphaelites, of whom Jones was soon enamoured.[8]

In his mid-forties, A. S. Hartrick was the most eminent artist on staff. He was a founding member of the Society of Illustrators and a member of the New English Art Club. He had been a close friend of Van Gogh and had known Degas, Gauguin, Toulouse-Lautrec, Beardsley, and Whistler. (In class he mimicked Whistler mimicking Rossetti, Swinburne, Sandys, and Beardsley.) John Sargent had recommended him for this teaching post. A gifted teacher, he saw immediately what had gone wrong with Jones's drawing. It was not, he said, that he had imitated bad art but that he had imitated at all. Instead of technique, which is imitable, Hartrick stressed accurate observation integrated with feeling and exact control.[9]

Wanting pupils to see and draw first the outline of an object, he taught drawing in two

1. *Lions*, 1910

styles. The first employs a thick, emphatic contour line used by the Pre-Raphaelites and Millet in a tradition extending back through Poussin and Rubens to Michelangelo. This is the style of Jones's drawing of a medieval soldier being advised by an old man (fig. 2) and would typify his drawing into the late 1920s. The other style is drawing the contour thinly, with the pencil point, which, Hartrick contended, made the best draughtsmen. Stressing this style, he traced it back through Legros and Ingres, to Raphael and the early Italian masters. It had the advantage, Hartrick said, of diminishing subjective self-expression and personal mannerisms. Recent exemplars of this style included the mid-century illustrators, among whom he praised especially Frederick Walker and, pre-eminently, Charles Keene of *Punch*. In his later work, Jones would primarily draw with the point. For most of his life, even as a painter, he would be primarily a draughtsman for whom, as he said, 'line is everything'.[10]

Hartrick fired Jones's enthusiasm for drawing for its own sake, and he was now drawing well. To the others, Hartrick sometimes commented, 'Look at that, you see, Jones leaves out everything but the magic' – which Jones later thought 'the nicest thing ever said about' his work. But when his attempts were too tentative or elaborate, Hartrick would urge, 'Make a frank statement, Jones. Make a frank statement.'[11]

2. *Soldier and Old Man*, 1914

Along with drawing with the point, Impressionist colour-technique would inform Jones's mature style, and this, too, he owed to Hartrick, who taught him to paint not in gradations of light and dark but in alternating warm and cool colours. 'That is *the* secret,' Jones later said. 'It doesn't matter what the colours contrasted are, so long as one is cold and the other warm.'[12]

Hartrick diverged from prevailing art-school emphasis on oil painting in promoting painting in watercolours. He conveyed in his teaching a sense of its history, praising Turner, Girtin, Cotman, and the founders of the old Watercolour Society and tracing the origins of the tradition to eighth- and ninth-century illuminators, beginning with the Book of Kells and the Lindisfarne Gospels.[13] But Jones's only surviving painting done in Hartrick's class is an oil, of a fisherman (fig. 3), a portrait painted from life but resembling the label on Skipper Sardines because the same model posed for it. Demonstrating realistic proficiency, the painting won a class prize.[14]

Hartrick deplored 'slick surface smoothness', favoured by the Royal Academy, as robbing pictures of spontaneity and distracting from basic form. Jones began to share his contempt for academic pictures, which were, Hartrick said, 'machines'. Jones took to heart his warning that 'skill getting in advance of judgment ... can kill art' and would spend much of his life evading the tyranny of technical skill – his paradigm for such evasion being Cézanne.[15]

About the great Impressionists, Hartrick was, he said, 'vastly entertaining', and he was proud to have a teacher who had known them. For Hartrick, Gauguin and Van Gogh were models of artistic integrity and independence. He repeated what Gauguin had told him: 'In art there are only revolutionaries and plagiarists.' Recollecting his friend 'Vincent', Hartrick warned of the price of artistic integrity. He and the Impressionists would inspire Jones's subsequent independent development and originality, although, as a student, Jones later admitted, he was merely trying 'to emulate the varying techniques of the changing art-masters'.[16]

3. *The Skipper, c.* 1913

He probably visited the first post-Impressionist exhibition at the Grafton Gallery in December or early January 1911, to see the work of Gauguin, Van Gogh, and Cézanne. He certainly went to the second post-Impressionist exhibition in 1912, featuring Matisse and Picasso. Reacting to the cubist and futurist paintings dominating the exhibit, Hartrick warned against 'isms' and stunts that attract attention but are ephemeral. He told his students that all permanent change in painting arises out of the art itself, not ideas about it.[17]

Hartrick introduced Jones to the work of the best living illustrators, many of whom he knew personally. These included Paul Renouard and E. J. Sullivan, to whom he gave his highest praise. He drew special attention to Sullivan's 'Gardener' (in *The Yellow Book*), saying it was originally designed to illustrate the Man with the Muckrake in *The Pilgrim's Progress* – a picture Jones would recall in *In Parenthesis* (174). Hartrick also praised Adolph Menzel for including immense detail without loss of dramatic form, Daniel Vierge for lightness of skill, Phil May for economy and vitality of line, and Aubrey Beardsley for clear thinking, immense power, and design.[18]

Hartrick also exposed him to the full history of European art. On the walls of his classroom studio hung full-size photographs of drawings by the old masters. He held classes in the National Gallery and in the British Museum Prints and Drawings Room (where Jones, Hawkins, and

Medworth spent hours together on their own looking through the folios of prints and drawings). Hartrick had students copy an old master's work, put the copy away, and draw it again from memory, forgetting incidental detail and retaining the essentials of design. Possibly for this exercise, Jones copied Rubens's *Judgement of Paris*, a 'bloody difficult' task. Emphasising drawing with the point, Hartrick showed his students Greek vases; drawings by Mantegna, and pen drawings by Raphael and Ingres. He introduced his students to Holbein's drawn portraits, praising them for their principle of 'no more than enough'. Jones would always admire these, his favourite being *John Fisher*. Hartrick ascribed his own artistic inclination to Celtic blood and, in the British Museum, pointed out the La Tène bronze Battersea shield, saying, 'They knew what they were up to, Jones.' While insisting that they look to the past, Hartrick's chief interest was the present. The great masters were to be studied for methods 'to express the spirit of to-day', which had, for him, a 'mystical' aspect – 'the final charm of beauty' being 'the suggestion of the infinite'.[19]

Late in life, Jones wrote that Hartrick's 'vision ... had an abiding effect' and said that he learned more from him than from any other teacher. And no other artist would subsequently influence him as much. Many of Hartrick's perceptions became his, and Hartrick set for him the standard of what an artist ought to be as a person. Jones most liked about his teacher's best work that it was 'lyrical', tentative, and with a 'sense of design & understanding of form'.[20] His own work would have these qualities.

* * *

A Victorian storytelling impulse pervaded the school, art being seen as an extension of historical, often medieval, narrative. Savage sent students on Saturdays to the Victoria and Albert Museum to sketch period rooms.[21] Wearing historical dress produced in the class in 'Costume Design and Dressmaking', students posed in tableaux, including Jones dressed as a friar blessing a half-naked barbarian (fig. 4) and as an eclectic bard with Celtic harp, Saxon cross-gartering, and Viking helmet (fig. 5), possibly the costume of Cadwal at the 1910 Christmas party.

Although Jones took few courses, and those repeatedly, his experience at Camberwell was not narrow. An enduring interest in historical costume and embroidery began with work by female students enrolled in 'Dressmaking, Textile, and Embroidery'. He attended extra lectures illustrated by lantern slides – one given by Arthur Kendrick possibly

4. Jones as Friar, c. 1912

planting the seed of his later interest in medieval tapestry. And for three and a half years, he was required to take a weekly one-hour class in English Literature, in which he read Emerson, whom he liked 'a good bit', and Ruskin, who led him to Turner.[22]

Turner's paintings were seldom shown and would remain in obscurity for decades, but Jones loved them, especially the later 'more impressionistic ones', which he considered 'real miracles'. He would praise Turner as 'easily . . . the greatest of all British painters by world standards' and be influenced by him but only years later, in diffusing colours as an antidote to the flat, hard-edged style then dominating contemporary painting.[23]

* * *

5. Jones as Bard, c. 1912

Jones was now an avid reader. He read translations of Bede, *The Anglo-Saxon Chronicle* and *The Song of Roland* – associating dying Roland with *The Dying Gaul*. He read 'a little Chaucer'; Langland; Shakespeare ('mainly the historical plays' and *Macbeth*); John Skelton; Hugh Latimer's sermons; the Scottish ballads; 'some Milton'; Gibbon; 'bits of Coleridge' (his favourite being *The Rime of the Ancient Mariner*); *Percy's Reliques*; Robert Browning; and the Pre-Raphaelites, chiefly Morris. He also read George Borrow (preferring *Lavengro* and *Romany Rye* to *Wild Wales*), and Stowe's *Survey* of Elizabethan London – a basis for imaginative restoration as he walked through central London, experience that would inform the central monologue of *The Anathemata*. He read Fenimore Cooper's *The Last of the Mohicans*, which gave him his 'first conscious awareness of a dichotomy' between civilisation and 'indigenous cultures', American Indians being analogous to the medieval Welsh. (Sympathy with cultures falling to civilisations would immunise him against what he called 'the nonsense about "progress" with a capital P'.) Much of his reading was romance: in 1910, Malory 'in bits' and Maurice Hewlett's modern romances of medieval intrigue; in 1913, *Aucassin and Nicolette*, which impressed him deeply and would influence his poetry. (He never reread it but could recall it vividly half a century later.) He read and loved Lewis Carroll's Alice books.[24]

Much of his reading concerned Wales, an enthusiasm encouraged by his father, who gave him Edwards's *Short History of Wales* and Lloyd's *The History of Wales from the Earliest Times to the Edwardian Conquest*, the best history of Wales in English. In it he read of the killing of the Welsh prince Llywelyn ap Gruffydd on 11 December 1282, a death terminating a lineage that had ruled Gwynedd for nearly a millennium and, he realised, abolishing Welsh political identity. Llywelyn's death would occupy his thoughts on

11 December for the rest of his life. For his sixteenth birthday, his father gave him a Welsh–English dictionary and Rhys and Brynmor Jones's *The Welsh People*, which would remain important to him. He also read the Welsh triplets, Guest's translation of *The Mabinogion*, and Giraldus Cambrensis. In his sixteenth year, he began in earnest studying Welsh and would continue on and off for the rest of his life, achieving basic reading comprehension but never being able to pronounce it like a native. His inability to master Welsh would be his 'bitterest grief'.[25]

He was fascinated with etymology – an interest sparked by Butter's *Etymological Spelling Book* – so much so that, despite foregoing grammar school, he considered becoming a philologist. He revelled in the layers of meaning of words rooting the present in the past. This interest would inform later regret at not having an academic education in which he might have learned research methods and languages. He would think his going to art school 'years too young a great mistake'.[26*]

* * *

Despite seeing a good deal of naked female flesh in life class, during his years at Camberwell he knew little about sex. The same was true of Medworth and Hawkins, who were, like many middle-class young people, sexually inhibited and puritanical. (David's mother first spoke to his sister about sex in 1917 on the eve of her wedding, saying: 'I suppose you know what you're in for. You won't like it but you'll get used to it.') Ignorance coexisted with longing. Jones collected picture postcards of contemporary beauties, including Lily Elsie and Zena Dare. In an early draft of *In Parenthesis*, he writes about 'a quite new & terrible desire to talk to' his older sister Cissy's friend, 'who would smile at him, when his sister wasn't looking – and stand so, slightly leaning, her flowered frock like a casement opening on her ~~bosom~~ loveliness'. The girl with the deleted bosom may have been Cissy's friend Edith Levitt, though the object of his amorous interest was her younger sister Elsie, a tall, big-boned brunette with a pleasant voice. They may have dated. He later shocked his cousin Kathleen Bradshaw by saying that, if you take a girl to the cinema, it is a good idea to sit in the back where you can put your arm round her without others noticing.[27]

* * *

* Near the end of his life, however, he would be glad he had missed an academic education. The chief advantage of escaping grammar school was that his thinking and imagining remained predominantly spatial, and this would make him, as he later realised, unique among modern poets in his approach to literary form.

In the summer of 1913, when students were expected to produce work for an autumn exhibition, he visited Wales with a school friend named Whitaker, a hunchback with dirty blond hair and a face like young T. S. Eliot. They stayed for three months just outside Tregaron in a hillside bungalow belonging to 'a jolly nice Englishwoman'. The town was a sheep-selling and small-farm centre. East of it spread the central Welsh moorlands, grassy hills rising to 1,600 feet, on which Bronze Age people had left cairns and Iron Age people built circular forts, such as Castell Rhyfel three miles to the east. Jones and Whitaker went out daily to paint. Jones made an oil painting of the tower of the town's fourteenth-century church of St Caron and sold it to a townswoman, a friend of his mother. From the heights above, he painted the town-in-landscape. A distant relative, Maria Evans, in Tregaron visiting her husband's parents, wanted this painting, and he promised to send it when it dried. He later decided not to, but his father insisted he keep his promise, so he posted it to her.[28] Murky and dull, it and two other paintings survive from this summer.

One Sunday evening, he and Whitaker visited a Calvinist Methodist chapel. The *hwyl* of the preacher was highly emotional, the congregation 'rather fierce looking', 'swaying to the singing', which was 'like a torrent', so that Jones felt 'quite afraid'. But outside after, the congregation was 'chattering and smiling' – the change startled him. He would remember, 'if we had drunk all the tea that was offered us we would have drowned'.[29]

With Whitaker, he liked walking to nearby Cors Goch Glanteifi, the largest peat-bog in Wales – a vast 'purple reddish brown' saucer of undrained wilderness, whitened with the tassels of cotton sedge and noisy with marsh birds. The mist drifting over it in the early morning reminded him of Gwyddion's magic mist in *The Mabinogion*. On the south side of the bog grew Scots pines, which he disliked for lacking deciduous irregularity and movement. Here they watched men cutting peat for fuel. In a little cottage on the bog, they came upon a woman attempting to stoke a dying peat fire with a leaky bellows. It seemed to Jones the work of a local craftsman. He expressed admiration for it, so she gave it to him, despite attempts to hand it back. The next morning he bought a new bellows in town and took it to her. She was delighted because, he later said quizzically, 'of course it worked better'.[30]

With Whitaker, he travelled in a horse-drawn trap via Ystrad Meurig to Pontrhydfendigaid, which he thought a 'jolly beautiful name'. Here the River Teifi tumbles down from the moors under a single-arched stone bridge. He loved the 'peaty, rusty-coloured stream water' that looks 'dark like some sort of beer but when you lap it in your hand it's quite clear'. And he admired the formidable beauty of the surrounding wild, bare, wind-swept moors. He and Whitaker travelled on to Strata Florida, the most important Cistercian abbey in medieval Wales, now merely a 'desolate arch and a little walling'.

They explored the country to the north, then considered the wildest in Wales, where getting lost could cost your life. He was impressed by the 'astounding beauty' of 'all that part of Ceredigion'.[31]

Along with his childhood trips to Wales, this extended visit gave personally-experienced contemporary setting to the history and legend of his reading. For Jones Welshness was largely an imaginative acquisition. He was chiefly interested in its medieval past and origins as expressed in Arthurian romances, which are to the post-classical Western world what the Homeric epics were to the ancient world. His Welsh admirers would claim him as their own, and he loved when they did; but, to borrow the language of Gestalt psychology, his intellectual-imaginary Welshness figured against a London-English social-cultural ground.

* * *

Balancing his deepening love of his father's nation was a compensatory movement towards the theology of his mother. She was a High Church fifth column in their evangelical home, introducing what Jones would later call 'a decided undercurrent or ground-swell of a sacramental and Catholic nature'. On Sunday evenings, the family went to the nearby tiny red-brick mission church of St George where his father conducted Matins and Evensong and preached. Earlier in the day, during Communion services at St James, Hatcham, at the creedal statement that God 'was made man', David felt 'almost . . . a compulsion' to kneel, especially at Christmas. Such papist behaviour was 'greatly disliked and subject to rebuke', so he dropped his handkerchief and knelt ostensibly to retrieve it. His mother asked him to stop for his father's sake, but he argued that his father couldn't see him from where he stood and it was no business of anyone else anyway. He could not understand Protestant hostility to bodily action.[32]

It bothered him that most Anglicans reject the doctrine of the real presence yet believe in Jesus as God incarnate. He found it easier to believe in the real presence once you believe in the divinity of Jesus than to believe in the divinity of Jesus. By the time he was eighteen, the service of the Church of England seemed to him 'arid'. Convinced that the pastor at St James was not exercising a sacramental ministry, he stopped attending and went instead – sometimes perhaps with his mother – to High Church St Cyprian's at the corner of Brockley Road and Adelaide Avenue.[33]

* * *

Jones attended annual costume balls for art students, once as a medieval bowman. For that costume, Cissy knit a long wool shirt, which aluminium paint transformed into chain mail. To go to the Chelsea Arts Ball as a jovial friar, he went to the Carmelite monastery in Church Street, Kensington and asked to borrow a pattern to make a habit. The porter summoned the superior, who lent him a habit.[34]

When Frank Medworth received his art teacher's certificates on 18 March 1913, photographs were taken. Jones joined in, posing on the front steps of the entrance to the school (fig. 6). He would later be fussy about what he wore, preferring the best quality in clothes and shoes – a sartorial inclination evidently now already well established.[35]

By 1914, Jones, Hawkins, and Medworth were painting 'all day, every day, except Sunday'. On Saturdays and summer evenings, they went to a studio for an open life class in a former warehouse in Kennington near the Oval, a mile-and-a-half west of the art school. Run by a man named Fripp, the place was like a French atelier, with large dusty plaster casts, including Jones's favourites, the *Venus de Milo* and, in a corner, *The Dying Gaul*.[36]

Dedicated totally to art, Jones did not take the Board of Education examinations to qualify as an art master, and he was determined to avoid commercial art. He wanted to draw animals and illustrate medieval Welsh subjects but had no idea how to earn a living at it. Deciding that being an artist precluded supporting a family, he resolved to forgo marriage. That he did so between the ages of fifteen and eighteen, before seriously trying to sell pictures, suggests other than economic considerations, the nature of which he would explore decades later. For now he was committed to art, poverty, and, consequently, bachelorhood.[37]

6. Jones (far left) and Medworth (behind on left), Hawkins (far right), March 1913

While at Camberwell, he had his handwriting analysed and saved the graphologist's report, which in later years he inscribed in big red capitals 'NB', suggesting that he considered it accurate:

This writing shows a good deal of energy and ardour, but more in the mental than physical realm. The writer is rather reserved and somewhat sensitive, is kind hearted and does not appear to be selfish. He shows however a certain amount of conceit and he has a fairly strong will, & is determined. He is persevering but not strikingly ambitious. He has a quick imagination which almost runs ahead of his pen. I should say he is rather quick-tempered & excitable. He shows some originality, & has the sense of the artistic. He is very critical but shows excellent powers of deduction, i.e. has a good judgment. He is generous but his generosity is controlled by prudence. There are slight signs of a temporary physical weakness, or struggle with obstacles in the way.

On 5 August 1914, Jones bought half a dozen newspapers, including *The Times*, its front page consisting entirely of the headline: BRITAIN AT WAR.* Wanting to be part of history (and to ride a horse), he went to enlist with the Royal Welsh Yeomanry but was advised instead to join the infantry. On 29 September, he attended an address by Lloyd George about raising a Welsh Army Corps with a London-Welsh battalion.† Jones applied to join but, hearing nothing and growing impatient, went to enlist in the Queen's Westminster Rifles. Refused his choice of regiment, he tried to enlist in the Artists' Rifles but was rejected for 'deficient chest measurement'. He donned running shorts and jogged through Brockley and Lewisham in a vain attempt to enlarge his chest. Then physical requirements relaxed, and he enlisted on 2 January 1915 in the newly constituted London-Welsh battalion of the Royal Welch Fusiliers for the duration of the war.[1]

In mid-January, he went to Llandudno to join the 15th Battalion of the 113th Brigade of the 23rd Foot in the 38th (Welsh) Division. His battalion consisted mostly of Cockneys, a few middle-class Englishmen, and mainly Welsh officers. He was in the 6th platoon of B Company. On St David's Day, he again heard Lloyd George speak, and was moved, but later, reading the speech in the papers, found it 'appalling bloody tripe'.[2]

He was now immersed in a mixture of Welsh and English languages, accents, idioms, and dispositions. Most members of the other battalions of the brigade spoke Welsh and the centuries-old Welsh English of Shakespeare's Fluellen. Overwhelmingly

1. Private David Jones, 1915

* For a much expanded account of Jones's war experience, see T. Dilworth, *David Jones in the Great War* (London: Enitharmon Press, 2012).

† Boasting of historical Welsh valour in his speech, Lloyd George referred to Crécy, as would the boasting archetypal soldier at the heart of *In Parenthesis* (79–84), who shares the chancellor's first name and rhetorical panache.

2. 'Pro Patria', *Graphic*, 11 December 1915

Welsh, the brigade was now his nomadic home. There were twelve battalions in the division, widely evoking the Twelve Tribes of Israel and underlying Old Testament allusions in *In Parenthesis*. In August 1915, the brigade joined the other brigades of the 38th Division in an immense camp north of Winchester on Winnall Down.[3]

On leave to say goodbye, Jones was photographed (fig. 1) and visited Hartrick, who, as art editor of the *Graphic*, asked for a drawing to publish. Near the end of November, Jones sent 'Pro Patria', which appeared in the issue of 11 December 1915 (fig. 2). The prominence of the knight and the foremost sleeper implies the correspondence between medieval and modern warriors then characteristic of propaganda posters.

Rifles arrived in mid-November, and his battalion went to Salisbury Plain for musketry instruction. They were billeted in large circular bell-tents on Larkhill. Each morning he woke to a view of Stonehenge two miles away across the plain. After two weeks of practice, he was rated 'a first class shot'.[4]

On 1 December they marched seventeen miles to the Southampton docks. Not yet at his full height of 5 feet 7½ inches, Jones was smaller than most but carried the same burden – seventy-seven pounds on a dry day, increased by rain (as now) to a hundred pounds, approximately his body weight. The next night in a rough sea they crossed the Channel in the *Queen Alexandra*, disembarking in Le Havre, and spent two weeks training in the village of Warne, where, on especially wet days, they assembled in a barn for lectures by battalion officers. The most popular was the medical officer, 'Doc Day', speaking vividly and comically about venereal disease. It was the frankest, lewdest sexual talk Jones had heard.[5]

On 19 December, they went to Riez Bailleul, a group of small farms. Jones was about to enter a barn when his lieutenant asked, 'Have you a match, Jones?' 'Oh yes,' he replied, forgetting protocol, 'I have some here.' His sergeant heard the exchange and, the lieutenant having left, began upbraiding Jones for improperly addressing a commissioned officer, then stopped and ducked into the barn. Jones stood transfixed, sensing it coming – a long-range heavy shell. It struck in an apotheosis of violence fifty yards away, leaving a gaping hole and muck and turnip-sap spattering the breech-block of a nearby field-gun. He was shaken. The explosion, which he would poetically commemorate (*IP* 24), tore time in two, separating his early years from all to follow.[6] That night the battalion walked the remaining four miles to the front line, the last three-quarters of a mile through flooded communication trenches. In the firing-trench they fixed bayonets, and settled in. A hundred and fifty yards ahead was the German firing-trench.

Jones preferred life in the trenches to the empty routine and irksome discipline of training. The previous year had been 'frightful'. He hated the endless drill, the parade-ground renunciation of personality, the saluting, the bullying and insults. (Bayonet practice was especially 'revolting', being urged to shout obscenely, to hate, to aim for the enemy's eyes and genitals.) At drill he was 'grotesquely incompetent … a parade's despair' (*IP* xv), telling with difficulty his right hand from his left (though never incurring a penalty for blunders during drill, parade, or inspection). Only now did military life acquire meaning. It was also more relaxed. Camaraderie increased. People of all ranks 'who could be jolly horrible', he later said, 'were so much nicer to each other'. He 'much preferred being in the line' to being anywhere else in the army. Though always 'a parade's despair', he would soon, as a combat soldier, be canny, efficient, adept at survival.[7]

Night and day the men followed a staggered schedule: three hours of sentry duty, then three hours on fatigue duty, then three hours for sleep. The men were always tired, chronic weariness sometimes becoming torment. When Jones slept it was soundly. Once he woke to find biscuits gone from his greatcoat pockets – rats had crawled over his body, beneath the coat, to eat through the pocket lining.[8]

Extreme weariness, boredom, occasional hunger and thirst (fear made men thirsty), this was life in the trenches, punctuated by sudden violence and hurried effort, made hateful by rain and mud. The winter of 1915–16 was bitter, sunless, and wet. Jones had inherited from his mother a sensitivity to cold and thought the war '*could* not possibly last another winter – no one would "stick it"'. But he would never be so healthy, partly because the sick were not coddled and, since illness brought none of the benefits he had known as a child, he ceased being ill, and partly because fear increased adrenalin, supercharging the immune system. He would catch cold almost immediately upon returning home on leave.[9]

Life in the trenches had aesthetic compensations. He appreciated beauty in 'improvisations, such as bits of sand-bag tied round' legs, by which men acquired 'character & "picturesqueness"'. Fond of all things interwoven, he admired the wattled revetments of the French. At morning stand-to, facing east over no-man's-land, he saw 'marvellously beautiful dawns' accompanied by the morning song of birds. And, for him, the devastated landscape had a 'beauty of a strange sort' that, he later wrote, 'remains imprinted on the mind forever'. He carried in his pack a 7 by 4½ inch sketchbook in which he drew landscapes and, chiefly, platoon mates in their soft service caps, alone or in groups.[10]

On night sentry duty, he wryly repeated to himself the circular chant of his childhood: 'It was a dark and stormy night…' In later years, when it came to mind, he would associate it with memories of soldiers huddled together. He also bolstered his 'timid spirit' (his words) by reciting to himself memorised parts of Macaulay's *Lays of Ancient Rome*.[11]

Jones and his companions enjoyed the intimate, open society of the slum. His best friends were Reggie Allen, a machine-gunner from Abertillery, north-west of Newport; Leslie Poulter, a signaller from London, well educated, multilingual, widely read, and unfailingly amusing; and Harry Cook also a signaller, regularly promoted for courage and efficiency and regularly demoted for drunkenness. They were middle class and intelligent. Another friend was Arthur Pritchard-Williams, a sniper aspiring to be a dentist. Lazarus Black, an East End Cockney Jew with a wife and children, 'attached himself' to Jones.[12]

On Christmas morning, Jones heard Germans singing carols and Cockneys loudly drowning them out with 'Casey Jones' (see *IP* 67–8).[13]

On 28 December, the battalion withdrew from the trenches. Jones hated leaving any place he was used to, and, even though he was 'pretty scared in them', always '*positively disliked* coming out of the trenches'. (He thought himself 'average' in experiencing fear, and, although 'bloody frightened' in the trenches, felt 'a curious kind of exhilaration'.) After a week in reserve training, they entered trenches at Richebourg-Saint-Vaast, 'a ghastly place', where on 10 January 1916, they experienced their first

3. 'shrapnel burst, 1916 Givenchy, supports', 1916

enemy barrage, an appalling trial lasting four hours and leaving two dead and five wounded. This was the start of five months of four-to-seven-day periods rotating between the front line, support trenches, reserve trenches, and divisional reserve in the Richebourg, Neuve-Chapelle and Givenchy sectors. Givenchy was the most desolate place he had seen, with only 'a solid briary brake of red rusted entanglements of wire' separating them from the enemy.[14] The soldiers called it, simply, 'the craters', after huge cavities caused by undermining and countermining. Mortar fire was sometimes nearly constant here. All this winter these trenches were the hardest part of the Western front to hold, and casualties were high.

Whenever possible he volunteered for night patrol in no-man's-land because it exempted him from fatigue duty and patrols were exciting and, he thought, only slightly more dangerous. When his lieutenant saw that he could draw, he was regularly assigned to night patrol to make maps of no-man's-land. One night he and three others went out. They crawled up to the enemy wire – he could see the sentry's steel helmet moving back and forth in the trench – and someone loudly kicked a tin. They shook with stifled laughter, which increased the danger, which increased their hilarity and their desperation to suppress it. Minutes later hysteria subsided and, Jones would remember, 'we crept back as fast as we bloody well could'.[15]

At Festubert, a mile north of Givenchy, swampy ground allowed only isolated surface sandbag breastworks. The 'Islands' or 'Grouse-Butts', as they were called, could be reached only over open ground on duckboard tracks at night. Here, once, when crossing a ditch on a plank, unaccountable terror paralysed him – an eruption into consciousness of the dread he habitually repressed.[16] For the rest of the war, he would never consciously be so afraid.

In four months, the battalion lost 105 men – 25 killed, 80 wounded. Five days at Givenchy in April cost them five dead, nineteen wounded.

On 13 April the battalion received steel helmets. The 'tin hats' resembled those of medieval infantry and confirmed a felt affinity with the medieval past already suggested, for Jones, by the eighteen-inch short sword bayonet (fig. 4), which, when not fixed to the rifle, hung in a scabbard reaching to the knee. He felt this

4. 'Front line 1916 – why not fixed bayonette?', 1916

affinity with the past 'only when' in 'the Forward Area'. Never merely a matter of physical resemblance, it was awareness that 'this is what chaps must have felt like during recent or remote historical combat'. In his opinion, 'men behaved in much the same way as . . . past heroes had behaved'.[17]

On the night of 7 May at Fauquissart, Jones took part in guarding the flank of their first raid. The few prisoners taken shook with fear. The sergeant major, who had not been involved in the action, grabbed one, twisted his arm up behind his back, and began frogmarching him down the trench. Jones and his companions stopped him, saying, 'You can't do that, sir.' (Sergeant majors were, he later said, 'almost all bastards'.) British casualties included only two dead, whom he could see the next day on the enemy wire – 'hung like rag-merchants' stock' (*IP* 106). One was a lieutenant he had especially liked, 'an attractive man, very absent minded, and . . . fair-haired', resembling the bareheaded squire in Uccello's *The Rout of San Romano* (see *IP* 2, 106).[18]

Because the army was running out of front-line junior officers, ranks were being combed for promotable privates. Jones's accent was middle class, so his colonel, J. C. Bell, sent for him and asked why he was not commissioned. Jones said he was 'incapable of ordering people about'. Bell asked, 'What is your school?' Jones replied, 'Camberwell School of Arts and Crafts'. 'Oh', said Bell, ending the interview. He never again urged him to accept a commission.

Jones admired and imitated the manners of educated lieutenants and used their slang ('chaps', 'blokes', 'Boche'), but he disliked the officer class because most were arrogant and lacked humour, of which his fellow privates had plenty. He was later offered the position of batman, an officer's servant exempt from fatigues and carrying a pack, but declined, preferring privates to officers and wishing to stay with his friends.[19]

On 11 June in the Neuve-Chapelle line, the regiment began marching south to take part in the Battle of the Somme.

After water-logged trenches, consecutive days of rapid marching with full packs blistered the feet of many men but not Jones. His mother had sent him soft woollen socks to wear under the rough grey army issue. Throughout the war, she sent him a new pair every few weeks. He would never have blisters, nor did he mind marching.[20]

Exhausted, the battalion arrived at the Somme at midnight on 1 July, and for the next four days was marched back and forth behind the lines. In a forward trench throughout the 6th and 7th, they endured continuous, systematic bombardment by enemy howitzers – casualties were fifty-eight killed and wounded, including victims of shell shock. From the 8th to the 10th they marched back and up and back and up and back again, each man carrying eighty-five pounds (full pack plus additional ammunition in two bandoliers round the neck), demoralised and exhausted. After midnight on

10 July, Captain Thomas Elias brought new orders to attack Mametz Wood.* The wood was a mile deep and roughly three-quarters of a mile wide. Its flanks strongly defended by machine-gun emplacements, the wood was considered so nearly impregnable that it had been omitted as an objective in the initial attack of 1 July. At 4.15 a.m., the 14th and 16th Battalions attacked up the open middle in clear view of the enemy, while Jones and his battalion moved into Queens Nullah, a long, deep ditch on high ground immediately fronting the wood. Moving up, he saw waves of men slowly advancing towards the wood – to him 'an impressive sight'.[21]

Doubting whether the new recruits of his Fourth Army could retain discipline in a frontal assault on strongly fortified positions, General Henry Rawlinson had decided that they would attack at a leisurely walk, forbidding running until twenty yards from the enemy trench. He also neglected to coordinate artillery fire on enemy batteries, which, as a result, took an appalling toll on the slow-walking infantry.

Shells burst in the nullah. Casualties mounted. Noise was deafening, the air thick with smoke and chalk dust. Jones hugged the earth. Nearby, his colonel nonchalantly stood exposed. Another officer called out to him, 'Well, Bell!' – a memorable rhyme (*IP* 154) – and they reminisced about service together in India, a conversation soon obscured by the screaming of a badly wounded man. Despite unmodulated thundering drumfire, Jones heard on his right 'one of the most moving things' he would ever hear, the 14th Battalion singing in Welsh 'Jesu, lover of my soul' (*IP* 160). Faintly, he heard a shrill whistle and, seeing his lieutenant, R. G. Rees, wave them forward, clambered over the top. Almost immediately, Rees, just ahead of him, fell – a death commemorated movingly in *In Parenthesis* (166).[22]

Slowly Jones's battalion crossed sixty yards of plateau, scurried down a steep incline, and walked up a gradually rising slope towards the enemy: 500 yards taking them over five minutes, a passage through a maelstrom of bullets and shrapnel flying at every angle – a myriad of potential deaths and maimings with no protecting cover. German machine-guns, methodically sweeping the waves of slowly walking men, ravaged especially the Welsh to the right. His own battalion was slightly sheltered by a fortunate alignment of ground. Nevertheless, a third of them fell.[23]

Rushing the enemy trench at the edge of the wood, he tripped and fell flat but, to his surprise, was not bayoneted in the back – the trench was occupied by corpses.[24] He rose and entered the wood. Fighting until 9 a.m., he and the others pushed 600 yards forward until enfilading machine-gun fire pinned them down. They laid low for the rest of the morning, taking casualties from British heavy artillery falling short. At 1 p.m., the enemy

---

* A few years later, Jones was startled when reading in Malory 'Captain Elias came on the morn' to do battle.

machine-gunners eliminated, they pushed forward. Jones saw a German accidentally drop a grenade and throw another over the bush in which he was hiding. In response, he threw one of his own, wounding or killing the man, whose dropped stick-bomb he examined, admiring the label on its handle. Pushing forward, he saw haggard enemy prisoners resembling sleepwalkers – the battalion would capture ninety that day, including officers whose long-skirted field-grey greatcoats 'with ... red-piping of exactly the right hue & proportion' he admired.[25]

At 6 p.m., within forty yards of the northern edge of the wood, they came under heavy fire from the German second line and were ordered back 250 yards. Retreating, Jones passed the corpses of acquaintances, some mutilated beyond recognition but wearing on their sleeves the yellow badge of the battalion.

In the dark, he began stalking a German whom he recognised in time to be Major Jack Edwards, second-in-command of the battalion.

A corporal from headquarters ordered Jones into line firing from a prone position along with others. One near him was shot. Jones tried in vain to stop the bleeding. With the help of captured German picks, they managed to dig a shallow trench and prepared to hold for the night.[26]

Probably after midnight, Jones was sent to help clear another portion of the wood. While advancing, he felt his left leg slammed hard and he fell. Realising he had been shot, he crawled back towards the British line. A Welsh corporal hoisted him onto his back and carried him till Major Edwards told him, 'Drop the bugger here', and asked, 'Don't you know there's a sod of a war on?' The question amused Jones, who resumed crawling until he was found by stretcher-bearers. They carried him back through the still-heavily-shelled valley of approach.[27]

He had been shot through the calf half-an-inch behind the bone. At a forward dressing station a medical orderly exclaimed, 'What a beautiful blighty!' and extracted the bullet. It had struck at near muzzle velocity – Jones's leg a livid bruise from toes to hip.[28]

He was moved to a casualty clearing station ten miles behind the line and slept. A cultivated, upper-class nurse asking how he felt startled him awake, her voice to him 'the nicest thing in the world' – the first female English voice he had heard in seven months. It 'brought back a "civilized" world' he had 'almost forgotten existed'. In later years he remembered that voice as having left 'an indelible mark' and speculated about its possibly making him especially sensitive to the power of 'a certain sort of voice as if it were a *physical touch* – a healing thing it is almost'.

Every July, for the rest of his life, he would relive his experience at the Somme, saying in 1971, 'my mind can't be rid of it'.[29]

* * *

On the night of 15 July, Jones crossed the channel in the *St David* and in the morning was moved to a hospital in Birmingham. On the 20th, he was sent to the idyllic Warwickshire village of Shipston-on-Stour to convalesce in Park House Hospital at 40 Church Street on the north edge of the village. There he fell in love with a tall, shapely, unregistered Voluntary Aid Detachment nurse named Elsie Hancock, with reddish, chestnut hair (fig. 5). She was, he later said, 'the object of my adoration', but, with no opportunity for embracing, 'it wasn't a real love affair'. She told him that she was engaged to an officer who had earlier recovered from a leg wound, but she felt affection for Jones and gave him photographs of herself.

5. 'Yours ever Elsie', 1916

She lived next door at number 36, and, though patients were forbidden to visit the homes of nurses, one afternoon in September they went for tea with her mother in the garden. The next morning he was visited by Dr McTaggart, the hospital director. After moralising about the Ten Commandments and 'inflexible laws governing the universe', he said that Jones had broken a regulation by visiting Nurse Hancock's home and, so, would be discharged. Elsie later told him that the doctor's daughter, the hospital matron, had seen them from a top-floor window and told her father. Fifty years later Jones would say with considerable passion, 'Christ forgive me, I could wring her bloody neck.'[30]

During his two-week post-convalescent leave, he made a brightly coloured pastel drawing of a knight bearing a damsel on his charger (fig. 6), subsequently known in the family as *Lancelot and Guinevere*. With prominent chin, the knight resembles the artist. With reddish chestnut hair worn up at the back, the damsel resembles Elsie Hancock.* He and Elsie wrote to each other for the rest of the war, she sending him more photographs of herself.

After leaving Shipston, in London on his way to his parents' house, Jones had visited Hartrick and recounted the assault on Mametz Wood as a sort of comedy.[31] Hartrick asked for a drawing of it for the *Graphic*. Jones made and delivered 'Close Quarters', which was published on 9 September (fig. 7), accompanied by a caption referring to 'the Welsh Division – helmeted like their ancestors at Agincourt'.

* J. Miles and D. Shiel misidentify Guinevere (*Maker Unmade*, p. 215), their mistake originating with Jones's mother, who knew nothing of Elsie Hancock and, referring to the picture, used to say, 'That's David and Elsie', meaning Elsie Levitt, a brunette.

6. *Lancelot and Guinevere*, 1916

Also while on leave, Jones gave his parents a two-page essay entitled 'A French Vision', his earliest surviving writing. Recording thoughts and feelings about his combat experience, he describes his battalion first approaching the front line through a flooded communication trench and contrasts modern 'wholesale butchery' with war in 'the old days'. But, recalling the Battle of Agincourt, he asks, 'Was it worthwhile for these men, five centuries . . . ago? By their fierce conflict, and their outpoured blood, they freed the land from the tyrant's yoke!' And, returning to the present, 'The trench is still cold and wet; eyes still ache, and hands freeze. But it's worth it!' He later confessed that during the war he was immature and, unlike Wilfred Owen, believed 'the old lie'.[32] Like many in wartime, he anesthetised himself with euphemism and comforting cliché. The essay reflects the 500th anniversary of Agincourt in the previous year, which pervaded the consciousness of soldiers and would inform their memoirs. Although jingoistic, the essay is the seed of *In Parenthesis*, which also includes a journey through a flooded communication trench and alludes to Agincourt, though contradicting the nationalistic warmongering of Shakespeare's Henry V.

* * *

7. 'Close Quarters', *Graphic*, 9 September 1916

Jones rejoined his battalion at the most violent area of the front north of Ypres. On 24 October 1916, now as a member of the 14th Platoon of D Company, he went into reserve dugouts in the south-west bank of the Yser Canal, a place he recognised years later in Chaucer's description of the Temple of Mars in 'The Knight's Tale': a dead forest of sharp stubs, harsh wind, cold, dimness, black smoke, and frightening noises.[33]

He saw that the war had changed. It was now a matter of wholesale, mechanised force. There was more artillery, much of it forward, firing in the open. Ammunition dumps 'rose like slag heaps on every available bit of ground'. The enthusiasm of before the Somme was gone. Life now seemed 'an endless repetition with no foreseeable end'. Half the men of the battalion were now strangers to him. He began insulating himself emotionally. He continued to sketch but his subjects were no longer men but equipment (fig. 8) and landscapes with ruined buildings (fig. 9). The shift reflects withdrawal from companions, who were subject to killing and maiming. Images of 'wounded men' would haunt him for the rest of his life.[34]

Assigned to Battalion Headquarters, a dugout in the Canal Bank, he was given a little dugout of his own in the support line. During the day he drew maps at headquarters,

8. *Equipment, 1917*

9. *Breilen Aug 18, 1917, N.W. of Ypres Mark I or Mark IV Tank?*

most nights accompanying the intelligence officer on patrol making sketch-maps.[35] Although diaries were forbidden, he kept one. On 2 November, all but a few pages of it were destroyed, along with his dugout, by five rounds of artillery.

Soon after, he was assigned to the 2nd Field Survey Company and sent to Observation Group B, Royal Engineers, for three weeks' training in survey principles, map reading, and the operation of a theodolite in locating enemy batteries by cross-observation or flash-spotting. He was then sent south to a unit observing from three posts overlooking Ploegsteert Wood. His job was to plot coordinates to pinpoint German batteries. He was unsuccessful. Flashes in quick succession confused him, and, in the dark, he sometimes had difficulty finding the speaking end of the telephone. He often jostled the scope, losing the bearing, and approximating it. By the end of February 1917, he was discharged from the Survey on the trumped-up charge of not getting a haircut.[36]

On 12 December 1916, Germany had proposed peace, which, to his regret, Britain and France rejected. He sent a drawing to Hartrick, who published it in January 1917 in the *Graphic* over the caption 'Germany and Peace' (fig. 10). A Teutonic knight approaches the alluring

10. 'Germany and Peace', *Graphic*, 20 January 1917

and vulnerable angel Peace, resembling Elsie Hancock, eroticised with bare shoulders.

Also while with the Survey, he had sent an essay to his father, who published an edited version in the *Christian Herald* on 17 May 1917. In it Jones writes that though 'the triumph of the Entente over the war lords of Odin' has not occurred, 'the Bosch [*sic*] is . . . "up against it"', and he wonders whether any of the 'Bosch prisoners' had 'with vandal joy, . . . gloated over a prostrate and stricken Belgium'.

On 29 March he was back at the Canal Bank and again assigned to headquarters to draw maps. For much of the next year, he went on night patrols. He also helped repulse two raids. From reserve positions, he watched the shelling of Ypres to the south, which, at night, reminded him of fireworks at the Crystal Palace seen from the Hilly Fields. He saw enemy artillery flatten the remnant of the famous Ypres tower.[37]

About this time, one night in a communication trench, he encountered a 'shit wallah' (assigned to empty a latrine) carrying two full buckets. Recognising Evan Evans from a Welsh battalion, he said, 'You've got a dirty bloody job.' Evans replied, 'Bloody job indeed. The army of Artaxerxes was utterly destroyed for lack of sanitation', and he urged Jones to read some history. Evans would join Lloyd George as a prototype for Dai Greatcoat, the archetypal soldier remembering past warfare at the centre of *In Parenthesis*.[38]

In the left pocket of his tunic, Jones kept letters from home, including one in which his mother wrote, 'Really, David, the spelling in your last letter was a disgrace to the family. A child of four would do better.' One evening, while removing his clothes, he discovered to his surprise that a ricochet bullet had penetrated the pocket, the packet of letters, his cardigan, waistcoat, shirt, and underwear vest, just grazing his chest. He could not remember feeling the impact.[39]

Early in 1917, his helmet saved his life. He was in the firing trench when a mine exploded. In the rain of debris, a large piece of metal struck his helmet, knocking him unconscious. He came to with the helmet pressed down around his ears and a herringbone pattern imprinted across its inside. For a week he had a very stiff neck. After the war, Poulter (fig. 11), who was 6 feet 2 inches tall and strong, recounted picking him up, tucking him under one arm, and running with him to safety.[40] This may have been the occasion – Jones would not recall being carried but then he had been unconscious.

While off duty one rainy Sunday and wandering alone between support and reserve lines looking for firewood, Jones came upon a byre that might contain dry wood. Putting his eye to a crack in the paling, he saw two gusty

11. Leslie Poulter, c. 1917

candle flames and the back of a man in liturgical vestments facing a stack of ammunition boxes covered by a white cloth. Half a dozen men in muddied tunics were kneeling on the straw-covered floor. The tinkling of a little bell broke the silence, followed faintly by mysterious words. This, Jones realised, was a Catholic Mass. It seemed like the Last Supper – never had he experienced at an Anglican service the unity he sensed between these men. So close to the front line, in a panorama of desolation, this was 'a great marvel' and would remain, in memory, a numinous experience.[41]

At 10 a.m. on 24 April, a heavy German bombardment fell all along their front. In the firing trench, he was worried about Harry Cook, whom he had not seen all day. Noticing Poulter running down another trench, he shouted against the noise of explosions, 'HAVE YOU SEEN HARRY?' Poulter yelled, 'I SAW YOUNG HARRY WITH HIS BEAVER ON.' Jones realised that Cook was alive and knew that a beaver was a medieval face-guard, but Poulter had been quoting something, which, a while later, he recalled as *Henry IV, Part I*.[42] Poulter's spontaneous allusion subsequently epitomised for Jones the penetration of the present by the past in the minds of infantrymen.

In this sector at about this time at an intersection of trenches, he was shaving when the Prince of Wales appeared, wearing a short 'British Warm' coat and light woollen scarf. He asked, 'Do you happen to know which of these trenches leads directly to' a certain post 'in the forward trench?' Embarrassed, his face lathered and in a tattered weskit, Jones indicated the trench and advised caution by a certain trench-sign. The Prince said, 'Thanks, can't have a fag with you – an awful hurry', and vanished. A few minutes later, a breathless colonel stuck his head round the revetment and asked, 'Have you seen Wales?' Jones said yes, that he had directed him to the forward trench. The colonel asked, 'Why didn't you stop him?' and ran off, Jones calling after him, 'HOW COULD I, SIR?'[43]

On 6 May, Reggie Allen was killed by a trench-mortar projectile. Being a soldier was a job, death and mutilation commonplace, but this death turned Jones's chief solace, friendship, into his sharpest grief.[44]*

Artillery fire was frightful, its main target not opposing artillery, as before the Somme, but infantry in the trenches. And it was more accurate. Dawn bombardments were routine, followed by irregular shelling. On 17 June, heavy shelling killed thirty and wounded sixty. On the 22nd, according to the battalion diarist, shelling caused 'a great amount of damage to trenches & personnel'. On the 23rd, huddled with others in a dugout, Jones endured seven hours and fifteen minutes of continuous shelling.[45] In a light bombardment, one shell a minute landed in the immediate vicinity. A heavy bombardment involved a heavy gun for every twenty yards under fire and a

---

* In 1937 he would dedicate *In Parenthesis* 'especially' to 'PTE. R.A. LEWIS-GUNNER' – using only his initials lest 'someone who loved him might chance to see it & be upset'.

field gun for every ten yards, so that a shell landed in a company sector every two or three seconds. Most dangerous was shrapnel from anti-aircraft shells, arriving with approximately every four heavy howitzer shells and bursting in air like oversize grenades. In a concentrated bombardment, the interval between explosions disappeared. In a dugout, the earth shook. Up above, it heaved like the sea in storm. In Jones's experience, there were 'chaps who fear' most 'being caught underground & those who fear most the nakedness of above ground'. He was among the latter.[46] Continual experience, day after day, of even light bombardments was enervating – a numbness like shock set in, leaving a sadness that lengthened into malaise.

Jones and his battalion spent the night of 23–24 July digging a narrow (2 feet wide, 7 feet deep) assembly trench in preparation for the Third Battle of Ypres, later known as Passchendaele. They worked within 200 yards of the German line, amid exploding anti-aircraft, howitzer, and gas shells. The night was, he later recalled, 'the worst of all'. Gas masks 'became a filthy mess of condensation inside'. He dug all night, thinking 'this is the end; they've got us this time'. But 'in the morning . . . not a single person' in the work party had been hit, though, for the first time, members of the brigade were blinded by mustard gas.[47]

On the morning of 25 July, his platoon helped guard the flanks of a party raiding Pilckem Ridge. Two evenings later, his platoon went forward again to guard a flank of a raiding party, which was annihilated (more than a hundred killed or wounded), and Jones's platoon 'badly cut up'.

His regiment was to initiate the battle of Passchendaele. Jones was assigned to 'battalion nuclear reserve' – a group from which the battalion, if wiped out, could be reconstituted. He wanted to be with his friends in the attack, so he asked to trade places with a married man. The adjutant berated him for 'pretending to wish to be a bloody hero', while knowing full well that men detailed had no choice in the matter. The night of 31 July, Jones was with the nucleus 'beneath the trajectory / zone' of artillery fire (WP 33) when the others assaulted Pilckem Village, taking heavy casualties, but gaining the ridge.[48] On 1 August, he joined them there. On the 4th, they returned to the Canal Bank.

Now too weak for combat, the battalion was sent, on 25 September, to the usually quiet Bois-Grenier sector, where they were subjected to heavy shelling for days. Jones was granted leave but astonished the adjutant by postponing it to avoid having to help his parents move house. His leave (ten days including travel time) began on 14 October. He arrived at Victoria Station crawling with lice and went straight to his parents' new house in Howson Road. Without pausing, he went upstairs to the bathroom, removed his uniform and underclothes, and threw them out the window. (His mother had insisted that he discard his lousy clothing this way.) Seeing his sister approach the clothing, he shouted, 'FOR CHRIST SAKE, LEAVE

THE FUCKING THINGS ALONE.' Such language had not been heard in the Jones home. Mortified, he bathed and put on civilian clothes, which no longer fitted.[49]

He happily returned to trenches at Bois-Grenier. They were old, the communication trenches 'quite beautiful' with flowering morning glory and other convolvuli tangling over the revetment frames. The battalion would remain here through most of the autumn of 1917 and return in January and February 1918. The quietest front Jones had experienced, with opposing firing trenches 300 yards apart, here he 'had quite a nice time'. Again he was attached to the intelligence officer at Battalion Headquarters and went with him on night patrols, making sketch-maps of enemy saps and trenches. He also drew finished maps and wrote reports.[50]*

Mapping no-man's-land since early 1916 intensified Jones's spatial imagination in ways that would influence his art. His imagination had a decade-long incubation period – important experiences taking approximately ten years to gestate and emerge from his subconscious in painting or poetry. His visual art of a decade later, and increasingly from then on, would consist of irregular areas of colour, wandering lines, and broken perspectives that give them affinity with maps. He felt considerable affection for the single wavering line typical of British defences, the kind of line he would draw 'with the point' and which he later thought differentiated the British imagination from that of other nations. And in his poetry after *In Parenthesis*, narrative and rhetorical 'lines' would waver freely to chart the geography of his imagination.

In the Bois-Grenier sector, sleeping alone in a little dugout in the support line, Jones ignored standing orders to keep boots on. He was awakened on the night of 25 October by 'a hurricane of enemy shelling' – the worst he had ever experienced. His 'little dug-out shook with the vibrations of near H.E. bursts'. 'Half awake and . . . bewildered', he also heard low bursts of medium shrapnel, long-distance 'nine-fives', and twelve-inch shells trundling far over the support line. A barrage in such depth usually heralded an attack. You could not run safely through the trenches with bare feet. He put on a boot but could not find the other. He lit the stub end of a candle, quickly extinguished by the ground's shaking. In what seemed an endless nightmare, he felt frantically for the other boot, eventually finding it tangled in his equipment. He put it on and emerged into 'a tornado of violence'. Never again would he disobey standing orders about boots.[51]

He had long ago acquired two anthologies of poetry, *Palgrave's Golden Treasury* and *The Oxford Book of English Verse 1250–1900*. He carried one or the other into the trenches to read but in secret because Cockneys considered

---

* He would commemorate himself as cartographer in a character named 'Private W. Map' (*IP* 127). According to the Welsh colloquial practice of identifying a person by occupation, 'Walter Map' identifies someone named Walter David Jones who makes maps.

poetry-readers sissies. Now he was finding it difficult to enjoy poetry because most writers 'knew no calamity comparable to what we knew' and 'wrote of death and hurts and despair in highfalutin' terms, without our close-up, day by day contact with such things'.[52] He would affect a rapprochement with literary tradition in *In Parenthesis* by combining allusion to the poetry in his anthologies with allusions to romances, which afford more intense expression of crisis and horror than most 'realistic' lyric writing.

In the spring of 1917, he became friendly with the Catholic brigade chaplain, Daniel Hughes SJ. Stationed with a Methodist Welsh battalion, for company Hughes visited the Londoners, who were less scandalised by his drinking whisky with the men. Jones thought him 'a hell of a nice chap, . . . a remarkable man and of great bravery'. (He had won the Military Cross.) Moved by his glimpse of the Mass in the Ypres sector months earlier, Jones spoke to him about the Catholic Church and borrowed from him St Francis de Sales's *Introduction to the Devout Life*.[53]

To Jones the only antidote to the catastrophe of war was metaphysical. The virtues of infantrymen implied for him significance of the sort that de Sales emphasises in his book. For Jones, Anglican Christianity had become a matter of dead routine. 'There was something pretty unlovable about those official "church parades"', he would recall, 'very Erastian' (subordinate to the state) 'and totally devoid of the sacramental'. He now felt 'inside, a Catholic'.[54]

Poulter, too, was drawn to Catholicism. In Jones's dugout, they talked about their new shared interest over whisky pilfered by Poulter from the regimental sergeant major. Poulter entered the Catholic Church during the war, but Jones procrastinated: this was a big decision. Furthermore, most Catholics were not as appealing as Hughes. A number of rosary-praying Irishmen in his battalion were 'crude, revolting', and 'unchristian' in their 'discourtesy'.[55]

In November, Jones produced a short pseudo-medieval allegory in the style of William Morris's late prose romances entitled *The Quest* and printed by his father as a New Year's card. On the cover (fig. 12), a knight and bare-shouldered damsel, idealisations of himself and Elsie, travel with a minstrel, also resembling Jones, and a monkish scholar. Together they seek a classless society in 'the Castle called Heart's Desire'. An angelic voice

12. *The Quest*, New Year, 1918

urges the knight to fight only for liberty and justice and says that the 'mighty king, who rules in equity' shall guide them to his castle, the heavenly reward for chivalric behaviour.

* * *

Except while on leave, in reserve, and with the Survey, for the past three years Jones had experienced enemy shelling daily and an extensive bombardment, on average, twice a week. Now artillery 'crashes' or salvos fell suddenly all along the forward and support lines and then immediately ceased, causing far more casualties than continual bombardment. One casualty of this nerve-racking tactic was quiet, a condition no longer of equanimity but of apprehension. Up to the autumn of 1916, he had been deeply, irrationally convinced that he would survive the war; now he felt he would not. He was rated a third-class shot – he 'just ... didn't care anymore'. 'Indifference, tedium' masked post-traumatic stress, then known as shell shock.[56]

The basic symptom of shell shock was unbearable fear. Cases were hysteric or neurasthenic. The hysteric is the stereotype: a man suddenly cringing in terror, weeping, clinging to a companion (*IP* 153). Far more common were the neurasthenic, resolute under fire, their underlying fear emerging later in breakdowns or lingering neuroses. Jones was one of these. His years under fire in the trenches may not have been the sole cause of later unhappiness but they were sufficient cause.

Depleted by casualties, the brigade disbanded his battalion, its companies going in mid-February 1918 to the other three battalions. For Jones, this was devastating, and – possibly, he thought, as a consequence – he came down with trench fever, a disease related to typhus. Excused all duty, he was sent to divisional reserve, his fever at 105°F (40.5°C) for several days. His neck and face swelled and his tongue turned green. It was a severe case, involving 'disorderly action of the heart'. He was evacuated to Base Hospital, where he nearly died, and was sent to a hospital in north London for three months. In newspapers, he followed the great German offensive of late March, convinced that trench fever had saved

13. 'Civilisation bound by the Black Knight of Prussia', *Graphic*, 13 July 1918

his life.[57] With no known cure, the illness ran its course, and he completed his convalescence in nursing homes.

Jones's years of combat were over. He had seen more active duty in the war than any other British writer. With time subtracted for convalescence and leave, he spent a total of 117 weeks at the front – at least two months longer than Edmund Blunden, formerly regarded as having served longest. Jones later said, 'I'm not sure I killed anyone, though I ought to have done. What I didn't like was the Mills bomb, tossing it down into a German dugout, killing or maiming someone you couldn't see. It was horrible. On the other hand, shooting a chap … seems quite a respectable thing to do.'[58]

While convalescing, he made a final drawing for the *Graphic*, entitled 'Civilisation bound by the Black Knight of Prussia, who is challenged by another Knight, who represents the Allies' (fig. 13). Civilisation resembles, once again, Elsie Hancock, more eroticised than ever. Like his other pictures for the *Graphic*, this one reflects his belief that he was fighting to save France, Belgium, and Western culture.

* * *

After post-convalescent leave and tedious military training near Liverpool, in August 1918, Jones was sent to the 3rd Battalion of the Royal Welch Fusiliers at the New Barracks on the southern edge of Limerick, Ireland.

During assault training there, he badly sprained an ankle. A medical officer gave him a walking stick and permission to use it. As he hobbled across the barracks parade-ground, a regimental sergeant major commanded, 'Put that stick down!' Jones explained that the MO had given him permission to use it. The sergeant major repeated the order, was refused twice more, and arrested him. Awaiting court martial, Jones spent three days and nights in the guardroom, which reminded him of Cruikshank's engravings of the Tower of London and Byron's 'The Prisoner of Chillon'. A friendly lieutenant named Evans convinced the sergeant major to reduce the charge to 'hesitation in obeying an order'. Jones was confined to barracks for two weeks. The medical officer had not intervened, he later told Jones, because 'we officers have to stick together'. His cowardice and the injustice rankled for a long time.[59]

Since before the war, Jones had favoured Irish independence. He realised that British propaganda about the sanctity of small nations and their right to self-determination contradicted British rule of Ireland. He bought a copy of the 1916 Proclamation and hung it on the barrack-room wall, where other soldiers read it with interest and respect. Members of rebel paramilitary units were regularly arrested and held in the New Barracks. At the main gate, their mothers and sisters accosted sentries shouting, 'Murderer!' (Their screeching and jeering had made one of his nights in the guardroom nightmarish.) Their courage reminded him of unarmed Gordon on the stairs at Khartoum. Jones dreaded being called out for policing and worried about what he would do in 'a real showdown'. Probably, he thought, he would follow orders.⁶⁰ Having fought for three years 'in defence of the Empire', he was reminded of first-century Romans subjugating British Celts.

He later wrote that Ireland 'made a fairly vivid impression especially the soft rain & the intense blueness of the distance & also the great beauty of young women very dirty in *red* skirts bare footed & in white shifts or blouses'. Once especially he was affected by a young beauty. In the second week of November 1918, taking part in daylong manoeuvres in the hills north of Cork, he and four companions passed a barefoot, red-haired beauty driving a cow. She was 'a wild & almost savage figure' with 'the carriage of a princess', the reds of her hair and skirt bright in the lateral light. She looked to Jones 'like the daughter of the High King of all Eire' or, he later thought, Helen of Troy. She entered a long, low farm building, thatched and overgrown. He followed her in and saw, sitting beside a small duck pond in the dirt floor, an old woman hunched before a pot over a peat fire. 'Here,' he thought, 'is the Bronze Age or Iron Age.' But the peasant princess had vanished.⁶¹ It was as if he had walked into a tale about an Irish hag who had temporarily transformed into a young beauty.

Later he frequently recalled this experience and that of the Mass north of Ypres in 1917. They were like psychologically significant, recurring dreams. In both he is alone approaching a building. In the earlier, he experiences a numinous sight. In the later, beauty vanishes in old age. The first involves surprising fulfillment and inward liberation; the second, disappointment. If a Freudian were to interpret his Irish vision, the old woman would be a mother-figure, suggesting Oedipal fear of what a beautiful young woman might become or actually be.

On 11 November 1918, the Armistice was declared. He had survived the war – his only accomplishment that surprised those who later knew him.

Just before leaving Ireland for Wimbledon to be 'disembodied', he leaned his rifle on the outside of a latrine wall and emerged to find it stolen. He was frantic. To lose your rifle is among the worst of military crimes. On 18 December at Wimbledon, with mounting anxiety, he walked up to the desk where he was to turn in his rifle, noticed a stack of rifles nearby, took one, and handed it over as his own. He walked away, convinced that someone would check the serial number and discover his ruse. Back in Brockley, he waited anxiously for the military police, convinced that sooner or later they would come for him.⁶²

With characteristic perspective, Jones would not regard the war as an important historic watershed. But it was the single most important public event of his life, occupying the last four of his formative years, indelibly staining the litmus of his identity. Decades afterwards, a door slamming or a car backfiring would startle him back to the trenches. In distant thunder, he heard artillery. Like an Ancient Mariner, he retold war anecdotes. In his final years, he said, 'the memory of [the war] is like a disease ... I still think about it more than anything else.'⁶³

PART TWO

NEW BEGINNINGS

CHAPTER 4: 1919–21

I n the spring of 1919, Jones visited Shipston-on-Stour to see Elsie Hancock. She would not break her engagement (to Thomas Bullock), so, sadly for him, they parted. At the end of his life, he would confide that his love for her had never been 'wholly eradicated'.[1]

London now seemed alien, except for the scream of tramcars sounding like incoming shells. He met with Poulter. Both felt on an extended leave and disliked civilian life. They decided to join the Archangel Expedition fighting the Bolsheviks in Russia. But Jones's father argued against his going, and Poulter went alone – Jones letting himself be convinced because he was eager to resume painting. His enthusiasm was fueled by the appearance in London galleries of post-Impressionist works and the anti-academic movement led by Wyndham Lewis.[2]

The Joneses' new home was 'Hillcrest' on Howson Road (fig. 1). Jones took over the back bedroom as a studio. It was 12 by 24 feet, with a large east-facing window. He worked at a table facing the window, at night by the light of an oil lamp and a gas jet. His mother wished to carpet the floor, but he wanted it bare to resemble the deck of a ship.[3]

He renewed his friendships with Frank Medworth and Harold Hawkins. Both had been wounded at the Somme, Hawkins so severely that he could paint only by supporting his right hand with his left arm. And both thought that Jones was suffering from shell shock. The three of them returned to the Kensington open life-class, and in the summer went on sketching trips together in the countryside of Kent and Surrey.[4] Jones and Hawkins accompanied Medworth on Sunday visits to Rotherhithe, where they patronised the Paradise pub (*IP* 112–13).

At the Medworth house, Jones met Frank's purported Great-aunt Mary (née Stewart), who was actually, Frank had discovered, his paternal grandmother. A Rotherhithe Cockney and former mistress of a German nobleman in the

1. Hillcrest, 115 Howson Road, 1934

circle of Edward VII, 'Auntie', as they called her, was delightful, one of the best talkers Jones would ever meet. Now in her seventies, she entertained them uproariously with stories of Edward and his friends. Auntie Mary would be the principal model for 'the Lady of the Pool' in *The Anathemata* (one of whose archetypes is Jesus's mother Mary), a great talker who had acquired worldly knowledge while giving and receiving carnal knowledge.[5]

Led by Hawkins, Jones and Medworth went to Shakespeare plays at the New Court Theatre. During a performance of *King John*, in which one character repeatedly says 'and bastards', they laughed hysterically and were threatened with expulsion. Jones and Medworth would repeatedly see Nigel Playfair's 1920 revival of *The Beggar's Opera*, which contributed to Jones's sense of London's living past. He would soon cease going to the theatre, later writing about drama, 'I think that of all the arts it's the most hard to get right.'[6]

Jones, Hawkins, and Medworth re-enrolled at the Camberwell art school on government grants to study 'Commercial Design and Illustration'. The other, younger students looked up to them. Jones was attractive, gentle, witty, well spoken, quiet, wistful, his home-county accent slightly Cockney, with a remarkable voice – rich, slightly off-timbre, not sonorous or deep, slightly foggy. A dozen young women were infatuated with him, including two sisters, Doreen and Evelyn Dillon, the latter for a time in earnest pursuit. To all of them he was unresponsive.[7]

2. *The Betrayal*, 1921

With Hartrick now teaching elsewhere, the most interesting art master at Camberwell was Walter Bayes, a very good artist, Jones thought, and a 'marvellous man'. Bayes emphasised what he called 'the science' of art: perspective and geometric proportion centred on 'the axis' as the 'essence' of solid form. His influence is evident in Jones's sketch for a painting of the betrayal of Jesus in Gethsemane, in which figures are located in a chiasmic recession of octagons drawn flat on the ground, with Jesus at the centre (fig. 2). The notion of axile spatiality would inform the innovative chiasmic structure of *The Anathemata*, which concludes with reference to the cross of Jesus as 'the Axile tree' (243).[8]

In 1919, Jones made important discoveries. One was El Greco's *Christ on the Mount of Olives*, newly arrived in the National Gallery. He visited it repeatedly, in 1923 calling it 'the best picture in the world'. And at the Tate he discovered Blake, revering him as a draughtsman of 'powerful linear' form. He would later say that he was influenced more by El Greco and Blake than by anything he had learned in art school. He also admired Samuel Palmer, who, he thought, sometimes painted better than Blake (Jones travelled to Shoreham especially to see Palmer's 'valley of vision'), and Piero della Francesca's *The Baptism of Christ* and *The Nativity*.[9]

In hopes of attracting attention and selling pictures, Jones, Hawkins, and Medworth called themselves 'The Three Musketeers' and took their portfolios together to galleries. They were included in the first important series of post-war exhibitions in London, in William Marchant's Goupil Gallery, in 1919, and were praised as a group by the critic for the *Observer*. Two oil paintings by Jones were exhibited, priced at £63 each: *The Reclaimers* and *The Military*. Of the latter only the final drawing survives (fig. 3), in which Jesus and the two thieves are crucified on high crosses (suggesting the influence of Tintoretto or Mantegna) by soldiers in helmets. While praising the painting's 'superb design', one critic objected to the modern British helmets as 'apt to give offence'.[10] The Three Musketeers exhibited pictures at the Goupil through 1920 and also, that year, at the Chester Gallery.

Early in the winter term of 1920, Bayes resigned from Camberwell to replace his friend and mentor, Walter

3. *The Military*, 1919

4. '1920–1 West[minister]', 1921

Sickert, as headmaster at Westminster School of Art. At his urging, the Musketeers moved with him, transferring their government grants in March 1921. The school occupied the upper floors of the Westminster Technical Institute at 77 Vincent Square, a short walk from Victoria Station. Jones enrolled in Bernard Meninsky's life class and found him 'of great help and encouragement' especially in achieving 'recession in drawing'. His influence can be seen in the most elaborate of Jones's surviving Westminster drawings, of a model with her back to a mirror reflecting vaguely the artist drawing her (fig. 4).[11]

The genius loci of the school was Sickert, who lectured once a week. A brilliant conversationalist, he clarified Jones's ideas about art. Sickert praised Turner above all other painters – Jones was the only student in the school who agreed – and undermined Jones's admiration for the Pre-Raphaelites. In his lectures, he propounded rules which Bayes enforced and Jones complied with but thought silly. Yet he regarded Sickert as 'the best English painter since Turner' and himself as 'school of Sickert', imitating his out-of-fashion Impressionist style. From Sickert he learned how colour tones change in value depending on juxtaposition with other colours and first heard about 'distortion' as a source of vitality in art. Distortion was the primary trait of post-Impressionism but, he realised, no innovation since it characterised all visual art in varying degrees, El Greco being an extreme example. Sickert encouraged him to shift to watercolours as a neglected medium and therefore one of opportunity, even though they fetched a third the price of oil paintings and, over time, faded with exposure to light. Tongue in cheek, Jones considered forming a Society for Painters of Impermanent Pictures.[12]

* * *

Jones and his friends felt, in his words, 'the imperative need to break away ... from the academic "laws of composition"'. Impressionism had 'marked the end ... of "fidelity to nature"', and the post-Impressionists 'blew most of the walls down!' Impressionism had emphasised colour and was, despite its theory, romantic; post-Impressionism re-established balance with Classicism by emphasising linear form. He saw all he could of the new art from Paris, including his now favourite – Pierre Bonnard, whom Sickert praised along with Gauguin as the greatest of the post-Impressionists. Jones was also 'very impressed' by André Derain's still lifes, which seemed to him 'monumental & ageless'.[13]

Jones was intrigued by Bloomsbury post-Impressionist theory as expounded in Clive Bell's *Art* (1914), which Sickert had urged him to read. In 1920, Roger Fry affirmed Bell's formalism in *Vision and Design*, repeating Ruskin's contention that art is neither useful nor moral. In 1922, Bell's *Since Cézanne* consolidated Bloomsbury aesthetics, its title becoming for the next few years Jones's slogan for modernity. According to Fry and Bell, abstract, intrinsic, 'significant form' gives a work of art distinctive being. In agreement was another book Jones liked, T. E. Hulme's *Speculations* (1924), emphasising 'geometric' form.[14] Of all the propositions of post-Impressionist theory, Jones especially valued Fry's declaration that a painting is not an imitation or impression but a thing in itself: a painting of a girl 're-presents' (hyphen required) the girl 'under another form'. Because it 'effects what it signifies', Jones thought artistic depiction sacramental and especially like the Eucharist. This may explain why he always spoke of a picture only in terms of its subject: it was a tree, a ship, a cat, a woman, re-presented.[15]

*   *   *

Jones had many art-school friends, including the sculptor Stephen Tomlin; Mirita Blunt, with whom he was briefly in love (see *IP* 32); and Mollie Higgins, whom he considered 'the most beautiful girl in Bloomsbury', to whom he gave two drawings. They mostly met in The Old Lady's, a one-room eatery in Artillery Row, and in nearby pubs, discussing art, art theory, artists, and politics. When one of them gushed about Communism meaning the end of war, Jones said, 'Don't be stupid, you'll fight each other about what you mean by Communism.' With ex-servicemen he reminisced about the war.[16]

Sometimes friends 'enticed' him to concerts, which he 'endured' and, if Mozart was performed, enjoyed. From Wagner, he 'fled to the bar'. Once 'dragged' to a performance of *Parsifal* and finding 'the sheer noise … the stage sets & the attitudinizing' by actors unbearable, he left and rode the Circle Line, read until the end of the performance, and rejoined his friends emerging from the theatre.[17]

By the summer of 1921, he was in love with one of his art-school friends, vivacious, unconventional Dorothea de Halpert (fig. 5), a protégée of Sickert and a Catholic. A Russophile, she 'dragged' him to see *Uncle Vanya* and other Russian plays. (They seemed to him 'much the same … a general moan,

5. Dorothea de Halpert, c. 1920

a lot of long diminutives and pistol shots off stage'.) She 'made' him read Tolstoy's *Tales of Army Life* and the short stories of Gogol. She 'dragged' him to a performance of Russian ballet, which he liked 'a bit' though it seemed largely 'whimsy'. Through her, he met former Slade students, including Leila Reynolds, an atheist Communist who ridiculed him as 'the holiest young man' she knew, drawing him in caricature dancing naked with a large rosary around his neck, its crucifix strategically placed.[18]

Dorothea rented a tiny, one-room ground floor studio in Vincent Square, where he and others spent time between classes. There he told her that when about to begin a painting he felt a great dread that 'was enough to stop anyone painting ever'. On a gas ring in her studio they boiled gelatin for priming canvas. One 'bitter winter day', snuggling close together, they fell asleep, and nearly died – the unlit gas was on.[19] The knocking of a visiting friend woke them, saving their lives.

Possibly with her – it was shortly after the war with a young woman he wanted particularly to impress – he was in an Underground station when up walked his old platoon-mate Lazarus Black, looking like a comic music-hall Jew with a gaudy tiepin and shoes like mirrors. He threw his arms around Jones's neck saying, 'David, what are you doing?' Jones icily replied, 'Very well, actually.' After further failures to initiate conversation, Black walked sadly away. 'Who was that horrible man?' the woman asked. 'Do you know people like that?' Jones replied, 'Just someone I was with during the war.' In later years, he told this story as one in which 'I come off rather badly.'[20]

Dorothea was engaged to an American named Forrest Travis but was having second thoughts. She and Jones 'almost became engaged', he later said, but were not sexually intimate. When, sitting beside her in her tiny

6. Jones, possibly by Dorothea de Halpert or Frank Medworth, c. 1920

studio, he made advances, she jerked away, saying 'Don't ever do that again.'
He never forgot those words. Decades later, memory of the rebuff prompted
him to confide, 'I don't really understand this blasted sex thing.' She steered
their relationship back to being just friends and married Travis in February
1922. Jones subsequently visited her upper-class mother, Beatrix, who was
now fond of 'our David', 'very pleasant and entertaining as he always is in his
unaffected natural way'. For the rest of his life, he and Dorothea remained
friends, visiting, writing, and exchanging gifts.[21]

*   *   *

In 1919, Jones's reading of Jessie Weston's *From Ritual to Romance* and
especially Frazer's *The Golden Bough* precipitated a religious crisis by revealing
similarities between Christianity and paganism. Then, the same year, he
read *The Goddess of Ghosts* (1915), a collection of stories by the classicist
C. C. Martindale SJ, which resolved his doubts by disclosing the spiritual
intimations of paganism as validated by Christianity and what Jones would
call 'the Vegetation Rites of the Redeemer'. Martindale's book was a major
influence – Jones said, 'formative'.[22]

In January 1919, for the Camberwell School of Arts Sketch Club prize,
Jones had chosen G. K. Chesterton's *Orthodoxy*, a witty argument for
Catholic Christianity. Jones was increasingly drawn to Catholicism. With
his father he attended a debate between a Dominican priest and a leading
representative of the Protestant Truth Society – a debate which, to his
father's chagrin, Jones thought the priest won. By 1921, he was reading the
Roman missal and slipping out of life class to attend
'at least a bit of High Mass' in nearby Westminster
Cathedral.[23]

Conversation with Catholic art-school friends
and Poulter, back from Russia in 1920, convinced
him to seek formal instruction. He accompanied one
of his art-school friends, Frank Wall, to Yorkshire in
the early summer of 1920. Wall introduced him to
an intelligent, cultured Catholic priest named John
O'Connor (fig. 7) at St Cuthbert's Church in Heaton.
On subsequent visits to Yorkshire, staying with Wall's
aunts in Wharfedale, Jones visited O'Connor evenings,
with the aid of two Bibles and a bottle of whisky,
discussing theology late into the night.[24] O'Connor was
a friend of G. K. Chesterton and the prototype of his
fictional detective, Father Brown, though Jones could
see little resemblance. Theologically sophisticated,
O'Connor was convinced that doctrinal formulae were

7. John O'Connor, c. 1925

of limited use, that terms like substance, accidents, and transubstantiation were 'inadequate', as even the Council of Trent admitted, 'to convey … reality'. He emphasised the Mass as sacrifice, and Jones 'felt' for himself its 'sacrificial nature … as against the "memorial meal" of Protestant theology'. O'Connor told him that the real presence made the Eucharist and the Incarnation closely analogous, an idea that would inform *The Anathemata*. Jones confided that he was disenchanted with art school and uncertain about the place of art in the modern world. O'Connor mentioned having met the sculptor Eric Gill, who had recently co-founded a guild of Catholic craftsmen in Sussex. Jones was interested, and O'Connor wrote to Gill arranging a meeting.[25]

On 28 January 1921, Jones and Wall went to Portslade, west of Brighton, where Jones's parents had the loan of a house on the beach. The next morning they walked to Ditchling Common and found Gill in his workshop. He was energetic, friendly, responsive, inclined to grin while conversing. Jones expressed dissatisfaction with art school and misgivings about his role as an artist. Gill spoke about the workmen of the Guild integrating life, work, religion, and local rural culture. While talking (in a voice at once husky and slight, like that of Greta Garbo), he carved letters in stone. Jones was impressed – he admired Roman inscriptions, having 'felt the majesty and power' of those on the plaster casts of Trajan's Column at Camberwell and Westminster and in the Wroxeter forum inscription at the Victoria and Albert Museum. His own attempts at Roman lettering and those of fellow students had been pathetic or boring, but Gill was carving 'living lettering'. Jones and Wall met the other craftsmen, ate supper with the Gill family, and left at eight in the evening. Jones had enjoyed Gill's Socratic conversation and wanted to return and work with him.[26]

Jones finished the winter term at Westminster and, during the 1921 spring holiday in mid-May, for three days walked with Wall the old Pilgrim's Road (from Orpington) to Canterbury, entering Canterbury on 17 May. In the cathedral, Jones came to the tomb of Archbishop John Peckham, who had helped Edward I conquer Wales. Roused to historical fury and muttering army execrations (and hoping no verger was watching), Jones gave his effigy 'a whack', hurting his hand. From Canterbury he sent Gill a postcard. Upon returning to his parents' home, he experienced inexplicable anxiety, depression, and insomnia, which lasted a few days, the first definitive intimations of emotional distress to come.[27]

During his walk to Canterbury, he had made a sketch of the Kentish hills that he used as a study for a large oil painting (27 by 39 inches), finished that summer in Dorothea's studio and entitled *North Downs* (fig. 8). He submitted it to the London Group. On 21 October, Dorothea's mother records in her diary, 'Poor Jones is depressed as his picture was rejected

8. *North Downs*, 1921

9. *Our Lady of the Hills*, 1921

– it is too large I think.' He gave it to Dorothea. The study for the painting was shown in the November–December 1921 Goupil Exhibition, priced at £4.4s., along with an oil entitled *Our Lady of the Hills* (£3.1s.). In the latter (fig. 9), Mary, with sorrowful eyes, foresees Calvary, one of the hills of the title. Neither picture sold.

* * *

About whether or not to enter the Catholic Church, Jones was uncertain. On 12 July, O'Connor wrote that Jones had '*negative* doubt or nervous misgivings about almost everything', that this was part of his general post-war disillusionment.

Visiting Ditchling a second time, on 20 July, Jones told Gill that he could not see how anyone could be sure that the Catholic Church was what it claimed to be. Gill said that only the Catholic Church originated in New Testament times, professed to be universal in membership, and claimed absolute moral and religious authority. He then drew three triangular shapes: the lines of one did not meet at one angle, those of a second were even more disconnected, and those of a third met. He asked Jones to pick the triangle. Pointing to the last, Jones said, 'I like that one.' Gill said, 'I didn't ask which you prefer. That isn't a better triangle. The others aren't triangles at all. Either it's a triangle or it's not.' There was only one. It was the Catholic Church. That day, Jones made up his mind to join it.[28] *

* * *

* In their biographies of Gill, Robert Speaight and Fiona MacCarthy recount the anecdote of the triangles without indicating its meaning, which Jones related to me and W. Blissett in conversation.

10. Desmond Chute, 1919

11. Hilary Pepler, 1921

Invited by Gill to help paint the incised letters of his war memorial for New College, Oxford, on 3 August 1921 Jones returned to Ditchling. He was given a place to sleep in the attic of the dairy behind Gill's house with Denis Tegetmeier, another former art-student and ex-serviceman. Jones thought the unpainted memorial 'marvellous', that Gill had solved the problem of inscribing English by forgetting 'what the words mean altogether & just' making 'as even as possible a pattern of incised lines covering equally the whole panel'. Gill wanted the letters painted with red ochre, and intermittently throughout August, Jones and Tegetmeier helped paint them.[29] Jones also drew for Gill a sombre, burdened infantryman to incorporate into a war memorial in Trumperton.

Jones saw Desmond Chute engraving with a burin on the end of a boxwood block, and expressed interest. Chute (fig. 10) was a co-founder of the Guild, who had studied at the Slade and was a friend of Stanley Spencer. With Gill, he had co-founded the Society of Wood Engravers, which had first exhibited in England in 1920. Chute taught Jones how to engrave and had him read R. J. Beedham's manual, *Wood Engraving* (St Dominic's Press, 1919). Wood engraving had been replaced as a journalistic craft by photo-engraving; and now, following the example of Bewick, Blake, and Calvert, artists were beginning to engrave their own drawings. Gill encouraged Jones to engrave as an antidote to art-school training, its difficulty as a medium forcing a post-Impressionist corrective to close imitation of nature. Engraving requires simplification and emphasises design, of which Jones was already a master. Within days, Chute knew that his pupil had surpassed him. Having joined the vanguard of the revival of the art form, Jones showed Medworth and Hawkins how to engrave – it was, he would say, the only thing he ever taught anyone. For the next ten years he habitually carried his graver in one coat pocket and the block he was engraving in the other.[30]

He visited Hilary Pepler (fig. 11), the Reeve of the Common and the third co-founder of the Guild. He and his family lived on a farm on the south side of the Common. His classical good looks combined with a cast in one eye to make his appearance uncanny.* Benign, reserved, amiable, witty, he wrote plays for community production and was interested in puppetry and mime. He ran the Guild's press, which he and Gill used largely for propaganda, thinking this their right and duty by virtue of their association with

* Jones would remember this effect when referring in *The Anathemata* to the 'cast' eye of Aphrodite (194 n. 2).

the Dominicans, officially the Order of Preachers. Pepler showed Jones his three presses and told him that he could use any wood engravings Jones made.[31]

The Guild of Saints Joseph and Dominic, as it was called, was a manifestation of the Arts and Crafts movement, originating in the 1880s with William Morris. The Guild craftsmen were regarded as workmen, free of the preciousness of the fine arts; they were not socialists, like Morris, but 'Distributists', dedicated to distributing rather than abolishing private ownership. (The movement derived from the papal encyclical *Rerum Novarum* and was expounded by Belloc in *The Servile State* [1912], which Jones read later and would increasingly regard as prophetic.) The Guild was a cooperative, owning a small brick chapel and the houses and workshops which workers rented, each worker owning his own tools, the products of his work, and his earnings. Members were Gill, Pepler, Chute, and Joseph Cribb (a stone carver), wives being denied membership because they worked in the house and garden, not the workshop.[32]

The Guild members and their families were retrieving the values and modes of pre-industrial rural life. On Pepler's farm, they mowed hay with a scythe, cut corn with a swophook, threshed barley with a flail, and winnowed it with a fan. They wore smocks in imitation of old local farmers and shepherds. They ate homemade bread, drank home-brewed beer, and wore homespun clothing. The community involved fellowship like that Jones had known as a soldier. (Gill, Tegetmeier, and Laurie Cribb, Gill's apprentice, were ex-servicemen, the latter two having seen combat.) Like infantrymen, they argued among themselves at all hours. Jones often went to Gill's house in the evening, sometimes for supper, sometimes with Tegetmeier and Chute. Topics of discussion included the inadequacies of art schools, their inimical emphasis on technique, and the need for artists to regard themselves solely as workmen.[33]

*　　*　　*

Jones wrote home announcing his decision to become a Catholic. His father replied that he was 'amazed' at his joining 'the Romish Church', which 'has always barred the spread of the Bible' and 'always has been the enemy of progress and Enlightenment, the friend and helper of the assassin & murderer'; that he (David) would be giving 'first place' to the Pope instead of the king and become a worshiper of 'idols of wood, stone & brass', to say nothing of 'the horrors of the Confessional'. It is 'the *Church first* & Bible second ... God *de*-throned – Man enthroned! ... your new name ought to be Reuben!' – seller of his brother (Genesis 37) and forfeiter of his birthright by defiling his father's bed (1 Chronicles 5:1). His mother, too, was greatly upset.

He notified O'Connor that he was ready to enter the Church, and O'Connor invited him to stay at the rectory. The baptism – 'conditional' upon his Anglican baptism being invalid – took place on 7 September 1921, Frank Wall serving as godfather.* O'Connor had wanted Jones to have a baptismal middle name, and he agreed to 'Michael', which was unregistered. He would sign his name 'David Michael' as late as 1931 but only when writing to friends from Ditchling days. Subsequently he dropped it altogether, saying, 'I use no other form either publicly or privately or legally than David Jones.' The baptism washed away forever the initial 'W' for Walter.[34]

He considered O'Connor 'a remarkable man & full of wisdom'. Now he saw his light side, which included dramatic recitation (Villon, Robert Browning, Kipling, Shakespeare) and singing ('The Croppy Boy', Gilbert and Sullivan, Italian peasant songs). Jones would dedicate his last poem, 'The Kensington Mass', to this 'altogether astonishing Irishman from Meath'. But O'Connor was sometimes severe, thinking that Jones needed 'discipline' – an impression originating in returning to the rectory to see water flowing from the front door, down the steps, and along the pavement. After an early bath, Jones had gone for a walk without emptying the tub or turning off the hot water.[35]

Jones did not become a Catholic to save his soul. He regarded the conciliar statement that 'there is no salvation outside of the Church' as nonsense. As for 'piety, sincerity, goodness, knowledge of the Scriptures and the Fathers, and deep devotion to the Passion & effectual grace', there was more of these in many Protestants he knew 'than in most Catholics'. But he was convinced that the Catholic Church was 'real' as no other Church was – the very point Gill had made with the triangular shapes. He felt its reality in the chant during high Mass at Westminster Cathedral, so different from the 'elegant, sophisticated but unreal sung Evensong at Kings College Cambridge'. It was, he said, 'the reality ... that seldom if ever seemed quite there among the many, many different kinds of Protestants I've known'.[36]

He also liked the rootedness of the Church in the past. Anglicans and Protestants originated culturally in the Renaissance, Catholicism in the classical world. He would write, 'it seems to me that only by becoming a Catholic can one establish continuity with Antiquity'. He was aware of the Anglican apologetical claim of continuity with the ancient Celtic-British Church and emphasis on the late sixth-century antipathy between Celtic '"ancient paths" and the "Roman obedience" of Canterbury'. But there had been no such antipathy earlier, when Britain was a diocese of the

---

* Five years later, Jones asked Philip Hagreen, 'What are the duties of a godson to his godfather?' Hagreen: 'None.' Jones: 'I hope you are right because mine has just lapsed.'

prefecture of Gaul. Celtic Christianity was, he knew, 'as Roman in origin as the Welsh dragon'.[37]

Moreover, the past of the Church was its presence in mythic contemporaneity. This was the effect of the time-abolishing presence of Jesus in the Eucharist. Experience of the 'numinous', of 'Mystery', of 'incomprehensible otherness' fed in Jones deep liturgical devotion that would last the rest of his life.

When not at Mass, he often read his missal as though it were a scriptural text – as, indeed, it largely is. Repetitions (such as of a psalm verse or scriptural quotation in the Introit and Gradual) he 'always found moving'. They sometimes recalled the childhood circle rhyme 'It was a dark and stormy night', which in turn recalled companionship with others huddled together in the trenches. These blended somehow with the fellowship he felt at Mass. He came to appreciate the shape of the Mass, regarding it as 'a supreme art-form ... perfected' by 'centuries of usage'. Performance aside, he was enthralled by its written and choreographed form-meaning, to which everything individually personal and subjective was subordinate. Even now the Mass was for him the paradigm of symbols, capable of containing and interpreting legend, myth, and pagan religion. As art, it was essentially modernist: paratactic, without linear continuity, moving by juxtaposition and accumulation. It contradicted 'the ludicrous division' between abstract and non-abstract art, 'for nothing,' he said, 'could ... be more "abstract" than the Mass, or *less "realistic"* or *more "real"* '. It would be the work of art he most loved.[38]

*   *   *

Convinced of the futility of art-school training, he was encouraged to leave by Sickert, who believed that no one should be more than three years in art school – Jones was in his seventh year – and that you should either enter the market or begin your education all over again by unlearning art-school habits. Bayes, too, urged him to go.[39]

On the evening of 23 November, Jones left for his second extended visit to Ditchling, where he engraved for Pepler, ground and mixed paint colours with Gill, and made a large nativity scene for the chapel with Joseph Cribb, Jones painting the figures of Mary, Joseph, and St Dominic.[40] He returned to Brockley for Christmas.

There he attended his first Christmas Midnight Mass, a short walk north of his parents' house, at St Mary Magdalen Church, now his local parish church. He thought the building 'hideous', a 'little tail-end of imitation baroque', but the parish 'lovely'. He especially liked Vespers on Sunday evenings, sung 'with great fervour by the choir & a large part of the congregation' and involving the censing of the altar, for him 'one of the most moving things'. Of the parish's three Augustinian priests, he especially liked Bernardine Balfontaine, from the south of France, who would stay through 1929. His sermons were short and the best Jones ever heard. Balfontaine frequently paraphrased St Athanasius: 'God became man so that you might become gods' (see *A* 129 n. 4). In 1964, Jones confided that Balfontaine influenced him 'more than any other' priest he had known and said, 'I often think of him.'[41]

Early in January 1922, Jones withdrew from art school, moved to Ditchling Common, and apprenticed himself, at Gill's suggestion, to a newly arrived carpenter, George Maxwell. Wearing a smock over shirt and trousers, Jones woodworked floors and beams, thinking of his now favourite bit of scripture about the heavenly Jerusalem 'built as a city strongly interjoined' (Psalm 122:3).[1]

The day began with the Angelus at 6 a.m. and continued with meetings of the workmen at set times in the chapel to read aloud the hours of the Little Office of the Blessed Virgin, a short form of the Divine Office, concluding at 9 p.m. with Compline. Afternoons on Sundays and feast days were given over to sports, long walks, and picnics. On holiday evenings, Gill's daughters sang folk-songs, which were now Jones's favourite secular music.[2]

He loved best Gregorian chant. For him it was an 'overwhelming' experience, 'so infallibly what the heart desires', lifting up 'the whole being'.* After hearing the sung night office in St Hugh's Charterhouse, at Parkminster, in January, he told Gill that he felt he ought to become a monk. The feeling persisted, and in November 1922 he underwent a ten-day retreat there to discern whether he had a religious vocation. He stayed in the guest house, receiving spiritual direction from Paschal Jefferys, who, thinking he loved the chant mainly for its beauty, insisted that he stop attending night office. The prior, Peter Pepin, realised that his chief interest was art and advised him 'to find a good Catholic girl' and have a family. Jones said, 'I don't reckon that's up my street either.' When, back in Brockley, Fr Balfontaine urged him to join a religious order, Jones replied, 'I am told that I have no vocation to the religious life.' He may have felt confirmation of this non-vocation when, after walking twelve miles to the Charterhouse in the summer of 1923, he rested on a bench in the cloister. A passing monk asked him whether he was comfortable. He answered, 'Yes, thank you.' The monk said, 'Then think whether our Lord was comfortable on the cross.' Rising immediately, Jones quick-marched to the nearest pub and made himself even more comfortable.[3]

---

* He would always prefer it to any other music, writing, 'it makes all other musical forms however stupendous and of no matter what greatness – even Bach – seem ... self-consciously "grand." ... Air-borne? Well yes, but ... one is aware of the engines. Whereas in the Chant the gravitas and gaiety & lightness seem more like the unconscious flight & song of a bird.' It would be a model for his poetry; in the chant, form and content being indistinguishable since words are not subordinate to melody.

At Ditchling he became, as he always subsequently claimed to be, a Thomist. The Gills, Peplers, and Maxwell were Dominican tertiaries (lay associates) and were visited regularly by Dominican friars, who were all Thomists and, consequently, broadly cultured and comfortable in the world. (They were also in sympathy with workers and the poor.) Dominicans argued for hours in the scholastic manner, and Jones liked the 'invigorating, sense-making, illuminating precision' of their thinking. He would experience it in conversation for the next quarter century. For him, Aquinas's most important teaching was the goodness of nature, eliminating moral dualism between matter and spirit, which, he now realised, had characterised his pre-Catholic Christianity. Like Aquinas, he had an analogical sensibility: he adopted the Thomistic (following Aristotle) soul or 'form' as the 'informing principle' of the body to the single 'form-content' without which, for Jones, a work of art failed fully to exist.[4]

* * *

With Tegetmeier and another bachelor, Reginald Lawson, he was housed in a small converted carriage shed. To commemorate taking possession in the spring of 1923, he painted in oils on the newly whitewashed kitchen walls a mural of Jesus entering Jerusalem on Palm Sunday (fig. 1). Inspired by the surface – he exclaimed to Lawson, '*That's* a wall!' – he painted it with immense enjoyment, exclaiming, 'There's people for you! The people of God, and who is this but Christ the Lord to keep you company.'[5]

1. *Entry into Jerusalem*, or *Cum Floribus et Palmis*, 1923

He wanted to revive the art of wall painting on a grand scale, an aspiration rooted in boyhood viewing of the painted hall in the Naval College at Greenwich and encouragement at Camberwell.* After reading Cennini's treatise on quattrocento painting, he painted crucifixions over the door and the fireplace of the cottage and, on the whitewashed walls of the carpentry shop, a small crucifixion scene, a round-faced St Dominic, and the mocking of Jesus.[6]

Gill decided that Jones, Tegetmeier, and Lawson were 'novices' under obedience to him, and decreed Lawson head of the house and cook and Tegetmeier housekeeper. (Lawson later said, 'We spoiled David.') Raising rabbits and pigs, keeping bees, and operating a hayrick, the bachelors were soon partaking in the Guild's Distributist experiment. To others in the community the bachelors seemed indecisive and depressed. Gill's eldest daughter, Betty, called them 'the Sorrowful Mysteries', and that became the name of their cottage.[7]

* * *

Jones's murals and many small watercolour drawings were, as he later said, 'imitative of primitive Christian art' as an antidote to 'the "Academic", ... the slick, and ... the sentimental'. Post-Impressionist in downplaying technique, they were sculptural, emphasising contour, solidity, and volume. Reacting against conventional shading, Jones 'smooch[ed] the edges with black' in a version of his thick-line Camberwell style. Later he would say that it was 'awfully reflective of ... "London Group" technique' and the current 'tendency' against 'looseness, naturalism & impressionism' in favour of simplified 'formal shapes'.[8]

Some of his smaller pictures were inspired by the *Roman Martyrology* read aloud daily at lunch with the Gills (fig. 2). Brief, often ludicrous accounts of the lives of martyrs, they promoted mirth and sometimes ribaldry. A ridiculously funny favourite of Jones concerned a saint who refused as an infant to look at his mother's breasts on Friday, the day Catholics abstained from meat.[9]

2. *Sancta Helena*, 18 August 1922

* * *

* In 1910–11, Gerald Moira gave a series of public lectures there on murals, and the course in design co-taught by Savage and Hartrick in 1913–14 was partly devoted to 'Mural Decoration'.

As an apprentice carpenter, Jones learned about wood and the care and sharpening of tools but was unable to cut and plane straight-and-square in order to mortise and tenon. Dovetails should be air-tight – his were out by an eighth of an inch. He was incompetent at measurement and arithmetic and often used the wrong tool. Shown how to twist bolts into wood with an Archimedean driver, he locked it and laboriously turned it round and round like a wrench. Within a year, it was apparent that he would never be a carpenter, and he quit his apprenticeship. But joinery would influence his poetry, its manuscripts revealing an inclination to fit together pieces of writing in sequence or one within another, *emboîtement* (interfitting) fashion.[10]

By late spring 1922, he was, like others at Ditchling, bearded and wore his smock everywhere. But after his appearance horrified his visiting parents, he shaved his beard, discarded his smock when travelling, and, before long (disobeying Gill), ceased wearing it altogether.[11]

* * *

Early in 1922, Jones was impressed by an article in a Catholic paper summarising a claim by Maurice de la Taille SJ that the Last Supper, the crucifixion, and the Mass were one sacrifice in differing modalities: unbloody oblation, bloody immolation, and unbloody re-enactment. Jones enthusiastically endorsed this theory to the workmen and to Vincent McNabb, a Dominican priest, who vehemently denounced it as heretical, saying that it denied the crucifixion as the sole cause of salvation. When McNabb subsided, Jones calmly said that, for him, this view 'appeared to open windows'. From now on, the three-fold relationship in de la Taille's theory informed Jones's experience of Mass – it would underlie the triple image concluding *The Anathemata*.[12]

* * *

The dominant figure in the Guild was Eric Gill. He was optimistic, direct, accessible, curious, quick to laugh, a lover of jokes, and radiated benevolence, understanding, wisdom, confidence, strength, and energy. The freshness of his reactions made him enjoyable company – it was a quality Jones shared, making their relationship mutually delightful. Gill was a good listener but disputatious, logical but often simplistic and naïve – truth being, for him, syllogistic. He expected understanding and agreement or else (Jones thought this ridiculous) compliance. Jones later recalled, 'he would ... get very angry with me for letting slip a perfectly subjective & personal objection – I often copped out in that way!'[13]

According to those close to them, they were like father and son (fig. 3). Gill's daughter Petra said, 'it was rather a subordinate relationship'. A friend of both, Prudence Pelham, was remembered as saying that Gill dominated

3. Jones and Eric Gill, Bristol, by G. Methven Brownlee, 1926

Jones. But Philip Hagreen recalled him in 1924 as 'strangely independent', uninterested in learning anything Gill could teach, 'affectionate' yet 'detached'. Gill chastised him for the disorder of his work space; Jones continued to clutter his worktable and put out cigarettes in his paintbox. He disagreed in principle with Gill's insistence on order, which he thought unnatural and inimical to artistic creation.[14]

Jones's greater understanding of art precluded a complete takeover. While continuing to admire Gill's letter carving, he disliked the slick technical expertise of his other work. He decided that Gill's doctrine of undoing art training and beginning again as a craftsman was destructive. Sensing the danger for himself and knowing that he wanted to continue drawing and painting, he, as he later put it, said 'no' to Gill.[15]

About art they disagreed fundamentally. Gill used it as social and moral propaganda and erotic stimulus. Jones thought that these uses diminished aesthetic purpose. He agreed with Gill about the innocence of sexual activity and did not mind frank sexual talk, but beauty, not goodness or sexual titillation, was the goal of art.[16]

There were other areas of disagreement. Gill regretted the absence of a living tradition to sustain artistic work; Jones rejoiced that, for the first time in history, the absence of tradition freed artists. Gill felt antipathy to modernism; Jones did not. Gill loved Bridges's *The Testament of Beauty*; Jones thought it 'a bloody bore'. Gill thought cultural anthropology and history wastes of time; Jones found them fascinating. Later Jones described Gill as 'someone to whom one owes a debt of gratitude at a certain period of one's life but with whom one disagreed in all sorts of ways, but whose friendship remained altogether independent of the disagreements'.[17]

* * *

The chief intellectual preoccupation of Guild members was the thinking of Jacques Maritain, a Neo-Thomist whose *Art et Scholastique* (1920) John O'Connor was translating for publication by St Dominic's Press as *The Philosophy of Art* (1923). A 'great truth' Jones especially valued was Maritain's Aristotelian distinction between doing (*praxis*) and making (*poesis*), the former governed by morality, the latter by aesthetics – this, for Jones, refuted moral objections to 'art for art's sake'. Maritain emphasises art as objective 'sign', which became one of Jones's key words. Maritain contends that art is fundamentally sacramental, partly because every beauty emanates from God as primal Beauty. Making art is therefore a kind of prayer. For Jones, this notion resolved a tension between religion and art that had troubled him since adolescence, when he felt that he was 'serving two masters' and art a good deal more than God. Maritain affirms the 'unity of all made things'. Jones found support for this idea in Vivian Bickford's *Certainty*, which proposes as a criterion of knowledge 'unity of indirect reference', by which a multitude of apparently unrelated things indirectly indicate the encompassing truth of Christianity. For Jones this unity expanded Thomistic analogy. Much of his later poetry would achieve thematic unity by indirect reference – it would be the operating premise of *The Anathemata*. Jones would read and reread Maritain's book, urging friends to buy it. It was, one of them, Ernest Hawkins, said, his 'bible' – no book influenced him more. By 1924, it would be to his mind as a map to a place. To Maritain's ideas, he added one of his own, that beauty is achievable in art as it is not in nature, since art escapes the effects of the Fall. Over the coming decades he would speak about these things to friends, one of whom (Jim Ede) would remember, 'He talked about practically nothing else.'[18]

* * *

In July 1922, Jones visited Oxford. He had become friends with Martin D'Arcy at Ditchling, a young Jesuit of penetrating intelligence who had excelled in Classics at Oxford and had a fresh doctorate in theology from the Gregorian D'Arcy (fig. 4), who would come to regard Jones as 'the dearest of people', invited him to stay at

4. Martin D'Arcy, by Howard Coster, 1938

the Jesuit house in Oxford, Campion Hall, then in St Giles Street. At meals there, Jones discussed the relationship of paganism to Christianity with Cyril Martindale, the most sensitive, intelligent, well-rounded person he had met, 'an amazing chap'. He also visited the Dominicans at nearby Blackfriars, where his closest friend was John-Baptist Reeves, highly intelligent, a sympathetic listener, and a much sought-after confessor.[19]

Jones visited London, where he spent much of the autumn of 1923 painting letters of a Gill inscription for the Royal Navy Hospital, sometimes bringing Gill home to Brockley. His parents 'adored Eric'. He and Gill went to galleries, and on 10 November to Burlington House to see an exhibit of English Primitives. Jones had 'many long talks' with 'various old pals', chief among them Medworth, now teaching at Westminster. He visited Hawkins's studio, where a photograph was taken of him engraving (fig. 5), his hair combed back in the direction he pushed it as he worked or talked. His suit was of ginger-coloured tweed woven by Petra Gill. He had taken the cloth to a tailor, who asked what sort of suit he

5. Jones engraving, 1923

wanted. Jones replied, 'I am only interested in the things eternal.' After pausing to take this in, the tailor explained the different styles, one of which suited Jones. It was, Hawkins's brother Ernest remembered, the hairiest tweed he ever saw, the trousers so scratchy they had to be lined with silk.[20]

*　　*　　*

Jones concentrated on engraving, working in a shed next to the press. Pepler paid him a small amount per inch, the engraved blocks to be used and reused at Pepler's discretion, mainly as illustrations for the press, chiefly for the *Game*, a small monthly magazine.[21]

Loving the look and feel of the wood he engraved led Jones to an important compositional innovation. For engravings wider than two inches, blocks were bolted together, leaving a visible line where the grains met. Often he introduced a vertical division (a door edge, a roof support) to coincide with this line, which became, paradoxically, a unifying device (fig. 6). He used it often. It would inform the structure of *In Parenthesis*, *The Anathemata*, and 'The Sleeping Lord'.

Following Gill's example, Jones turned unsuccessful engravings into small boxwood sculptures, including crucifixes, for Gill, Petra, and himself,

6. Woodcutters and family, 1923

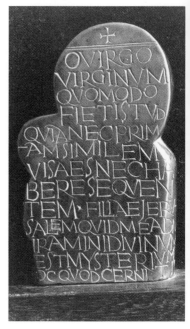

7. *Mater Castissima*, back, 1924

and a relief of Petra in profile, which was shown (priced at £12.10s.) with two watercolours in the autumn 1923 Goupil exhibition. The only large sculpture he made was of St Dominic (29 inches tall), carved in 1923 of what he later remembered as 'bloody hard' oak (see chapter 14, fig. 6). One of the best and largest of the small carvings and one Gill especially loved was *Mater Castissima* (1924), on the back and side of which he carved a Latin inscription (fig. 7). He wanted to fix the carving onto a base but had no idea how – Philip Hagreen did it for him. Jones exhibited it at the Goupil Gallery and later sold it to Maxwell. These carvings, though miniature, are monumental. Gill later claimed that they 'alone would place him in the first rank of modern artists'.[22]

* * *

Early in 1924, working beside one another, Jones and Philip Hagreen became friends. They talked about artists. Hagreen would remember that Jones was enthralled with pictures by the Gill children. He objected to the academic elevation of Raphael – he had 'no time for him' – and of Rembrandt. Jones said he admired Renoir and loved his *Umbrellas* in the National Gallery. The fall of Richard II was his current historical obsession. It included the Wilton Diptych and Shakespeare's play. (Mirrors 'always' reminded him of the scene at the end of Act Four.) Speaking about literature, he quoted from Chesterton's *Ballad of the White Horse* and recited Belloc's 'The Birds'. He read Hagreen's copy of *Moby-Dick*, partly on Gill's recommendation.[23]

8. 'The Presentation', *A Child's Rosary Book*, 1924

* * *

Escape from carpentry released in Jones a surge of creativity. In 1924 he illustrated for Pepler *A Child's Rosary Book* with fifteen packed, emphatic engravings. Involving Gallo-Roman groupings of squat figures with oversized heads, some are fascinating in design: for example, 'The Presentation' (fig. 8), in which figures and columns rise to eye level and culminate in reverberating haloes, heads, and arches.

While still engraving for the *Rosary Book*, he became interested in more exciting work. Pepler was popping in and reciting satirical rhymes composed for Jones to illustrate, and he engraved without hesitation, spontaneously. Pepler printed a book of the illustrated rhymes, *Libellus Lapidum* (1924). In the engraving on the cover Jones sits with a giant graver behind Pepler astride a wingless, bucking Pegasus (fig. 9). These engravings are remarkably free, showing an important advance in liveliness and ease that would make Jones, in Hagreen's estimation, an engraver equal to Hogarth, Bewick, and Blake.[24]

* * *

Jones began walking out with Petra Gill. She was natural, lovely, warm, and shy. He spoke to her about the war; his little niece Stella, whom he loved; and Welsh history. He walked quickly. One afternoon, her father asked her, 'Did you have a nice walk?' She said, 'David had a nice walk. I had a nice run.' On 13 December 1924, Gill records

9. Cover, *Libellus Lapidum*, 1924

in a letter to Chute, 'supper's finished and Petra is sewing & David J. is reading *Twelfth Night* to her!' She thought him 'quite interested in plays'. He read poetry to her. She would remember, he was 'very humorous' and 'a very, very dear person, . . . very affectionate. He used to love . . . holding my hand, and we would have kisses and a certain sort of cuddling, but apart from that it was rather immature, really.' They became engaged – she recalled, 'We almost drifted into it', his proposal being something like 'Well, we must get married.'[25] He was 29; she 18.

On 22 April 1924, he told Gill, who insisted on a formal betrothal ceremony, which took place after Compline two days later, before the entire community with John O'Connor presiding. Jones gave Hagreen a silver shilling from which to make an engagement ring, on the outer edge of which Hagreen engraved in Latin from the Song of Songs: 'My beloved is mine and I am his' (2:16). He charged Jones ten shillings, and Jones, deadpan, told Petra that she should pay since she was going to wear it.[26]

Eric Gill thought Jones the most highly sexed man he had ever known and regarded his chastity as a marvellous spiritual achievement.* Gill told Hagreen that Jones would only kiss Petra but never fully embrace because 'his sex-works work too easily' – he later referred to himself as 'poor old hair-trigger Jones'. Told about this affliction decades later, Petra was surprised and said, 'I saw nothing of that.' She thought fastidiousness might have inhibited him. She would remember their engagement as 'a brother and sister relationship, rather a religious, idealised, thing'. They behaved, she said, like a couple of seventeen-year-olds. 'We were quite happy just to kiss goodnight or walk along hand in hand, that sort of thing.' Copulation was out of the question – she did not want a baby out of wedlock, and, she later said, 'We had a sort of terrific feeling that it was wrong.'† But there was more physical intimacy than she admitted

---

* Tom Burns, who knew Jones well a few years later, also said that he thought him 'very highly sexed'.

† Jones did not know that Eric Gill's sexual behavior had included incest, since Tom Burns, with whom Jones would have confided about it, did not know. Gill's sexual relations with his eldest daughter, Betty, were frequent though not coital. Eric's diary discloses that in 1920 he approached Petra intending anal intercourse. Touching her slightly, without penetration, he was so appalled at himself that he stopped. He never again touched Petra sexually, never sexually touched Joanna, and eventually, in 1921, ended sexual relations with Betty. Accomplished with much internal struggle and the help of confessors, Gill's change of behaviour was an impressive moral achievement. In 1924 Petra was not, therefore – as D. Shiel and J. Miles have thought (*Maker Unmade*, pp. 151, 246, 248) – sexually reticent owing to recent erotic attention by Eric. Nor, as Merlin James assumes, did he ever try to dissuade her from marrying (*A Map of the Artist's Mind*, p. 25). For the extent of Eric Gill's sexual conduct, see F. MacCarthy, *Eric Gill* (London: Faber, 1989), pp. 155ff.

10. *The Garden Enclosed*, 1924

to. Out on the Downs, in what he later called 'the secret places lovers know', clothing was displaced, and they enjoyed the pleasures of mutual masturbation.[27]

Some evenings they visited the Hagreen cottage. Once after the Hagreens carried up to bed their four-year-old daughter clinging to a toy horse on wheels, Jones said, 'Strange how early in life one wants to take what one loves to bed with one.' On another occasion Petra said that she did not understand how something just recounted could be true. He explained, and she said, 'I still don't see.' He explained again, again without success. Patiently, more fully, he explained a third time, again unsuccessfully. Turning to Hagreen, he said, 'Tell me, Philip, is there anything in marriage to make up for having to keep your temper with a woman?'[28]

His small portraits of her seem uninspired, and a small oil, *The Garden Enclosed* (9 by 10 inches, fig. 10), portends trouble. The garden in the title alludes to the words in the Song of Songs, 'a garden is my sister, my spouse' (4:12), a problematic apposition. On the ground at the divergence of paths is Petra's doll (carved for her as a little girl by her father), dropped to indicate transition to womanhood. Stretching phallic necks across the middle distance, geese penetrate a tumescent grove but leave the joined couple, who are not erotic but wooden, like the doll and like the joined buildings behind them.[29] They kiss, but the female figure leans back, placing a hand between them. Is her leaning away and gesture of resistance projected hesitation on his part? Did he feel the tension between the right fork of the path and the leftward movement of animal nature, a divergence (repeated in tree branches) suggesting tension between marital sexuality and bachelorhood? He showed this picture in the 1924 Goupil Salon Exhibition, priced at £15.15s.

* * *

In early April 1924, Jones became a 'postulant' of the Guild, promising to live and work according to its rules and spirit – he would never be a full member. And on 17 April, he became a third-order Dominican, something that would matter to him for several years – until 1929 he sometimes wrote 'T.O.S.D.' after his name.[30]

In June, he accompanied Gill to Bradford to help install (and paint the lettering of) stations of the cross for O'Connor's church, and Gill asked Jones to move with him to Wales, since Gill was breaking with Pepler, whom he considered financially dishonest. He planned to rent an abandoned monastery in Wales. Jones demurred and refused to take sides, thinking the conflict basically a difference in temperament. At a Guild meeting on 29 June, Pepler and Maxwell voted to reorganise the community on socialist lines, contravening Distributist insistence on private property and depriving Gill of ownership of his blocks engraved for the press (which Pepler had not bought). Pepler insisted on keeping them – for this Gill would not forgive him. On 13 July, the Gills, the Hagreens, and the Brennans (a farm labourer and his wife) left what seemed to Jones 'a very desolate Ditchling'. Petra and he stayed, she to complete her training as a weaver with Ethel Mairet in Ditchling Village, he to finish his first external commission.[31]

Gill had shown *Libellus Lapidum* to Harold Monro, the publisher and proprietor of the Poetry Bookshop, who had asked Jones to illustrate Eleanor Farjeon's *The Town Child's Alphabet* (1924). The job required an ink drawing for each letter and the cover (fig. 11), all reproduced with line-blocks in two colours. He spent the last two weeks of August on these drawings, which are contemporary (very 1920s) in style.[32]

That project finished, he was unable to earn a living at Ditchling and 'with much hesitation' returned to Brockley. He went with Medworth to Hawkins's studio, where he learned dry-point etching. At his father's printing room, a retiring trade engraver gave him the full set of engraving tools he had used since the 1860s. The well-made tools, separation from Gill, the stimulus of working with Medworth, and the return to a studio setting all made a difference. Only now, he said, did he 'start fire' as an engraver. And now he first had his characteristic pudding-basin haircut (fig. 3), his hair falling over his forehead in a fringe.[33]

Petra visited Brockley for weekends in June and October. She was invited so infrequently because, Jones explained, overnight guests put too much strain on his mother. During these visits, it seemed to Petra that his parents did not 'really understand him' – 'the war perhaps' had separated him from them. There was no open talk at table, his mother quiet, his father doing his best to amuse and keep the conversation going. Clearly to Petra, his mother disapproved of their engagement. Although she and Petra spoke during the washing-up (and then she seemed 'sweet' and 'kind'), his mother was otherwise 'reserved', and Petra 'felt an intruder'. Feeling the tension, David arranged usually to be out of the house. He and Petra walked to the top of the Hilly Fields. They went into London to visit galleries. They visited Medworth, with whom, she thought, he had 'an intellectual relationship' and 'talked a lot about life'. They also went for tea to his sister, who now had a second daughter, Mollie. During the four months he lived in Brockley, he never visited Petra at Ditchling, possibly because he lacked train fare. He often wrote but not, she thought, as often as he might.[34]

In early October 1924, Eric Gill visited, sleeping in Jones's studio for six nights. He convinced Jones to resign as a Guild postulant and to visit him in Wales.[35]

11. Cover, *The Town Child's Alphabet*, 1924

CHAPTER 6: 1924–27

On 22 December 1924, intending only to visit, not 'in any sense to join' Gill, Jones arrived at Capel-y-ffin in the Ewys Valley in the wildest reaches of the Black Mountains. Nestled at 1,300 feet on a low slope of the south-west ridge (fig. 1), the former Benedictine monastery was a two-storey, neo-Gothic quadrangle beside an uncompleted church, roofless and open at the front. Jones was reunited with the Hagreens, Tegetmeier, and Donald Attwater, a Gill devotee he had known at Ditchling, and he met three monks from Caldey and a nineteen-year-old Latin tutor named René Hague. Jones was given a monk's cell in the monastery attic under bare rafters and divided from its neighbours by seven-foot-high pine partitions – a cold place to sleep in a cold, damp building shaded from the sun. At dinner in the Gills' kitchen, the men wore overcoats and the women heavy woollen shawls.[1]

The next day, Jones went down the valley in a two-wheeled cart to Llanfihangel to meet Petra, arriving for Christmas. Anxious to return before night, he tried in vain to make the horse gallop, standing like a charioteer, yelling and lashing with the reins. In another cart, Eric's wife, Mary, and Betty met them. Since he feared driving further in the dark, Mary drove Petra the rest of the way, and Betty drove him – ignominious conclusion to a romantic reunion.[2]

At Christmas dinner, Eric read from the *Roman Martyrology*, and Jones heard for the first time the elaborate dating of the Nativity, on which he would model the dating of the paschal events in *The Anathemata*. He gave out copies of his recent engraving *By the Mystery of thy Holy Incarnation* (fig. 2) and gave Gill a copy of Coventry Patmore's *Religio Poetae*.[3]

Except for the cold, Jones loved everything about Capel. The Gill daughters were, he thought, 'wonderful characters of great strength & wisdom'. He was fond of

1. The monastery at Capel-y-ffin

2. *By the Mystery of thy Holy Incarnation*, 1924

the family cats and visually interested in the farm animals though finding pigs and sheep hard to draw. He loved animals but only 'to look at', Joanna Gill would remember: 'He absolutely loved cows but wouldn't have liked to milk one.' He spent the long dark evenings with the Gills reading, sometimes listening to Eric read aloud from *Morte D'Arthur*. The family sang shanties, carols, and folksongs – Jones singing 'Six Dukes', 'She Was Poor But She Was Honest', and comical army songs. All together they sang his remembered wartime song, 'Close the door they're coming through the windows, close the windows they're coming through the door'.[4]

He loved the majestic, irregular landscape. Small wild ponies grazing on the slopes seemed to him suspended there and, from the hill opposite, appeared larger than life. He loved how a pair of herons, 'the most superb of birds', flew 'with the necks & heads curved back' up the valley each evening and back in the morning. Fetching milk from a nearby farm, he and Hagreen paused on a narrow wooden bridge over the Honddu to listen to the stream and spoke of how Eric, who considered the beauty of nature a bourgeois notion, would think they were wasting time.[5]

Partly because of the cold, Jones painted watercolours outdoors quickly and freely, liberating himself from the rigidly iconic Ditchling style. Place also precipitated stylistic change. In *Tir y Blaenau* (fig. 3), high, irregular, upward hill-curves pull against the downward curves of the Honddu, opening the picture. Pivoting perspective bends space. Viewing it from top to bottom, you feel as though rising into the air. Nothing in this picture is straight, symmetrical, or still. If the water flows, so does the land. *Tir y Blaenau* would hang over his bed in the 1960s, the work from which, he said, all his 'subsequent water-colour thing ... developed'.[6]

3. *Tir y Blaenau*, December 1924–January 1925

Staying on after Petra's return to Ditchling in January 1925, he contributed pictures to the monastery building, the largest on the north wall of the temporary chapel, soon to be Gill's studio. The mural was oil paint on the limewashed wall, a crucifixion flanked by lettering (fig. 4). (He would later like only the lettering.) When the new chapel was complete in the northern attic, he painted a chi-rho and Agnus Dei on the tabernacle door, with a bordering Latin inscription he especially liked about being fed with 'honey out of the rock' (*petra*) – words with personal meaning for him.[7]

4. Mural, Capel-y-ffin, 1925

*   *   *

On 3 March, to escape the cold at Capel, Jones went with Eric to Caldey Island, off the Pembrokeshire coast. After a few days, Gill left and Jones stayed. He was so poor, using a rope instead of a belt to hold up his trousers, that the prior, Wilfred Upson, let him live and eat in the monastery (instead of the guesthouse). He wore his overcoat tied at the waist for extra warmth, even on warm days, and even – the monks thought this odd – at meals in the refectory. He attended Mass and the office and worked in the scriptorium, beside an artist-monk, Theodore Bailey, and sometimes Upson, who was a script-writer and illuminator.[8]

The island was, Jones thought, 'marvellous', with an intriguing 'strange light'. Accompanied often by Bailey, who sketched his companion (fig. 5), he got to know 'every inch' of the 550-acre island. He loved the bays with clifftop perspectives and from high on Chapel Point watched the huge Atlantic waves.[9] He visited the ruins of the tiny Norman Old Priory, its chapel containing a sixth-century ogham stone, inscribed with a memorial probably of St Illtud. Bailey took him to a shallow niche, called Nana's

5. Jones by Dom Theodore Bailey, 1927

6. *Ship off Ynys Byr,* 1925

Cave, north-east of the abbey, where Roman-age antiquities had recently been found. Moved by the island having been an outpost of Christianity in the early Dark Ages, Jones ruminated about the Celtic saints here and on other such islands after the fall of Rome bringing Christianity to the newly pagan cultures of England and the continent.

In mid-March, clement weather allowed him to paint outdoors. It was his first time painting the sea, which was a fluid complement to the heights of Capel-y-ffin in having a liberating effect. He saw the sea as a source of light consisting of varying pure tones minimally informed. Mostly he painted Drinkim Bay, which gave him a sheltered feeling. To paint the whole of it, he imaginatively projected point of view 300 feet above where he had to stand, at the cliff edge, to see any of it. One of the best early paintings of the bay is *Ship off Ynys Byr* (fig. 6). The steamship near the horizon is like a nail on which the round bay hangs. Its outer arms squeeze the water, pressing it towards the viewer. Resisting the pressure is wind – indicated only by the blown branches of a single tree in the foreground, free of watery pressure and waving to the ship floating equally free above. It is a picture of weight and pressure transcended.

Most of the time Jones worked in the scriptorium engraving illustrations for *Gulliver's Travels.* Just before they left Capel, Gill had shown Jones's engravings to Robert Gibbings, who, with his wife, Moira, ran the Golden Cockerel Press, and the Gibbingses had commissioned Jones to illustrate Swift's book with forty-two engravings. But Jones soon tired of the job. There were far too many engravings, and it was, he thought, 'such a boring book'. (All utopias, including Thomas More's 'bloody dull book', bored him.)[10] But some of these engravings accommodate spatial constraints ingeniously. In his depiction of the female

7. *Gulliver's Travels* illustration 35, 1925

Yahoo embracing Gulliver in the pond (fig. 7), the visual rhyme of buttocks and breasts jars against that of oblong back-bent heads. The forced embrace, cramped within the edges of the pond and the picture edges, vividly conveys suffocating sexual fear. Indicative or not of the artist's inner life, it is the most powerfully felt of these engravings and not, like many of them, a demonstration merely of competent technique and design.

He stayed on Caldey a month longer than he had stayed at Capel-y-ffin, and he left not for Capel, although Petra had been there since early April, but for Brockley. The impression that he lived chiefly at Capel during this period is mistaken: he lived mostly at Brockley, made a few extended visits to Capel and fewer but longer to Caldey, recording his home address in the guestbook as 115 Howson Rd. Because Capel was so far from London, Gill rented a basement flat in a building in Halls Road, where Jones often met him or Tegetmeier, who had a room in the same building.[11]

* * *

The *Gulliver* engravings took their toll in eye strain. In June 1925, Jones received from an optometrist one prescription for drops to soothe sore eyes and another for new glasses to correct minor nearsightedness, slight astigmatism, and a muscle imbalance pulling his right eye one degree off true.* The correction was so slight that for most people glasses would have been unnecessary, but engraving was close, exacting work.

Since the spring of 1924, he had been visiting Harold Stanley (Jim) Ede, assistant to the keeper at the Tate (known prior to 1931 as the National Gallery, Millbank). Its only curator who appreciated the work of living artists, he encouraged those who visited. Ede invited him home for supper to number 1 Elm Row in Hampstead, a small house he had divided into flats, the Edes

---

* The prescription was for the right eye $-.50/+.25$ and for the left $-.25$.

8. *St Helena*, 1925

and their two daughters occupying the lower flat. Ede's wife, Helen, to her surprise, immediately began calling Jones 'David'. When he took Petra to meet them, Petra found her open-hearted and warm but Jim distant, effete, puritanical. Ede kept some of Jones's work at the Tate, showing and praising it to prospective buyers.[12]

On 10 July 1925, Jones returned to Caldey and then to Capel for a reunion with Petra. In a room on the south side of the quadrangle designated for her weaving (which he associated with the wattling he loved), she spun and worked at her loom, and he drew and engraved at a high, deep windowsill to catch the light. She wove for him a fine woollen cloth, which she dyed indigo and he had made into a jacket and waistcoat.[13] He carved in relief and gave her a Madonna and Child and, on 18 August, for the feast of St Helena – Petra's middle name was Helen – an exquisite little boxwood pendant, carved in the round (fig. 8).

Jones and Petra walked to a shaded dingle where a small stream fell to the Honddu. Across the Honddu they ascended a shepherd's path to Blaen Bwch, a ruined cottage where they could be alone. They walked up the valley onto the high plateau. Sometimes they went north along the western ridge to a waterfall, the 'Sixty-Footer', 'marvellous,' he would remember. In this lush, Edenic spot, you can stand behind the falling water and bathe in the 'deep, chilly' pool.[14]

He felt great affection for Laurie Cribb, now at Capel working as Gill's assistant and, for Jones, a typical 'old soldier'. Cribb had served with a transport company during the Battle of Mons and then in Salonica. Like a Cockney private, he complained constantly, even retrospectively, about the cold in the Greek mountains and his feet freezing. This and (ironically) his aversion to intellectual discussion, would inform the complaint near the heart of *In Parenthesis*: 'I am '62 Socrates, my feet are colder than you think on this/Potidaean duck-board' (80). Inevitably, his complaining climaxed in vituperation against mules. He is the prototype of Jones's Emeritus Nodens who complains about camels (*SL* 98).* As he worked, Cribb sang the songs of the army, including one about a toreador named Alphonso, to which Jones would allude (*IP* 103).[15]

Jones's best friend at Capel was twenty-year-old René Hague (fig. 9). Lean, spectacled, with thick, straight, dark auburn hair, he was energetic,

---

* 'Camels' is a textual error. In May 1974, Jones wrote that he 'actually *meant*' Nodens to complain about 'mules'.

playful, witty, irascible – the eternal boy. He spoke in a rich voice precisely, quickly, confidently. A prodigy at Ampleforth, he had gone to Oriel College, Oxford, on a Classics scholarship but was sent down for spending (and being unable to repay) the funds of a drama society. He joined then quit the Jesuit noviciate and tutored monks on Caldey in Latin. In love with Gill's daughter Joanna, he was now working for a local sheep farmer and sleeping in a cell next to Jones's. Over the dividing partition, they read Malory aloud to one another before falling asleep. They joked continually, Petra recalled, Hague making outlandish statements, each pulling the other's leg. Jones respected his 'razor-like intelligence' and Classical learning.[16] For the rest of his life, René would be one of his closest friends.

9. René Hague, c. 1925

On 29 October, with Gill, Jones visited Gibbings, at Waltham St Lawrence, who proposed having the *Gulliver* engravings hand-painted. Jones objected, then said, 'I suppose you might try it' and indicated on trial prints what colours should be used. He got on especially well with Moira and enjoyed talking with her. All four collaborated in making joke-sketches and off-colour limericks.[*] That evening, Gill danced nude with the Gibbingses, Jones taking no part in these revels, possibly unaware of them. He subsequently thought that painting the *Gulliver* prints ruined them and he managed to erase most of the colour in his copy using Milton, a mouthwash containing a bleaching agent. Though he disliked the book, it was hailed by the *New Statesman* as 'the most pleasing of all modern editions of Gulliver', with especially 'delightful' maps.[17]

Jones spent a fortnight over Christmas at Capel with Gill, Petra, and Hague, returned to Brockley, and, in the spring of 1926, to Capel, where he painted, among other works, *Y Twmpa, Nant Honddu* (fig. 10). In it, the wooded area on the Twmpa emerges from the slope and seems to hang forward, not far behind the nearest trees, a not-fanciful visual effect. On clear bright days, the sides of the Twmpa and the eastern valley ridge appeared to him to advance closer, pressing 'in on every side'. Roughly mirroring the peak, this irregular V-shape narrows to the top of the large trees. These, the V-shape, the looming

---

* One example is a drawing of a high-kicking woman in a transparent dress, to which Jones contributed the head and hair. The Gibbings estate withholds permission to reproduce it, but in the verse (paraphrasing the Gibbingses' contributions and identifying authors in parenthesis): the woman is named Moira . . . (Moira) 'Who said: "my left thigh? Oh! Ta-rá-ra!"' (Jones) / 'when she kicks, there's no flaccid phallus' (Robert) / 'From Cape Horn to the drawing rooms of Tara' (Gill).

10. *Y Twmpa, Nant Honddu*, 1926

summit, and the cloud above create a diffused column of vertical force that steadies the picture. Irregular diagonal lines in the middle-ground and foreground generate contrasting forces. Distances are uncertain. (The four trees to the left of the V-shape are impossibly big.) Planes abut. Linear delineations break spatial continuity. He was beginning to relinquish the thick line and emphatic edge of the Michelangelo–Pre-Raphaelite tradition for the thin, freer point-line that speeds drawing, encouraging spontaneity.

Till now, his style had been derivative. Asserting 'the rectilineal and angular', he had emphasised continuous hard-edged contours and strictly divided surfaces following the Classical convention in which clear boundaries command the picture. Now his style was incorporating a degree of 'chaos' that conveys motion. He had taken a long time – he was now over thirty – but he was finding a style distinctively his own, involving distortion, 'our old & familiar friend', which, he later wrote, 'has to be infallibly right & requisite to the occasion or it is *worse* than all the academic tediums'. Moving away from thick, definite solidity, he would soon be evaluating his works in these terms: 'I think it's all right – it's freer.' He would later say that 'from 1926 onwards' there was 'a fairly recognisable direction' in his work, that his paintings were now what he 'personally would ask a painting to be'.[18]

Back in Brockley in the summer of 1926, in the firebox beneath the washing copper in the scullery, Jones burned all he had of his pre-1925 paintings and drawings except his wartime sketches and some art-school studies. An extraordinarily decisive act, it indicated how ruthlessly critical of his own work he was.[19]

For most of the next six months, he worked at home, painting mostly from his studio window looking out on the back garden and achieving a compromise between sculptural vividness and freedom from uniform perspective. The definite, recognisable forms of these paintings make them easy to see. They represent a pause in development, one step back to Westminster after taking two steps forward at Capel and Caldey.

The Town Garden (fig. 11) bends perspective, looking down at the foreground and straight out at the background. The wavy irregularity of the living bare branches contrasts with the linear fences with their linear slats.

His parents' dog, Michael, looks up, wagging his tail; and, in collusion, the waggly branches seem to greet the viewer with wild happiness. This exemplifies a foundational principle for Jones, that once a person 'has put two marks on the drawing paper – he has made, not two marks, but three, & it is by that third invisible "mark" that we know whether the other two have significance'. Perspective splits, each foreground fence being seen from a good deal the other side of centre, opening the picture. The tops of houses march into the left background from a perspective all their own. The life of this painting is in the changes required to see it.

In London Jones visited friends, including Hague, who had left Capel at the beginning of February 1926, sometimes going with him to meetings of the Distributist League in the Devereaux Pub in Essex Street. Weaver Hawkins had moved to France. Jones visited Medworth in his rooms in Kensington and sometimes drew with him in the life class at Westminster – his last visit there would be in 1928. Each Monday evening at 6.30 they went for a pub crawl, a ritual observed through the early 1930s. Also in pubs he met Poulter, who was working as a railway clerk and playing rugby for the London Welsh. At his insistence, Jones read *The Brothers Karamazov*, the only long Russian novel he would read. With Gill he attended meetings of the Society of Wood Engravers, where he met John and Paul Nash, Gwen Raverat, Noel Rooke, and sixty-three-year-old, white-bearded Lucien Pissarro, the first modern artist to engrave his own drawings.[20]

Sometimes with Gill, Jones visited Oliver Lodge, a Gill disciple and satellite of Bloomsbury, in his Chelsea studio. As they drew together, Lodge commented on Jones having a new hat, and Jones explained that he was merely its custodian. A friend who had entered a monastery the previous week had given it to him, saying he no longer needed it. But he would be expelled in a few weeks, he said, and would need it back. The friend was Denis Tegetmeier. Motivated by secret passion for Petra Gill, he had become a Cistercian postulant – the passing of the hat a symbolic act, as would be its return six months later when Tegetmeier resumed life as a layman.[21]

Jones visited the London Dominicans, who, in the July 1926 issue of their journal, *Blackfriars*, published his first essay since the war, 'Beauty in Catholic Churches', in which he contends that art must express

11. *The Town Garden*, 1926

12. *The Book of Jonah* illustration 13, 1926

contemporary culture and that, since today we are generally unable to create 'a thing of beauty', the only hope for authentic art is a counter culture determined 'to avoid . . . the general decline'.

During the early months of 1926, he illustrated *The Book of Jonah* for Gibbings's press with thirteen wood engravings. The project may reflect recent assertions by Gill that the Christian artist must be a prophet.[22] Jones depicts Jonah's Nineveh as a modern city, thereby implying his affinity with the biblical prophet – 'Jonah' being a near homonym for 'Jones'. The best of these engravings is the last (fig. 12). In it the prophet complains under his rocking shelter in the windy heat; the worm in the gourd plant evokes the serpent in Eden; Jonah's near nakedness resembles that of Jesus on the cross: all suggesting an intriguing correspondence between the Fall, Jonah's reluctance, and the redemption. Vital in its subtle variety, this brilliant combination of black-line and intaglio engraving expressing the delirium of heat is Jones's most impressive engraving to date.

Most of the other *Jonah* engravings indicate, however, that he was stalled in his development, owing to the influence of Gibbings and Gill. Like all printers, Gibbings wanted linear clarity of the sort Gill excelled at, and most of the *Jonah* engravings resemble Gill's – they are 'pure Eric', Jones said, and for that reason he would dislike them.[23] However, he achieves visual correspondences that chiasmically pair ten of the thirteen engravings. He was beginning to combine linear sequence with spatial symmetry in a new kind of unity that would inform his subsequent illustrated books and his long poems.

* * *

Back at Capel in the late summer of 1926, Jones saw a good deal of Douglas Cleverdon, a twenty-four-year-old Bristol bookseller. Welsh on his mother's side, he was a recent graduate from Oxford in Classics, religiously non-aligned, benign, gentle, warm, enthusiastic. When they had first met that spring, Jones had seemed to him 'unassuming and gentle, . . . charitable in his judgements and free of malice' with 'a lively sense of humour' and 'an endearing chuckle'. Cleverdon wanted to publish artistic books. His bookshop was in the ground floor of 18 Charlotte Street, where he lived in a third-floor flat as a lodger and flatmate of G. Methven Brownlee, a forty-nine-year-old photographer. In her studio, she took portrait photographs of Cleverdon (fig. 13), Jones in his indigo coat (fig. 14), Jones with Gill (chapter 5, fig. 3), and Petra (fig. 15).[24]

Kept indoors by the cold at Capel the previous winter, Jones had begun engraving in copper. The transition from wood engraving had been difficult: at first his burin slithered over the surface, so that he held it too tight, resulting in stiff over-control. But he liked copper-plate prints having been 'pressed into the paper', and he improved. Cleverdon bought some, and Stanley Morison saw them. Morison (fig. 16), whom Jones had met at Ditchling, was the foremost British typographical designer.* He commissioned Jones to illustrate a booklet entitled *Seven Fables of*

13. Douglas Cleverdon, by G. Methven Brownlee, 1924

14. Jones, by Brownlee, 1926

15. Petra Gill, by Brownlee, 1926

* He would design the Times New Roman typeface in 1929 and later the page layouts for *The Times* and the *Tablet*.

16. Stanley Morison, 1933

17. *Seven Fables of Aesop* illustration 1, 1928

Aesop, to serve as a type-specimen of a new font designed for the Lanston Monotype Corporation.[25]

Jones spent the spring of 1927 on the seven small (2½ by 3¼ inch) *Aesop* engravings, economising line by simplifying design. They are technically impressive. When shown a copy in 1974, he would say that he thought the animals 'bloody good', that he disliked the sculptor in the fifth engraving, and that, in the first engraving, he liked the man's hand on his hip as he smites the lion, a posture he had seen in the trenches (fig. 17).

In these engravings and a large Christmas card, he more than doubled his experience in copper and made technical advances – one being the use of short multiple dry-point scratches to evoke the sheen of sea surface and the contour of limbs. He was now achieving a 'flowing style', an effect 'of linear freedom and firmness hardly obtainable in any other material'. As he was finding with watercolours, the more exacting the medium 'the more free and flowing the ultimate result'.[26] Benefiting from working for a press free from Gill's influence and Gibbings's requirements, he was exorcising 'the instinct of self-preservation in a talent', Sickert's definition of genius. Moreover, he was applying to wood engraving what he was learning in copper.

He had received a commission from the Gregynog Press to illustrate an edition of the Book of Ecclesiastes in Welsh, *Llyfr y Pregeth-wr*. He cut two wood engravings: a vignette for the title page and a large crucifixion scene for the frontispiece (fig. 18), both masterful shallow intaglio engravings. No longer cutting the wood, his extremely sharp graver glided in free curves across its surface like a burin or dry-point needle on copper. This new style produced a block difficult to print. Too little ink greys the black areas, and the slightest excess blocks up the thin scratchings. When properly printed, however, the image has remarkable intricacy, richness, and sense of movement. In these engravings, he transformed the medium from one of mere ornament and illustration to art independent and interesting in itself. This, his first public work for Wales, is a prelude to his supreme achievement as a wood engraver.

Gibbings commissioned him to illustrate *The Chester Play of the Deluge* with ten engravings for £100 and, recognising the brilliance of the Ecclesiastes frontispiece, ceased insisting on easy-to-print linear simplicity. For the *Deluge*, Jones gave a lot of attention to preliminary design and made studies of animals in the London and Bristol zoos. Deeply absorbed and working with intense concentration, he engraved in his new intaglio style. The blocks were large for wood engravings (5½ by 6½ inches) and, except the penultimate illustration, busy, full yet harmonious, charged with rhythmic movement. They demonstrate in grouping figures a mastery not seen in British art since Blake and establish Jones as one of the foremost modern animal artists. He finished his 'sumptuous work', as he called it, in Brockley at the end of June 1927. His own favourite of these engravings is no. 6 (fig. 19), the animals boarding the Ark. (In the upper left are the herons he liked to watch flying in the valley of the Honddu.)[27]

18. *Llyfr y Pregeth-wr*, 1927

Consistent in style and quality, the ten *Deluge* engravings have the overall structure he had begun to discover in *The Book of Jonah*. While following the temporal sequence of the medieval play, they achieve multiple, chiasmic correspondences, each engraving having its mirroring counterpart, the first five with the second five in inverse sequence.*

The Deluge is archetypally autobiographical. Jones had read Maritain asserting continuity between boatbuilding and art. As builder of the ark, Noah is therefore a type of the artist. Jones cannot have worked on these engravings for

19. *Deluge 6, The Chester Play of the Deluge*, 1927

* For explication of this pattern of pairings, see T. Dilworth, *Reading David Jones* (Cardiff: University of Wales, 2008), pp. 9–19.

20. *Deluge 9, The Chester Play of the Deluge,* 1927

half a year without associating the biblical flood with the Thames flood of 6–7 January 1926, filling the lower floor of the Tate where Jim Ede was keeping some of Jones's watercolours and (much more important to both of them) 19,000 Turner watercolours and drawings, submerged but kept dry by ark-tight carpentry of a set of cabinets.[28] (Jones appreciated this feat of carpentry as only a poor carpenter can.) When he drew and cut the tenth engraving, in which Noah stands at an altar before sacrificial fire, did he remember his burning of drawings and paintings months before? That, too, was a sacrifice heralding a new creation, which now included these engravings. He regarded industrialism as, at once, a destroying flood and the start of a new dark age. During the historical Dark Ages, the Church had been an ark (and its monasteries, arks) preserving Christianity and Classical culture. In the new dark age, his art might be such an ark. Gill had often called the Guild at Ditchling an ark.[29] At Capel, Jones stayed in a building perched part way up its own Mount Ararat (see fig. 20) and arking twelve adults and seven children in close proximity to animals. When it rained there, it deluged. That he was conscious of these associations is implied by affinity between the second *Deluge* engraving, in which Noah's family bends to work, and Jones's 1926 painting *Mr Gill's Hay Harvest*, in which those living at Capel work in the monastery field. At Ditchling and Capel, Gill was Noah and Jones his prospective son-in-law. Now, here, Jones was Noah, the archetype of Noah's ark joining with the Dark Age preservation of Christian culture by Celtic monks in a myth of personal vocation.

The Deluge is one of the great illustrated books but not as printed in 1927. Jones complained that the printers used hard paper and omitted damping. The paper was hard but, according to Gibbings, damped. Where Gibbings erred was in printing blocks and type simultaneously, for seldom do they respond equally to uniform pressure. He instructed the printers to ink the blocks lightly to avoid filling in the shallow, fine lines – a far lesser evil than over-inking, but they printed grey. Jones regarded the Golden Cockerel prints as 'utterly worthless'. (Decades later, after the press made a set for a Council for the Encouragement of Music and the Arts exhibition, he urged republication of the book but with 'the most careful printing as the lines are extremely delicate and get easily filled up – and the quality gets lost and the effect coarsened'.) In his later years, he thought the *Deluge* wood engravings the first 'in any way representative of' his subsequent development, the only ones he would allow to be reproduced. Acting as a broker arranging sales of *Deluge* prints, Ede asked for a framed set to take to Paris. Jones delayed and then declined, saying he could not 'imagine the French being impressed by the work of a third rate English Artist'.[30]

On the strength of the Ecclesiastes and *Deluge* engravings, Jones was elected in 1927 to the Society of Wood Engravers. With him was elected Eric Ravilious, whose work Jones admired above that of all other wood engravers and whom he considered 'one of the nicest people' he knew. On 26 November 1928 Jones would help to hang the Society's show at the Redfern Gallery.[31]

*   *   *

Jim Ede had introduced Jones's work to Arthur Howell, a former Cardiff draper who owned the St George Gallery in Hanover Square. Howell thought Jones's pictures 'entirely new'. In early July 1925, Jones had asked him for an exhibition. Howell offered instead to act as his exclusive agent, showing chosen pictures to select clients and building interest for a possible exhibition the following year. Jones left, hoping to get an exhibition elsewhere. A year later, he returned and nervously agreed to Howell's offer. Impressed by the newer paintings, particularly those done at Brockley, Howell arranged a package deal: cash down for delivery of 'a score or so' of watercolours. (Gill figured that the price per picture was something like £2.5s.9¼d. 'precisely like an article in a draper's shop', and they laughed at that.) Knowing that Jones's pictures were not easy to grasp at first sight, Howell adopted a method learned from Ede. He showed an art critic three pictures, which the critic disliked, and, leaving them propped against his desk, kept him in conversation for half an hour. A month later, he did it again. The following month, again, and the critic would exclaim, 'I have been too hasty – these are good.' In the spring of 1927, Howell proposed a shared exhibition with Gill. Gill agreed but, knowing his work inferior to Jones's, wrote, 'let us both pray that the collaboration won't hurt you'. The exhibition took place in April and May and included twenty-seven pictures by Jones, mostly done at Capel, Caldey, and Brockley. To Howell's surprise and Jones's delight, many viewers came, most pictures sold, and reviews were favourable. Writing anonymously in *The Times*, Ede acutely described Jones's landscapes as 'half maps and half pictures, with the distance between near and far abolished, but with considerable emphasis upon the relief of individual parts – such as the folds of hills' and containing 'hints of Giotto, Cézanne, and – in the peculiar flexibility of the designs – Blake, but in total effect it is strongly original'.[32]

Ede had told Edward Marsh about Jones, and, during the exhibition, introduced them. Marsh was Churchill's private secretary and one of the few perceptive early English collectors of modern art. He admired Jones's pictures, bought one, and, as the founder and secretary of the Contemporary Art Society, ensured that it also bought one – Jones's first sale to a public institution. Marsh used his influence to have him included in the Daily Express Young Artists' Show, which had previously rejected his work. In this he colluded with Ede, directing Jones to take pictures to Ede, who had 'the matter in hand'. Jones thought Marsh 'very smart' and was impressed by his knowing 'everybody of importance' while being 'totally devoid of snobbishness'. They would meet at exhibitions, Marsh would continue to buy his work, and Jones would remain grateful for the early encouragement.[33]

Ede had Jones to supper on 22 June 1927 with the pianist Vera Moore and the painters Ben and Winifred Nicholson. From then on Jones visited the Edes nearly weekly, sometimes staying overnight. (On 6 August, closing the shutters in the spare room, he broke a narrow-based Staite Murray vase, which Murray subsequently repaired.) Jones painted the front garden (*Number One Elm Row*). He and Ede walked together on the heath and went to Kew to sketch and to the zoo. On 13 September, Jones had him home to Brockley.[34]

On the advice of Ede and Gill, Jones discontinued his arrangement with Howell, which earned him less than half of what he would get on straight commission. (Artists then got two-thirds of the sale price.)[35] Hoping to sell fewer pictures for more money, Jones placed works in the Goupil Gallery Exhibition of October–November and the South London Group Exhibition at Camberwell.

On 27 November and 4 December 1927, at supper with the Edes, he mentioned how deeply impressed he was by the recent Blake Centenary Exhibition at the Tate. He regarded Blake as 'infinitely the greatest of all Britishers'. Having just returned from two weeks in Paris, Ede was full of anecdotes about meetings with Picasso, Braque, Brancusi, Chagall, Miro, Rousseau, and Gertrude Stein.[36]*

* * *

Since leaving Ditchling, Jones had spent little time with Petra, and their relationship was troubled. He repeatedly postponed setting a wedding date,

* Ede had said, 'Oh Miss Stein I'm so glad to meet you. I've been longing to see your Picassos.' She turned abruptly and walked away. Picasso later told him, 'You shouldn't have mentioned me to her because she's very possessive and also she wants to be noticed for herself and not for the pictures she's got.'

saying, 'I can't get married until I've got more money.' He seemed to her to want the sexual and material comforts of marriage without having to support a family. Living with his parents was out of the question, so she assumed they would live at Capel, though he did not want to live with her parents and be so far from London galleries.[37]

The difficulty was not solely monetary. He would tease her by saying, 'Come on, you old dear wife', which she disliked. Joanna Gill and Hague thought he took her for granted, as though already married. 'He may have found me terribly dull,' Petra later said, 'because I wasn't intellectual at all', not 'sophisticated enough. Perhaps he found me rather boring.' Hagreen thought they had nothing in common. She was simple, straightforward, without his depth of sensitivity or breadth of interests. Hagreen said that Betty 'was a joy' and Joanna 'was a joy', but Petra 'was a lump' and there was 'a kind of numbness' to her.[38] Having revised his opinion about Jones being highly sexed, Gill wrote to Gibbings on 3 October 1925, 'D.J.'s "crow" is better than his cock.'

Contributing to Jones's strain were neurotic symptoms. They surfaced soon after he reunited with Petra at Capel in the summer of 1926. Strolling with her in the valley, he told her, 'I feel as though I'm walking two feet above the earth', an experience with striking affinity to his panic attack on the plank at Festubert in April 1916 – psychologists attribute such sensations to fear and desire to escape. This experience was followed by debilitating anxiety, depression, and insomnia of the sort that had afflicted him in 1921 after returning to Brockley from Canterbury. In this woeful condition, he was taken in mid-July to Bristol to stay with Chute and his mother in order to see a physician, Dr Newman Field. He prescribed two stimulants, Easton Syrup and a strychnine tonic, and told him, 'Don't worry, you'll be all right.' Two weeks after it began, the depression lifted and the anxiety and insomnia abated, though Jones would refill the prescription in October.[39]

While at Capel, he feared mixing with people. He had always found the local Welsh farmers strange and frightening and now would not accompany Petra into Hay-on-Wye or join weekly excursions to Abergavenny. He seemed to her to want just to paint and engrave without any other concerns. 'The slightest thing upset him,' she said, and he would have a stomach ache or diarrhoea and stay in bed. He was 'always getting colds', always had a sore throat, always worried about his health. He was so often ill, that she got used to taking up his meals and waiting on him. He behaved, as she put it, 'like a helpless child'.

The engagement became increasingly tenuous. Friends of the family, including O'Connor and Reeves, were for breaking it off, but the betrothal ceremony had been so weddingish, Petra remembered, that ending the engagement seemed unthinkable. Jones, too, was paralysed. It was, she recalled, 'a frightful crisis for him'. In September, all the Gills but Petra having left Capel to winter in the south of France at Salies-de-Béarn, Petra suggested that she and Jones have a period apart, during which he could make up his mind.[40]

He went home to Brockley and then, on 3 October, to Caldey, devoting most of his days to painting out of doors and spending evenings with the McHardy family, who worked the island farm.[41] About his quandary over Petra, he confided by post to Ede. Thinking of Maritain's view that the artist must channel energies into art, Jones wrote on 4 November, 'The whole question of sublimation – suppression "canalization" . . . is a very vexed one – & hideously complicated for me . . . largely by there being no general standard of practice, or accepted ethics in the world at the moment.' Religious celibacy was analogous: even though 'we *all* admit that God alone can satisfy our affections', Jones knows that turning 'all one's energies . . . into spiritual channels . . . is *only the vocation of the few*' mystics, whereas, he says, 'I can't imagine anyone more bound up in terrestrial comforts than I – it revolts me to think of it.'

While in London in July, he had confided his dilemma to Tegetmeier, who irritably asked whether or not he was marrying her and listened with obvious impatience as he waffled. Jones later said to Petra, 'I don't understand. Denis was very off-hand with me . . . We've always had such good talks together. He was very unfriendly.'[42]

Learning after Christmas that Jones was still on Caldey, Tegetmeier went to Capel to court her. A month later, she accepted his proposal of marriage. On 4 February 1927, she wrote two letters, neither of which survives, one to Jones, the other to her parents. Gill replied from Salies on 6 February:

> it is the very best thing you could have told us . . . I am filled with joy in your happiness. For years it has been evident that David was more reluctant than any man ought to be who is betrothed. You know very well that I love him dearly and I shall always do so. Had it not been so I could never have borne his coolness to you so patiently. He is one of the best artists now living and one of the best and dearest of men, but neither of these things spells marriage . . . I feel sure that David himself will be very much relieved and grateful for the step you've taken. I think he would have broken off the engagement himself long ago had he not felt that loyalty to you and his promise came before any personal reluctance or fear that he might feel . . . Know, though mother and I have often wished that what you have done could be done . . . Certainly I should not think unkindly of David. I cannot understand his state of mind – I was never thus – but I know he has suffered a great deal. His love for you is real enough but it is not 'married love'. Neither do I think he will think ill of you for what you have done or of me for thus wholeheartedly, completely and enthusiastically agreeing with you.[43]

In her letter to Jones she said, as she remembered, that she 'felt the time had come to break it off because obviously it wasn't going to work out'. She was unhappy with the thought of him 'just taking any old job in order to get married' and wanted him to go on with his work. She said that Tegetmeier had proposed marriage and they were now engaged, and she asked him 'to release' her to marry him. Jones was with the McHardys when he opened her letter. Thirteen-year-old Monica McHardy watched him read it, heard him exclaim 'Oh no!', and saw him smash his fist into a stone wall.[44] *

He wanted to go to Petra immediately but the last boat for the mainland had left. That night McHardy gave him whisky, which he was unused to. He became violently ill. The next day the sea was rough, and, badly hungover, he stayed in bed. By the following day, he decided not to go: she had made her decision, and who was he to interfere? He responded by post. She burned the letter along with his love letters but later recalled that he expressed shock and surprise. 'He couldn't understand my attitude,' she said, and his rival was 'Denis of all people! They were friends!' About Jones's state of mind during the following weeks, a young novice then in the monastery would remember in old age that he 'was very depressed, desperate, almost suicidal'.[45] With nowhere else to go, he remained on Caldey through Easter, extending his stay to seven months.

The assumption that the breaking of the engagement was a relief for Jones is a Gill-family myth originated by Gill and perpetuated by Hague. In March, Jones wrote to Hagreen, 'you can imagine, I expect, the pain & strain & general mental mix of it all. Lord!! However, one deserves it for one's sins ... My mind is still chaotic.' He blamed himself. In a letter to Ede in November, he apologised for not writing sooner, adding, 'it is really beyond words disgusting I know – but then I am disgusting to my friends & I suppose most disgusting to my best friends – hence my loss of Petra I expect'. Guilt feelings would endure on some level for the rest of his life. In his final years, when calling bishops hypocrites for discarding the language and forms of the Catholic liturgy, he used this analogy: 'You fall in love with a girl, visit her often, kiss her, tell her many times and in many ways that you love her; then you visit her less and less often, give her an occasional peck, tell her that she has your esteem.'† And he concluded indignantly, 'What you do in religion as in love is a sign of what you are.'[46]

Back in London, Jones fully revealed his misery to Ede and acted, Ede remembered, 'as if she was everything'. To distract him, Ede proposed a quick trip to Paris. They went and, on 27 April, Jones met and talked with Gill there and went with Mary to the Louvre. Back in London, two days later, he met Gill again. (In May, Gill proposed that Jones 'ghost' on commissions which

* The account by J. Miles and D. Shiel of Jones repeatedly hitting 'his head slowly against the stone' wall, though unattributed, derives from an unreliable source who was not an eyewitness.

† When I recounted these words to Petra, she acknowledged that this was what their engagement had been like.

Gill would touch up and claim as entirely his own work; Jones refused.) It was Ede to whom he unburdened his heart, telling him what he wanted and yet would not and could not. After one visit, Ede wrote, 'You need I am sure physical expression . . . You need to stroke your cat (Whatever it is you want to "stroke" – stroke it & get relief – . . . your denial is suicide.) & not just to think of the beauty of stroking . . . You are ill for Petra & the blank it has made . . . Yes you are right it is a pain loving people . . .' During the rest of the year, Jones continued seeing Gill, Hague, and Tegetmeier but could not bear to see Petra. He would later see two things as determining the course of his life, not going to university and not marrying Petra.[47]

21. *Self-portrait*, 1928

He drew and painted pictures that contained images of himself, but only one would be entitled *Self-portrait* (fig. 21). He would paint it, in oils, in 1928, in his Brockley studio. It is sombre in tone. The mirrored face and upper torso do not easily 'fit in' or belong to the background, a disconcerting effect owing to fractured perspective. The face has a haggard look missing from a contemporary passport photograph (chapter 7, fig. 3), in which Jones wears the same coat, shirt, and tie. The face and torso are effectively severed from his (absent) lower body in a sort of castration. The left side of the mirror hangs disconcertingly over the edge of the table on which it is propped. A lack of significant formal interrelationship contributes to a feeling of desolation. The candles – two, as on an altar – are phallic, as they are also in their reflection in the mirror, pointing (accusingly?) towards him. The odd, expanding, long white shape, indicating the side of the table, which is clothed like an altar, is incongruously straight-edged, knife-like, pointing, like the candles, piercing in relationship to his chest. This is the altar of art, at which the artist in the mirror is sacrificed and reconstituted. His face is harrowed yet also impassive, distracted from grief by the act of painting. This is a dedicated artist, mentally and emotionally fully aware of the cost of his dedication. He would later misdate this painting '1927', perhaps associating it with the traumatic event of this year.

PART THREE

WONDER YEARS

CHAPTER 7: 1927–30

n mid-August 1927, Jones joined his parents in Portslade at 5 Western Esplanade (fig. 1), an elegant stone house on the tideline, lent to his father by the owner of the *Christian Herald*. During four weeks here in August and September, Jones did 'a lot' of painting, mostly of the open sea under an empty sky. The sea was, he said, 'quite a *big* influence' making his work 'more "pure" somehow as water-colour painting'. From now on the fluidity and movement of the sea would inform even the land in his pictures. Concerned chiefly with the transitory effects of light and weather, he painted atmosphere, remembering Ruskin writing that in Turner the sea, however calm, is redolent of storm. That, he thought, is 'more than half' the secret 'of good painting, of good art ... it is both peace *and* war'. He would write in 1962 that his Portslade pictures 'are, probably, quite the best I've done'. On 1 October 1927, he went to Caldey for three weeks to paint land-and-seascapes.[1]

* * *

His main attachment was now not to Gill but Ede (fig. 2), who facilitated his aesthetic transformation by understanding it. They shared, for example, belief in the importance of a sense of movement, which was, after unity, Jones's 'criterion in assessing the worth of any picture'. It had to 'flow in some way', and he adopted as a motto Galileo's statement about the solar system – *Eppur si muove*, 'Nevertheless it moves'.[2]

1. Hove Seaside Villas, *c.* 1927. Number 5 is the third from foremost

2 Jim Ede, c. 1936

Jones was now often at the Edes' Hampstead flat, which had, like Jim Ede, a precious, *noli-me-tangere* quality. Jones would 'just wander in unannounced', Jim recalled, and often stayed overnight, sometimes for days. He was the Edes' most constant family friend, finding in them the familial intimacy he had lost with the Gills. The spare bedroom was considered his.[3]

He stayed largely for Jim's wife, Helen, whom he considered 'real'. Lovely and delightful, with a wonderful pealing laugh, she was solicitous towards him. In 1928, she knitted him a pair of red socks so that he and Jim could be equally fashionably outrageous. Jones often stayed when Jim left for work. When Jim went on a month-long US lecture tour, Jones spent a week with her and her daughters. For him she was, Jim thought, sexually 'safe'. She knew many famous people but told her daughter Mary, 'There are only two men in this world worth knowing: one is Jim Ede; the other is David Jones.'[4]

The Edes hosted a salon. At 4 p.m. each Sunday, tea, toast, and marmalade were served to usually half a dozen guests, mostly entertainers – classical actors, performers in the Ziegfeld Follies, musicians – and the wealthy, invited to meet poor artists. Jones enjoyed them all, Ede remembered, especially liking Margaret Gerstley, an actress who returned his affection chastely, accompanied as she usually was by her South African girlfriend. At about 9.30 all visitors were shown the door except Jones, who stayed on to share a light supper.[5]

He also came to supper on Wednesdays, sometimes with another guest, once the painter Georges Braque, Jim acting as interpreter. (Jones later wrote of Braque, 'I always liked him' and thought him far 'better than Matisse ... but not as good as Bonnard'.) Other regular visitors included Ben and Winifred Nicholson, Ivor Hitchens, Edward (Teddy) Wolfe, Barbara Hepworth, and Staite Murray. On 26 August 1930, Jim introduced Jones to Penelope Chetwode and, later at the Café Royal, to her fiancé, John Betjeman, who had just run noisily down the stairs waving a toy gun and shouting 'Bang! Bang! You're dead!'[6]

Jones and Jim talked about 'anything', Jim remembered, and that included *Ulysses*, mutual acquaintances, and 'often' Freud and psychoanalysis. But chiefly they spoke of 'the spiritual meaning of life'. Agnostic, leaning towards Buddhism, Jim thought that 'body and spirit are one and the same' and that, therefore, 'God is a strawberry.' (Jones later confided to Kathleen Raine, 'Jim has a soft centre.') Jim regarded the Catholic Church as repressive; Jones explained that it 'only (ideally) shapes & modifies & rightly orders the emotions', adding 'anyone might' not 'like the "shapes" it makes of people's lives' but that is 'like saying of a man playing tennis that one prefers rugby football'. When he stayed over at the Edes on a Saturday night, he attended Sunday Mass at the Dominican house in Haverstock Hill over two miles away. Jim expressed amazement at his rising early and walking so far. Jones said, 'If you knew that your dearest friend was arriving in Paddington at eleven thirty you would be only too pleased to go and meet him.' He was, Jim said, 'fundamentally spiritual'.[7]

*   *   *

Jones and Ben Nicholson became friends. Nicholson was aesthetically narrow, rejecting art not resembling his own, Ede said, whereas 'David was prepared to like anything.' Completely modern, Nicholson was insensitive to (a now favourite expression of Jones) 'degradation and decay'. But they agreed in valuing freedom in painting and in loving the early Italian primitives and, among the moderns, Cézanne, Rousseau, Matisse, Derain, Braque, and Picasso. Nicholson signed postcards to Jones 'love Ben' and, according to Ede, 'felt that as an artist and a person David was something'. Because Nicholson admired Jones's recent paintings, especially *Tir y Blaenau* (chapter 6, fig. 3), and because of the advocacy of Ede, at a meeting of the 7 & 5 Society on 26 January 1928, Nicholson nominated Jones for membership, Percy Jowett seconding the nomination, and Jones was elected.[8]

The 7 & 5 Society was a cooperative founded in 1919 to break the exhibiting monopoly of the London Group and share exhibition costs. Nicholson was now chairman, and Ede its spokesman, having written the foreword to the catalogue for their 1926 exhibition. Apart from basic post-Impressionist doctrine, the 7 & 5 was theory-free, and, from 1926 to 1932 exhibited most of the best British art of the time, upstaging the larger London Group.

*   *   *

Painting for Jones involved 'fierce concentration'. A friend, Harman Grisewood, would remember Jones's 'whole physical being mobilised' as if 'wrestling' with the picture. And success depended, Jones said, '*wholly …* upon' a 'final extra kick' of concentrated energy. So illness precluded painting. Suffering from flu at Portslade in late March or early April 1928, he retreated to bed. But feeling he 'had to do something', sitting up in bed, he made 'lots of drawings' of infantrymen 'and little brief pieces of writing'. He intended the drawings to be designs for 'etchings' and the writing to be 'word pictures as a sort of running commentary, … the writing to be definitely subsidiary'. The project originated in his sense of himself as a book illustrator, though now he would also provide the text.

3. Jones passport photograph, 1928

He may have had in mind the example of Blake's illuminated books since he later told a reporter, Blake 'has influenced me more than any other writer or artist'.* He composed 'some sentences' set on the morning before embarkation that would 'be the initial passages' of his war epic, *In Parenthesis*. He proceeded by recalling a specific event, experience, sight, or feeling, and then remembering what immediately preceded or followed it. Wanting to 'find out . . . in what way' negotiations between realism and aesthetics in visual art took place in writing, he discovered there was 'almost no difference' – they 'proceed on the same principles': 'a word or sequence of words' might belong to the content or 'subject' but be wrong formally. Easier to alter than painting, writing was 'not *quite* so exhausting'. It soon outgrew what could be appended to pictures. Without anticipating publication, he decided to call it 'In Parenthesis', 'almost the first words' he wrote and later claimed, 'the only words not' subsequently 'altered a dozen times'.[9]

Recovering from the flu, he returned to painting during the day, writing in 'spare time and evenings' in his room with the door closed – he needed privacy to write. His parents worried. His father repeatedly came to the door calling, 'What on earth are you doing?' When David confessed that he was writing, his father said he was wasting his time. So strong and persistent was his disapproval that David hid his activity, writing 'in terrible secrecy'.[10]

* * *

On 26 March 1928 Jones (fig. 3) joined Gill and Robert Gibbings on a trip to France. Visiting the Louvre – or it may have been in the National Gallery in London (later he could not remember which) – Jones came upon a man copying a, to Jones, uninteresting painting. They began arguing, the argument became heated and loud, and attendants expelled Jones from the building. On the afternoon of 15 April, he accompanied the Edes to the Louvre, where he especially liked Michelangelo's *Rebellious Slave* because 'it simply twirls you round . . . instinctively to

* He thought Blake a better artist, in his '*best* drawings & designs', than poet and a better engraver than painter. He admired Blake's poetry but not the long 'prophetic' books, in which he disliked the 'transference of Neo-platonic concepts & Classical' ideas 'into Hebrew or Hebraic-sounding & therefore Hebrew evoking' names, such as Thel, Ahania, Urizen, and Los: 'I don't believe you can introduce an invented or altogether foreign nomenclature. Because names themselves set up all sorts of other forms & undertones & this causes difficulties within a tradition – it won't work in my view'.

follow its spiral'. Then they visited the Musée Cluny and its large unicorn tapestries, where he contracted an enthusiasm for unicorns that would influence his engraving and poetry.[11]

On the 16th with the Gills, he visited Chartres Cathedral and wandered the medieval town below, visiting its church of St Pierre. Afterwards, on the train to Salies-de-Béarn, where Gill was part-owner of a villa, Gill praised the cathedral as the best building in the world. Jones infuriated him by saying he preferred St Pierre and later, light-filled Gothic architecture. He was guarding his independence: although not 'fond of gothic' and preferring Romanesque and Norman architecture, he did think Chartres by far the most beautiful building he had seen and 'the most breath-taking *gothic* building in the world', one that 'makes all other *Gothic* buildings seem nothing'.[12]

Staying at the Ville des Palmiers in Salies, Jones painted prolifically, and in seventeen days finished over a dozen large watercolours. Looser and wilder than his previous landscapes, most are bright in pigment with a broad palette inspired by the southern light. With the Gills he went sightseeing to Sauveterre and the nearby churches of St Martin and the Vierge Noire; to Licq-Athérey, which he sketched (fig. 4); Oloron-Sainte-Marie; Pau; Saint-Pé-de-Bigorre; and Lourdes. Near Lourdes they visited the Hagreens, to whom Jones praised the twelfth-century carvings over the west door of the church at Oloron. From Salies, Mary Gill pointed out the Brèche de Roland, forty-three miles south and, near the end of his stay, Jones and Eric visited the forested ravine, an experience that would influence his poetry (*IP* 80; *A* 57).[13]

Petra was about to arrive at Salies, so Jones left on 5 May to stay with the Hagreens in the Chalet St Vincent. Also staying was an old Yorkshire woman, Miss Best, whose surname would find its way into *In Parenthesis* (4). At the adjacent Dominican convent he attended the office, sung with 'a more marvellous beauty' than he had heard. From the chalet he could see,

at Lourdes, just over half a mile upriver, thousands of pilgrims with candles, a river of light winding towards the grotto, where the Virgin had appeared in 1858.[14] He would associate it with Eleusis (where pagans had prayed to Demeter) in his poetry (*IP* 39; *A* 95, 230).

Visiting the grotto, he thought its church buildings a 'concentrated horror', admired the 'amazingly simple' devotion of the pilgrims, and liked the old buildings in town but not the street leading to the grotto: 'it's like … a Woolworths store on the summit of the Mount of Olives'. He visited old churches nearby, arranging

4. *Licq-Athérey*, 1928

photographs to be taken of the large crucifix at Arrens-Marsous and the fifteenth-century carving of St Anne in the church of Germincy-de-Prés.[15]

The landscape did not at first inspire him. He looked at the mountains for weeks before they gradually began 'to mean something … as kinds of lights hung in the sky'. Then he carried a portfolio and easel outdoors for miles, enduring discomforts that included a threatening farm dog and 'a blasted snake', because, he told Hagreen, 'he needed to struggle with unwilling material to produce the tensions & stresses that make a live painting'; he found that painting indoors from memory produced only easy lines and boring rhythms.[16] Among his successful paintings was *Montes et Omnes Colles* (fig. 5). In it the landscape and river writhe against gravity and perspective. Trees happily wave as though in compliance with Psalm 148, which the title alludes to, which urges mountains, hills, and trees to praise the Lord. Not so happy, the equally restless mountains seem to brood. In 1930, the Whitworth in Manchester would buy this painting – his first sale to a public gallery.

He went with Hagreen to Arcachon on the coast and to Cap Ferret, where, when not painting, he poured out his grief over Petra. According to Hagreen, her rejection had thrown him 'into the abyss'. He noticed the back of a girl hanging laundry and moaned, 'Why will she look so like Petra?' Hagreen said that Jones had been 'sailing with a fair wind' until the break-up 'snapped' his 'mast' so that now he 'could only row'.[17]

On 7 June, Jones returned to Paris, staying for a few days with Ede, whom he accompanied to a house to see a large number of big Picassos,

5. *Montes et Omnes Colles*, 1928

which had a great impact on him. Walking the boulevards, he was haunted by the medieval city he would have much preferred, which had been destroyed in the previous century. Most memorable about his 'few & brief visits' to Paris was 'a peculiar quality of the atmosphere – of light'.[18]

Largely because of the painting he had done in his ten weeks in France, his exhibition in the autumn at the Goupil Gallery was a success, earning him for 1927–28 an income (after expenses) of £180.8s.9d. This windfall required him for the first time to fill out income-tax forms, for which he hired Ethel Watts, the first female chartered accountant in Britain, who would continue to do his taxes and become a friend.[19]

* * *

In the spring of 1927, Cleverdon had commissioned Jones to make copper engravings for the work Jones most wanted to illustrate, Coleridge's *The Rime of the Ancient Mariner*. Morison would design the layout. Doubting his technical ability, Jones asked to engrave in wood, but Cleverdon insisted – he wanted by Christmas 1927 eight 7½ by 5 inch copper engravings and a smaller headpiece and tailpiece. Jones wanted £5 per large engraving, since they would be 'hard work'. He collected thirty-four photographs of sailing ships from newspapers and magazines plus a photograph of an albatross. He visited the South Kensington Museum to see historic models of ships. He sought detailed diagrams of rigging and wanted to know what happens on deck during the raising of sails. But painting postponed engraving. Not until July 1928 did he buy for his studio a small press, small for maximum pressure.[20]

Changes are difficult in copper, so each design had to be 'as sure as possible'. As with the *Aesop* engravings, he economised, simplifying lines reinforced sparingly by cross-hatching, a style he came to regard as truest to the medium, with 'a lyricism inherent in the clean, furrowed, free, fluent engraved line'. He made between 150 and 200 preliminary pencil drawings with the point – he 'designed and redesigned, eliminated and eliminated' – destroying all but the final drawings for each engraving.[21]

In mid-August, his eyes were so sore that he had to stop working. The family doctor said he 'quite obviously' should quit engraving. But he found that by working between long periods of rest, he could keep going.[22]

When five engravings were more-or-less complete, Cleverdon learned that they were 7 by 5½ inches instead of 7½ by 5. Not wanting to distress Jones, he and Morison silently changed the layout. An edition of thirteen 'first state proofs' that collectors buy was printed by Collins and Dear. These were too clean for Jones, who wanted a unifying undertone. He searched for another printer, eventually selecting Walter L. Colls.[23]

6. *The Rime of the Ancient Mariner 6, 1929*

7. *The Rime of the Ancient Mariner 8, 1929*

After completing the engravings in mid-January 1929, Jones made an edition of thirty, which is unique in that he chose the paper and ink, inked the plates, wiped them, and pulled the prints himself. He wanted black ink for the book but acquiesced to green-black. He, Morison, and Cleverdon were present when Colls began printing the engravings and later when the Fanfare Press began printing the type.[24]

The Rime of the Ancient Mariner is the first important copper-engraved, illustrated book since Blake's *The Book of Job* (1826). As with the *Deluge*, the large engravings form a chiasmic pattern of corresponding pairs.* He matted his favourites among them, the last four, in a single frame and hung them in his parents' sitting room. Of these, visually the most extraordinary is no. 6 (fig. 6), in which animated corpses work ropes as the corposant shimmers in the rigging. The effect is ghastly, achieved through wavering tones and unnerving diagonals. No. 8 (fig. 7), with a central wall dividing arches, exemplifies his structural principle of dividing to unite, which, by chiasmic expansion, unifies the entire series.

Upon finishing *The Ancient Mariner*, he experienced the first of what would be several depressions following major creation. The published book was immediately recognised as the best illustration of Coleridge's poem. In 1943 it would be called 'one of the perfect partnerships between author and illustrator in modern times'. But the Great Depression doomed it to financial failure. In 1933, the last seventy copies, originally priced at £2.20, were remaindered by Blackwells at 37½ pence.[25]

In the summer of 1929, Jones began engraving in wood to illustrate *Everyman* for Gibbings but finding the medieval morality play 'utterly' uncongenial, abandoned it.[26]

---

* For explication of this pattern, see the Afterword of S. T. Coleridge, *The Rime of the Ancient Mariner*, illustrated by David Jones, ed. T. Dilworth (London: Enitharmon, 2005), pp. 82–116.

In early October 1929, in his little studio in Brockley, he painted the site of his labours (fig. 8). *The Artist's Worktable* is energised by contrast between drawing (sharp, hard tactile objects) and painting (non-linear tones). The pinned-up curtain in the upper right balances the open drawer in the lower left, the drawer rhyming with the open portion of window, in both of which particulars are sharply defined. This simultaneous opening in and out anticipates, in his poetry, his breaking open already-written texts to write within them. The loosening of form in this painting results from what the engraver Simon Brett calls deliberately naïve seeing. As an art student, Jones had learned unnaturally to view wholes. Now he was reverting selectively to prioritising constituent particulars. The tree on the horizon, window locks, scissors, inkpot: these are rendered in the sharp focus of untrained seeing.[27] Noticing little things

8. *The Artist's Worktable*, 1929

conveys immediacy and tactility, which reflects his habit of physically handling things. Now many of his pictures exist as a jumble of parts achieving communal unity.

* * *

Painting on Caldey in October 1928, he had missed the Benedictines, who had moved to Pinknash in Gloucestershire. On 8 May 1929, he visited them for a fortnight, staying in the abbey, formerly a hunting lodge of Henry VIII, the sole building on a vast wooded slope of the Cotswolds. The monks asked what he thought of the place. He said, 'It's too green', words they gleefully remembered for sixty years as exemplifying his eccentricity. (He was quoting François Boucher, who said that for painters, 'Nature is too green and badly lit.') He left a donation of four guineas. With two friends he would return for another visit in the summer of 1931.[28]

* * *

On 5 September 1923, Jones had shown around Ditchling a visiting Stonyhurst schoolboy named Tom Burns. In 1926 Burns had been working at the Catholic publishing house Sheed & Ward. Jones walked in and asked, 'Do you remember me?' Burns said, 'Of course I do' and took him to lunch.

9. Tom Burns, c. 1928

Thereafter they saw each other once or twice a week, Jones entering the office any time, interrupting Burns's work for conversation. Burns was then enthusiastic about the seventeenth-century Jesuit spiritual writer Jean de Caussade and later remembered Jones as sharing his enthusiasm for Caussade's idea of the 'sacrament of the present moment'.[29]

Born in Chile in 1906 and raised in Wimbledon, Burns (fig. 9) was tall, with strong Basque features: large head, broad forehead, eyebrows thick at the outside like wings, and a pronounced underbite. Energetic, confident, gregarious, affable, enterprising, and intellectually curious, he had spent a year in Paris among a group of Catholic thinkers presided over by Maritain. Back in England he became a street evangelist for the Catholic Evidence Guild. Not in the least sanctimonious, he attended balls and cocktail parties and frequented nightclubs, his favourite being 'Hell'. He was physically forceful, socially adventurous, aggressive in pursuit of women, and decisive – all traits Jones lacked and admired, calling him 'South American Joe' because he was so macho. Theirs was 'a very easy companionship', Ede remembered, in which 'David felt happy', and if 'Tom was a sort of jolly Spanish pirate', he was also, for him, 'a kind of harbour'. Tom lived with his older brother, Charles, a psychiatrist, at 40 St Leonard's Terrace in Chelsea.[30]

Jones spent, as he said, 'half my time' in the Burnses' house, a good part of it drinking Italian vermouth with Tom in his bedsitter/study. Tom remembered him as a 'constant' presence, 'an anchor-man' at regular Saturday lunches and evening parties, during which he 'crouched on the corner of a divan with two or three graceful girls draped round' him 'in earnest discussion'. By the end of the evening, 'all the beautiful girls would be with David getting his wisdom and charm' – the essence of which was, according to one of these girls, Vicky Reid, his 'great love for people'. He also said something original and convincing on almost any subject. At the end of the evening, he caught the last train to Brockley at 11.10 or stayed the night or several nights. This became, after the Edes', his second alternative home.[31]

*　*　*

In the autumn of 1928, Gill had moved his family to Pigotts, an Elizabethan farmstead five miles north of High Wycombe in Buckinghamshire, an hour-and-a-half from London. Jones visited for the weekend of 2 February 1929 and spoke with Petra for the first time since their break-up, though they had seen each other briefly the previous June at Evelyn Waugh's wedding. Jones stayed away for the rest of the winter because Pigotts was 'so bloody cold' but returned in May for several weeks. He came down frequently in warm weather, taking a taxi from High Wycombe instead of the bus. He slept in a room above Gill's engraving workshop.[32]

In late June 1929, Oliver Lodge arrived by car from London with Enid Furminger, a stunning brunette wearing a long fur coat and nothing beneath. She posed for Lodge, Gill, and Jones. Jones's drawing, augmented by delicate washes of grey-green and purple (fig. 10), was so erotic that he thought it pornographic. He sold it to Cleverdon for £5 on the condition that it not be exhibited in his (Jones's) lifetime. Later he wished he had burned it and he diminished the erotic appeal of the female form in his art.[33]

10. *Nude* (Enid Furminger), 1929

Subsequently Lodge had tall twenty-three-year-old Diana Uppington pose for them. She thought Jones 'shy' – she danced naked round the room between sittings.[34] He liked her and drew for her a nude (fig. 11) with Matisse-like sureness of continuous line.

To the south of the quadrangle at Pigotts were extensive gardens, where, in the summer of 1929, Jones urged Petra to leave Tegetmeier and marry him. She thought this 'wild', told him so, and refused.[35] For sixty years, no one else would know of this proposal or surmise the desperation behind it.

At Pigotts on 7 January 1930, assailed by gnawing thoughts of what might have been, he served Petra's nuptial Mass. He and Gill signed as witnesses. His wedding present was a large Capel landscape painted during their engagement.

11. *Nude*, for Diana Lodge, c. 1930

For a frontispiece to Walter Shewring's *Hermia, and Some Other Poems* (1930) he made his penultimate and favourite wood engraving, *The Bride* (fig. 13), a remaking of a failed first illustration for *The Ancient Mariner* in which he had wanted to evoke a nun taking the veil and the numinousness of '*sacramentum hoc magnum est*'. He employed 'the technique' (taken from Bewick) of setting off whites and greys against 'very small areas of solid black' such as the spiked hearse with candles – he was 'jolly fond' of such spikes. Romanesque windows repeat

12. Denis and Petra Tegetmeier and Joanna Gill, 7 January 1930

13. *The Bride*, 1930

the curves of the bride's breasts, their upper portions exposed like the sky in the windows. In one window is the hart of Psalm 42, homonymous with her heart which desires the bridegroom. The wrinkles in her dress and chiffon sleeves suggest vegetation. Her archetype is Mother Earth. Flowers and candles promise an intercourse daringly intimated by the nail in the vulval wound in Jesus's foot. Her high forehead is Petra's (see fig. 12), but symbolically her groom is the Saviour, an archetype with which Jones identified. The left calf of crucified Jesus has a blemish close to the location of the scar of Jones's bullet wound.[36]

The newly married Tegetmeiers lived in the cottage across the yard from his bedroom window, from which he liked watching Petra washing dishes in the sink. To Jones's surprise, he found that now she was married, he got on better with her.[37] From his window (fig. 14), he painted the farmyard (fig. 15).

14. Pigotts farmyard from Jones's bedroom window

15. *Pigotts Farmyard*, 1930

He compressed the facing cottages, removing two gables and three windows; lightened the tones of the buildings so that they blend into the landscape, opening the enclosure; and painted as if from a hundred feet above-and-behind his window. Free and irregular, the picture rocks with life.

Hague and Joanna Gill married on 19 November 1930 and took over the cottage next to the Tegetmeiers. Jones gave them a portrait he had painted of Joanna. On their kitchen wall hung a drawing he had made years earlier of St Nicholas presenting them with a cheque for £10,000 so they could marry. Now when visiting Pigotts, he stayed with them. Through 1939 he visited for most of every summer, arriving in early June and remaining till late August and sometimes longer.[38]

Helping to reconcile him to Petra's marriage was growing affection for Prudence Pelham (chapter 9, fig. 9). He had met her in the spring of 1929 when she was nineteen and learning letter-cutting from Gill. The second daughter of the sixth Earl of Chichester, she had studied sculpture in Paris. Reacting against her family background, she dressed like a gypsy with her hair unkempt, passing with bohemian ease through class barriers. She felt happy at Pigotts, away from the social inhibitions of relatives and, after twice repulsing Gill's never-subtle advances, free from sexual pursuit. Her friend Miriam Rothschild recalled, 'She had more sex appeal than anyone I've ever met.' When in Paris 'we walked down the street, men turned round like marionettes and followed us'. In pubs men came to her 'like moths round a candle'. Tom Burns pursued her aggressively, until she rejected his marriage proposal in October 1930.[39]

Prudence loved Jones. They walked together in the thick beechwood surrounding Pigotts. (Like all woods, it reminded him of 'woodlands in ... legend & history'.) In early summer 1930, he painted her in the Hagues' parlour (fig. 16). Burns would later claim to have bought this picture, and Jones would claim not to have sold it – a source of lasting tension between them. Sometimes Burns had the picture, sometimes Jones, who exhibited it on the condition that it not be sold.[40]

In 1929, Jones, Hague, Gill, and Prudence began reading Hamish MacLaren's *Private Opinions of a British Blue-jacket* (1929), which became one of Jones's most loved books. Recording the near stream-of-consciousness of a sailor named Taplow, it became for the four of them a personal lexicon of screwball, cute Southampton Cockney, rife with

16. *Lady Prudence Pelham*, 1930

malapropisms and spelling eccentricities. Speaking and in letters, Jones would break into Taplowese: a meal was 'a primb feed'; an acquaintance, 'a nise tipe of gurl'.

*   *   *

In 1927 Ede had introduced Jones to Helen Sutherland, one of the richest women in England (chapter 8, fig. 9). A forty-seven-year-old Quaker and former social worker, she was intelligent, sensitive, always exquisitely dressed. She regarded her fortune, inherited from her mother, as a trust for the support of impoverished artists, buying only pictures she liked, often to give away. In March 1929, at a party at her house in Belgravia, she invited Jones to Rock Hall, a large castellated house she leased four miles north of Alnwick, in Northumberland. In August 1929, he went up by train with Helen Ede and her daughters. Helen Sutherland wanted to buy a picture from him, to which he tried to add another as a gift – she bought both. He now would spend the spring and autumn with her in Northumberland, staying so long because she wanted to support him and because, she said, 'he's bad at going'.[41] Preferring his refined and delicate paintings to work by any other living artist, she became his patron, the chief collector of his work.

*   *   *

Now an important force in the revival of watercolour painting in Britain, Jones painted increasingly in that medium. He preferred it as suiting his sense of the world, in which he detected 'a feeling of transparency and … metamorphosis'. When he painted in oils, he used lots of turpentine to get the effect of watercolours. But he also sometimes thickened watercolour to look like oils, using an impasto of Chinese White. 'He was always impatient of the medium he was working in', Grisewood later remembered.[42]

Membership in the 7 & 5 boosted Jones's sales and reputation. Knowing that a major exhibit annually awaited his work contributed to the years from 1929 to 1932 being, in his reckoning, his 'most fruitful – the best watercolours & the largest number'. His best year for drawing was 1929, he later said, but the creative surge had begun earlier, just after the break-up with Petra. He worked 'in a kind of fierce concentration', quickly, without plan or preliminary sketches. Since 1927 he painted over fifty successful pictures a year. 'I painted all the time', he remembered, and 'was most able to concentrate on getting towards what I wanted in painting'. Colour was now as important as line, and, influenced by his engravings, line was fine, delicately irregular, sometimes wandering like loose threads within and across boundaries. In 1984, John Rothenstein would say that Jones's large watercolours of this period 'are among the most original creations in modern painting'.[43]

Artists in the 7 & 5 of whom Jones was fond were Winifred Nicholson, Sophie Fedorovitch, Kit Wood, Cedric Morris, and, especially, Teddy Wolfe. Those outside the 7 & 5 with whom he was most friendly would be Henry Moore, William Coldstream, and Ceri Richards. But his closest friends were not artists. Competition or envy played no part in this – he disliked hearing negative criticism of living artists and tried always to see the good in their work. He was genuinely unambitious, uninterested in recognition and fame, which, as goals, he considered vulgar.[44]

* * *

Jones's closest friends were those he met at St Leonard's Terrace for Saturday lunch and discussion, which often lasted into the next morning. They believed in a Christian-humanist analogue to Einstein's Unified Field Theory, its basis Baron Friedrich von Hügel's assertion that religion, philosophy, science, art, literature, and politics are 'closely inter-related parts of one great whole'. Jones was 'quite addicted' to von Hügel's writings 'in the late '20s & early '30s'. Stressing that God and his grace is everywhere, von Hügel encouraged in the group a radical ecumenism in which unity in grace overrides doctrinal differences.[45]

Mostly Catholic, they saw themselves as an alternative to Bloomsbury, which was agnostic, Fabian, and pro-Soviet. The Chelsea Group included Donald Attwater, Alec Dru, and occasionally Douglas Woodruff, then writing lead articles for *The Times*. Jones brought in René Hague, Cedric Morris (who brought along his male lover), and John Betjeman. Martin D'Arcy brought in Georges Cattaui, under-attaché at the Egyptian embassy (a Jewish Catholic aficionado of Proust), and Oxford undergraduates, including Stephen Spender, Robert Speaight, and Bernard Wall. Wall brought in Edmond Howard, a son of the British ambassador to Washington, who brought in his elder brother Francis, who brought in Jack Hamson, a Cambridge don specialising in international law. Tom Burns's brother Charles brought in Dr Douglas McClean, a Bloomsbury atheist, who gave discussion an argumentative edge. Tom brought in the culture historian Christopher Dawson, whose recently published *Progress and Religion* (1929) was a basis for discussion – they endorsed its main premise that religion is the basis of culture. Jones found the scope, depth, and clarity of Dawson's conversation breathtaking and would read most of Dawson's many publications. Dawson brought in the philosopher E. I. Watkin. In the summer of 1929, Hague brought in twenty-three-year-old Harman Grisewood, who had been junior to him at Ampleforth.

Grisewood had gone to Oxford on scholarship to read History but, having partied continually, left without a degree and was now a member of the BBC Repertory Company (fig. 17).[46]

17. Harman Grisewood, c. 1935

Tom Burns, Jones, Hague, Wall, and Grisewood: these five were the heart of the group. They were, Kathleen Raine later said, 'like brothers'. Each of the others regarded Jones as his best friend. According to Cleverdon, Grisewood was Jones's most intimate friend. Jones's relationship with Hague was more playful but he found Grisewood the most 'wholly sympathetic', later describing him as *without doubt* the one person who understands my states of mind over the years'.[47]

Tom Burns introduced newly Catholic Evelyn Waugh, whom Jones mostly met outside the group – with Burns or Grisewood. Jones found Waugh 'screamingly funny ... even when you hated what he said' but also infuriating 'because of his absurd exaggerations of all sorts of things, brainless stuff'. Waugh once urged him to stop brushing his hair down over his forehead because, 'you look like a bloody artist', to which he replied, 'I am a bloody artist.' Occasional visitors included Waugh's closest friend Christopher Sykes and Christopher Hollis, a friend of Woodruff. They, with Waugh, indulged in an uncritical Bellocian Catholic triumphalism that the others rejected – Stanley Morison vehemently.[48]

At Tom Burns's request, Jones brought in Eric Gill. Jones, Gill, and Dawson (who disliked Gill) tended to preside over discussion: Gill by virtue of his personality, Dawson because he knew so much, and Jones in matters artistic; but no one led for long. Theological and philosophical aspects of discussion found expression in Watkin's *The Bow in the Clouds* (1931), which then became the basis for further discussion.[49]

Literary talk included Ezra Pound's *The Spirit of Romance* (1910), which was, Grisewood said, 'really important' to Jones. The group supported D. H. Lawrence in his reaction to Victorian prudery, agreeing that sex could be ego-perverted and that, to prevent this, it should be spontaneous, natural, ecstatic. Without endorsing Lawrence's belief that orgasm can be a mystical experience, they thought him a prophet in the Cambridge–Bloomsbury wilderness for regarding an approach to God as the basic concern of life. They admired *The Waste Land*, which Jones had first read probably in 1926, his initial response being '*That's it!*' – at last a poem modern in form, a work of '*extraordinary* authenticity' that 'mirrors our civilizational phase with absolute validity'.[50] They read and discussed *Time and Western Man* (1927), in which Wyndham Lewis prefers a spatial sense of reality (which is classical, rational, and objective) to a temporal sense (romantic, impressionistic, and subjective), a distinction that would possibly encourage an inclination towards spatial form in

Jones's poetry. Tom Burns and Wall led discussion about Joyce, who was, Burns said, 'very much background of our lives. We were very conversant with the text of *Ulysses.*' (In 1932 Jones would begin reading it but not get far.) Burns later thought that Jones read *A Portrait of the Artist* at this time, but Jones would not read *Dubliners* till 1960, his favourite of its stories being 'The Sisters'.[51]

Joyce became hugely important for him in the summer of 1930, when Hague read aloud to him from the newly published *Anna Livia Plurabelle* (chapter 8 of *Finnegans Wake*). 'That', Jones said, 'made a great impression on me'. Soon after, Grisewood played for him the recording of Joyce reading its final pages, and Jones was enthralled – Grisewood gave him the record. Hague then read him more of the chapter, and Jones acquired a copy of the text, learning by heart the recorded pages and reciting them to himself while out walking. From now on, he would regard Joyce as the pre-eminent modern writer and the *Wake* as the paradigm of literary art.[52]

Discussion ranged through the history of philosophy. The fourteenth-century nominalist William of Ockham was responsible, they agreed, for much that was wrong in Western thought and culture. Jones's main objection was to 'Ockham's razor', which forbade the positing of unnecessary entities. This led to Protestantism, to the minimalist dualism of Descartes, to the scepticism of Hume and the English empiricists, and to positivist reductionism – why have angels? why saints? why God? the less the better! Jones sympathised with positivist scepticism, which he found 'everywhere, not least in my own tormented mind', but he was convinced that the perception of reality 'as finite' is the 'peculiar weakness' of positivism. It was this impoverishment, he and his friends thought, that made the partial metaphysics of Marxism and fascism appealing to so many.[53]

They opposed dualism, exemplified for Jones by Plato (in contrast to Aristotle) and Yeats (in contrast to Joyce). The 'Aristotle–Plato thing' was now Jones's fundamental critical distinction. They thought that the integrating vision of Francis of Assisi had first healed Platonic-Augustinian dualism, which was overcome by Aquinas's 'realist' return to nature and the senses. This 'realism' had, for Jones, an analogue in writing: 'I believe', he said in 1944, 'that all good poetry must hold up a clear bodily image & that the work is done by that *image* – so that the general shines out from the particular.' The Protestant attempt to reject religious symbol while keeping religious meaning led to the loss of both. This and reversion to dualism by Counter-Reformation Catholics led, partly through Descartes, to pragmatism, resulting in what Jones and his friends called 'The Break' from a culturally healthier past. The term translates Nietzsche's *Aufbruch* – at Ditchling, Jones had called it 'the gap' and seen it in shoddy modern craftsmanship and poor taste. For the next forty years, as The Break became increasingly apparent, he would seek to overcome it. Socially, he realised, nothing could be done, but in his art and writing, he might provide a bridge over the gap, an ark for the flood.[54]

Discussing these issues, Jones developed an original theory of culture – by synthesising Spengler's distinction between culture and civilisation with gratuity and utility, the two basic psychological attitudes of Bloomsbury aesthetics. Culture concerns gratuitous acts and objects such as goodnight kisses and birthday cakes, which are innately symbolic. Civilisation concerns utilitarian acts (fixing a tap) and objects (a wrench) not innately symbolic. Lacking gratuitous expression, the present phase of Western civilisation is culturally impoverished. Tom Burns was the first to expound this theory in print, in a preface for *Essays on Order* (1931), but admitted that Jones was its 'originator'.[55] Jones would articulate it thoroughly in 'Art and Sacrament' (*EA* 143–79) and succinctly in 'Use and Sign' (*DG* 177–85), a theory that informs all his later poetry.*

In politics, they dismissed Liberalism as watered-down Christianity everywhere defeated or in retreat. Declining to choose between the Left and Right, both of which absolutised the state, and rejecting Marxism for denying the spiritual dimension of reality, they endorsed Belloc's polemic against socialism and capitalism in *The Servile State*. Jones read Belloc's *Europe and the Faith* (1921) and his essays, particularly liking 'The Servants of the Rich'. The group dissented, however, from Belloc's equation of Europe with Catholicism. They discussed Charles Maurras, leader of the right-wing *Action Française*, whom Jones and Burns especially found sympathetic, but rejected his idea of Catholic politics, preferring the call of Henri Massis in *Defence of the West* (1927) for a Europe morally and intellectually unified by ideas rooted in the Catholic faith. In this sense they opposed the Left and considered themselves 'avant-garde in a rightist Catholic European style'.[56]

The group was especially impressed by the Italian priest Luigi Sturzo, a sociologist indebted to Aquinas and the social encyclicals of Leo XIII. Sturzo stressed personal freedom and responsibility. He had founded the Christian Democratic movement, which became the Italian Popular Party, which the fascists had suppressed, exiling Sturzo, who was now in England and in touch with Wall and Tom Burns.

Jones and his friends discussed everything in relation to Catholic Christianity without feeling restrained by doctrinal terminology, which God transcended. Dogma was not the absolute truth prelates afflicted with 'ecclesiastic materialism' pretended it to be. Far more important were momentary intuitions of divine presence. These did not make you a mystic, defined by Watkin as having heightened, vivid, all-consuming awareness of

---

* Nothing resembling Jones's culture theory would appear in English until Jacques Ellul's *The Technological Society* (1964), which Jones read in 1966 with enthusiastic agreement.

union with God. In his last years Jones would complain, 'critics call me a visionary and a mystic – would to God I were!'[57]*

They embraced Neo-Thomism, which implicitly criticised clericalism (superstitious attribution of numinous value to clergymen) and the Vatican fiction that the Church is monolithic. They abhorred Catholic intellectual stultification and its cause, the 'monstrous' papal condemnation of theological modernism and its affirmation that reason is the principal approach to truth. Catholic institutionalism was no better, they thought, than its Soviet counterpart – both devalue the person. Counteracting it, Neo-Thomism stressed Aquinas's doctrine that God created and approved of human freedom.† Only hypocrisy sustained the moral self-esteem of the Church, which, as an institution, Jones found 'pretty worrying really – it's almost like another religion', nearly as bad, he thought, as the Royal Academy, despite having a 'reality' that the Royal Academy did not.[58]

He and his friends regarded as inessential to the faith late doctrinal formulations that would have been alien to most Catholics throughout the ages. They were sure that Catholics could deviate from Vatican ideology while remaining fully 'orthodox', as Jones always considered himself. Seeking to understand the meaning behind biblical myth and ecclesiastical dogma, he found 'the truths of religion ... so different from what they appear at first sight – & much *truer*'. When Grisewood confided that he could not believe in the flames of purgatory, Jones said, 'No, of course not. That's just fanciful language, but that there is some kind of purgatorial process, yes.'[59]

The group agreed that the doctrine of the Fall could not be taken literally, since the notion of transmissible moral fault was absurd. Adam and Eve made sense only as the first humanoids to evolve into people. Grisewood recalled Jones saying, 'We don't know what original sin was but we do know its effect in nature. You don't ever have a perfect leaf; you only have an idea of a perfect leaf.' Furthermore, fossil evidence showed that suffering, violence, and imperfection preceded human evolution. For the rest of his life, Jones would wonder 'what precisely' the Fall is but accepted 'that something pretty fundamental has gone awry & ... that great misery & appalling wrongness abound'. But since the Fall was the precondition for the Incarnation and Redemption, he believed it a felix culpa.[60]

---

* Jones's remark, made to me and Blissett in 1971, is mistaken by J. Miles and D. Shiel as indicating distress at failing 'to approach more closely into [sic] communion with God' and preoccupation with 'the concept of mysticism ... throughout his life' (*Maker Unmade*, p. 138). According to Grisewood, Jones always said about mysticism, 'It's not for me.'

† Jones admired the writing of Abbot Marmion, who, combining Aquinas with the best of Tridentine Catholicism, asserts that divine life through 'grace' is inherent in the human soul.

He regretted the Council of Trent making the Church oppositional, narrow, and sectarian and in particular nursed a grudge against its declaration (in Session 25, 3–4 Dec. 1563) that art should be edifying. That, he said, corrupts art.[61]

Their discussions gave rise to the idea of reforming the English Catholic Church. Tom Burns took the lead by founding the journal *Order*. It was named after the Thomistic hierarchy of being and echoed Aquinas's Latin on its masthead about 'ordering things right'. Jones contributed for its cover a large wood engraving (5 by 4 inches) of a unicorn in an enclosing 'O' for order (fig. 18). The engraving suggests what order meant to him, a reverberation of circles: within the circular fence, a circular pond; on the unicorn's neckband, a circular collar with circular loop; and on its body, circular spots. The implication is that within the outer

18. *Order*, 1929

circle are many circles with many centres, though the animal's posture affirms the large circularity of the fence – the implied ur-centre of all being the heart of the Christ-symbolising unicorn. Four numbers of *Order* appeared, but in late 1929 the demands of Burns's job forced him to shut down the journal. He began co-editing with Dawson a series of short books called 'Essays in Order', for the covers of which Jones made a small wood engraving of a unicorn.

In the Chelsea Group and apart from it, 'endlessly' according to Tom Burns, Jones talked about psychology with Charles Burns (fig. 19). As a psychiatrist, he was primarily an Adlerian and preferred Jung to Freud because Jung valued spiritual awareness. From Charles, Jones learned about archetypes, an idea now influencing his work, and about Jungean 'free association', which resembled Thomistic analogical thinking. (Asked whether Jones had read Jung, Tom Burns replied, 'I'm pretty sure, yes.') Often participating in these discussions was Charles's close friend Eric Strauss, a Freudian Catholic convert retaining his Jewish faith. They were sceptical of Freud's anthropological speculations and dismissed his reduction of religion to neurosis but valued his concepts of unconscious motivation and repression. After

19. Charles Burns, c. 1936

undergoing Freudian analysis in the early 1930s, Charles would prefer Freud to Adler and Jung, especially for tearing off 'the mask of hypocrisy' and as a 'guide to health and perhaps even to holiness'. Jones would follow him in his conversion.[62]

The wide-ranging discussions of the Chelsea Group lasted throughout the 1930s, assisting Jones in the formulation of his mature ideas about history, literature, religion, and culture. These discussions would be the matrix of the new *Tablet*, which Tom Burns would edit; of the BBC Third Programme, which Grisewood would develop; and of *The Anathemata*.

* * *

Jones read little war poetry but over a dozen war books.* He thought that they exaggerated fear and calamity, failed to convey war as 'like ordinary life . . . only more intensified', failed to convey the sense of historical continuity that he and others had felt, and failed to show the 'extreme *tenderness* of men in action to one another'. They also failed to find a language true both to the war and to the modern present. In the spring of 1929 at St Leonard's Terrace, he finished reading Remarque's *All Quiet on the Western Front* and, setting it down, said, 'Bugger it, I can do better than that. I'm going to write a book.' He resumed his writing, which now became 'a serious obsession'.[63]

Composition of what would become *In Parenthesis* progressed in overlapping draft foliations, back in ink, forward in pencil. Jones limited narrated time to the seven months culminating in the Battle of the Somme, a period he remembered vividly. Writing was, he found, like weaving a tapestry, the result 'renewing . . . because . . . the past takes on a new form'. The process involved free association, encouraged by Lowes's *The Road to Xanadu* (1927), read after finishing *The Ancient Mariner* engravings. Free association produced allusions, which were always rooted in a word, reaction, feeling, or thought remembered from the war.[64] (Allusions to Malory and Welsh legend are present in the earliest drafts.)

In late 1929 or early 1930, Jones read an early draft of the opening pages to Grisewood, who responded, 'You must jolly well go on with this.' Grisewood, too, was writing poetry, so they began discussing their writing

---

* These included those by C. E. Montague, of which Jones especially liked *Fiery Particles* (1923); Patrick Miller's *The Natural Man* (1924, 'awfully good'); Edmund Blunden's *Undertones of War* (1928); Robert Graves's *Goodbye to All That* (1929); Richard Aldington's *Death of a Hero* (1929); Ernst Jünger's *The Storm of Steel* (tr. 1929) and *Copse 125* (tr. 1930); Siegfried Sassoon's *Memoirs of an Infantry Officer* (1930); Frederic Manning's *Her Privates We* (1930); Herbert Read's *In Retreat* (1925, 'absolutely . . . superb', 'one of the best bits of writing about the war'); L. W. Griffith's *Up to Mametz and Beyond* (1931); and Frank Richards's *Old Soldiers Never Die* (1933).

regularly in the restaurant of Simpson's-in-the-Strand. Meeting for lunch or supper, they mostly sat at a table near the bar, talking over drinks for hours, sometimes continuing at St Leonard's Terrace. Jones read new or revised work aloud, and they analysed it. He sought to make language mean as much as possible while being contemporary, using 'the words you heard people using'. For him, writing was largely a matter of 'deliberate juxtaposition', which is, he thought, 'the crucial *conscious* concern' of any artist. Together they examined the position of a word in its line, sentence, and passage. 'It was the position,' Grisewood remembered, 'that made it poetry instead of prose.'[65]

Jones alternated between run-on lines (prose form) and end lines (verse). 'There was a sliding scale', Grisewood said, in which prose lines involved a 'lessening of tension'. Jones later wrote, 'it is "poetry" that matters, whether the medium is ... so-called "verse" or "prose"'. When asked later by Laurence Binyon whether he was, in certain run-on passages, intentionally writing blank verse, he answered, 'I just have to let the thing grow as it will ... but curbing it & coaxing it or kicking it to give the form I feel best expresses what I want to say.' His 'overriding consideration was that the words used & their juxtaposition with other words should have as many overtones & undertones as possible apropos the content'.[66]

Jones's primary model for poetic use of colloquial language was *Anna Livia Plurabelle* – he wanted his words to have the same effect. Another model was Robert Browning's 'Bishop Blougram's Apology'. For fragmentation, which would distinguish the whole of Part 7, there was *The Waste Land*. For rhythmic freedom, there was plainchant; and for disjunctive meditative interiority, St-John Perse's *Anabasis* in Eliot's translation (1930), which he said 'had a really direct influence on me'. He would say in 1971 that Perse 'influenced me in the deepest sense'.[67]

For linguistic vividness, vitality, and economy, an important model was the poetry of Gerard Manley Hopkins, which Jones had first heard read in Oxford in 1927 and had been reading himself since Christmas 1930. He was also interested in Walt Whitman, but more impressed by Hopkins, whom he found 'more interesting ... than almost any poet for centuries. He really understood what poetry was all about & how it is a made thing with a shape – He really "makes" his poems in a way that can be said of few poets.' (Jones appreciated 'The Wreck of the Deutschland' as his 'greatest' poem, but had a special liking for 'The Leaden Echo and the Golden Echo' and 'Spelt from Sibyl's Leaves'.) Influenced by medieval Welsh *cynghanedd* (multiple alliterations) in ways that anticipate the linguistic pyrotechnics of *Finnegans Wake*, Hopkins's poetry was for him the prime literary example of making the past contemporary. He would later wonder why so many academics claimed that he was influenced by Pound (whose poetry he had not read) but seldom saw or mentioned the 'very great influence' of Hopkins.[68]

In his writing, Jones created a new range of literary English, modulating between Cockney and a heightened, artificial, epic language influenced by the Authorised Bible. In drafts of early sections, Cockney ludicrously breaks intimacy with the reader. In later drafts he preserved Cockney syntax, rhythms, and vocabulary without orthographically indicating pronunciation. Then he de-Kiplingised the earlier sections, making 'it not *realistic*'.[69] He eliminated from early drafts (characteristically Cockney) coarse language – its impact on the page being greater, he found, than when spoken – so 'fucking obliged' became 'signally obliged'. And he de-Fluellenises the Welsh English in early drafts. As a result of meticulous adjustments during years of revision, dramatic voices operate like the unifying middle tone in a painting, their medial language allowing easy modulation between coarse lower-class eloquence and more formal 'literary' expression.

Proceeding uncertainly, tentatively, doubtful of the quality of the writing, he was repeatedly tempted to quit. But Grisewood 'made' him 'stick to it'. Jones was now also reading it to Hague, the Edes, Helen Sutherland, and other close friends – wherever he went, he carried the current draft in a black foolscap binder. He tested everything repeatedly by reading aloud: 'Unless it sounds right,' he said, 'it's no good at all.' But only with Grisewood did he discuss it technically. But for Grisewood, he said, 'there wouldn't be an *In Parenthesis*' – though he added, 'I was deeply interested in the experiment – so I might have proceeded, in any case.'[70]

Jones regarded it entirely as an aesthetic challenge. The analogy between writing and painting remaining his guiding principle, he tried 'to make every part both concrete & particular & yet with a recession of meanings', never 'writing "about" the thing' but 'making the thing itself in words'. He was convinced that his being 'first and almost wholly a visual artist' made his writing 'different'. As with a picture, the meaning was in the relationships, and the relationships were multiple, complex, and subtle, changing with revision. Thirty years later, when asked, 'Did you work hard?' he replied, 'Oh, oh, oh, terribly', adding with some exaggeration, 'Everything was written hundreds of times, actually.'[71]

* * *

Coming up to London at least twice a week, Jones met on a regular weekday with Chelsea Group friends at La Commercio, a tiny, inexpensive family-run Italian restaurant on Charlotte Street in Soho. There was a good deal of flirtation with waitresses, the beautiful daughters of the family. Jones's favourite was lovely, reposeful Francesca, for him a standard of beauty – looking at a picture or speaking of a person, he would say, 'She's like Francesca.' Occasionally he drew her from memory. Or they ate at the Gourmet in Lyle Street. He went to the special exhibitions at Burlington House, the most important for him being Italian Masters in January 1930. There he preferred works by early painters, including his beloved Piero della Francesca, and Botticelli's *Birth of Venus* and *Primavera*. He also greatly admired the Tintorettos – his favourite being *The Rescue of Arsinoe*. Though 'not, on the whole, *very* fond of Leonardo' and thinking his writing on art 'bloody silly', he thought the da Vinci cartoon, *The Virgin and Child with St Anne*, 'stupendous' and 'far more interesting ... than the painting he made from it, now at the Louvre'. It was 'a miracle ... the sort of thing that's done only once in human history'.* He looked at pictures with powerful, raw openness, being overwhelmed by the work, good or bad. Only when away from the pictures would he talk about them.[72]

He visited exhibitions of contemporary art at the Royal Academy sometimes with Grisewood, who remembered his response to pictures as mainly wincing in recoil as though physically hurt, shutting his eyes, exclaiming, 'Agh, God!' He thought the 'mediocrity' of the Royal Academy owing to its being 'typical of the age when it was founded – but without much subsequent reality'. On 10 June 1932, he wrote to a friend, 'For some obscure reason I ventured alone & unprotected into the Royal Academy one day last week – its horror is beyond expression – I always fondly think that perhaps a good picture will filter in by accident – but no.' Entering Burlington House, he thought of the words inscribed above the entrance to Dante's hell, 'Abandon hope all ye who enter here.'[73]

In 1929 Jones had gone to the library of the V&A to check details for his writing and met one of its librarians, Arthur Wheen, the translator of *All Quiet on the Western Front*. They became friends, and the library became another of his regular London stops. An Australian and former Rhodes scholar, Wheen was a friend of T. S. Eliot and Herbert Read and had a quick, deep, and subtle mind. Having lost the use of his left arm at the Somme, he

---

* About art and artists, Jones would also say over the years that he liked Tiepolo, whom he associated with Roman fresco painting; he liked early Renaissance painting but not Raphael (except, in the V&A tapestry-cartoon for *The Miraculous Draught of Fishes*, 'I like those birds standing on the shore'); he loved Rubens, Nicholas Hilliard; Dürer, Martin Schongauer, the Maître de Moulins, Fouquet (particularly his *Conversion of St Hubert*); Pisanello's *Vision of St Eustace*, early Renaissance engraving, Bellini's *Madonna of the Meadow*, and Mantegna's *Agony in the Garden* and *Dead Christ*. Jones did not like 'Rembrandt at all for most of his life' but in later years would feel him 'a bit more', liking best *The Conspiracy of Julius Civilis: The Oath*. He admired Cruikshank, and was annoyed at the president of the Royal Academy blaming him for failing to copy reality exactly. He admired William Etty. He disliked Van Gogh's expressionist distortions, projecting inward emotion. Though he admired Picasso, he thought that Braque, in his fidelity to detail, showed more love. For more on Jones's interest in European and English artists and for an exposition of their influence, see P. Hills, *The Art of David Jones, Vision and Memory* (London: Lund Humphries, 2015), pp. 109–21.

was haunted by the war. He had published *Two Masters* (1929), a fictionalised account of having, as a spy, killed his best friend – Jones read and, according to Tom Burns, 'enormously' admired it. Wheen encouraged the writing of *In Parenthesis* through all the years of its composition. He was one of those for whom it was written.[74]

Jones and he often went together to exhibitions. The price of a Jones picture was too steep for Wheen, but at his prodding the V&A bought six of them and, as soon as his salary allowed, he began to buy them with instalments of £5. Thinking that artists should benefit from increased value of their work, after full payment was made, he periodically sent Jones a cheque 'in further payment'. Jones thought him 'a rather splendid sort of chap'.[75]

In 1930, Jones accompanied Tom Burns and Grisewood to the first British performance of Stravinsky's *Symphony of Psalms*, which moved him deeply. That year he saw and loved *The Blue Angel* – he had, Burns remembered, 'a craze for Dietrich' – and several times saw the film adaptation of *All Quiet on the Western Front*, whose lead actor, Lew Ayres, bore an uncanny resemblance to him. He went once with Petra, telling her 'it wasn't too over exaggerated', and once with Burns and Prudence Pelham. But he usually declined invitations to go to the cinema because, he later said, 'All my life, my retinas retained the image a fraction of a second too long.' Possibly encouraging transparent layering in his paintings, this condition results from lack of pigment in the photoreceptors in the retina which continue firing an image to the brain. The cause is Vitamin-A deficiency, which also represses the immune system, lowers body temperature, and causes eye strain and depression. It results from, or is aggravated by, heavy drinking.[76]

He continued seeing Frank Medworth, who was keeping company with a Westminster student named Muriel (Mog) Anderson. Medworth and Mog went on holiday to Spain to visit Weaver Hawkins in Barcelona. When they returned, she was pregnant, and Medworth consulted Jones, who said, 'You'll have to marry the girl.' The official ceremony took place on 5 July 1929 at the Chelsea Register Office with Jones and Gill as witnesses. Jones and Medworth continued to meet until January 1934, when Medworth moved to Hull to be principal of an art school.[77]*

---

* Medworth eventually emigrated to Australia, became principal of Sydney Art School, and, in 1947, attended a UN conference in Mexico City, where altitude diminishes air pressure. He gave a nonsensical speech, attributed by listeners to drunkenness but caused by his brain expanding into a hole in his skull acquired at the Somme. That evening, he killed himself, a delayed casualty of the war. Jones would always regard him as an 'astounding man'.

Through the sculptor Frank Dobson, Jones met the novelist and spiritualist Leo H. Myers and his wife, Elsie – she liked Jones and his work. He visited the family in London and twice at their country house, Twyford Lodge, where he painted the sea from his bedroom. He was smitten with their twenty-one-year-old daughter, 'E.Q.' She was tall, big-eyed like her mother, serene, and oblivious to his infatuation–he did not pursue her.[78*]

He also visited the home of Wilfrid Meynell, the grand old man of Catholic journalism, to whom Tom Burns had introducd him. At the family's farmstead-compound at Greatham in the West Sussex Downs Jones met G. K. Chesterton, who laughed so much towards the conclusions of his stories that his listeners, also laughing, could not hear them. Here, in the summer of 1930, Jones's hosts made him 'do country dancing which was hell – it's really too ghastly'.[79]

The regularity and narrowness of his parents' life in Brockley contrasted with his expanding interests and widening circles of friends. He was unhappy about living at home in his mid-thirties. Returning to the house, a 'fog of depression' often descended upon him – he did not know why. He would later write to a friend that at home he 'was always ... deeply depressed inside', a depression 'camouflaged by an appearance of cheerfulness of a sort'.[80]

On the morning of his thirty-fifth birthday in 1930, alone in his bedroom, he opened his copy of the *Oxford Book of English Verse* and sang 'Jerusalem, my happy home' ('The New Jerusalem') in honour of All Saints, his favourite of all religious feasts 'because it's so good to have a day on which are commemorated all the men of good will from the foundation of the world – jolly good'.[81]

In the autumn of 1930, he was reading Newman, the Scanlan translation of *Art and Scholasticism*, bits of Abbot Butler, bits of von Hügel, Naomi Mitchison's *When the Bough Breaks and Other Stories* (1924) ('most awfully good') and *The Conquered*, about Caesar's war in Gaul. He illustrated his second Ariel poem, Roy Campbell's *The Gum Trees* (fig. 21).[†] He was 'trying to paint each day' and finding it not always easy to work at home, although 'it *should* be'. His father did the outside work, but on one occasion David had had to mow the lawn – he wrote to Petra, 'that was an event I think worth recording – a hateful job!' He was chagrined at the cook-housekeeper, Cissy Robertson, who, he was convinced, stole his Jaeger underpants for her brother. (David's mother made his undershirts.)[82]

20. Cover illustration, *The Gum Trees*, 1929

* E.Q. (Elsie Queen) Myers married Ben Nicholson's brother Kit.

† Jones had illustrated Harold Monro's 'The Winter Solstice' in 1928.

Jones was now painting extraordinary portraits in watercolours, using the whiteness of the paper and achieving a visual shallowness rare in portraits, as though thinning away roundness of personality to reveal the archetype. Ede thought them a radical new beginning that, if Jones were to continue making them, would establish him as the modern Gainsborough. Jones protested, 'I think you've gone a bit far about the Gainsborough analogy!' but agreed that he was headed in that direction. What he now sought in a painting is implied by his reaction to a London Group exhibition in late October 1929: a painting by Sickert was good because it 'had an "idea"' while the rest, all '"able" paintings of various sorts', seemed 'only seen with the eye of the flesh'.[83]

I n the summer of 1928, Cleverdon had asked Jones to illustrate an edition of *Morte D'Arthur* with thirty wood engravings. Although engraving paid far less than painting, he was prepared to devote 1930 to the job but, after beginning work on a title page, was forced by sore eyes to quit.* The inclination to illustrate Malory persisted, however, and in early 1930 he finished a dry-point pietà, entitled *Wounded Knight*, possibly of Arthur's death. In the last week of February 1930, while in bed (for five weeks) with the flu, he made a little (8 by 10 inches) engraving-like painting 'for Morte D'Arthur' on wood, entitled *Merlin Appears in the Form of a Child to Arthur Sleeping*, called *Merlin Land* for short (fig. 1). Malory then went underground in his imagination but was emerging as an allusive subtext of *In Parenthesis* – so that instead of illustrating Malory, Malory would, in a sense, illustrate Jones.

He realised that *Merlin Land* had affinity with surrealism but was unimpressed by the surrealist pictures now appearing in London. He disliked Dali, 'a kind of "show-man" of huge ability indeed, but lacking that "tenderness" which is, after all … an essential ingredient of the poetic art'. And he was put off by surrealist theory, which, he wrote to Ben Nicholson, holds 'that the isolation of something immemorially present in painting is the one thing that matters'. But he thought Paul Delvaux a 'great' artist, who gave our 'post-Freudian age … its most "gentle" & thence most "poetic" expression'. Jones suspected

1. *Merlin Land*, 1930–32

* Cleverdon also proposed that Jones illustrate Christopher Smart's 'A Song of David', which he might have attempted despite eye strain, since, for him, it stood out in English poetry 'very bright and clear', 'beyond the frontiers of criticism and reservation'. But the Depression killed the market for illustrated books, and Cleverdon dropped the project. Jones admired Smart's 'child-delight' in animals. In a 1939 review of Smart's newly dis-covered *Jubilate Agno*, he wrote that Smart 'prayed always in every line of his poem, for each line is a praise'. Lists in Jones's later poetry owe much to Smart's example.

2. Christopher Dawson, c. 1935

his admiration 'was purely sensual – it's so damned easy to deceive oneself', until Herbert Read confirmed for him Delvaux's 'real poetry' in *A Letter to a Young Painter* (1962).[1]

Jones read Dawson's latest book, *The Making of Europe*, in proof and discussed it with him in June. He sometimes visited Dawson (fig. 2) in his dark London flat ('the Mausoleum') in Queen's Gate Terrace. Jones admired Dawson's combination of 'great knowledge ... with *deep humility*' and learned more from him than from anyone else. His enthusiasm about him was unreserved; and Dawson admired Jones. When Jones borrowed and annotated Louis Bussell's copy of Dawson's *The Age of the Gods* (1928), Bussell mentioned it to Dawson, who said that he would very much like to see those annotations. According to one of Dawson's daughters, he and Jones loved one another, but Dawson was usually depressed, and Jones sometimes 'got utterly worn out' talking with him.[2]

*　　*　　*

Jones's shows in 1930, in July at Heal and Son and in October at the Mansard Gallery, were 'important' for him because they included his '*best & freer sort*' of animal pictures, with affinity with prehistoric cave paintings. Since 1928, he had gone to Regent's Park Zoo to draw and paint deer, wolves, and big cats in order to capture the feeling and rhythm of their movement.

3. *Agag*, 1930

He used 'pencil and watercolour ... at the same time', making no alterations after leaving the animal. In 1930 in the Small Cat House, he made what he regarded as one of his best, of a serval cat whose ghosted forelegs convey motion. He called it *Agag* (fig. 3) after I Samuel 15:32: 'And Agag came unto him delicately', an association that came to him 'immediately' as he drew.* His favourite of these drawings was a panther (1931), purchased by the Walker Gallery. According to Guy Davenport, they establish him as perhaps the best modern animal artist.[3]

* He thought 'revolting' the story of Samuel hewing the defenceless king to pieces after his people had been massacred, though the use of the word 'delicately' raised the passage 'to pure poetry'.

Occasionally at the zoo, Jones went to the Lion House just before feeding time, and telephoned Tom Burns in his office to let him hear the lions roar. Once, working close to a heavy wire fence, Jones watched a lion cub leaping sideways – lamblike, he thought – but hard into the fence where he stood, knocking him over (terrified of its claws and disgusted by its smell) to uproarious laughter of nearby children.[4]

* * *

In 1931 Jones and Prudence Pelham became godparents to René and Joanna's first born, christened, to Jones's delight, Michael Mary Immanuel Patrick Joseph Vesey Hague. The boy would grow up to remember 'Dai' as 'just part of the family', for whom the Hagues' marriage was a rock. (From his Ditchling days, his closest friends called him 'Dai', Welsh diminutive of 'David'.)[5]

At Pigotts Jones sometimes finished two paintings a day. When not painting, he worked on *In Parenthesis* at a table in the Hagues' sitting room or lying in bed. At Pigotts in the summer of 1931, he painted a watercolour portrait of Jack Hansom's fiancée. Hansom 'reckoned she was jolly beautiful', Jones said, 'but ... I found her jolly hard to draw because I could *not* beat up any real feeling about her ... . I didn't know which she was Athena or Diana or Persephone or whatever. & if you don't know the archetype how can you draw the type?'[6]

One of his most successful pictures this summer was *Curtained Outlook* (fig. 4), a watercolour done from a bedroom in the Tegetmeier cottage. In the painting, the window floats, freed by fractured perspective, the cluttered tabletop beneath seeming to sink into impossible space within the wall, so that the sill hovers over it. Through a gossamer curtain looms the gabled end of Gill's house. Countering the

4. *Curtained Outlook*, 1931

inward pressure of the house is the vase of flowers, its profusion tending at once to centre and decentre the picture. Objects on the table restrain the eye's inclination to fly through the window. A daring picture, it only just avoids chaos partly by the off-rhyme between window frame and table. 'There are ... many ways of doing it,' he wrote, 'but ... unity one must get, or, anyway, always have in mind.'[7]

Jones celebrated Petra's birthday in his pocket calendar with Xs (a kiss for each year) and a little painting of her (fig. 5). This was also to celebrate a painting, *Petra im Rosenhag*. Initially she sat each afternoon for a couple of hours silently – 'He was too concentrating' for conversation, she said, and 'very excited'. He worked on it for a month (fig. 6). Virginal (like Renaissance madonnas *im Rosenhag)* and a fertility figure, with flowers on her dress, she is Welsh Blodeuwedd and Flora, goddess of springtime in Botticelli's *Primavera*. The diffusion of light shining through her makes her visually numinous. Tonally weaker than her rocking background, she sinks into it, a uniform wholeness calming it. Yet her posture is ambiguously unbalanced, and, while her mouth welcomes, her eyes warn you to keep your distance. Her archetypes are Diana and Flora, virgin and mother. Kenneth Clark would think this picture has 'more of' Jones's 'mind in it than almost anything else he did'.[8]

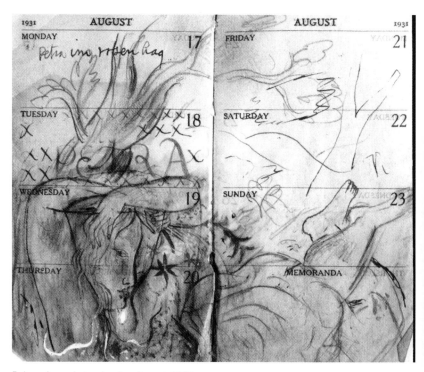

5. Jones's pocket calendar, August 1931

6. *Petra im Rosenhag*, 1931

*   *   *

With Tom Burns and Grisewood, Jones went to Caldey in late September 1931 for two weeks, staying in a large cottage called Ty Gwyn. In the mornings, Jones painted outdoors despite viciously biting flies, which he found 'horrible and enraging'. In the afternoon, he sometimes joined his friends in exploring the island. In the evening they talked and drank whisky or read. Or he wrote – he was finishing a draft of Part 3 of In Parenthesis and starting Part 4.[9] He also wrote most of a twelve-page joke arrest warrant for 'Lecher Hague', completed on the evening of 2 October.*

One afternoon, strolling with Grisewood along the beach of Priory Bay, Jones expressed his views on sex and love. He said that with Petra he had wanted sex and she had wanted marriage. Now he was earning enough money to support a family but wanted to avoid emotional entanglement. Breaking with her had released creative energy. In anyone energy is limited, and art is all-consuming, 'totalitarian'. As a monk dedicates himself to God through celibacy, he said, he was dedicating himself to art. Confirming his dedication was William Orpen having been ruined as a painter by a social-climbing wife. Not that there is anything wrong with sex, he said, and he had no objection to premarital or extramarital sexual relationships. Grisewood demurred, and Jones asked, 'What do you think our sexual organs are for? The sexual act itself can never be wrong. Quite possibly it is the only thing a human being does that is free of the taint of original sin.' But in the Thomistic hierarchy of values, he said, art ranks above sensory pleasure. Every inclination to love is God-given and erotic, from the bottom where you copulate to the top where you unite with God. Advancing involves discernment. For him fastidiousness was an additional factor. He said, 'I don't want to wake up with a girl beside me. That would be revolting to me in some way.'[10]

He returned to London with a stack of new paintings, many remarkable. When Ben Nicholson saw them, he 'said he liked them very much' and urged Jones to send them to the Lefevre Gallery, one of the most important in London, where they were shown in November.[11]

*   *   *

On 4 August 1931, Jones made his third visit to Northumberland. Helen Sutherland sent him a third-class rail ticket to which he added money to travel first class. He did this, as in London he took taxis, not extravagantly as friends thought but because agoraphobic. Shortly before arriving at

---

* For a description of this document, see T. Dilworth, 'Under Arrest: "Lecher Hague" by David Jones', Times Literary Supplement, 4/2/2011, pp. 14–15.

7. Rock Hall, c. 1935

Alnmouth, he moved to a third-class coach from which he emerged to be met by her chauffeur, 'the gloomy Mills', and driven eight miles through rolling farmland to Rock.[12]

Rock Hall (fig. 7) was an Elizabethan manor house built round a Peel tower. On the first floor were Helen's suite and study, guest bedrooms, and a gallery with pictures on shelves round the walls. By the end of the decade, these shelves would hold about thirty Ben Nicholsons and more Joneses – the numbers varying as she acquired and gave them away. Jones was usually assigned a small bedroom in the original tower, over Helen's study above the main entrance, from which he looked out on a small Norman church, its graveyard, a large pond surrounded by chestnuts and oaks, and the tiny village of Rock. Between the church and the house was a park where sheep grazed and pheasants ran. It was for him a place of 'calm & bird's-song'.[13]

From his bedroom he painted *The Chapel in the Park* (fig. 8). The view sheep-less at the time, he drew some sheep from memory, one of them turning out, he thought, 'very comical'. Because some of the colour floats free of drawing, the picture has affinity with a palimpsest or double exposure, the primary image a drawing, the other a painting. He later disliked the dark green bush on the lower right.[14]

The '*heavenly*' country around Rock was historically redolent for him. Until about 400 AD, it had belonged to his Celtic ancestors, the Votodini. Then it became the kingdom of Rheged, defended against Angles by Urien and his son Owain – after Arthur, the most renowned heroes of Celtic-British legend, passing into romance as Urein and Yvain. At the start and finish of each visit, Jones was driven past the Duke of Northumberland's sprawling castle, which, Helen told him, was on the site of Lancelot's castle, Joyous Guard, and the supposed place of his burial. With this

8. *The Chapel in the Park*, 1931

association in mind, Jones referred to the church at Rock as 'the Chapel Perilous', the place of terrifying enchantment that Lancelot enters – an episode in Malory that reminded him of his experience at night in Mametz Wood.[15]

Almost every morning, Jones walked nearly a mile to the pub in the village of Rennington. For cigarettes he went even in rain. There he drank a Guinness or, on warm days, a gin-and-tonic and refilled his whisky flask – Helen provided no whisky (or beer) – returning for lunch smelling of alcohol, to her chagrin, and longing to be with Burns and Grisewood drinking 'a vast quantity' of beer. At Rock wine was offered but rarely and frugally.[16]

A perfectionist, Helen (fig. 9) chastised anyone late for meals. Jones dreaded being late for breakfast, at 9.30, but often was. He was sometimes late for supper, too, when in his room where he was unable to hear the summoning gong. Guests were expected to sleep with windows open – he pulled the Welsh rug up over the eiderdown – and they were told not to waste water or electricity and not to make or receive telephone calls. They were to be clean, dress properly, and converse well. Literary discussion was of a high order. She was ruthless to anyone who spoke frivolously. When she said it was time, guests retired for the night. According to Kathleen Raine, Jones was 'very frightened' of her.[17]

9. Helen Sutherland, c. 1950

A connoisseur of people as well as pictures, she considered herself a sort of mother, needing to create a 'family'. By 1932 the friends she loved most were David Jones, Helen Ede, Ben Nicholson, and the pianist Vera Moore, whose playing and company Jones enjoyed. Of these, she considered Vera Moore and Jones to be, as she put it, 'my *own*'. Kathleen Raine said, 'she loved David's work best and she loved David best. She thought he was perfect. She wouldn't forgive Jim Ede a thing. She would forgive Ben Nicholson a good deal. She would forgive David absolutely everything.' He was comfortable in the role of favourite child. Like his mother, Helen was tiny (just over 5 feet), and could withhold affection from those who erred, as from Jim Ede when he presented her with flowers from her own garden. Jones was on his best behaviour with her, which largely meant watching his language. But their relationship cannot be reduced to a psychological paradigm: they were friends, and she realised that he was in many respects more than her equal.[18]

At Rock he saw the Edes, Teddy Wolfe, and Ben and Winifred Nicholson. One of the guests, Edward Hodgkin, would remember Ben praising at some length the beauty of a refrigerator – 'What beautiful lines!' – and Jones, across the table, responding, 'What a lot of balls!'[19]

He met new people here, including Jelly d'Arányi and Adila Fachiri, violinists; Arthur Waley, the translator; and Peter Quennell, the poet, scholar, and editor. On 7 August 1931, he met Earl Grey and heard him speak 'in the Liberal interest'. He met the Byzantine historian Steven Runciman, with whom he discussed the Crusades – about which Jones talked with anyone interested. (He 'never really understood' their '"religious" aspect' and positively disliked St Louis for his 'muscular Xtianity'.)[20]

Among many 'Harris-tweed, worthy, scholarly, early-to-bed-earlier-to-rise chaps', he met Robert (Robin) Hodgkin, an Oxford history don, one of 'the older generation' of which he 'was a bit scared' – he felt he might offend him if he said 'blast it' at dinner but found him 'lovely' to talk to. Jones liked his deep sympathy with the Angles and Saxons and his wanting to be fair to the Romano-Celts. He thought Hodgkin's *History of the Anglo-Saxons*, a birthday gift from Helen in 1935, 'beautifully done', and while

> a bit superior about the Welsh ... at *least* he admits that with the loss of the Island to the 'steady, prudent', etc., Teutons they in their hills wove, as he would say, a web of magic & imagination round the story of their defeat which in turn gave the world the Arthurian Cycle. Which is indeed worth the loss of many islands & continents. Seeing that nothing succeeds like failure as Chesterton might say.

He and Hodgkin spoke about *Italy and Her Invaders*, by Hodgkin's father, Thomas. Jones had read all eight volumes. It was, Grisewood said, 'a really important influence' on him, the only book in which he could read in detail about the barbarians. He admired its scope and long perspective on political and cultural consequences of events. He also liked the illustrations, one of which was of the *Ara Pacis*, which would be important in his poetry (*SL* 15–23).[21]

He very much liked Hodgkin's sons, Thomas (Tommy) and Edward (Teddy). In 1930, Thomas was at Balliol reading Greats (Ancient History and Philosophy); Edward was at Eton and went up in 1932 to read History. Jones visited them in Oxford, beginning with Thomas in the autumn of 1930. That year, he had painted Thomas's portrait, which Helen bought for £30. In 1931, he painted another picture of the view from his bedroom at Rock, which he let Thomas buy for £15.[22]

He discussed history with the Hodgkin boys. Edward remembered that Jones saw historic figures almost as still living and the events as still happening. After loaning him John Morris's *The Welsh Wars of Edward I* (1901), Edward was astonished at Jones's detailed memory of it – he seemed to know the soldiers and their circumstances in the wet Welsh hills as if they had been his own battalion in the war. His knowledge of history was, Edward said, fuller in every respect than what could be learned at Oxford, especially about the early Church, the Celtic Church, and medieval Catholicism.[23]

At Rock Jones met Helen's goddaughter, Nicolete Binyon, the severe, precocious nineteen-year-old daughter of the poet and art-historian Laurence Binyon. She was reading medieval history at Oxford and active in the Arts Club. Because she was utterly confident in her judgements, Jones and his close friends called her 'little Nicky know-all'. On 14 June 1930, she had arranged for Sickert to address the Arts Club at St John's College. Jones attended, and the *Oxford Mail* published a photograph (fig. 10) in which he stands between her and his old teacher. Jones thought 'she

10. Michael Sadler, Walter Sickert, Jones, and Nicolete Binyon, *Oxford Mail*, 14 June 1930

ought to be dolled-up a lot ... that she ought to rouge her lips', as he probably told her, since she informed him by letter that she had done her hair 'differently with "a curly fringe"' – he joked with Hague, 'slight porno touch here'. He mentored her, introducing her to Maritain's *The Philosophy of Art*. She confided to a friend that if he asked she would marry him. Her mother, Cecily, abhorred his being a Catholic and, fearing his influence on her daughter, asked Helen not to invite her when he was there. In her studies, Nicolete concentrated on St Augustine, whose writing converted her to Catholicism – Jones told an Anglican friend, 'that was not my fault'.[24] She introduced him to her friend Alison Debenham, a painter and Catholic who would be, like Nicolete, a lifelong friend.

In 1930, he had become friends with Dick Owen Brown, the thirty-seven-year-old Low Church vicar at Rock. After supper at Rock Hall, they had long theological conversations, sometimes with Helen. Jones visited him at his rectory in Rennington, where Brown was often confined to bed by asthma, sometimes struggling for breath, a sight that alarmed Jones. They had much in common, including, Edward Hodgkin said, incapacity for pretence.[25]

Helen frequently organised group excursions to places soon familiar to Jones, among them the many castles in the area. They visited Ros Castle, the highest hill in the Kyloe range and, in the park below, saw the last surviving wild herd of indigenous big-horned Chillingham white cattle, whose forbears had freely roamed the island. He visited them repeatedly. Helen liked walking all day, fifteen miles or so and at a good clip, stopping for a sandwich lunch out of haversacks. When she announced an excursion, Jones would think, 'Oh God! a bloody route march & no rum ration.' Occasionally they took a boat to the Farne Islands. Sometimes they visited local fishing villages, which he loved, his favourites being Alnmouth and 'ramshackle' Eyemouth. In Embleton Bay, he saw boats with markings in their bows suggestive of eyes, to which he would refer in his poetry (*A* 99, 148).[26]

Several times they went to Lindisfarne or Holy Island, accessible at low tide over nearly three miles of sand – from Beal they crossed barefoot, the water 'just over … feet & ankles'. At quarter-mile intervals for those cut off by the tide were posts topped by wicker baskets, which appealed to his 'innate affection for any kind of plaited or twined thing'. (Trudging along, Jones remembered the bloody fight of Urien against Angles for three days and three nights on this crossing and, on the brink of victory, Urien's betrayal and murder, which allowed the Angles to spill from their beachhead to conquer Rheged. While making the crossing in 1930, he had mentioned this battle to the Hodgkin boys and Nicolete and was surprised by their not having heard of it or of Urien.) They visited the eleventh-century abbey ruins and sometimes the castle, owned by friends of Helen. Jones wished to slip away to an island pub for a double Scotch and soda but, knowing that it would be 'fatal to attempt the operation & *fail*', remained with the party. They returned to explore the coast, which had, he thought, 'no special charm'.[27]

When the excursion was to Hadrian's Wall, he would 'curse inwardly' at having to make what Helen called 'a really early start' and always tried to beg off, but she insisted. They drove, then walked 'for miles' up to and along the Wall. Several times they visited its most impressive fort, Housesteads. Here beneath an archway over the *via principalis* were ruts in the stone showing the gauge of wagon, cart, and chariot wheels, a sight that moved him deeply. The Wall and this fort gave him 'the feeling of the past still living in the present' as though he 'might meet a Roman legionary round the next bend'. Never wanting to go, he was always glad he did.[28]

On 28 April 1932, Jones accompanied Helen Ede from Rock to Edinburgh. On the way, he enjoyed the countryside, especially 'that Lowland part … where Cunedda lived' (in the fourth century). In Edinburgh he walked the Royal Mile expecting to see 'superb architecture' but was disappointed. 'There's nothing really. Holyrood Palace is a crashing bore & everything is a dismal colour – the Cathedral of St. Giles is the worst Gothic building I *ever* saw – a congested & constipated affair – but the Rock & Castle – magnificent' and he thought the Forth Bridge 'superb' and the city unique for its light, which seemed 'to have a special clarity'. He later said it was the only beautiful *big* city I'd seen in Britain'. And he liked the Scots for not being 'prepossessing'.[29]

By 1932, Jones was one of the people in London whom Helen Sutherland most wanted to visit. They exchanged many hundreds of letters and he valued what she called his 'beautiful & so rich mind & heart & wisdom'. She appreciated what she considered his Cockney sense of fun and 'contemporary folk language'. 'She liked him,' Edward Hodgkin remembered, 'because he was genuine, and because he talked so well – about art, literature, and religion.' Jones liked her pared-down Quaker simplicity – and, as she ascended to High Anglicanism, they increasingly agreed theologically. Although she was 'very exacting', Hodgkin said, it was 'a very easy relationship' – 'a tribute to both of them that it worked out so well'.[30]

*　　*　　*

After making some commercial engravings for London Transport, in 1932 he made the last of his 207 engravings, *He Frees the Waters in Helyon* (fig. 11), inspired by a large (6 by 9½ inch) irregular end-grain block. Like *Merlin Land*, it resembles a photographic negative. The subject is a medieval legend in which a unicorn representing Christ purifies poisoned waters. The ivory horn in redemptive intercourse with the stream is continuous with the rays of Venus, here the Christmas star. The broken wall alludes to Ephesians 2:12–14. Symbolising renewal of the waste land is the Grail with erect spear, evoking fertility imagery from Jessie Weston's *From Ritual to Romance* (1920).[31] Owing to eye strain, he did not finish it, but it would

11. *He Frees the Waters in Helyon*, 1932

remain a favourite. It is symbolically autobiographical for, like the unicorn
he was trying to redeem modern civilisation with gravure, brush, or pen
in place of a unicorn horn.

* * *

He spent 23 January 1931 at Brockley painting what he called in his
pocket diary a 'self-portrait', later entitled *Human Being* (fig. 12). The
initial inspiration was the (largely hidden) hands in Jean Fouquet's *Charles
VII*, 'that stupendous painting'.[32] The eyes, unsynchronised, direct our
view to the ear, which sticks out like a storefront sign. Listening, he is
intent above, relaxed below, a self divided.

Important to most of Jones's work now was the juxtaposition of near
and far largely by eliminating perspective and continuity-in-depth. In this
he was helped by filling the picture with sea and sky in his best Portslade
paintings. *Calypso's Seaward Prospect* is one of these (fig. 13), in which his
parents' bedroom doors open to a pink terrace indistinguishable from the
beach. Sky, sea, and terrace shimmer – light has taken over. Lightest of all
are the interiors of beams, a post, and doors, which are not, as they would
realistically be, in silhouette. The eye is momentarily jerked from all this
shimmer to foreground specifics, which focus vision, then luminosity

absorbs it once again. Another example
of such juxtaposition is *Manawydan's
Glass Door*, the same scene but in a
storm with doors shut, completed, like
other large watercolours now, within
three days.[33]

In late 1931 or early 1932 in the
Brockley studio, Grisewood sat for a
portrait in oils. Jones nearly finished
a frontal view but, during the second
sitting, uttering fusilier oaths the likes
of which Grisewood had never heard,
furiously knifed the picture to ribbons.
Grisewood sat twice more, for a profile
view, facing the window (fig. 14). Jones
called it *Portrait of a Maker* – Grisewood
being a poet. The overcoat worn by
him in the picture is the one Jones wears
in *Human Being* – it was a gift from
Grisewood, a green coat which Jones
dyed black, his 'greatcoat' or, jokingly,
his 'little coat'. Grisewood noticed that

12. *Human Being*, 1931

13. *Calypso's Seaward Prospect, 1931*

the bottle on the mantel was of Eno's Fruit Salts, a nerve tonic for those feeling 'languid – tired – "blue"'. Jones had replaced its commercial label with his own lettering in the belief that even ordinary domestic things should be beautiful.[34]

In the 7 & 5 show at the Leicester Gallery in February 1932, sixty-four works were exhibited: six each by Jones, Ben Nicholson, and by newly elected Henry Moore, and fewer by each of the others. Jones thought it 'a jolly nice show'. All six of his sold, more than by any other. (Nicholson sold three; Henry Moore, one). Michael Sadler bought *Portrait of a Maker.* Helen Sutherland bought *Human Being* and hung it in her library between a Nicholson and her only Seurat. Gallery owners who had rejected his

14. *Portrait of a Maker*, 1932

work wrote to say they had always admired it.[35]

In early January 1932, he had gone with Gill to Burlington House to see the exhibition of French Art 1200–1900. For Jones 'the best thing at the Show' was Fouquet's portrait of *Charles VII*, and he 'spent long in gazing at' it. He thought it 'the very image of an epoch', 'timeless', and 'unforgettable'. He also loved the virgin in Fouquet's *Melun Diptych*, which prompted him to say, 'What more can be asked of an art-work than that it displays [*sic*] an archetype?' Retaining a vivid memory of it, he wrote twenty years later, 'I don't suppose that "this flesh" . . . has ever been delineated with more uncompromising verisimilitude, yet seen *sub specie aeternitatis*.' On 15 February he would go again to the exhibition with Gill.[36]

* * *

Nicholson had left Winifred and their three children in 1931 to live with Barbara Hepworth. Jones thought Ben's act a terrible betrayal without being immoral. He understood romantic love as an undeniable imperative, and he liked Aristotle's *Nicomachean Ethics* ('three bloody cheers') for advocating a flexible standard of measurement, 'like the leaden rule'. Yet he was not romantic about Ben's decision. When Ben proclaimed to him a new morality and said that Barbara was the first woman who fully understood him, Jones replied, 'Come now Ben. You've got a nice young girl to sleep with. Lucky you!'[37]

In 1929, Tom Burns had introduced Jones to Gwendolen Plunket Greene, the niece in von Hügel's *Letters to a Niece*, a book Jones loved. Gwen and her daughter had lately leapt from High Anglicanism into the Catholic Church. A fine violinist, Gwen sensitised Jones, and to a greater extent Grisewood, to Bach, Beethoven, and Schubert. For Grisewood and Burns, the main attraction was Gwen's daughter, Olivia, a beautiful big-eyed flapper, enamoured of the Charleston, jazz, whisky, and sex, preferably with Negroes but, after a mystical experience, now celibate. Grisewood thought her a genius. Jones distrusted her impulsiveness. When she spoke to him in earnest about mysticism, he went glassy-eyed and later told Grisewood, 'I don't care for all that, you know. It's no good to me, that sort of thing.' He preferred Gwen, 'a most wonderful character'. (He also liked the maid, Mrs Parker, an 'admirable woman'.) He came to their Bloomsbury flat for Sunday teas, seeing there his sculptor-friend Stephen Tomlin and Evelyn Waugh, whose confidante Olivia had become after his first wife left him. The talk was enthusiastic, wide ranging, full of banter and jokes. Like participants in the Chelsea Group, Gwen advocated an all-inclusive Christianity and believed that faith ought to enrich humanity and increase affection.[38]

Once Gwen complained about being unable to get a decent pudding basin, and Jones responded passionately, 'I know. They're so shallow. The bloody sods will not make the thing properly. It represents cultural decline.' More pertinent for him was the spoon: 'in the Renaissance', it 'reached a point of beauty, and it should have been left alone. But chaps had to go on changing the shape and getting it wrong.' He would search antique-dealers' shops 'for a single spoon that does not affront the senses'. The 'impedimenta' of modern life were, he thought, mostly 'mediocre, shoddy and slick', shaking his conviction that man is essentially an artistic maker.[39]

He would later include Gwen Plunket Greene 'and hence Von Hügel' among 'those blokes' to whom he owed 'nearly *everything*' in that they 'offered me some comprehension of the stuff of 'Catholic "*cult* & culture"''. She published her thoughts in *The Prophet Child* (1935) – a book of spiritual psychology with which he 'utterly' agreed, letting her use *He Frees the Waters* as a frontispiece. In her book she writes about the heroism of mundane virtue, which was by now a major theme of *In Parenthesis*. The Plunket Greenes remained close friends of Jones until the end of the decade, when they moved to Wiltshire because Gwen could no longer afford her son David's heroin addiction.[40]

In 1930, Tom Burns had introduced Jones to Victoria (Vicky) Reid, whom he often visited at her family home at 72 Grosvenor Street in Mayfair. Following a by-now well-established pattern, he went chiefly to talk with her mother, Lady Susan Reid. Born a Baring and extremely well educated (by a French governess), she had been a lady-in-waiting to Queen Victoria and her husband had been the Queen's physician. Vicky studied violin. Living with the family, Cécile Geoffroy-Dechaume studied piano. When Jones arrived, they stopped practising ('he was so nice', Vicky said) but not without feeling inconvenienced. He visited several times a week, always muffled up, often saying he had a cold and couldn't work, and usually staying most of the day. He was full of humour, Vicky remembered: 'we laughed endlessly'. He was thirteen years older than they but did not, to them, 'feel older'. They loved him, felt uninhibited with him, sensed no sexual pressure from him. He 'didn't seem like an ordinary man', Vicky remembered, not 'dominant enough to cope with marriage'. Vicky referred to herself, Cécile, and Nicolete, who also visited, as 'David's wives'.[41]

In 1932, when Charles Burns married and moved to Birmingham to found a child guidance clinic, Tom left St Leonard's Terrace and, with his newly widowed mother and youngest sister, Margaret, moved to 10 Jubilee Place. There he had a studio on the top floor with a skylight and divan-bed. Grisewood took a room in the basement. He and Jones spent long hours in Tom's top-floor studio bedroom.[42]

There, 'on one or two occasions', Jones had 'a look at' the unpublished notebooks of Gerard Manley Hopkins, loaned to Burns by D'Arcy. Although Burns remembered him as showing only 'mild interest', so they may have been no influence, the descriptive language of *In Parenthesis* has striking affinity with Hopkins's visually vivid and acoustically rich lyrical notebook descriptions.[43]

In the summer of 1932, Jones met Jacques Maritain. Burns drove them together to Pigotts. Jones later remembered, 'Maritain & I carried on a conversation about the arts with Tom as interpreter.' At one point, they stopped and urinated by the side of the road, Maritain saying, 'You know our proverb? *Qui pisse contre vent mouille ses pantalons.*' Afterwards, Jones and Burns would quote this to each other apropos of their efforts to invigorate the Catholic Church in England.[44]

* * *

Jones and his closest friends were, Tom Burns remembered, 'endlessly' joking and laughing. Raised in the late Victorian and Edwardian heydays of joke-telling, Jones told jokes well, with flawless timing. His specialty was shaggy-dog stories. Burns recalled him telling a favourite:

> A chap comes into a shop and says, 'Can you make me a bun in the shape of an S?' The baker says, 'Yes, come in tomorrow and it'll be ready for you.' The chap returns the next morning and the baker shows him the bun.
>
> 'No, no, it isn't *really* an S. You haven't got the curves right, have you. They're too tight and it's too long.'
>
> 'I'm so sorry. I'll try again. Come back tomorrow morning.'
>
> So he comes back in the morning and the baker shows him a new bun.
>
> 'I'm sorry but it isn't right, the curves are too rounded, too wide, you know, they have to be, well, more like the curves of an S.'
>
> 'Yes, I see, well, I'm sure I can get it right. Come back in the morning and I'll have it for you.'
>
> The next morning, the chap returns and is shown another bun.

'Oh, very good, you've almost got it. The curves are right, but the width of the curving line is a bit too thick.'

'Hmm, well, I'll try again. If you come in the morning, I'm sure I'll get it right this time.'

So, the next morning the chap comes back again and is shown the new bun.

'Well, that's a pretty good S, a pretty good S. Yes, that's it, that's just what I want.'

'I'm so glad. Can I parcel it up for you?'

'That's all right, I'll eat it here.'

Jones also liked telling this story:

A man goes into a milk-bar and asks for a drink. The bar-attendant asks, 'What flavour do you want in your milkshake?' He says, 'I think I want one without flavouring.' She says, 'But what sort of flavour do you want it without?' He says, 'Ah, that depends on what flavours you have.' She says, 'Strawberry, orange, lemon, vanilla & lime.' He says, 'I'll have mine without lemon.' She looks through the bottles and says, 'I'm awfully sorry sir, but I'm afraid we're out of lemon.' He says, 'Very well, if I can't have a drink without lemon flavour, I won't have a drink at all', and angrily walks out.

Yet another concerns the story of the theft of the Soissons vase by one of Clovis's soldiers, which goes on too long to include here.[45] Jones had deep affinity for such stories – his conversations and letters tended to be long and 'shaggy'. The same may be said of *The Anathemata*, which if it conforms to any known genre, may be a shaggy-dog story.

*   *   *

The spring and summer of 1932 was the most prolific period in Jones's life. He had a contract with Ernest Brown of the Leicester Gallery to supply forty pictures in the autumn. He went to Caldey with the Burns brothers to paint, then to Rock, where he made four watercolours, fewer than he had hoped. But among them was *Briar Cup* (fig. 15).[46]

In it, viewpoint pivots: you look down at the table and horizontally beyond. Tonally light circular shapes of table and containers attract and still vision, which vegetation sends off. Tension between containment and departure (mediated in quasi-roundnesses of flowers and leaves) is inscribed by two long briar branches: one bending into circularity (partly mirroring the teapot handle); the other extending to balance a shell-burst of trees.

15. *Briar Cup*, 1932

These also unify by pulling the eye down into their convergence. The table is before a window whose frame has vanished. The meaning of the picture is the relationship of order to wildness (including war) by interpenetration of indoors and outdoors, culture (hinting at fertility imagery in Jessie Weston), and nature. Neither staying in nor going out, this painting encourages endless viewing. In its lightness, vitality, and stillness, it is a harbinger of Jones's great chalice paintings of the 1950s. Helen Sutherland bought it.

In its erasure of walls, this and other paintings include what Ede calls a 'sense of substance being insubstantial'. As Simon Brett writes, Jones's full or partial disappearances reproduce awareness of actual seeing, in which focusing beyond an object (or past a window frame) renders it unseen or transparent. Most are unconscious of such naïve seeing owing partly to familiarity with photography, which cannot reproduce it.[47] Jones's presentation of seeing may owe a great deal to his habit of gazing out of windows during long illnesses.

Painting and writing, he was now super productive. He painted enough to exhibit over the next few years in many galleries: the Leicester, Tooths, the Lefevre, the Redfern, the Beaux Art, the Wertheim, the Goupil, and the Zwemmer. And on 9 April 1932, he began what would be nearly 300 foolscap pages of overlapping drafts of Part 7 of *In Parenthesis*. Able to 'be immersed in' only 'one thing at a time', he alternated between painting and writing and, when writing, regretted this.[48]

According to his note on the manuscript, he finished the draft of Part 7 'at Pigotts Aug 18th 1932', bringing the poem to chronological completion in a manuscript draft of 281 pages, which distils more than 1,137 surviving foolscap pages in three stages of draft. After four years of writing, the initial stage of composition was done. Burns had the manuscript typed, and Jones and Hague deposited it in Barclays Bank in Reading.[49]

Already *In Parenthesis* had remarkable cumulative force, for which Jones's models were Malory; *Wuthering Heights*; the Mass; the Last Gospel within the Mass; and *Moby-Dick,* which he said, 'gathers depth and drive as it proceeds toward the final disaster' and is surpassed in this only by Malory.[50]

He intended a limited edition printed by Hague, but in the spring of 1932 Jim Ede had given a glowing account of Jones's writing to Richard de la Mare at Faber, who asked to read it for possible trade publication. Jones replied, 'It is not finished … now is the difficult task of interminable revision.'[51]

At Pigotts in June he had gone to see the newly opened grave of 'a supposed Neolithic man' at Wycombe, and it was 'awfully exciting seeing him'.[52] The experience would inform his later poetry having to do with 'sleeping lords' (*A* 65, 77, 80; *SL* 70–96).

* * *

In his tiny bedroom in the Hagues' cottage, Jones painted René (fig. 16), his alert, intelligent face topped by a mess of hair matching his rumpled clothing. This is the man – alive in a mixture of intensity, alertness, and tumbling chaos. Jones kept it for himself, five years later entitling it, *The Translator of the Chanson de Roland.* He thought it 'the best … "likeness" of any' he had attempted.[53]

The 1932 paintings liberate light from line, as in nearly line-less, Winifred Nicholson-influenced still lifes of the summer. Especially beautiful

16. *The Translator of the Chanson de Roland*, 1932

is *July Change, Flowers on a Table* (fig 17). Dissolving objects in fields of colour approach abstraction, and he was, he later said, 'strongly tempted to go abstract' at this time. These paintings are entirely free of the tightness that he felt was a danger for him. He would remember, they 'got nearest to what I had in mind – but a *very long way from the goal*'. He 'was conscious for some long time ... that I was straining every nerve to do something more than I had power to do'.[54]

In the summer and autumn of 1932, in addition to finishing the continuous draft of *In Parenthesis*, he made sixty paintings: fifty large, free, fast watercolours and ten oils. The watercolours included his last portrait – of Petra, entitled *The Seated Mother* (fig. 18), bought by Helen Sutherland. In 1946, unobserved, Kathleen Raine would see him prop it against a chair in Helen's drawing room, and gaze with 'unforgettable ... pondering sweetness' that no one was meant to see. It would be the last picture he painted for years.[55]

* * *

In the second week of October Jones suffered a nervous breakdown. There had been signs: agoraphobia, neurotic anxiety about illness, fear of germs and animals (snakes, dogs, horses, wasps), and depression accompanying 'colds of a certain kind'. In August, he began feeling anxious and sad and lost sleep. Then he ceased talking. Severe depression alternated with panic in which he could scarcely breathe, his heart pounding – he broke into a sweat, his legs went weak, and he felt dizzy and nauseated. The Hagues pretended not to notice or joked: at breakfast, René asked, 'Were you biting the blankets much?' Jones replied in a thin, far-off voice, 'Mmm' (pause) 'yes' (pause) 'pretty rough' (pause) 'he's been sending over a lot of stuff'. The artillery metaphor is suggestive, but he and René both saw the cause as 'girl trouble'. René would ask, 'The old pornos, Dai?' and he would murmur, 'Ah' (pause) 'yes' (pause) 'the old trouble'. He was

17. *July Change, Flowers on a Table*, 1932

in love with Prudence Pelham, but, according to Prudence, his collapse was caused by his still being in love with Petra.[56] He may have found the presence at Pigotts of both disconcerting. Whatever the causes, the collapse was precipitated by explosive creativity.

But he blamed writing. In 1939 he said, 'I sometimes wonder if doing it didn't partly bring on this breakdown' and 'if I hadn't . . . I should probably be painting still.' Imaginatively reliving traumatic war experience might trigger a breakdown, but finishing a major work always left him enervated and depressed – even finishing a 'quite small work' left him feeling 'peculiar'. He also wondered whether being half Welsh was a cause.[57]

Jones's condition persisting, the Hagues drove him to his parents in Brockley – he later said, 'that was a mistake'. He remained there during

18. *The Seated Mother*, 1932

the long months of nervous collapse. His insomnia was, he said, total: 'I did not sleep for nine months – no one I've told has believed me.' Lying in bed he heard the chiming of his father's clock 'every' quarter hour. In the morning he dressed and descended for breakfast as if nothing was wrong – which was, he said, 'the thing to do in those days'. He could not bear to talk, write, read, or go out. But at the end of October 1933 he dragged himself to Harley Street to consult a neurologist, James C. Woods, whose diagnosis was neurasthenia owing to shell shock, a 'severe ... Depressive Psychosis'. Jones told him that painting made him feel worse. Woods said, 'Cultivate a masterly inactivity.' Chest X-rays were taken, which Jones found 'rather beautiful'. He was to take a tonic, drink Ovaltine, and reduce smoking to a few cigarettes a day – this he found 'a bit of a curse'. When he could, he read Wordsworth, Pepys, and Evelyn's *Diary*, went for a walk, or worked at revising *In Parenthesis*.[58]

During the whole of 1933 Jones vacillated between depression, anxiety, and terror. He told Nicolete, 'I can look at the coal scuttle and be absolutely terrified.' Inexplicable, meaningless fear was intolerable, 'the chief misery ... never knowing what or why or when'. Agoraphobia worsened. Being alone in public brought on extreme agitation, a sense of impending disaster, an impulse to flee.* He feared panicking, not knowing when the terror might strike, dreading embarrassing loss of control. When walking alone, and even sometimes with a friend, he would rush ahead fearfully, fleeing the unknown horror he sensed behind him, like a child rushing up from a dark cellar, but there was no escape – this happened when walking with Prudence.[59]

His Christmas card for 1933 is a symbolic self-portrait. Noah's Ark rides the flood (fig. 19) not, as earlier, in relatively calm waters at dawn (chapter 6, fig. 20) but in rough water at night. The interior flood tosses

* In 1938, riding east on the District Line with his niece Stella, Jones frantically rushed away before coming to his stop, exclaiming over her protest, 'I must get out!'

the ark of himself and his art. From the sky a divine hand — its stigma recalling that Jesus, too, suffered — blesses the imperilled vessel. The accompanying inscription translates, 'strengthen our souls for passing through intolerable waters'. In 1940 he would write to Charles Burns of the arid state of his inner life:

19. Christmas card, 1933

> This nervous collapse of mine over these many years has, I think, taught me that not many of the popular & accepted & believed-in theories or convictions about 'heavenly consolation' etc. hold much water . . . all such clichés as, say, 'God will help you' are as misleading as 'you must pull yourself together' — 'exercise the will' — 'there is nothing really the matter with you' etc. etc. (all those imbecile but well-meant suggestions that people make constantly to anyone with 'neurasthenia'). The thing is, I suppose, one has somehow got to hold on to the fact that 'God is helping me' . . . in the very pit of some psychological-pathological state. This seems to reduce the matter to a pure intellectual conception. But it's the best I can do at present.

He was, Tom Burns thought, experiencing what John of the Cross called 'the Dark night of the soul'.[60]

Before his breakdown, he had been fairly robust. From now on, he would be frail and physically withdrawn, hunching his shoulders, making himself small, a lesser target, retreating from 'the barrage' into the dugout of his body. He would never fully return to the lightness of spirit and apparent happiness of his first thirty-seven years. His suffering was grim and showed in his face, which took on a grey pallor and, in repose, a haggard, unutterably sad expression. In 1968 he would write of his 1932 breakdown, 'it has persisted'.[61]

PART FOUR

TIME BETWEEN

CHAPTER 9: 1933–37

From New Year's till April 1933, Jones's pocket diary is blank – three months of insomnia, anxiety, and depression. But in early 1934 he was seeing friends, including Gill. On New Year's Day, he had supper at Tom Burns's flat with Ede, John Betjeman, the painter Robin Ironside, Nicolete (formerly Binyon) Gray and her husband, Basil Gray. When invited in early February 1934 to bring new works for the exhibition of the 7 & 5, he did not respond. On 26 February at the Edes, he ate with Henry Moore, whom he met there frequently this year.* But his friends could see how depressed he was and decided he needed a rest cure.[1]

Tom Burns arranged a trip to Cairo and Jerusalem, paid for by him, Ede, and, chiefly, Helen Sutherland. 'Bewildered' and '*frantic*', Jones at first refused to go but was persuaded. He was too indecisive to shop for the trip. (Out with Grisewood he bought a yellow shirt which, upon returning home, he put in the dustbin, and, with Burns, unable to decide between a heavy dressing gown and a light one, bought both.) So Burns shopped for him. Vicky Reid helped him pack. (He put into a large trunk Spengler's *Decline of the West*, his Everyman Malory and a bottle of Eno's but could decide on nothing else. Vicky chose the rest for him.) In gratitude, he gave her a painting. On the morning of departure, 6 April, he said he could not go – he had no 'little coat' for warmer temperatures. Burns, who had taken a holiday to accompany him to Cairo, promised, 'We'll get you a little coat before it's too hot. I've bought all your tropical clothes and we've got the tickets – you've just *got* to go.' Burns 'only just' managed to get him aboard the P&O ship *Malaja*. Petra saw him into his second-class cabin – it was, for him, 'heavenly' having her there. Under way in the Channel, he had his first full night's sleep in nine months.[2]

It was a twelve-day voyage. Initially he remained below, his Goanese steward bringing him meals in bed. At Gibraltar, Jones declined to join passengers disembarking for the afternoon in a crowded lighter, then said, 'Bugger me, let's go', so Burns hired a dinghy. Together they

1. Jones in his 'little coat' on the *Malaja*, 1934

---

* Jones considered 'Harry' Moore 'remarkable ... a most solid character & impossible not to like, transparently sincere'. An ex-serviceman from West Yorkshire, Moore is commemorated in *In Parenthesis* as 'Harry of Ilkley' (114), Ilkley being Cockney rhyming slang for 'Ilkley Moor'/Moore.

walked round Gibraltar, where Burns bought him a light tweed 'little coat'. By the time they put in at Alexandria, Jones was noticeably better, talking to others, even playing deck quoits and shuffleboard. On 18 April, they reached Port Said and went by train to Cairo.[3]

Through Georges Cattaui, Burns had arranged to stay with Ralph and Manya Harari – he a wealthy Egyptian Jew, a diplomat, and former colonel in the British army; she a lovely Russian Jew, chic, very intelligent. They lived on the west bank of the Nile in the top flat of palatial 'L'Immeuble Eliaki', overlooking the river and the old city with its domed mosques and minarets. The garden ran down to a gated wall, where, in the mornings, Jones watched fleets of dhows slowly passing – he sketched them in a letter to Petra (fig. 2). The hot afternoons he spent behind shuttered windows, draped over a leather sofa sipping Napoleon Brandy or gin and soda. His stomach was 'perpetually out of order'. Mornings were especially 'bad'.[4]

After 5 p.m., when the heat decreased, he ventured out, staying near the riverbank in the modern city, which he thought 'noisy & boring'. The Hararis took them (until Burns returned to England) on excursions: to mosques, including the Ibn Tulun Mosque with its 'heavenly' ninth-century twisting brick piers, which reminded him of *Arabian Nights*; to the National Museum with its Tutankhamun treasure, 'meretricious & boring'; to the Citadel and through the old town, *Arabian Nights* again. Jones loved seeing animals on the roads with children running beside them: camels, herds of

2. Dhows, 26 April 1934

long-haired goats, 'white Fra-Angelico asses', and water buffaloes he thought 'grand' (fig. 3). On 4 May they drove to the pyramids at Giza, which he thought 'utterly supurb' and 'pretty astonishing', and the Sphinx 'absolutely grand' and 'a 1st class artwork – its proportions are so interesting'. A few days later they drove to the necropolis of Memphis, where he saw the step-pyramid of Zozer, which he sketched (fig. 4).[5]

He loved his hosts, especially 'Momma Harari'. With Burns gone and her husband at work, she was his principal companion. She had been received into the Catholic Church two years before and, during recent summers in England, had attended meetings of the Chelsea Group.[6]

After six weeks with them, Jones left for Jerusalem on 28 May, flying to Lydda. Disappointed with 'the almost tram-car even & steady uneventfulness', he read Malory during the flight. From Lydda he took the bus to Jerusalem, where he stayed at the Austrian Hospice – at the first

3. Buffalo, ass, pyramids, 26 April 1934

turning of the Via Dolorosa in the centre of the Muslim Quarter, the tallest building on the north slope of the old city. It had been recommended to Gill (who booked Jones's room) by Thomas Hodgkin, then working as secretary to the British High Commissioner. Hodgkin and Gill were living there, Gill while completing decorative panels for the Rockefeller Archaeology Museum.

Jones's room was on the top floor to the right of the stairway, with two windows and a balcony facing south.[7]

Jones hated the heat and the sun, preferring to look at the city from his high window where he spent much of each day. Occasionally he did 'creep out' for cigarettes and wandered 'the densely crowded & incredibly noisy streets' (too narrow for motorised traffic) 'and the Suq'. The old city was almost entirely Arabic. He liked the 'nice pet sheep with

4. Zozer pyramid, 1934

blue-bead collars'. There was lots of noise: talking, shouting, and music on gramophones and radios. In a café under his window, Arabic music played from 4.30 a.m. till midnight 'and sometimes Mozart' to his 'astonishment'. From the minaret across the street, a mullah sang out the haunting, melancholy plainchant of Islam. It was a city of smells – coffee, tamarind, and baked desserts in large round pans. At the Damascus Gate, men unloaded camels. And he repeatedly visited the nearby Armenian church, admiring its mosaics and primitive, Giotto-like paintings. He greatly preferred the old city to the 'new town of horrible buildings' to the south and west, especially hating the 'awful' Cook's Travel Office, which 'frightened' him.

So he kept to the old city, preferring to walk in the cool, less crowded evening, seeing Arab men relaxing in front of houses, being shaved or ordering coffee and the hubble-bubble.[8]

Most evenings, he walked east past the site of the Roman Fortress Antonia, through St Stephen's Gate to stand among the graves of the Muslim cemetery and look towards the Mount of Olives, illuminated by the setting sun, 'lovely' despite 'two appalling churches'.[9] Near the foot of the Mount was Gethsemane, the olive garden of Jesus's agony. Whenever leaving or returning to the hospice, he walked the Via Dolorosa and sometimes thought of Jesus carrying his cross.

In the evening of 29 May, Jones walked with Gill to the Church of the Holy Sepulchre, crowded and thickly over-ornamented with marble, silver lamps, candles, icons, and mosaics. When Hodgkin later tried to take him again, he said, 'No, I think I'll stay right here and have a double scotch.'[10]

With Gill and Laurie Cribb he went to the Temple Mount, visiting the cavernous, black-domed Al-Aqsa Mosque and the Dome of the Rock – he liked its white, slightly undulating stone base. At its centre is a large black outcropping, traditionally regarded as the *omphalos* of the world (*A* 58), where Abraham came to sacrifice Isaac (*A* 232–33). Jones disliked the surrounding fence, which reminded him of the alligator pool in the London zoo.[11]

On 31 May, the feast of Corpus Christi, in the hospice chapel he attended his first Mass in Jerusalem. (It was originally scheduled for 6 a.m.; he requested a delay till 7, which granted, he 'cursed himself' for not asking 'for 8'.) At Mass three-quarters of a mile from where the words of consecration were first spoken, spatial proximity combined with sacramental annihilation of time in an experience that would inform meditative presence at the Last Supper during Mass in *The Anathemata*, in 'The Kensington Mass', and in other Mass poems (*RQ* 87–106). On Sunday 17 June, Hodgkin joined him and the Gills (Mary and Joanna had arrived on 8 June) in the chapel for a high Mass celebrated by German Benedictines. Jones gave Hodgkin a running commentary, whispering, during a final, celebratory *Te Deum*, 'It's probably because the Germans have taken Paris.'[12]

Extraordinarily for Jones, one hot afternoon he made a two-mile pilgrimage over the Mount of Olives to Bethany, where Jesus spent nights while preaching in Jerusalem, where he raised Lazarus, and where Mary poured 'costly ointment' over Jesus's head – for Jones, a paradigmatic act of gratuitousness (*DG* 183; *WP* 36).

At a Franciscan monastery on an important site in Trajan's Jewish war he saw an inscribed stone still in place, marking the cookhouse of a section of the legion whose members had been first ashore in Britain in 55 BC. That moved him at the time more than anything else he had seen in Palestine.[13]

Jones was not getting on well with Gill, who regarded depression as a moral failure. Hodgkin was more sympathetic, so he spent most evenings talking with him. Jones claimed to be 'wretched' – his stomach still bad, he ate little and lost fourteen pounds, which worried him. 'He does look ill,' wrote Hodgkin, but 'is magnificent company … Talking seems to be about the only thing that he enjoys doing, and he is so learned and witty that I always enjoy these conversations that go on intermittently from six till eleven at night.' They discussed Jews, Arabs, the British Empire, and the Crusades. Jones expressed fascination with the battle of Hattin, where Saladin defeated the Crusaders, later regretting not visiting the site. He read Hodgkin's copy of Burton's *Anatomy of Melancholy* in a vain attempt to understand his distress. In the afternoon, the worst time of day for him, 'he was too wretched to talk'.[14]

On 23 June, Hodgkin arranged a tour for him and the Gills, but Jones declined, to avoid the heat and Gill. Instead, he stayed in his room, gazing at the old city and meditating on

> the sharp contrast of the old world of herds & olives & immemorial
> ways of life immeasurably slow, dusty, full of pain, disease, & full
> of grace, … & this other way of *our* world – wired, lit, pipe-lined,
> hideous … [the] mechanized state … seems not friendly to the …
> earth [and] seems to only arrive at anything like unity & a feeling of
> rightness in the air or on the sea. I mean … an air-plane seems to
> not at all insult the sky by its mass-produced contraptions. Neither,
> I think, does a mechanized ship seem incongruous on the sea even
> though a ship of sail seems a million times more lovely … My mind
> runs that way as I look out of my window.[15]

He saw helmeted British soldiers marching in squads. With 'bronzed' bare limbs, riot shields, batons 'in each right fist … the ring of the hob-nailed service-boots on the stone sets and the sharp commands', they reminded him of Roman soldiers. As weeks passed, the association 'became established': the British Mandate and memories of service in

5. View from Jones's room at the Austrian Hospice [1993]

Ireland allowed him vividly to imagine the ancient Roman occupation. He was convinced that these British soldiers were basically the same as those he had served with and the Roman soldiers here in the first century AD. About this, he mused 'a great deal'. The one thing about Jerusalem that made him happy, it would inform his later poetry (*SL* 10–59), in which the view from the walls of the Fortress Antonia (*SL* 28–30) is similar to that from his window (fig. 5). Directly or indirectly, as he later said, 'everything' he wrote after 1934 'has arisen' out of his experience of Jerusalem.[16]

He wanted to see Bethlehem, so Hodgkin took him on 30 June. High on a Judaean hill, the little town afforded a spectacular falling-away view of 'a lovely country of hills'. They visited the Church of the Nativity, a sixth-century basilica where Crusader kings had been crowned. Jones was excited to see Constantinian floor-mosaics being uncovered. Bethlehem was, he thought, 'convincing' and 'very beautiful'.[17]

On 7 July, after more than five weeks in Jerusalem, together with the Gills and Cribb, Jones left by train for Port Said, passing Battir station, where his biblical namesake slew Goliath (as Gill pointed out) and Ortas, where Solomon composed the Song of Songs. He wrote to Petra, 'it was very very like a hot & dry Capel-y-ffin ... we all thought so'.[18]

On 12 July they embarked in the SS *Dornala* and on the 18th visited Marseille and its ninth-century cathedral, with walls and pillars of the Roman Temple of Diana that had occupied the spot. On the 26th they reached Plymouth and on the 27th the Tilbury docks – concluding a westward voyage that would underlie ancient-and-medieval voyaging in *The Anathemata*.

*　*　*

As a cure, Jones's visit to the Middle East was 'bitterly disappointing'. It did allow him to resume work on *In Parenthesis*, and he felt 'a thousand times better' than in hot Jerusalem, but when he approached his Brockley home, the gloom set in. He stayed with his parents for less than a week, writing in his pocket diary, 'SENOJ DIVAD', a possible indication of the unease he felt. 'Still trying to get well by resting', he went to Rock with the Edes, then to Pigotts, and, in early September, returned to Brockley, again experiencing 'the jimjams'. Sometimes returning from the city, as he touched the front gate, he was overwhelmed with anxiety and, finding it impossible to enter, returned to central London. So he kept away, staying with the Edes or with Tom Burns, now living in the upper two floors of 3 Glebe Place, at the top of which was a spare room where Jones slept and took illnesses to bed, Burns's mother fretting over him.[19]

Calling Jones's neurosis 'Rosey', Tom would ask, 'How's Rosey today?' or, 'Here's old Rosy back again, tell her to bugger off. Come and have a beer.' To get Jones 'out of Rosy's clutches' Tom would tell a harrowing story of someone even worse off. Other friends were less helpful. Nicolete, for example, admonished him for moral laxity and insufficient will. Jones could not speak on the telephone, and Tom would call on his behalf a Dr Fothergill for advice and medicine. The only close friend fully to appreciate his condition was Charles Burns. Grisewood also sympathised but said that Jones fully confided only to Charles at this time and Charles was devoted to him.[20]

Jones paid no rent – the Burnses' sister Margaret thought him a scrounger – though periodically he gave Tom a drawing or a painting. The daily maid, Ethel, of whom Jones was fond, cooked and cleaned. There was a cat, Archibald, and soon another, Tim, a stray adopted by Tom. Whenever Tim brought fleas into the house, Jones (who abhorred fleas) had Ethel spray him round the legs to discourage migration. He and Tom went to Mass Sundays and sometimes during the week at nearby Holy Redeemer Church, Jones tending to sit near the back, sometimes ducking out during sermons for a cigarette. Nearly always, a drink at the King's Head and Eight Bells followed. On weekdays, Tom would often return from work saying, 'Come on, Dai, let's have a pint. I'm absolutely dying for a quick one.' After supper, they drank Haig whisky, easily getting through a bottle in an evening. Then, thinking this excessive, they waited for 10 p.m. to begin drinking – they worked at opposite ends of the dining-room table, between them a bottle of whisky and an alarm clock set for 10.[21]

One evening Evelyn Waugh visited. He and Jones argued over a point – probably of Renaissance English history, which Waugh was researching for his biography of Edmund Campion. Jones had a copy of the eleventh edition of the *Encyclopedia Britannica*, which he had moved into Glebe Place, and Waugh proposed, 'Your Encyclopaedia against £15'. Jones agreed, thinking it a joke, but, to his dismay, Waugh arrived next morning by taxi to collect the encyclopedia. Jones later told him that he thought his book on Campion (1935) 'frightfully good'.[22]

Jones visited Leslie Poulter, living in Blackheath with his wife, Amy – Jones had attended their wedding in 1924, giving them his painting *The Reclaimers*. He was unaware of smoldering resentment in Amy, an adamant Prince Edward Island Protestant who objected to artists and Catholics and considered him a freeloader. Once he stayed overnight and left without emptying his chamber pot. She furiously forbade further visits.[23]

On 5 September Jones left for Rock, where, by October, the news reached him that Barbara Hepworth had borne Nicholson triplets. 'I don't half feel sorry for them', he wrote, 'it really does seem too awful a thing to be possible – poor Ben', though years later, his face creasing with mirth, he would say, 'Served old Ben bloody right.' Feeling vindicated in his own decision not to marry and weeping with laughter, he continued, 'Had to marry the woman then, didn't he. Poor old Ben, didn't know what he'd taken on.'[24]

On 4 October Major-General Arthur Grenfell Wauchope, the High Commissioner of Palestine, arrived at Rock and 'rather put the fear of God into' Jones. The General observed, 'You seem to smoke rather a lot of cigarettes, young man. About how many a day?' Jones: 'About twenty, I suppose.' The General: 'Hmm. Well, better than thirty or forty.' Jones: 'And better than ten.' Edward Hodgkin remembered that Jones

> had a way of playing with a cigarette before he lit it, rolling it over in his fingers, squashing it out of shape, even pulling bits of tobacco out from the ends, and then perhaps holding it still in the fingers of both hands for quite a while, looking at it, pursing his lips and smiling, almost as if he expected it to say something . . . or simply light itself and take its own way to his mouth.[25]

Shortly after returning to London from Rock on 11 November 1934, Jones dined with T. S. Eliot, whom he had earlier met once, at lunch with Tom Burns in 1930. On that occasion Jones had not mentioned *In Parenthesis*. Now Eliot knew he was writing something but not precisely what – that was between Jones and de la Mare.[26]

Jones and Eliot may have discussed de la Taille's *Mystery of Faith*. Jones was reading the first volume, concerning 'the Eucharistic Sacrifice'. He found it 'Technical & tough. Grand & almost fierce in places'.[27] De la Taille writes that Jesus 'placed himself in the order of signs' – words important to Jones, which he would use as an epigraph for *Epoch and Artist*.

His agoraphobia made the congestion of London oppressive. He wrote to Helen, 'I seem to get "worked up" as soon as I'm in this town & all the alternatives & "horribles" always panic me.' He was now under doctor's orders to keep out of London as much as possible. He felt guilty 'to not be flourishing & useful' to his 'dear & good' parents, 'now that they are old' — a feeling surfacing frequently in his conversation and letters.[28]

In mid-November he stayed for ten days at Nicolete's invitation at her parents' country cottage on Westridge Farm near Streatley in Berkshire. In the evening 'old Binyon' looked at pictures and monologued, 'making great points over his graphics'. Jones had read his 1925 book on Blake's followers Calvert, Palmer, and Richmond, was surprised at his not noticing the decline in their later work, and wanted to discuss art with him. But, Jones wrote Hague, 'you know how difficult it is in talking to great men of the decade just past — you get curiously shy & feel an awful little impostor'. Though he thought Laurence Binyon's poetry terrible, he felt a Celtic affinity with him — 'Binyon' being an elided form of the Welsh 'Ap Einion' — and considered him 'a nice old chap', 'indeed delightful', but 'particularly hot' on the 'laws of prosody' and devoted (as Jones was not) to Milton.* Nicky and Basil Gray were also there for the week. Basil was officious and arrogant. With close friends, Jones joked that Basil's job, in the British Museum, was to set out the postcards. At one point during an evening while looking at him, he broke into laughter and 'had to make a joke to explain'.[29]

On 24 November, Jones went to stay for a week with the Betjemans at Garrard's Farm, Uffington, 'right up against the White Horse' in the hillside. He examined it up close and wondered how, in the first millennium BC, they could 'incise an exact & sweeping line of' such size and 'extraordinary rhythm'. He would commemorate this 'West horse-hill' in *The Anathemata* (55) and, years later, had a photograph of it on the wall of his room.[30]

He liked Betjeman's mind and values and thought him charming, envying his success with women (something for which he also envied Cyril Connolly). John was evangelical then and, with eyes fervently closed, played for Jones Protestant hymns on a harmonium. On 27 November, the Betjemans took him to visit a nearby Iron Age 'Camp & Stone Circle'.[31]

*   *   *

Jones wanted to flee Christmas in London. Helen Sutherland gave him money to sail to Cannes for warmth and rest, but Burns, joining him, decided on less-expensive Devonshire. Jones wanted to go to the warmer south coast, but, on

* Jones disliked *Paradise Lost* for its false, Latinate language, its facile (too rhythmically regular) verse, its psychologically-incredible elevated thoughts, and its dualism between intellect and emotions, morality and perception, reflecting Milton's Calvinistic theology: Satan is courageous but damned while the victorious Messiah is a milksop. Milton was the prime example of what he wanted not to be as a poet. Jones endorsed T. S. Eliot's 1936 essay criticising Milton. Eliot's reversal in his second Milton essay (1947) convinced him that Eliot had sold out to the English establishment.

Olivia Greene's recommendation, Burns chose the Quay Hotel at Hartland Point on the north coast. Jones liked the hotel and its wild setting. After Burns returned to London, he stayed on, enduring New Year's, a 'crashing bore' for him since it did not initiate a natural season. (He disliked Welsh enthusiasm for it.) The hotel was eating up his funds, so he wanted to sail either to Ireland or to Lundy Island, but examining sailing lists made him ill and he liked Hartland. A 'filthy cold' made leaving even less desirable and kept him in bed for over a week. He had brought with him to read Dawson's *Medieval Religion* and his 'regulars', Malory, *Alice in Wonderland*, MacLaren's 'Taplow', and T. S. Eliot. He was 'nibbling' at *In Parenthesis* and had begun writing something new, which he later entitled 'The Book of Balaam's Ass'.[32]

On 4 February 1935, Prudence Pelham visited, with René Hague, and drove Jones to Sidmouth, on the south coast. He had heard positive things about it from Dawson, whose daughters were at school there. Jones and Prudence took rooms in the Fort Hotel, a whitewashed early-Victorian building (fig. 6); across the road was a beach and the sea, warmed by a southern current. The Fort had central heating, and he had an electric heater in his room, so he was nearly always warm.

He began his day in bed with breakfast, *The Times*, and the post. About 10.45 he went to the Marine Hotel for 'a wet before lunch'. In the afternoon, he and Prudence read in the garden, she in the sun, he in shade, succumbing to 'that dreadful afternoon fatigue that Sidmouth is renowned for'. At 5.30, the maid – they called her 'Brellies' for her large breasts – brought tea to his room. In the evenings, he and Prudence adjourned to the Royal Clarence or the Marine till after midnight. She stayed for three weeks, driving him on excursions into the countryside, including, once, to Maiden Castle, the largest Iron Age hill fort in southern England.[33]

6. The Fort Hotel, Sidmouth

Jones disliked Sidmouth's red cliffs. 'On some days', he wrote to Ede, 'it's like living under a vast baulk of chocolate – they turn the bitter sea also into a kind of cocoa lake'. He regretted the hotel cost and considered moving to the countryside. Prudence scoured Sussex for a farm where he could stay, but less comfortable lodgings were, to him, intolerable. He adjusted to economic guilt, prolonging his first stay in Sidmouth to six months.[34] It would be his home for most of the next five years.

Outdoors he wore his floppy brimmed hat, his greatcoat, a muffler, and, on colder days, a second muffler. He walked the beach under the cliff for miles. 'One never gets tired of the sea', he wrote Petra, 'I do like living by it', its 'long taut' horizon line 'always "a good thing"' and the smell of wrack in the sunshine. He especially liked 'a high flat place above the sea' where he sat against a Neolithic standing stone, thinking.[35]

Each weekend Jones visited Dawson's daughters, Juliana and Christina, in the convent school of the Assumption. He liked attending Mass in its chapel, where, he thought, 'they sing the proper ... rather nicely ... innocently', though he was regularly appalled by the banality of sermons: 'it *is* a bloody shame ... to break the sequence of Mass with this stuff'. Sometimes he went in the evening to visit and listen to the nuns reciting Compline. To the Dawson girls, he seemed 'very poor', always 'tired'.[36]

Hague, Burns, and Prudence kept in touch with him by telephone. He rarely phoned them 'because you can say so little & it costs so much'. Prudence sent Admiral Collingwood's *Correspondence*, which was his 'kind of thing', 'so good in places'. In late February, she returned with the Hagues, and he and René discussed René's financial worries and planned the layout of *In Parenthesis*.[37]

As the weather warmed, Jones avoided the seafront in bright daylight and took to the country, where he liked seeing the snowdrops bloom, then the primroses. The strengthening sun gave him a headache and, even with

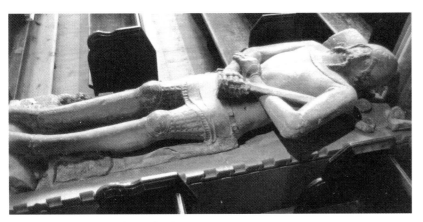

7. Otho de Grandisson, Ottery St Mary

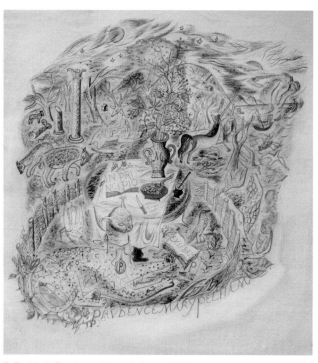

8. Ex Libris Prudence Mary Pelham, 1938

his hat on, hurt the top of his head. His practice was to walk quickly in the sun – 'that way you are out of it sooner'. He preferred 'grey days of a nondescript sort', with the front bare 'save for a doddering general or two'.[38]

Visiting again in late April, Prudence drove him to the parish church of Ottery St Mary, where he was impressed by a tomb effigy of a knight, Otho de Grandisson (d. 1359): 'glorious ... absolutely grand – one of the most moving Gothic carvings I've ever seen' (fig. 7). 'It's Our Lord & King Arthur Dead & Lancelot & Roland & Jonathan & all Xtian men dead.' He and Prudence commissioned a chemist to take photographs of it. If one turned out well, Jones planned to use it on the cover of *In Parenthesis*. They thought none good enough and returned them, then regretted not keeping them.[39]

Running out of money, Prudence left again. He missed her badly, longed to hear from her, and, as a memento, kept primroses they had picked together. He now found pubs depressing, 'not much good ... without a china' (plate/mate) – she was more than a mate in the Cockney sense but not sexually.[40] Their relationship was now the primary human context in which he felt, thought, and worked. In his adult life no woman had meant or would mean so much to him – on this all who knew him well agreed. His feeling for her would implicitly be expressed in a bookplate she commissioned in 1938, a picture he made too elaborate for proper reduction to bookplate size (fig. 8) – in it he gives prominence to the words 'In Principio', referring to her love for the opening of St John's gospel.

Tall, thin, brown-haired, with large blue eyes, Prudence was imaginative, intelligent, spontaneous, magnanimous, expressive (fig. 9). 'Tremendously musical', her voice was high, light, delicately modulated, enchanting – and Jones was especially sensitive to voices. When few women did, she drove a car (and could change a tyre) and drank in pubs with men. Her talk was vivid: Sidmouth was 'Sodmouth'; she disliked 'spy-chologists'; a favourite restaurant, the Hanover, was 'The Hangover'; when she overate she was 'stunned with food'; rain against glass was 'like machine gun fire'; the sky was 'constipated' with threatening snow; and Arabic in a film translated, 'There is no God by God & Mohamet is his profet' [*sic*]. She loved animals and cared strongly about people, books, art, and politics. She had little interest in Catholicism, which she did not really understand. Vaguely Christian, her beliefs were indefinite and loosely held; she greatly admired Nietzsche as the supreme debunker. Without a theology, she regarded life as absurd, and this sometimes caused her agonies.[41]

When not staying with friends, she lived with her mother, Lady Chichester (Ruth Pelham). Never wealthy by aristocratic standards and having been crippled by double death duties, the family had just enough to live independently. They moved between Stanmer House on the Chichester estate near Brighton, Mill House in nearby Falmer, and a London flat – in Hans Crescent and later in Chesham Place – where Jones visited her. Usually so fond of mothers of friends, he found hers 'terrifying'.[42]

9. Prudence Pelham, c. 1935

Prudence and Jones were happy together, sharing acute sensitivity, responsiveness, comic sense, and aversion to phoniness and arrogance. They gave each other haircuts. She mended his socks and stole clothing for him from rich friends. In London when he was ill, she moved into the Glebe Place flat to look after him. They went to pubs, the zoo, galleries – she once scouted an exhibition of 'Reubens & Co' at Burlington House to see whether it contained enough Reubens for him. She bought paintings from him, eventually owning eight with more on loan. Money meaning nothing to her, she telephoned him often and at length. She was fifteen years younger but theirs was basically a relationship of equals. (Whenever he affirmed something as generally accepted, she would say, 'Speak for y'rself.') She, too, loved *Finnegans Wake* and Christopher Smart. They read Catullus together, liking especially lyric LVIII, making pen-and-ink inscriptions of it and speculating gleefully about the erotic meaning of *glubit*. Together they read *The Song of Roland*, Hopkins, Lewis Carroll, and, above all, Malory. She sent him Lear's *Nonsense*, of which his favourite was 'The Dong with the Luminous Nose', whose protagonist suffers in love.[43]

When apart they now wrote one another twice weekly. Each remembered the thoughts and observations of the day or days to share with the other. He saved her letters; she kept only the pages of his with pictures or inscriptions, and most of these were subsequently lost.[44] She thanked him repeatedly for 'your lovely' letters, 'your angel letters', but also, in one, 'saw the white emptiness of your glass & thought it would never be filled'.

She addressed him warmly, even ardently, but not with a fervour equal to his. She objected to his signing off 'w kisses', though she once closed: 'Lay a kiss on your whiteness for me.' When separated, she missed him dreadfully. They embraced meeting and parting, but there was no sexual touching. This is not, as has been suggested, owing to inhibition on her part. During their friendship she had extended sexual affairs – with Victor Rothschild, though she preferred Jones as a companion, and with Claude Philmore, whom she considered marrying though she called him 'Prigmore'. Because she was so independent, Rothschild and others assumed she was promiscuous, and she complained to Jones of being often suspected of 'pornos'. But for her, sex was an expression of love, she suffered greatly from unhappy love affairs, and declined nearly all sexual invitations and many proposals of marriage. If Jones had approached her sexually, she would have reciprocated.* But, although warmly affectionate, he was, she later confided, 'completely unsexed' (not, perhaps, the right word), living solely in a world of ideas. Aware of his reserve, the check in him that sensitive women always felt, she took no sexual initiative.[45]

In an early draft of his Preface to In Parenthesis, he wrote that a list of those to thank might easily exclude 'for reticence, the one most helpful of them all', whom he thanks in the published version anonymously but 'very especially' (xv). This is Prudence. She was the muse of In Parenthesis, the most helpful certainly during the later phases of composition, an editorial influence. He sent her entire sections, she suggested changes, and he informed her by post of revisions. Sometime before December 1936 she wrote: 'I've been reading your book up & down & backwards & forwards through the insertions – it isn't half *bleeding* good. I like it best from chap IV onwards it gathers such terrific force from there. It would be a very great impertinence for me to do anything but praise it but I will tell you about some things in my next letter if you like!' How influential was she? Miriam Rothschild said that the style of In Parenthesis is more like Prudence's speech than her letters to Jones convey and that her letters to Miriam (now lost) read like In Parenthesis.[46] He and Prudence shared styles of speaking, including impolite language – her favourite line in the poem was 'who gives a bugger for / the Dolorous Stroke' (162). Influence was probably mutual, but she never regarded herself as his equal as a writer and was too embarrassed ever to show him the poetry she wrote.

Jones pressed her to come to Sidmouth often and for extended periods, but her mother, brother, and sister, unsure about their relationship and vaguely disapproving, were loth to lend her money for visits. After leaving Sidmouth in the spring of 1937 to stay with the Rothschilds in Switzerland, she wrote,

* The opinion of Robert Buhler, her second husband and an acquaintance of Jones from 1943.

So very dearest David most darling David how short it was – I did hate leaving you – I did not say it a lot because I knew I would have to go & I knew you didn't want me to & it is so difficult to primb yourself to it . . . Good night my sweet David please please be happy I can't bare it when you are miserable & I have made it worse. Bless you all the time. I will think at you all the time & send you what ever nise you would like.

('Primb' and 'nise' are Taplowese.) She sent him mountain flowers packed in snow and moss.[47]

*   *   *

On 3 May on the promenade, Jones and Prudence encountered Dawson. Impressed by his intelligence, after he left, she exclaimed, 'What a Tiger!' and from then on, to Jones and his friends, Dawson was known as Tiger Dawson. In Sidmouth Jones had meals with him and talked about Wales, a newly discovered *chanson de geste* (*The Song of William*), and the Church – their conversations beginning slowly as each emerged from the doldrums.[48]

When Prudence invited Jones in June to Stanmer to attend *The Magic Flute* at Glyndebourne, he suffered 'the usual misrub & come over', feeling 'pretty *terrified* of Lady Chichester & chaps coming & me all in rags & perhaps having a come over ill', so he declined.[49]

He was 'absolutely broke with these vast hotel expenses'. His yearly earnings had fallen to £147. And avoiding work, as Dr Woods advised, made little difference in his condition – 'it is such a *vile* life doing no work – & with so much I *would* do. Bugger.'[50]

He left for London to help Ede select his works for a touring exhibition of 'Welsh' artists being organised by Augustus John. In London, Dr Woods strengthened his medication, prescribing a bromide mixture (a sedative, causing drowsiness), aspirin, and tablets for an underactive thyroid. Jones then fled London with Dawson for Dawson's inherited family house, Hartlington Hall, near Skipton in Wharfedale in North Yorkshire.[51]

The Yorkshire dales were a 'welcome change', its 'romantic scenery . . . *absolutely heavenly*', 'exactly the kind . . . I like' with 'great hills & wooded streams'. On the morning of 3 July, he walked 'over the hills . . . & back under deep green places by the river & sat & shouted psalms in Welsh' from his Book of Common Prayer in English and Welsh. That afternoon he went with the Dawsons to see Grass Wood, the site of a British village and fortified hill that Dawson thought might have been the capital of Urien's Rheged. Dawson and Jones talked at length about medieval Welsh history and literature.[52]

After a fortnight with the Dawsons, Jones went to Rock. Helen put him to work reordering her picture gallery, in which his own work made him 'quite *sick* – it is all such a bloody old tangle'. To Grisewood he wrote that he has 'been going through pretty good mental miseries':

> I've always always as long as I can ever remember felt my business (however blindly) to be my work & always knew that everything had got to go for that. I've always felt ... that my own real life was that of judgment of the work to be made ... But now since this curious illness ... I feel rather like a Life Guardsman in a breast-plate & spurs without a horse in a mine-crater in a gas attack.[53]

On Sunday 21 July 1935, Helen had seventeen miners from the Ashington colliery to tea, some of them amateur painters whose work she was championing. She assigned Jones to show her pictures. Never having spoken in public, he 'was so frightened', 'but they were *so* nice – intelligent & sensitive, 20 times more "aware" than most people one meets'. The miners would remember 'his gentleness, his sincerity, and above all the poetry that is apparent in his every gesture'.[54]

Near the pond in the wood a gamekeeper showed him 'a lovely sparrow-hawk he shot ... with great speckled wings spread ... with heavenly legs with trousers of spotted tawny feathers'.[55] He would recall it when referring in *In Parenthesis* to 'the speckled kite of Maldon' (54).

Missing Prudence, he got Helen to invite her to Rock. Prudence asked him to wake her for her first breakfast. He knocked on her door to no avail, then entered and roused her. The maid saw him coming out and reported to Helen, who was infuriated at their (assumed) sleeping together under her roof. She was extremely cool towards him for some time. He felt chagrined at being subject to moral opprobrium without having enjoyed the immorality. He asked Prudence to cut his hair. They put down a sheet from his bed to catch the (she called them) 'hair feathers'. They bundled them in the sheet and carried it into the wood behind the house – only to be met by Helen returning from feeding birds. They confessed, and she coolly informed him that the chauffeur would have driven him to a barber. Finding the constraints at Rock unbearable, Prudence wrote the Hagues:

> This is a house of 'utter prevention' ... It has been *heavenly* seeing David ... but you are *so* frightened of being late for lunch & the pub is just too far to swil [*sic*] in & be back by 12.30. ... David leaps to doors & for coffee-cups I never saw him so agile. We sit by a small, nice pond for a bit nearly every day & complain and are happy in turns. I do think it *awful* that David is to stay here so long. I'm sure it will make him ill.

She escaped to Pigotts.[56] He wore a bracelet she left behind.

When visiting Rock, Jones usually stayed a few days at Barmour Castle, as a guest of Helen's friend Constance Sitwell (cousin by marriage to the three famous Sitwells) and her daughter Ann. It was a relief from Helen's strict regime. On 2 August he took the train there, and enjoyed not being driven with Helen: 'not so much – Mills this & now Mills that & do be careful not to run down that bunny-rabbit & remember you must call at Mrs Things & don't forget to take the other road – not to be later than 5.31 or 32 at the very latest'. The train paused at Lucker, where he thought, 'Christ what a temptation to alter the signs by night.' This summer he spent three weeks at Barmoor, 'lovely & free'. Sleeping here and at Rock 'with a crenellated place below for archers & pourers of boiling pitch' would inform his last poem, in which Norman sentries in a 'crenellated traverse bay' wake the captain of the castle 'in his ... chamber' (*SL* 94–5).[57]

When Helen left Rock for a while in October, Jones went to the Schooner Hotel in Alnmouth. The place had 'all the things' he liked, 'sandy dunes & mud-flats & a bridge across at just the right place & sea birds calling on the wrack left by the tide'. While walking here he met Augustus John, who, when later asked how Jones was, answered, 'He's better. He went down to the beach and drew a monster in the sands with a stick.' On 9 November, Mills retrieved him in the Rolls.[58]

* * *

Unable to paint or draw, when not revising *In Parenthesis* or talking with friends, Jones spent his days and evenings reading. He believed it necessary to read widely: 'whatever you think about it, you must ... read it'. This included novels, one of them John Gray's *Park* (1930).* He repeatedly reread, in addition to Taplow, George and Weedon Grossmith's *Diary of a Nobody* (1892) and, annually, John Collier's *His Monkey Wife* (1930), which exemplified one of his favourite axioms, 'Nothing excellent that is not odd'. And he occasionally reread Collier's 'terribly interesting' *Tom's a-Cold* (1933). He enjoyed Thackery (though 'second rate') and, in Dickens (who lacks 'any decent ideas ... about anything'), he enjoyed 'Pickwick & all the "Pickwickian" stuff in all his work – that's got really "praise", "Lauds" to it'.)[59]

Of Classical literature Jones loved most the *Odyssey*, in which the repelling (to him) savage conditions of Mycenaean culture were 'all the time' woven with 'suggestions of such tenderness & civility & sophistication ... it makes one jump – and weep also'. Despite (all of

---

* Jones wished he had a collected works of Gray, especially liked his poem, 'The Patriarch of Uz', and thought that 'in a difficult-to-describe way' Gray, whom he had first known at Ditchling, 'most certainly was an influence' on his own writing.

them, he thought) poor translations, the epic, 'rather like the Mass,' retains its 'terrific shape'. After reading the *Aeneid* for the first time in 1940, he would prefer Homer.[60] *

He reread early medieval poetry, sensing the vigour of 'the springtime of a culture'. He appreciated the technical mastery of medieval Welsh poetry in Welsh and read Anglo-Saxon poetry in translation, liking especially 'that great, grim "Battle of Maldon"' and even more the 'Battle of Finnsburg' and most of all the 'glorious' 'Dream of the Rood'.[61] In 1950 he would acquire Sweet's *Anglo-Saxon Reader* and painstakingly work through these in the original.

Jones did not enjoy all things medieval. The most celebrated medieval Welsh poet, Dafydd ap Gwilym, he found 'sickening. Of course its most cunningly contrived & all chaps who know Welsh properly are *unanimous* in their admiration of his technique & beauty of form, but as far as *I* can see he had not got two ideas in his head. I should think he was about as bad as [Robert] Burns . . . as far as ideas went.' And 'The Nordic stuff,' he thought, 'is *curiously* boring . . . like "Sitting Bull" & "Grey Wolf" & Red Indian stuff . . . In a way in which Greek, Celtic, Latin & whatnot myth stuff never is.' The sagas and eddas 'feel *to me* unmixed frightfulness . . . horror & . . . lack of humour'. He also disliked Dante, read in Binyon's translation, for his (to Jones, boring) interest in 'power politics' and because Beatrice is 'not a compelling girl' but 'a convenient figure necessary to his worked out scheme'.[62]

He loved *Sir Gawain and the Green Knight* ('magical') and Langland's *Piers Plowman*, and Shakespeare's plays, whose plots, he said, 'I usually can't follow' – 'it's the *poetry* . . . I like', and it is 'praise, praise, & praise all through'. The 'supreme book' remained the *Morte D'Arthur*, 'a constant companion', valued as 'a collection of instances of chaps putting that before this & this before that, according to their several natures & impulses – there is no trite "loved I not honour more" . . . for honour itself moves with the object of worship – everyone instinctively understands this'. A favourite part was the short first chapter of Book Twenty – 'the *impotence* of Gawain, Gareth & Co, the venom of Agravaine & the sense of imminent ruin' all 'in the space of the Hampstead tube lift. In fact from there on to the end . . . it's all simply matchless.' He liked Malory's presentation of chivalry, which he had 'a great affection for', and disliked *Don Quixote* for lampooning. Malory wrote late in the Middle Ages, 'just in time' to be true to the past but late enough to bridge to the

* In early Jones criticism, Hague's strong Virgilian bias obscured Jones's predominantly Homeric affinities. Like so much modernist writing, Jones's poetry is Homeric in its paratactic form – juxtaposition without explanatory coordination. As a writer, he regarded himself as a joiner, 'he who fits together', which is precisely what *hòm-éros* means. Jones considered Virgil a sycophant, no better in that respect than the later Latin poet Claudian.

future – a figure with whom he identified. In contrast, Spenser wrote about knights too late.[63]*

By the mid-1930s, Jones gave up reading contemporary British poetry, which he found ludicrous in its reversion to outdated conventional forms. He held the Contemporary Poetry Society in contempt for being timid and boring. He was convinced that little could be done with short lyrics, most anthologised poems of earlier centuries now seeming to him 'pretty silly'. About this he would not change his mind. He wrote in 1962, 'I still can't see that "poetry", bits of "verse", apart from great felicity and skill in handling language, has much to be said for it.' He thought that if all but the 'lines that are really on the spot' were eliminated from *The Oxford Book of English Verse*, it 'would be a pretty thin book'. He included Arthur Quiller-Couch, the anthologist, among the empty icons of the British cultural establishment: 'Q[uiller-Couch], Walter P[ater] and the R.A.'[64]

* * *

While revising *In Parenthesis*, Jones theorised that there is a Celtic tradition in English literature, distinguished by three factors. The first is realism, a 'vivid sense of the particular, the actual, the tangible', a certain affection for the intimate creatureliness of things – a care for, and appreciation of, the particular genius of places, men, trees, animals'. The second is 'a pervading sense of metamorphosis and mutability. That trees are men walking. That words "bind and loose material things"' – something evident in the woven texture of 'all of Julian of Norwich', in Malory where Lancelot visits Chapel Perilous, in much of Shakespeare, in Blake, in *The Rime of the Ancient Mariner*, at the end of 'Christabel', in Lewis Carroll, and pre-eminently throughout *Finnegans Wake*. The third factor is inclusiveness, there being 'always a bit of lion in your lamb ... no item on the list in the Benedicite Omnia Opera Dominum is denied or forgotten.' It was Celtic, he thought, 'to include "everything"', 'entirety or totality in a little ... space'.[65]

This Celtic aesthetic, there 'to make you weep' in early medieval works, becomes, he thought, heavy and dull in the later Middle Ages, then, with Shakespeare and the Metaphysical poets, 'happy, prouder, conscious, & having a regular fine old fling'. Largely destroyed by the Puritan Revolution (surviving in folk-songs), it was 'half' restored by the romantic revival and by Blake. The Pre-Raphaelites 'recognized' it but 'got every cart before all the wrong horses', already confused by 'that horrible "Celtic twilight" idea'. Hopkins revived the '"Celtic" thing of demanding intricate & complex forms of compactness and precision and producing in his case, because of his great

---

* Jones could not bear *The Faerie Queene* and its 'bogus' Red Cross Knight. And he was furious with Spenser for writing against the Irish: 'the attitude of that sod ... makes me speechless with rage'.

poetic genius, works which astonish, not only by their power but by their delicacy'. After its publication, Jones would say that *In Parenthesis* belonged to this Celtic Tradition.[66]

His identifying it with this tradition originated in noticing affinity between the wet landscape of Western Front and earliest Welsh writing: 'The folk tradition of the insular Celts seems to present to the mind a half-aquatic world – ... it introduces a feeling of transparency and interpenetration of one element with another, of transposition and metamorphosis.'[67] Much of *In Parenthesis* is metamorphic in setting and action, and in texture, which modulates between differing registers of language and different allusive ranges and between basic imaginative levels (satire, realism, romance, and myth).

In the autumn of 1935, Jones mined for epigraphs for *In Parenthesis* and each of its seven parts Edward Anwyl's translation of Aneirin's *Y Gododdin*, a sixth-century fragmented elegy for a Welsh war band annihilated at Catraeth. Only recently read by him for the first time, it confirmed his sense of the essential continuity of calamitous warfare throughout history. In 1961, he would write that the Celts 'are masters of defeat' and that 'indeed, the philosophy of defeat seems to me to be their great contribution to our culture'. Like them, he was transforming calamity into literature – not, he later said, to promote pacifism but to 're-present' war as it is.[68]

* * *

In October 1935 the main news was of Italy's invasion of Ethiopia. Jones thought 'it intolerable ... these damned air-planes, gas & the rest knocking hell out of chaps with spears'. Only half jokingly he considered going to 'fight for the Abyssinians'. The only 'nice thing' to come of the conflict was, he thought, a music-hall gag: '"Addis a baa baa black shirt / Don't lose your wool" – a true Cockney "art work"'.[69]

* * *

10. Jones revising, c. 1935

Revising *In Parenthesis* in mid-November 1935, he felt like 'an unpracticed & ignorant driver trying to control a whole team of very restive horses on a steep path – in fact some of the horses seemed to be oxen & some mules'. He thought 'the best things are in Parts III, IV & VII, especially the last part'. He now inserted into the centre of the poem the boast of Dai Greatcoat, the archetypal soldier. This he composed by repeatedly splitting material for new insertions – a procedure that continued into correcting proof. By December 1935, he thought 'the revision ... virtually finished' but continued revising whenever he looked at a section not read for a while. He had quoted bits of C. K. Scott Moncrieff's translation of *The Song of Roland*, but preferring Hague's new translation (in which the death of Oliver made him weep), changed all the quotations to that.[70]

Having emended and added to the typescript, Jones was now rewriting the whole, telling Ede 'there is still so much I really dislike', adding 'I feel limp & dissatisfied & wonder why I've troubled to do the damn thing at all. Its pretty good tripe in long stretches you know but here & there I still like it.' In February 1936, he gave the numbered divisions titles. Burns visited and took the last of the second full manuscript to Hague for typing.[71]

At the beginning of March, Hague began sending Jones the new typescript, which helped him to see it objectively. He found Part 4 'much better than' he had thought and 'quite enjoyed' the jokes 'like somebody else's stuff, after all this while'. But he continued to have doubts: 'it seems utterly bad in places – in most places in fact – but I'm incapable now of forming a judgement.'* Revision and proofreading seemed endless.[72]

On 23 March, Jones dined with Dawson, who was in Sidmouth after suffering a nervous collapse. Every afternoon they walked together or rode a bus to the top of Peak Hill, where they walked on Mutter's Moor, or to the top of neighbouring Salcombe Hill, where they walked in forests and heather. He gave Dawson 'most of' In Parenthesis to read and, to his immense relief ('thank God'), Dawson liked it. He recommended notes, so, in April, Jones started writing what became eighty pages of them. After deleting a great many, on 25 July he sent them to Burns for typing.[73]

Intending to illustrate In Parenthesis with wood engravings, in March Jones made 'some drawings'. One became the frontispiece (fig. 11), which he regarded as integral to the poem. In it he models an infantryman on the remembered tomb effigy at Ottery St Mary (fig. 7). Most of his clothing torn away and with one shoe missing (like the one-bare-footed medieval Welsh soldiers in drawings he had seen reproduced in J. R. Green's A Short History of the English People [1892] and like Jones during the barrage in 1917), the infantryman raises his elbows awkwardly from burned flesh or in self-protection. By juxtaposition of nearness and distance the rats on the lower right approximate in scale the men on fatigue above them, evoking the problematic relationship in the poem between rats, who by behaving naturally 'redeem the time of our uncharity', and soldiers.[74] The sparsely delineated area on the right (freed from perspective and bringing background forward) and tonal equivalence between foreground and background render him one with his setting – he is the waste land personified. And because the background is tonally darker, the

---

* Symptomatic of depression, his indecisiveness was also temperamentally innate. Readers familiar with the Myers-Briggs personality test will surmise that Jones belonged to the one per cent of the population which is Introverted, Intuitive, Thinking, and Perceiving (i.e. Procrastinating) – the sort of person who is highly self-critical and decides with difficulty.

11. Frontispiece, *In Parenthesis*, 1936

visual suggestion is that he is behind it, a giant symbolically equivalent to it all. The metamorphic reversibility of figure and ground has its counterpart in the allusive subtext of the poem tending to break through the surface narrative. In 1944 he would exhibit the frontispiece under the title 'The Victim'.

Because unwilling to go 'through it all again in another medium — another matter of years', Jones decided not to engrave illustrations. Now he wanted it to be 'simply printed ... without embellishments or additions of any kind', but he would always regret not engraving illustrations.[75]

In March 1936, the Germans reoccupied the Rhineland, and, like most in Britain, Jones approved. He was 'very worked up about Germany & these nasty type of Frog' and wished 'we could pall up to Germany proper & let the other buggers do what they choose'. Drawing and painting again, he sent Prudence one of his first pictures since his breakdown. He made for himself a drawing of Germany as 'a nice big girl' with her foot in the Rhine 'only for my private entertainment'. By the end of the summer, he completed five watercolours, which showed the same spontaneous character as those done in 1932.[76]

In February 1936, Rex Nan Kivell at the Redfern Gallery proposed an exhibition. He was New Zealand born – charming, encouraging, obviously homosexual. Jones liked him and respected his feeling for art. Ede undertook to organise the exhibition, gathering paintings from storage at the Tate, from Howell, the Brockley house, and various galleries. The pictures were, Jones thought, 'of "the second line"', though he liked many, especially one of a lynx (mistakenly called *Hyena* in the catalogue). After the exhibition opened, he added and rearranged so that, he felt, his pictures had never looked better together. The exhibition ran 2–25 April, and received accolades in the press, the critics especially praising *Heat Wave, Chelsea*, which Kenneth Clark bought. Jones managed to come up to London for a day to see the show and meet Helen Sutherland. At Nan Kivell's urging, he contracted to sell all future pictures through the Redfern Gallery.[77]

Soon after the opening, Jones received notice from the 7 & 5 Society that, a vote having been taken in which he had received only two votes, he was no longer a member. He regretted not having resigned a year earlier, 'but in a way', he wrote Ede, 'it's much nicer to be hooked out – certainly whatever happened I suppose my stuff would no longer "go with" their particular goodness.' Nicholson was purging the Society of representational art. Jones admired Nicholson's new abstract work. Much of the best art now was abstract, he thought, as is inevitable when modern man loses most of his non-aesthetic values.[*] Jones considered all art essentially abstract, 'pure abstraction' being a conscious isolation of the first artistic principle, the juxtaposition of forms.[78]

There were sales at the Redfern, but Nan Kivell would not disclose what Jones had earned. In June, Ede interceded, learning that the amount was £206.6s.1d., which was not the windfall it may seem, since Nan Kivell made only partial, delayed payments. The exhibition had been, in a sense, a gift from Ede, who hinted in vain that Jones might reciprocate by giving him a painting.[79]

* By 1960 Jones would modify his view of abstract art, considering no abstract painting great and seeing 'certain manifestations' of the abstract movement as 'almost as tedious and silly and as uninformed by the mind . . . as that dead, bloody academism that we loathed so much. In fact it is, I suppose, the new academism.' He doubted whether any art emptied of 'creatureliness . . . can be the proper subject for a humane work.'

In late July or August 1936, Jones visited Dawson in Yorkshire for over three weeks. Dawson commissioned him to paint the view from a bedroom window as a way to give him money and paid him four times the going rate – his daughter Christina remembered the price as £100.[80]

Near the end of July, Jones and Hague visited de la Mare in the Faber offices in Russell Square to ensure that Hague would print *In Parenthesis*. Jones wanted to help him financially and wanted to use Gill's Joanna type, which only Hague's press possessed. He wanted the pages to be foolscap-size with the text 'printed large' in long double columns 'like a newspaper' but with wide margins to make it look like a poem. 'Not "artistic" in any way', it was 'to look like … the new *Tablet Publishing Company's Memorandum & Article of Association* … with a limp greyish cover stiffened at back'. Hague had printed a sample crown folio with two columns in 12-point Joanna.[81]

Jones would have returned to Sidmouth but could not afford it. He had not received a penny from Nan Kivell. And the Artist's Annuity Fund had reduced weekly amounts, which he had begun receiving not long after his breakdown, from £2 to £1.[82] On 30 July 1936, he went to Rock to stay.

He painted *Window at Rock*, his most important watercolour since his breakdown (fig. 12) and, he thought, one of his best. The lower window frame stands architecturally unattached like a sculpture of light. Vine leaves soften the straightness of mullions and casing. The eye flashes back and forth as this fidgety picture opens from light foreground to darker, more focused background. Drawing combines with line-less painting as in some of his 1932 pictures. Painting it precipitated another emotional 'misrub'. To Helen, who bought the picture, he seemed worried chiefly about becoming ill again, so that the beginning of symptoms intensified them.[83]

*　*　*

Since mid-September 1935, Prudence had been journeying in the Middle East, and he worried about her. Through letters, he fretfully followed her progress as she crossed the Sinai on camelback and contracted blood poisoning and malaria. Between March and July 1936, she received none of his letters, so he sent telegrams. After a summer in Palestine, she sailed home from Aleppo. (Her voyage underlies that from Aleppo to London of the much-afflicted *Mary* at the centre of *The Anathemata* – Prudence's middle name was Mary.) In August they enjoyed a three-week holiday-reunion in Sidmouth.[84]

Jones submitted *In Parenthesis*, revised and, he thought, finished, to de la Mare probably in early August 1936 – a typescript with manuscript insertions. On 1 October, de la Mare wrote that the delayed response was owing to everyone in the firm wanting to read it slowly. It was 'splendid', Faber would be proud to publish it, but there were 'two knotty points'. One was printing in double columns, which would discourage sales. Jones agreed to forego that. The

12. *Window at Rock*, 1936

other was hand-setting by Hague, which would be too expensive and preclude keeping standing type for reprinting. But Jones insisted. So they compromised: the Temple Press at Letchworth would machine-set the type, which Hague would correct, adjust, and print.* This cost extra, diminishing royalties.† Jones

* Hague did not, as generally assumed, set the type (Gill's Petra). *In Parenthesis* was badly set, as noticed by reviewers, who complained of words eliding, making reading difficult. This was the fault of the Temple Press setting-machines, not Hague, who probably corrected enjambment where space allowed. Physically the book was not clearly readable. Reused ever since, the poor typesetting continues to discourage readers.

† Royalties were 10% for the first thousand copies, 12½% for the second thousand, 15% for 2,000–5,000, and, thereafter, 20%. For all paperbacks he was to receive 10%.

asked for and got a £15 advance upon signing to cover the cost of typing a clean copy for proofreading.[85]

Now a regular at the Fort, he enjoyed fellowship there and friendships in town. He, the managers and their family (the Griffins), 'little Tucker the porter', the maids, and a long-time resident, Miss Scopes, formed a little community. One day in the spring, returning from a walk, he presented a bouquet of snowdrops to Mrs Griffin as if, she thought, he was giving it to his mother. At Tucker's request, he painted him a small view of Sidmouth. He enjoyed conversations at the bars nearby. Prudence wrote, 'It makes me scream with laughter to think of all those racing-grey-hound owners shaking you by the hand in The Marine.' Those he knew in town included Charles and Barbara Evans (he a schoolmaster sharing his Welsh enthusiasms); a priest named Murray; the Misses Jervois; retired Colonel L. H. Hastings; a teacher named Deanesley; a woman named Spunday; his doctor, E. E. Lightwood, with whom he walked the shore and dined at the Fort; and a homosexual couple, who had a good library and liked talking about books.[86]

* * *

On 11 July 1936, civil war broke out in Spain, and British opinion divided. On the left were most intellectuals and artists, including friends of Jones. (Hague and Gill were now near-Communists.) Many Catholics opposed the Republicans for murdering, sometimes after torturing, 6,000 priests and monks and hundreds of nuns – atrocities Jones knew about. Bernard Wall and Grisewood were strongly pro-Franco, and so, Grisewood remembered, was Jones, 'because of his opposition to Communists'. But he was not vehemently partisan. Prudence, who was Pro-Republican, related that in December 1936, Burns's Jesuit brother, George, rejoiced at Franco's troops having '5000 machine guns, ammunition dumps, and 5000 prisoners – wonderful isn't it!' and Jones replied, 'Well, it depends which side you're on.'[87]

More important to Jones was the abdication of Edward VIII, the most popular person in Britain since publicly sympathising with the unemployed in 1932. Jones especially admired him for embracing and kissing a limbless man in a home for mutilated soldiers. He knew from Grisewood that Edward loved poetry, could recite from Shakespeare's plays, and cared for the cultural well-being of society. Jones thought him the modern Richard II, whom 'the people loved'. When, in November 1936, Edward remarked that 'Something must be done' about depressed mining areas in South Wales and The Times leader blamed him for interfering in politics, Jones was convinced that powerful forces were aligned against him. To these Jones now ascribed the pressure to abdicate, for which he did not consider Edward's marrying a divorcée valid cause. Edward abdicated on 10 December and sailed from England on the 11th, the anniversary, Jones bitterly noted, of the killing of the last authentic prince of Wales in 1282. At the Fort, he argued heatedly about the abdication with a vicar, who exclaimed, 'But it's a matter of divorce, and you, you're a Catholic!', to which he replied, 'And you're an Anglican. Your religion is founded on a divorce.' He had Edward in mind when including 'SECRET PRINCES' in his dedication to *In Parenthesis* and when inserting into Part 4, 'sweet princes by malignant interests deprived' (66). In the dark days to come he would regret Edward's departure.[88]

During the winter of 1937, Jones went to a pub for lunch in nearby Lyme Regis to meet the great Welsh scholar Sir John Edward Lloyd and the novelist Anthony Powell, a meeting probably arranged by Charles Evans. After introductions, Jones plunged immediately into Welsh history and archaeology, and continued, to their dismay, all afternoon, through supper, and into the evening.[89]

Ede resigned from the Tate. He could no longer bear its director, James B. Manson, a lazy philistine averse to modern art – Jones thought Manson 'ghastly' and fully sympathised. Ede had built a house near Tangier and at the end of July was moving there. Jones returned to London to see the family for the last time at Elm Row, and they dined on sausages among the packing cases. For him their home had been 'a harbour' in a city he now loathed. He said, 'I do not think I could have stood those years without coming.' Just the possibility of visiting had made him happy. On Sunday afternoons for the rest of his life, he would remember the Ede teas and how he 'used to look forward to them'. (Having quit, Ede forfeited his chance to replace Manson, dismissed in 1938, but Jones would console him, saying that the Tate was part of the '"academic" painting world' which was 'fundamentally bogus – a vast mis-apprehension of the nature of the arts'.) Ede had been important to Jones personally, for the sale of many of his paintings, and for the promised publication of *In Parenthesis*. Now, Jones thought, London would be 'a desert'.[90]

*   *   *

The fresh typescript became another working draft as Jones continued revising. In November 1936, he was amazed to discover that, when not feeling unwell, he was every day improving the work. Among late insertions are: the centre of Dai Greatcoat's boast (81–2) and the near-final section including his now favourite segment, the visitation of the dead by the Queen of the Wood (185–6), one of the most poignant passages in literature. After he corrected galley proofs, Hague printed page proofs, which Jones read slowly – otherwise he got 'unwell again' – and revised 'quite a lot' the whole way through. Hague printed new proofs and, by not charging him for changes, allowed him to continue revising. Jones moved to Pigotts to work more closely with him, and changed 'a good many things'.[91]

In January 1937, Jones saw the blurb for *In Parenthesis*, in which T. S. Eliot anonymously calls it 'a distillation of the essence of war books' and '*chanson de gestes* [song of deeds] of the Cockney in the Great War ... and behind them ... their ancestors who fought and toiled and died in the Britain of the Celt and of the Saxon ... one of the ... most exciting books that we have published'. Eliot was the first to recognise it as 'an early epic', like Homer's oral epics, rather than Virgil's literary epic.[92]

Completing the book left Jones feeling 'a vacuum'. It had been 'something always to fall to whenever possible during this long long weary unwellness', and without it he longed more than ever to be able to 'get down to painting properly again'. He came up from Sidmouth for the publication party on 10 June, his 'nerves' becoming 'bad again' as soon as he arrived and began seeing people.[93]

He received six author's copies, sending one to Laurence Binyon, who responded on 8 July 1937 that he thought it 'wonderful' with 'a wholeness of tissue throughout, in spite of a strange complexity of elements'. The soldiers 'are *there*, quite near & real ... I see, I hear, I smell with an acute distinctness ... this is not just a piece of writing, but of living ... through what it makes one's heart faint to think of.' Jones was 'greatly encouraged' by his letter.[94]

The reviews were mostly laudatory. James Agate in the *Daily Express* called it a 'masterpiece', the best book on the war likely ever to appear – a judgement endorsed by subsequent reviewers. In a review in the *Times Literary Supplement* – anonymous, as all its reviews then were – Herbert Read wrote what, for thirty years, Jones would think 'the best thing' on *In Parenthesis*: 'this is an epic of war ... like no other war-book because for the first time' all the realistic sensory experiences of infantrymen

> have been woven into a pattern which, while retaining all the authentic realism of the event, has the heroic ring which we associate with the old *chansons de gestes*. It is almost inconceivable that this should have been done without affectation, without parody or pedantry. But the miracle is here – a book which we can accept as a true record of our suffering and as a work of art in the romantic tradition of Malory and the *Mabinogion*. But the possibility is clear to those who realize that to be romantic in this tradition is to be profoundly true to human experience ... It is beautifully objective, and the words are as hard and bright as the things they signify ... But into this purely literary texture the author has threaded details which were not in literature before: not only the equipment *and* technique of modern warfare, but the slang, the songs, the sentiments of the private soldiers ...

To the realism and humour and inherent poetry of this book the author has then added a complex network of literary allusion, not awkwardly or wilfully, but because it was in the texture of his thoughts and experience ... The most sustained example of this literary allusion is the long 'boast' of a Welsh soldier in Part 4 ... which is as fine a poem as any modern poet has written ... this book is one of the most remarkable literary achievements of our time.

An acquaintance of Jones – Wheen had introduced them in 1932 – Read* published another review in the *London Mercury*, in which he was the first to call Jones 'a great poet'.[95]

The avalanche of rave reviews surprised Jones and delighted the people at Faber. De la Mare ordered a second printing, but sales then slowed owing, Jones realised, to the international political climate: 'recent preoccupation with, & fear of, newer, & dreadfuller, & equally meaningless wars has made ... the war I wrote about ... of very remote interest to anyone'.[96]

* * *

Jones and Eliot were seeing more of each other. In the summer of 1936, at dinner with Eliot and others, Jones had liked him 'a great lot'. In the second week in July 1937 at Faber, they talked alone for the first time. Eliot said with apologies that *In Parenthesis* reminded him of Kipling. Jones said, 'Yes, I can believe it.' In the poem, soldiers sing 'Casey Jones' (68), which Eliot told him was his favourite song, one he sang to himself while shaving. Jones found him 'quiet & unpretentious to talk with'.[97]

In Parenthesis is the only modern epic poem in English. It makes vividly real the physicality of the Great War and imbues it with broad, rich cultural resonance. Its romance associations convey frightful emotional intensity. Major historical and legendary battles alluded to are calamitous (Troy, Catraeth, Camlann, Roncesvalles), except Agincourt, which is seen through allusions to *Henry V* as a battle meaningless to the common soldier. The implied central archetype is the dying god of fertility ritual, who symbolises the waste land and its renewal, here consisting of the goodness of infantrymen turning physical desolation into a metaphysical garden. In this respect, the poem takes literary modernism beyond irony.

* Jones respected Read for having served bravely in one of the best line regiments in the army and liked his 'detachment, reasonableness & modesty', his 'remarkable perception & sensitivity as a critic & a creative writer', and his 'sweetness of disposition & kindness'.

When Eliot read it in typescript, he considered it 'a work of genius'. In 1954 W. H. Auden declared it 'the greatest book about the First World War'. In 1980, Graham Greene placed it 'among the great poems of the century'. In 1991, the war historian Michael Howard wrote of it as 'the most remarkable work of literature to emerge from either world war'. In 1996, Adam Thorpe wrote that 'it towers above any other prose or verse memorial of' the Great War '(indeed, of any war)'. The best work on war in English, it may be the greatest work of British literature between the wars. Jones's transforming revisions made after his breakdown are one of the great aesthetic and existential achievements of twentieth-century literature. 'I think I just turned the corner,' he wrote, 'but O Mary! what a conjuring trick it was.'[98]

Jones visited Prudence at Stanmer House for the second week of July 1937. On Sunday afternoon, the 11th, W. B. Yeats – a friend of her sister, Betty – came to tea. Informed in advance that Jones would be there, Yeats paused in the doorway and slowly bowed from the waist, intoning, 'I salute the author of *In Parenthesis*.' He proceeded to praise the work in such extravagant terms and in such grand style that Jones suspected he was being mocked. Then the ladies present gathered round Yeats, who, as Jones remembered, began 'muttering half audible "bardic" verse over the tea-cups'.[1] Later in the week Yeats returned, and, as Prudence wrote to Edward Hodgkin, 'We had a pretty long session of W-Bloody-bore-Yeats. He read a long long long thing (it took all the beautiful afternoon). Luckily I couldn't hear it all but what I did hear sounded a bit political & quite certainly fascist.'

Alone together, Jones and Prudence amused themselves for hours looking through old scrapbooks in the library. Some of the time, he worked at his new, 'Balaam's Ass' writing, as he had previously done only at Hartland and at Mill House and here. Later he would say about staying at Stanmer, 'There was a lot of marble – well, it was like heaven, really.'[2]

From there he went to Westridge Farm, where Binyon talked about prosody, which Jones thought unimportant and uninteresting. But they found common ground in the Arthurian tradition.[3]

Jones then went to Pigotts, for a reunion with John-Baptist Reeves (now the editor of the *Catholic Herald*), the source of one of his favourite sayings, 'It is the nature of iron to rust.' There he met and became friendly with a new generation of Dominicans: Victor White, Thomas Gilby, Richard Kehoe, and Illtud Evans. He also met Michael Richey, a nineteen-year-old Gill apprentice, who took his meals with the Hagues and now, therefore, with him. At their first meeting, Jones talked, Richey remembered, 'endlessly about the Great War'. Though Jones was forty-two, Richey felt no difference in age between them. He would later say that Jones was the most acutely sensitive ('raw') person he had ever met. Also present were eleven Gill grandchildren who – though Jones was, Petra said, 'shy of children' – thought him 'lovely', a sort of favourite uncle. 'Everybody loved Dai', Michael Hague later said.[4]

While at Pigotts, in a tiny, dark, north-facing room at the back of Gill's workshop, Jones painted *The Farm Door* (fig. 1), his best picture since *Window at Rock*. In it he reverses indoor dimness and outdoor lightness. Offsetting

1. *The Farm Door*, 1937

the stabilising effect of horizontal and vertical lines are shadows and erratic linear shapes that make this work subtly frantic. It is a picture about the unifying complementarity of inside and outside, vegetative and animal nature, curves and straight lines.

In early September 1937 at Rock, Jones received word that his mother was ill and returned to London, staying at 3 Glebe Place, then at Grisewood's mezzanine flat at 61 Kings Road. She was now senile, which was for him, 'bloody unnerving' – he told a friend, 'I mind that more than anything.' On 22 September, she died of a stroke. He spent that night with Prudence, who wrote 'he was pretty well done-in and shaky poor dear'. She walked him in the morning to Grisewood's flat. His mother had been 'part of' his 'landscape'. To his surprise, she continued to feel real, but he was anxious and felt homeless. Not long after her burial, he told Grisewood that his favourite songs were ' "Frankie and Johnnie" and "I'm going there [heaven] to meet my mother" – I do love that one.'⁵ He and Gill would design her gravestone, which Gill carved (for a fee of £15.15s.0d.).

After the funeral, Jones accompanied his father to North Wales, and found Rhos changed for the worse, a 'wilderness of villas & bungalows'. The ancient fishing weir was gone. St Trillo's Chapel, 'cleaned out and cared for, . . . lost half its numinous feeling'. Suburban sprawl covered even the lower slope of *Bryn Euryn*. At Holywell where had been a green hillside sloping to the sea were now rows of red-brick bungalows.⁶

They stayed with Effie and her husband, George Meek, who wondered why David had brought a large trunk. On the day of their departure, David asked to use the dustbin and proceeded to bring down armfuls of empty (mostly beer) bottles that he had transported from London. He explained that he had been in the midst of moving (from Glebe Place to Grisewood's flat in the King's Road), but they thought this extremely odd and were 'somewhat on their dignity'.⁷

Jones and his father went to Chester to visit his Aunt Polly and his Uncle Joe Jones, a buyer of linens for Browns, who fascinated David by explaining different qualities of weaves. David strolled through the town and round its medieval walls, gazing at the River Dee, the Roman Deva (*A* 67, 69, 136). He told his uncle that he was 'impressed . . . by the historical relics of the city'.⁸

After returning to London, Jones stayed briefly in Brockley, then retreated to King's Road but telephoned or visited his father daily. By November he was back at Glebe Place. With war coming, Tom Burns told him he needed a stout pair of shoes and a good overcoat and gave him his long Savile Row coat of green coachman's cloth, which Jones dyed black, shrinking it to his size, though it fell to his ankles and he looked odd wearing it.⁹

About this time, outside Harrods, he came upon a half dozen unemployed miners from the Rhondda singing Welsh hymns for pennies. He disliked hymns because 'the same thing goes on verse after verse', and he thought they lost all feeling when sung by organised choirs to accompaniment. Yet here, now, sotto voce, 'with the noise of the traffic . . . & rain pouring down, the purity of sound, the reality' made him gasp with feeling. They sang for him his favourite hymn, *Bryn Calfaria* ('Calvary Hill').[10] *

* * *

A new friend was lovely, tall Diana Creagh, renting the ground-floor flat in 3 Glebe Place and working with the foreign exchange at the telephone company. A frequent visitor to the Burns flat, she was secretly in love with Tom, who was involved with Ann Bowes-Lyon, a cousin of the Queen Consort. One evening when Burns was out, Jones asked Diana up for a drink. They chatted, she in a chair facing the fireplace, he on the divan. He asked her to come sit beside him. She did. He put his right arm around her, placing his right hand on her breast. She stiffened, he withdrew his arm, she returned to her chair.[11]

In 1938, she would move from Glebe Place in order to extricate herself emotionally from Burns, but she and Jones remained friends. He aroused in her 'a strange protective feeling'. She bought him meals and once, at least, visited him in Sidmouth. When she told him that he had a calming influence on her, he was surprised and said, 'I've never been other than pretty neurotic and agitated within myself.' They visited some of her friends, including Margaret Smith, a painter, who asked him, 'Is it true that you mix your paints with spittle?' Grimacing, he admitted that it sometimes was.[12]

Through Diana, he met Violet Clifton, who had him to dinner with Oliver St John Gogarty, the original of 'stately plump Buck Mulligan' in Joyce's *Ulysses*. Gogarty was a wealthy, long-winded monologuist who enjoyed a flexible relationship with truth. Jones later confided to Grisewood that Gogarty was an 'awfully boring sort of chap ... What *conceit* and noise these about-town kinds of Irishmen have.' But in 1951, he would like Gogarty's *As I was Going Down Sackville Street* for recording Joyce's declaration that boatbuilding is as much 'art' as making a poem, a statement consonant with Maritain.[13]

At La Commercio, Jones, Grisewood, and Herbert Read were conversing about history over a meal. Read questioned him about his antipathy to Saxons. Not wishing to discuss it, Jones became 'rather glassy eyed' and said, as though he had just passed one in the road, 'Well, visually they were so disgusting, I mean all that ghastly cross-gartering, like puttees in the war.'[14]

---

* In later years he would be moved, sometimes to tears, when Welsh rugby fans sang hymns during radio broadcasts. That surprised him, since he regarded himself as unemotional, and convinced him that 'this blood thing is strange & strong'. But then the Welsh also loved brass bands, persuading him that they were a 'mixture of deep-felt sensitivity and *total vulgarity*'.

In 1936, Tom Burns had introduced him to the novelist Graham Greene and his wife, whom Jones afterwards sometimes visited. Once on his way across Clapham Common to see them, he was twice accosted by prostitutes, like a character in a Greene novel.[15]

Jones often met Prudence in the company of the Hodgkin brothers. Thomas, now married, was in Cumberland teaching philosophy to unemployed miners. Edward was on the editorial staff of the *Manchester Guardian* and more often in London. He introduced Jones and Prudence to a circle of young Oxford fellows and dons including Isaiah Berlin, Maurice Bowra, John Sparrow, and Stuart Hampshire.[16]

Prudence became sexually involved with Edward, straining her relationship with Jones. When she and Edward planned to go off together on holidays – a few weeks in France in 1937, a week in Dublin in the autumn of 1938 – Jones experienced jealous anguish. He argued with her over the Dublin trip throughout a (for her) 'gruelling day' visiting galleries. At Christmas, when invited by him to Sidmouth and by Edward to the Cotswolds, she felt 'torn in two' and stayed home. Her affair with Edward would last until 1939.[17]

* * *

Cleverdon visited Jones in Sidmouth in January to discuss adapting *In Parenthesis* for radio. Recalling their aborted Malory project, he suggested that Jones break his idleness by making a picture 'about *Morte D'Arthur*', and within a week Jones began one. Bringing it near completion took seven weeks, partly because drawing brought back his worst symptoms, and partly because he needed daylight to work effectively but felt well enough to work only after dinner. Working intermittently was frustrating. To conserve energy, he stopped writing.[18]

The subject of the picture, entitled *Guinever*, is Lancelot bursting through a window into a chamber where captive Guinevere sleeps naked (Malory, XIX, 6). To draw Lancelot, he posed nude before the wardrobe mirror, bending his torso to imitate a kneeling knight in the thirteenth-century Winchester Psalter (fig. 2) to evoke 'veneration'. Then, wearing only a shirt, he drew a study of his right leg. He neglected to lock the door. A maid entered, 'gave a startled noise and fled', an experience he found 'highly embarrassing'.[19]

In this challenging painting (fig. 3), rescue is redemption, and 'Eros & Agape kiss each other'. Sleeping knights in the foreground lie like tomb effigies, evoking the dead. They derive from the Ottery St Mary effigy

2. Study for *Guinever*, 1938

3. *Guinever*, 1940

(chapter 9, fig. 7) and Mantegna's dead Christ.[20] Guinevere's nudity implies sex but is de-eroticised by her degendered upper body and awkward posture. Lancelot enters on the right through a barred window. He is hard to see because he is tonally one with the wall and windows, and he bends and steps so awkwardly. Guinevere's bed corresponds to the clothed altar behind her, and she, therefore, to the Eucharist. Her affinity with the tabernacle, its curtains draped to suggest a vulva, is emphasised by the altar also having its adjacent sleepers before it. Church and home are associated by the altar near her head complementing the hearth at her foot – the latter based on a drawing Jones had asked Gill to make of the hearth at Pigotts to use as a study.[21] The painting is haunting, like a dream in slow motion in this arched, tomb-like place of fallen bodies and sleep. Autobiographically, it is intriguing since Jesus, Lancelot, and the artist symbolically overlap – visible on the calf of Lancelot's right leg is Jones's battle scar. His Guinevere was, of course, Prudence Pelham.

Jones liked the picture but doubted others would. Its form suits the subject, reflecting medieval *horror vacui*. Unlike his pre-breakdown paintings, this is a constellation of parts, possibly reflecting his now sporadic method of painting. If, in the vividness of its images, *In Parenthesis* is a painter's poem, this is a writer's painting, bristling with explicit cultural referents and specific symbols. The 'things in it', he wrote to Ede, are 'packed tight & rather confused & [it] takes you an hour to see'. Its form is, he thought, 'Celtic', 'an extraordinary complexity and intricacy' that would characterise most of his important paintings from now on. While unlike any previous or contemporary picture, it nevertheless implies what he once told a visiting artist, 'I am a Pre-Raphaelite.'[22] He virtually finished it in March 1938 but would make minor adjustments over the next two years and date it '1940'.

In June 1938 he painted *Cricket Match in Sidmouth* but could still only work at night by electric light, which was unsuited to painting. So he reverted solely to writing, which kept him awake till 1.30 or 2. By June, he added forty pages to his (not yet entitled) Balaam's Ass manuscript. He didn't know 'if any of it is any good', he wrote to Grisewood, but writing made him feel less useless.[23]

* * *

He was notified that he was to receive the Hawthornden Prize, then the only important British literary award, for *In Parenthesis*. Having to go to London to give an acceptance speech terrified him. And leaving Sidmouth was wrenching because, unable to take all his work with him, he had to destroy manuscripts and sketches. On the hot afternoon of 26 June 1938, he entered a jammed Aeolian Hall in Bond Street. In the silence after the announcement of the winner, trembling 'like a taut sail in a wind', he gave his speech, saying that in writing *In Parenthesis* he

felt, more clearly than before, the unity of the Arts. Those same problems that face the painter confront the writer in almost identical proportion.

Form and content, the juxtaposition of ideas and shapes within a determined scheme, to so state the contingent as to display the necessary – an awareness of dissimilar threads of tradition and a conditioning of those traditions by our own contemporary sensitivity, the making of an object with its own way of behaviour; not so much to describe, imitate, or represent, but rather . . . to show anew under another species some already existing reality.

To make substantially and really present in one's medium what already is.

To do in a ritual manner what has already been done with actual immolation.

Hoping notoriety would boost sales but otherwise indifferent to the honour, he was glad for the prize, a cheque for £100 – 'heavens! one needs this bloody money badly'. Faber had Hague print another thousand copies. Congratulatory letters poured in. Evelyn Waugh wrote, 'yours is not only the sort of book that ought to get' this prize, 'it is the book'.[24]

* * *

Asked his political affiliation on the prize acceptance form, Jones had written 'none'. He was less interested in politics than any of his friends.* But, now compelled to attend to international affairs, he was, like most ex-servicemen, pro-appeasement. War would finish him as an artist, he thought, and bring civilisation to an end. The current behaviour of Germany did not warrant that.[25]

He accepted Hitler's portrayal of National Socialism (in speeches published in *The Times*) as a revolt by the dispossessed, the unemployed,

---

* Only twice did Jones vote in national elections: in 1918 'to get off parade for a few hours', he voted Liberal for Lloyd George; and in 1945 when, despite being put off by campaign rhetoric, at the urging of Julian Asquith, he went to the voting station undecided. The Conservative incumbent, Sir William Davison, was being berated by a Labour supporter for his '*dreadful* record': voting '*against* sanctions on Italy, *against* intervention in Spain & *for* Chamberlain right through'. So Jones voted for him. Later, protesting against threatened cuts to the BBC, Jones wrote to Davison saying that, 'a very un-politically minded person', he had voted for the Conservative party as 'the least materialist' and the most likely to 'guard the heritage of this country'.

and the humiliated against economic depression and the unfairly punitive Treaty of Versailles. The broad negativism of fascism targeted many of Jones's bugbears, including international finance and capitalist-industrial exploitation of workers. He wrote to Ede, 'I see this so-called Dictatorship v "Democracy" business as largely an affair of the sword against money.' Germany's expansionism seemed no different from that of other nations in the previous century, whose now established empires were hypocritically opposing it.[26]

The Nazis also opposed Marxism, which Jones, Grisewood, Burns, and Wall saw as ideologically ridiculous. The leftist criterion of whether a nation, faction, or movement was bourgeois or anti-bourgeois Jones thought silly. The 'unreality' of 'The Left League & Co . . . terrified' him, and he thought Soviet prioritising the state, collectivism, and egalitarianism guaranteed mediocrity, denied priority of the person, and ignored the psychology of ego-motivation.[27]

Tom Burns remembered, 'We couldn't bear the Communists because they were atheists and were monstrously unjust.' Jones knew about the persecution of Christianity in Mexico and the Soviet Union. He was fully apprised of Stalin's deliberate starvation of tens of millions of Ukrainians. A Chelsea pub acquaintance of his, met through Diana Creagh (Vladimir Korostovetz, an agent of the Ukrainian hetman, Pavlo Skoropadskyi), showed him smuggled photographs as proof. (Bolsheviks had murdered Korostovetz's mother and brother and raped and murdered his favourite cousin.) Compared to Stalin, Hitler had been gentle. And Jones thought that as a former front-line fighter (also wounded in Mametz Wood), Hitler could be trusted to avoid war.[28]

Jones had read a truncated edition of *Mein Kampf* (1933), which Diana Creagh had lent to Burns. Jones thought it 'made up of roughly equal parts of common sense and absolute rubbish'. He agreed with much of its naming of evils but not the brutal means proposed to correct them. He found irrational and repugnant the Nazi interpretation of life as communal narcissism. Much of Hitler's thinking was, he thought, ridiculous: a narrow falsifying sense of history, absurd racist biology, and idiotic anthropology. He disliked Hitler's crudeness, his relentless moralising, and his hatred of Jews.[29]

Sharing the then general British bias against Jews,[*] imbibed probably from his mother and encouraged by Gill, Jones associated Jews with the business world, which he detested, and international finance, which he abhorred. Not essentially racial, his bias – unknown to most of his friends and not present in his published writing (or 99.99% of his unpublished writing) – coexisted with genuine affection for Jewish friends. And, though

* See Tony Judt, 'Edge People', *New York Review of Books*, 25/3/2010.

he generally disliked art dealers, of the two he admired, Freddy Meyer of the Meyer Gallery, a 'genuine chap' with perception and honesty, was a Jew. (The other was Ernest Brown of the Leicester Gallery.) The Chelsea Group regarded Jew-hating as unchristian; Jones had disliked the 'anti-Perfidious Jew stuff' in St Augustine; and he now opposed Nazi anti-Semitism, which, he agreed with Dawson, was scapegoating. German persecution of the Jews had worried him since the passing of the Nuremburg Laws in 1935.[30]

In 1937 or '38, Jones was visited at Glebe Place by a senior cultural attaché of the German embassy who was amusing, erudite, delightful. After conversing for a while, Jones protested Nazi persecution of the Jews. The visitor rose to his feet and fulminated for five minutes on their 'iniquities'. Jones did not argue – there seemed no point. He later related this incident not to demonstrate political virtue (however minimal) but because the German concluded his tirade with 'The Jews, you kick them out the door and they come back in through the window', recalling the Great War song about the Germans, 'Close the door, they're coming through the window, close the window, they're coming through the door' – which he had last heard sung in 1928 by Teddy Wolfe, his 'artist friend, a very jovial chap of Jewish blood'.[31]

In April 1939, Jones summed up his impression of *Mein Kampf* in a letter to Grisewood:

> I'm reading the full edition . . . it is amazingly interesting in all kinds of ways – but pretty terrifying too. God, he's nearly right – but this hate thing mars his whole thing, I feel. I mean it just misses getting over the frontier into the saint thing – he won't stand any nonsense or illusions or talk – but, having got so far, the whole conception of the world in terms of race-struggle (that's what it boils down to) will hardly do . . . Compared with his opponents he is grand, but compared with the saints he is bloody. And I think I mean also by saints – lovers, and all kinds of unifying makers.

He agreed with Hitler's critique of parliamentary democracy as a mediocre form of government, which, long before reading Hitler, he had thought little more than 'plutocracy' (a word Hitler used but Jones had earlier acquired from anti-fascist Dawson), the wealthy alone being able to run for office or influence those who do.[32]

According to Grisewood and Richey, Jones preferred to democracy a pre-Tudor (non-tyrannical), medieval-style monarchy. It would involve an almost sacramental union between ruler and nation – the monarch representing the whole community rather than a political party. He or she would be fully responsible for government as no parliamentarian can be. Yet Richey was convinced that Jones would not have put up with an absolute monarch.[33]

For Jones, the solution to spiritual bankruptcy was not political but cultural and religious. Only a widespread appreciation of symbolic activity as expressing spiritual values could, he thought, fill the vacuum at the heart of modern civilisation. He realised that the Nazis were almost as hostile as Communists to religion, particularly Catholicism. Reviewing Herbert Read's *Poetry and Anarchism* in June 1938, Jones expressed profound scepticism about all things political and, instead, the need to 'keep our vanishing points outside Time'. Three years before, he had advised Thomas Hodgkin, 'Don't get too overcome by this curious type of world of appearances & complicated shadows. There is a magnificent reality behind the bloody mess – I do think that even in my worst moments ... but it's a *bugger* of a difficulty to sustain I must say.' Burns put it succinctly, 'Any notion of David as a fascist is all balls.'[34]

To investigate German politics and culture, Jones, Burns, and Grisewood formed a small study group led by two recent German émigrés: a stern schoolmaster named Egbert Munser and a young Jesuit named Joseph Roggendorf, both vehemently anti-Nazi. (Roggendorf had barely escaped the Gestapo, pursuing him for warning a Jew travelling to Germany against persecution there.) Burns later said, 'David adored Roggy, a very, very intelligent and spiritual man.' Despising Hitler, the two Germans disclosed Nazi atrocities, but these seemed to Jones and his friends unexceptional. Nazi persecution of Jews seemed no different from anti-Semitism throughout much of European history. Suspected of being pro-Nazi, the discussion group was investigated by British Intelligence until the politics of the two Germans was discovered and suspicion lifted.[35] The group disbanded in June 1940, when Roggendorf went to Tokyo to join the faculty of the English Department at Sophia University.

Jones was at Rock throughout the Munich Crisis in September 1938. One of Helen Sutherland's visitors was Leonard Ropner, taking a brief holiday from Hitler. Meeting him in the library, Jones asked, 'How are things going at Munich?' Ropner replied, 'Do you like Mendelssohn?' Never having been sat on quite so effectively, Jones thought that their exchange ought to have been recorded by a Boswell.[36]

On 30 September, the Munich Agreement was signed, approving German occupation of the Sudetenland, as well as an Anglo-German declaration of desire 'never to go to war with one another again'. Relieved, on 18 December, through Jelly d'Aranyi, Jones sent the prime minister, Neville Chamberlain, a copy of *In Parenthesis* 'as an expression of gratitude for all you have done & are continuing to do to mend things in Europe & to save us from the worst'. On 9 January 1939, Chamberlain responded with 'warm thanks for your understanding and sympathetic letter'. As hostility to Chamberlain's policy grew on all sides, Jones remained steadfast in his admiration of him. He thought Chamberlain's statesmanship informed by 'specifically "Christian virtues" . . . out of a kind of real "innocence" . . . that takes no account of the other party's faults & ill-will but' but is 'careful that . . . no reproach, or ill-humour, or insufficient understanding on his part shall be the cause of hostility or breakdown'. A year later, he still thought Chamberlain 'magnificent'.[37]

* * *

Jones left Rock for London on 5 October 1938, and was then invited to Oxford by D'Arcy, who was now master of Campion Hall, which had moved in 1935 to a new building on Brewer Street. At Oxford, he visited Robin Hodgkin and the Dominicans at Blackfriars. Among those he conversed with at Campion was the poet Roger Venables, who usually lunched there. He visited and talked long with Charles Williams, an Anglican author of theological romances and literary criticism – Jones later said he knew him 'very well'. They shared enthusiasm for Hopkins, Eliot, medieval Wales, and the Arthurian tradition. Jones read in proof Williams's church history, *The Descent of the Dove* (1939).[38]

D'Arcy introduced Jones to Katharine Asquith, the fifty-three-year-old war-widowed daughter-in-law of the former Prime Minister. She was gentle, quiet, astute, devout (a Catholic convert), and admired *In Parenthesis*. Jones liked her.[39]

She introduced him to her son Julian, who, having read Greats, was studying agriculture at Oxford. He lived in a house in St Aldgate's with David Harlick, Peter Wood, Charles Hope Petty-Fitzmaurice (the Marquis of Lansdowne), and Hugh Fraser (son of Lord Lovat). Jones visited in the evenings, drinking whisky with them and enthralling them with his conversation. He called Lansdowne 'Charlie Wag' and Fraser, who was 6 feet 2 inches tall, 'Huge Frazer'. Through Julian, he met eighteen-year-old Clarissa Spencer-Churchill (niece of Winston) and Ronald Knox, the Newman chaplain, whom Jones liked 'very much – he was obviously a deeply spiritual man and an absolutely first class' Classical scholar.[40]

With Prudence he visited Isaiah Berlin and Stuart Hampshire at All Souls. The main topic of conversation was the Munich Crisis. Hampshire later remembered Jones wishing Edward VIII would fly to Germany and secure peace.[41]

In mid-November, Jones returned to London and, suffering increased emotional distress, fled to Sidmouth, where he resumed writing, which went, as usual, slowly. He told Grisewood:

> I've got a miserable feeling that my new thing is not so 'tight' & 'made' as I.P. It tends to be descriptive in a way that bores me

– also rhetorical – my chief fear & danger . . . This bloody difficulty of writing about 'ideas' & somehow making them concrete is a bugger to surmount – but I believe it can be done.

He was thinking of calling it 'The Book of Balaam' or 'Balaam's Ass'. He would work at it through the war, then give up on it because 'it would not come together' but return to it decades later to include part in his last book (*SL* 97–111).[42] He was also writing 'Absalom Mass' (*RQ* 113–22).

On 14 March 1939, Germany invaded the disintegrating remains of Czechoslovakia, and even Chamberlain lost hope in peace through appeasement. With Hitler now demanding Danzig, Chamberlain announced in the Commons that Britain guaranteed Poland's independence. Jones felt 'misery in my heart'.[43]

Then, in mid-March, Prudence telephoned to say that she was marrying Guy Branch, a friend of her brother. Stunned, Jones felt an agony of loss. Burns and Hague rushed to Sidmouth to spend the weekend with him. Burns returned at Easter, and Jones poured out his grief to him. They also talked international politics, to which Jones's reactions were confused with grief over Prudence. On 22 March, he received from her a sensitive non-invitation to her wedding on the 25th, in which she concluded, 'I *do* send you so much love and I've thought about you continually but didn't know whether to come to Sid or not – perhaps not – but I longed to talk to you. Good night bless you. Bellybone.' (Without his knowing, she rewrote her will prior to the wedding, bequeathing him £1,000.) On the day of the wedding, his thoughts were 'tortured and muddled'. Two weeks later, he wrote to Ede, 'I love her very very much & our friendship has meant everything to me . . . She is such a marvellous & unique, truly intelligent, & beautiful person . . . we were so very alike in a lot of ways, however incredible that sounds.' To Grisewood he confided, 'I only feel a huge sense of *impoverishment* & loss.' Two months later he was still unsettled: 'O dear this old romantic love, the only type I understand, does let you down. I do see why Lancelot ran "wood mad" in the trackless forest for four years so that no man might know him.'[44]

Still hoping to avoid 'the suicide of Europe', Jones wrote for publication in the *Tablet* a long plea for peace, saying that world domination by force must be resisted, but we must first 'know, beyond any shadow of doubt, that this feared domination' is 'absolutely certain and absolutely the worst fate'. He notes that opponents of the dictators include 'instruments or creators of capitalist exploitation' and 'imperialist necessity' as well as 'true defenders of liberty'. He says Fascists and Nazis deserve 'sympathy' for attempting 'to cope with certain admitted corruptions in our civilization', which partly explains 'their brutality and suppression of individual freedom'. Hitler's ambitions resembling those behind the first and second British Empires, Jones thinks German incorporation of Moravia and Bohemia 'reasonable enough' and is willing to let the Czechs go, too, in deference to realpolitik. The essay was almost immediately unpublishable – it would have appeared pro-Nazi.*

* * *

On 10 June 1939 he went again to Campion Hall at the invitation of D'Arcy, who was harbouring Jewish refugees. Jones spoke with Rudolf Pfeiffer, the eminent German classicist, who had fled Germany with his Jewish wife, and rekindled friendship with Cyril Martindale. Discussion was continual, Jones remembered, about 'religion, sex, the structure of society, the arts & everything'. A Jesuit scholastic named Vincent Turner heard him say that he liked being in Oxford because 'it's always so easy here to have an excuse for doing something else'.[45]

Knowing of Jones's early ambition to paint murals, D'Arcy asked him to paint one in the Lady Chapel. Feeling 'far from well', he declined, so, instead, D'Arcy invited Stanley Spencer to paint one. Spencer came in June for 'half a week', and Jones found him 'extremely amusing . . . with the energy of a positive dynamo'. Spencer apparently intended to shock 'the Fathers', as he called them; and Jones, who disliked brash sexual talk in public, acted as a buffer between them. On one occasion, Spencer said to them, 'I never paint a woman I haven't slept with', adding that he intended to paint the backside of his current mistress, Daphne Charlton. He told D'Arcy, 'I've got two wives, one divorced and one not, and feel equally married to both.' Vigorously debating the respective advantages of celibacy and his own way of life, he rounded on a pale, intense young Jesuit and shouted, to the amusement of D'Arcy and Jones, 'HOW WOULD YOU LIKE TO KEEP TWO BLOODY WOMEN?'[46]

Spencer found Jones 'such a friend' and they talked 'so much', their 'sessions' taking up much of the evenings. Turner remembered them as constantly together, conversing at tea and at coffee after meals. Jones encouraged Spencer in planning a building to house his religious art, which was, he assured him, 'much nearer' than he thought 'to the particular religious quality of feeling' he was striving for. Jones 'found it really quite important talking to him'. Quoting from the harvest-festival hymn,

---

* Twenty double-spaced typed foolscap pages dated 11 May 1939, it was excluded from *Epoch and Artist* and *The Dying Gaul*. Edited solely to reduce length, it appears in T. Dilworth, 'David Jones and Fascism', *Journal of Modern Literature*, 13 (March 1986), pp. 143–59, reprinted in *David Jones, Man and Poet*, ed. John Mathias (Orono: National Poetry Foundation, 1989), pp. 143–63. It will appear unabridged in Tom Villis, 'The Hitler Typescripts', *Unpublished Writings of David Jones*, ed. Thomas Berenato *et al* (London: Bloomsbury, 2017).

Spencer spoke of all being 'safely gathered in' – words that became for Jones paradigmatic of what the artist does. Spencer told Jones that he could not take the commission since 'the spirit of his work was not congruent with the spirit of Catholicism'. Apart from this time together, they knew each other, Jones said, 'not extremely well, but we met on odd occasions'.[47] *

This was Jones's last visit to Oxford. He and D'Arcy would meet again in 1952 for dinner, after which Jones would comment, 'he has a most attractive & lively mind & is the most loveable of persons'.[48]

* * *

At Julian Asquith's invitation, Jones spent the latter half of July at the family manor in the ancient West Somerset village of Mells near Frome. The matriarch of the family, Lady Horner, was bitterly anti-Catholic. That didn't bother Jones, who thought her 'a very remarkable woman who made the most wonderful embroideries – *huge* great pieces of tapestry – and who was jolly interesting . . . for she had known some of the Pre-Raphaelites, Burne-Jones in particular, quite well'. He found anecdotes about the Pre-Raphaelites 'fascinating & usually extremely amusing'. Katharine Asquith, too, made tapestries, which he thought 'lovely', partly owing to 'the obvious beauty of the interweaving'.[49]

Katharine and Julian took him to Wells to see the cathedral and its 'noble, grey, . . . stone stair' winding up to the chapter house and they took him to Glastonbury, thought to have been the island of Avalon where Arthur was buried. Jones was impressed by the tor rising abruptly like an Aztec pyramid 500 feet from reclaimed swampland. But for him the place had no great imaginative resonance, owing to the whimsical layer of false legend being so thick.[50]

Also visiting Mells was the painter Henry Lamb, a Bloomsbury atheist who loved arguing about religion, although most conversation was about the immanence of war. Jones liked him, and was surprised that he could work at a portrait of Julian with people walking around him talking.[51]

Clarissa Spencer-Churchill visited. She was beautiful and intelligent with a deep, strong, commanding voice that could soften to appealing tenderness. Sensitive to voices as having an 'almost limitless power to deject, repel, bore, or elevate, enchant, console, attract', Jones found hers 'a healing thing . . . or anyway jolly nice'. She became part of his London circle.[52]

* On one of these occasions, Jones arrived at the Leicester Gallery to hear Spencer shouting to Ernest Brown, who was nearly deaf, about the women he was keeping and how much it was costing him. He was being widely overheard, and Jones said, 'Stanley, *shhhhh*.' 'I can't,' Spencer said. 'He's deaf. I have to speak up.' Jones said, 'Then talk about something else.' 'I can't,' Spencer said. 'He wants to hear about this.'

4. Mells Church, 1939

He had arrived at Mells depressed but soon cheered up, largely because of his affection for Katharine, and was able to paint. Just outside the window of his first-floor bedroom was the fifteenth-century parish church. Liking its 'great & extremely beautiful' sixteenth-century tower, he painted it through the window a hundred yards farther away than it is (fig. 4). The tower is a nearly empty column of transparency and movement contrasting with the greater tonal definitions of everything else. Jones wrote, 'I'm awfully glad I did' it. 'If I did almost a half a dozen of them perhaps two . . . might have got exactly what I wanted – however I think it has something, *if a bit enfeebled.*' Katharine bought it for twenty-seven guineas. He hoped it would not 'deteriorate on acquaintance' and explained that 'pictures ... sometimes ... seem to get better as you know them. Sometimes they get empty – & one can seldom tell which pictures are going to do which for certain.'[53]

He left Mells sooner than he would have liked because he felt increasingly agitated and anxious, a surprise to him in such a 'beautiful and interesting place'. It was the first time that a visit worsened his symptoms – an experience that soon precluded making overnight visits.

Upon his return to Glebe Place he began reading the Loeb translation of Petronius, partly out of curiosity about Trimalchio, the rich and gluttonous host of *The Satyricon* after whom Julian had been nicknamed 'Trim' in infancy.[54] The classical convention of the banquet, which is the setting of most of *The Satyricon*, would influence Jones's writing in which conversation takes place at a dinner party thrown by a 'Roman blimp' (*RQ* 155–84).

In August 1939, Jones took his *In Parenthesis* manuscripts and portrait of Prudence to Pigotts to ensure their safety. There he began writing about Romans stationed in Jerusalem, for a book tentatively entitled 'Conversations at the time of the Passion'. As with *In Parenthesis*, the creative consequence of life experience was delayed, 'rather like projectiles that penetrate the earth but are fused to explode sometime after'. Apparently influenced by the stream-of-consciousness technique in *Ulysses*, this new writing concerned, Grisewood remembered, 'a dinner party sometime after the Crucifixion' and 'was realistic, witty, satirical, in the style of a novel'. Jones thought it 'too prosy', lacking 'poetic texture and intensity, which,' he said, 'is all that interests me'.[1]

At the end of August, the Luftwaffe bombed Poland, and Britain and France declared war. Several times Jones meant to return to London but was unable to because of an 'intolerable fear of being unwell' especially on moving trains, from which there was no immediate escape. At the end of December, cold finally drove him to London. Shortly after, while out walking, he, Tom Burns and Grisewood took from the deserted Italian Consulate in Berkeley Square, or a nearby waste bin,* stacks of stationery with the letterhead '*Il Ministero della Cultura Popolare. Appunto per il Duce*' for joke letters to friends. Jones would use it to draft pages of *The Anathemata* concerning utilitarian civilisation as exemplified by Roman battering rams (176–8).[2]

Rex Nan Kivell gave Jones a one-man show at the Redfern Gallery in January 1940. It consisted of twenty-three paintings, most from the Brockley house. The reviews were positive, *The Times* calling him 'one of the most original of contemporary English artists'. Pictures totalling £500 sold, a remarkable success in the stagnant wartime art market. But earnings were meagre – Nan Kivell said that buyers were delaying paying.[3]

Visiting Hugh Fraser at his mother's house, Jones met the historian Arnold Toynbee, whom he subsequently visited twice at his flat. Toynbee was newly convinced of the cultural centrality of religion. He also believed in cultural progress – Jones disagreed, contending that 'the peculiar insight & perfections of' an early period 'never really *fulfils* itself in later expressions'. Instead the 'conditions & genius' that produce such

> 'perfection' … die for all *time* … this finality-of-oblitera-tion-in-time … makes one believe in 'an-other-world' if anything could or does. I mean *one just could* not have the perfections of

---

* Accounts by Burns and Grisewood differ.

Durham, the Parthenon, the Ajanta paintings, the air-plane, a Ben [Nicholson], a Cézanne, the 23rd Psalm, 'Ulysses' etc in the same physical world – their unity can only be found outside time.[4]

Snow fell heavily in mid- and late January, adding, for Jones, to the loveliness of London in the blackout but keeping him indoors. (Snow made him 'feel rather *peculiar* . . . a kind of ill-at-ease feeling almost of foreboding'.) When he did go out, he slipped and sprained an ankle.[5]

At the end of January, he returned to Sidmouth where, throughout most of Lent, instead of attending Mass (celebrated badly), he read in his room the liturgy, the Little Office, and his Welsh Prayer Book.[6]

In March 1940, Mussolini and Hitler met at the Brenner Pass purportedly to seek peace. Jones expressed hopefulness and gratitude to the two dictators in a short poem, entitled 'The Brenner' (*WP* 79). Then Germany invaded neutral Holland, Belgium, Denmark, and Norway, and he realised that Britain had to fight.[7]

In mid-April he came down with acute appendicitis and was rushed in extreme pain to hospital. He received the last rites. At midnight a surgeon arrived from Exeter just in time to save his life. Hospitalised for a month, he listened to radio accounts of combat in northern France, finding it hard to imagine this new, mobilised war. He returned to the Fort on 15 May, stayed in bed for seven days, then, as instructed, sat in the sun, which he found 'intolerable', and took a little walk each day. Weak, his belly bound in five yards of elastic bandage, wearing his winter coat, scarf, and hat, he struggled along the promenade crowded with sunbathers.[8]

In June he was in pubs drinking with British troops evacuated from Dunkirk and 'alarmed' by their low morale. One 'kept on saying "Christ! Jerry is hot, Jerry is hot!" It was so untypical, not a vestige of . . . wry humour.' When the Germans took Paris, he was appalled at the utter failure of the French to defend themselves. He now thought an invasion likely.[9]

Grisewood was engaged to Margaret Bailey, a tall twenty-three-year-old blue-eyed blonde (fig. 1). Travelling for a cosmetics firm, she visited Jones in June 1940. He wrote to Grisewood: 'She is just like one of our goddesses of Antiquity come to visit the lower zone.' On the Fort's lounge piano, she played for him Schubert's *Impromptu in B-flat Major* and some Chopin, which he liked, though she sensed that he was not much interested in music.[10]

Hard-pressed to afford rent after paying hospital bills, Jones moved to less expensive rooms until, in June, he occupied what had been a litter room. Owing money

1. Margaret Bailey, c. 1938

to Dr E. E. Lightwood, his Sidmouth physician, he wrote to Grisewood, 'I hope they don't run after you in street & market-places saying "Friends of Jones the debtor."' And he added, 'I must say "economics" are as important as Marx said – he merely truncated the hierarchy of Being.' Burns organised a monthly subsidy of £21 (he and Helen Sutherland supplying half of it, and she occasionally 'lent' Jones money for half repayment and sent him to her dentist at her expense). Charles Evans invited Jones to live with him and his bride, and Sutherland invited him to stay with her. But in July he returned to London to avoid being cut off from his father by an invasion. He took full possession of the Glebe Place flat, Burns having been recruited by Douglas Woodruff to the Ministry of Information and sent as a spy to the British embassy in Madrid to promote the continued neutrality of Spain.[11]

2. Douglas Woodruff, c. 1940

As Jones followed the war in the press, he was perturbed by 'all the old boring, dreary hypocrisies & half-lies', Woodruff's *Tablet* editorials being 'the *only reasonable*' press commentary. He dined often with the Woodruffs and liked Douglas 'more and more', finding him 'so humble underneath that somewhat forbidding exterior that I used to dislike a lot' (fig. 2). They agreed in thinking that German conquest of Europe might soon brutally end their world. The Nazis were unchristian and anti-Catholic, but Jones hoped that a larger Germany would eventually favour Christianity, its Diocletian (Hitler) eventually succeeded by a Constantinian 'baptized Fuhrership'. To close friends he said, 'Better a German civilization than no civilization at all.' But on 28 August, the 'balloon barrage . . . very high in the sky' made it seem, he wrote, 'as though the battlements of London were in heaven (as I devoutly hope they may be)'.[12]

On 7 September the Luftwaffe began bombing London. Jones found it '*bloody* annoying when these fucking sirens go just when you want to get somewhere, or get away from somewhere! Sometimes the busses stop & sometimes they don't.' He enjoyed the company of Ethel, the maid, 'a marvellous person & bloody philosophical' about the air raids. Indoors or out, he paid little attention to air-raid warnings and, agoraphobic, avoided bomb shelters. Twice a day he went to a pub – the Six Bells or, less frequently, the Eight Bells, where he met and talked with artists, including Charles Vyse, Mervyn Peake (a 'bloody nice chap'), and Augustus John. Working as a VAD nurse, Ann Bowes-Lyon visited. Sitting with her, he once touched the inside of her wrist, saying, 'This is the most beautiful part of a woman's body.' Occasionally in the evenings and usually on Sundays, he met Harman Grisewood at the Six Bells, sometimes with Margaret, and frequently visited their mezzanine flat at 61 King's Road.[13]

In the second week of September the Blitz came to Chelsea. Glebe Place was 'reserve lineish' now. The street behind was badly bombed. For him, the relationship of space and time was jarred loose: 'one feels there ought to be a fire-step where the chair is'. 'Sometimes I feel that the axes at Hastings are still hewing & that Troy has yet to burn.'[14]*

Jones found the Blitz 'real' and life in it 'immediate', a holiday from neurosis – real violence and danger a relief from apparently groundless anxiety. For this old soldier, life was back to normal. Booming of naval guns in Hyde Park and concussions of bombs were music to him. He listened appreciatively, commenting to Grisewood, 'Really good, that's really good.' He walked through the streets at night, shrapnel banging down around him. He was stirred by civilian heroics and liked seeing air-raid wardens in uniform and beautiful girls wearing steel helmets at jaunty angles – he drew one in revealing disarray (fig. 3). He thought 'some of the shelters & protective works . . . jolly nice'. The city was less crowded, friendships closer, and strangers friendlier regardless of class. It was like comradeship in the trenches. At 2 a.m. with the Grays over hot chocolate after a raid, he said, 'You know, Nicky, we'll never have it as good as this again.' Usually 'quite happy', he would, however, suddenly long 'like anything' for 'some completely invulnerable hole to go to'.[15]

3. Air-raid Warden, c. 1940

Jones began living with Harman and Margaret, sleeping in the dining room wearing his shoes and advising them, sleeping in the cellar, to do the same. (He had learned his lesson in October 1917.) One night the three of them were on a bus in the Brompton Road when a raid began, green and red German flares floating down. He praised their beauty. Grisewood and Margaret chimed in. An irate army officer unable to distinguish beauty from use led other passengers in furiously berating them, nearly throwing them off the bus.[16]

On 14 September 1940 at 12.30 in a civil ceremony, Grisewood and Margaret married, for Jones 'a marvellous exhilaration in the midst of this un-making'. He gave them *Agag* (chapter 8, fig. 3). After lunch and champagne at Hyde Park Hotel and a visit to the zoo, they retired to the flat for tea. Grisewood had night duty at the BBC, so

* For Jones, time easily became unfixed. In March 1946 he would twice date cheques 'October'. In 1966 he would date a cheque '1066' and have it returned for restoration of the missing centuries.

the wedding night belonged to Margaret and Jones. With shrapnel bursting high above, he played a recording of the Sistine Chapel Choir singing the 'Reproaches'. The next evening, he played Schubert's *Quintet in C-major*, with 'gun-fire & a plane' in the background.[17]

On the night of 12–13 September, he had written a wedding poem entitled 'Prothalamion' (*WP* 32–3). On the night of the 18th, he drafted a second, entitled 'Epithalamion', revised and expanded over the next few days (*WP* 34–44). It traces incarnations of Aphrodite from Classical times to Margaret in the present, the beauty of the goddess coexisting all the while with degrees of injustice. This remarkable poem anticipates *The Anathemata* in historical sweep and allusive density. He intended that Hague print these poems for private distribution, but there was a paper shortage and Hague was soon in the air force.[18] Unpublished for sixty-two years, they are among the best poems written during the war.

Helping with the washing-up, Jones walked round the table talking, Margaret remembered, 'drying one spoon for about an hour'. With Harman at work, she and Jones sometimes walked in old Chelsea Gardens or went to a pub where they held hands. (To her he seemed not sexual but merely loving and kind.) He told her he admired her tapered fingers and her feet – they 'are perfectly formed'. Critical of the current practice of applying lipstick beyond the outer line of lips, he said, 'You mustn't distort either your eyebrows or your mouth.' He teased her for admiring the art of the Italian high Renaissance, which he disliked. She hated modern art, so he advised her to 'look at the lines', saying that the artists she disliked achieve what they do because they draw well.[19]

On 28 September, the Grisewoods solemnised their marriage at Brompton Oratory. Afterwards they went with him by taxi to Brockley, which had been heavily bombed. His father's ceilings had fallen. David had urged him to go to Chester, but he refused, 'patient and happy', living, David wrote, 'interiorly & truly like old man Enoch "with God", it's amazing – I wish I knew how it was done.'[20] In October, he accompanied the Grisewoods on their honeymoon, a weekend visit to Pigotts.

For a few days in October Prudence stayed with him at Glebe Place after being hospitalised for partial paralysis attributed to stress. Her husband, a fighter pilot, had been shot down, was presumed dead, returned, was shot down again, and was again missing. Her distress 'terrible', she clung to the hope that he was a prisoner of war.[21]

Since early August, Jones had been working on a painting inspired by the story of Phryne, the beautiful courtesan whose counsel unclothed 'her splendours', which so impressed the judges that they declared her innocent (fig. 4). He first entitled it 'Iphigeneia in Aulis', then, for the next eight years, 'Aphrodite Pandemos', then 'Aphrodite', eventually adding 'in Aulis'. On an altar of sacrifice, she stands bearing the thigh

4. *Aphrodite in Aulis*, 1941

wound of Aphrodite at Troy and the stigmata of Jesus. Light from the diamond on her right hand and the stigma wound on her left emphasises the contrary qualities of Aphrodite: '*Urania* and *Pandemos*', spiritual and sexual. Unifying these is the statement by Dionysius, 'From Divine beauty is everything derived', implying metaphysical significance of erotic desire. The presence of ancient and modern soldiers, an anti-aircraft gun, and a barrage balloon establish her as an archetype transcending time. To the left of the point of the British soldier's lance-

5. *Margaret's Hands,* 1940

of-Longinus (which pierced the side of Jesus) is a cleft in the hillside, the vulval cult-object at Eleusis. Shackled at the ankle, she is a sexual-slave-as-Christ-figure. The cracks in the marble of her left shin identify her with Pygmalion's Galatea. Her stance and blown hair evoke Botticelli's *Birth of Venus.* Jones intended her 'to include *all* female cult-figures, all goddesses rolled into one – wounded . . . as are all things worthy of our worship'. Her painterly prototype is the Virgin (with one breast exposed) in Jean Fouquet's *Melun Diptych,* for whom Charles VII's mistress modelled. Her human prototype was Margaret, whose hands she has – he had drawn and painted them earlier (fig. 5) and incorporated them in a drawing entitled *Aphrodite* (fig. 6). Emerging from enthusiasm for her beauty and from repressed-sexual participation in Grisewood's love affair, the painting was made possible by the heating-up of the war alleviating his depression. Always special to him, he would not offer it for sale.[22]

6. *Aphrodite* 'for Harman', 1940

In the second week of November 1940, Eric Gill died. Jones felt the loss deeply. He owed him 'an enormous debt' and considered him '*inimitable*', 'endearing', 'greater as a man than as an artist'.[23]* But he missed the funeral because his father had a serious heart attack.

He visited his father daily in hospital and then in the Oak Lawn Nursing Home in Sydenham. It was a long journey, involving several bus changes, during which he saw a good

---

* Gill's work suffered, Jones thought, from 'preoccupation with "this flesh", somewhat diagrammatically expressed', lending 'a sort of slickness' especially to 'his later drawings & engravings'. He thought Gill's best work was his carved lettering and the designed printing types, Joanna being 'by far' his 'best type-face . . . strong & clear and firm' with 'great freedom & dignity combined'.

7. *Germania and Britannia*, 'Epiphany', 1941

deal of the damage caused by bombing, 'curiously interesting & jolly pathetic'.[24]

On 6 January 1941, Jones drew Britannia and Germania embracing above words of the Coventry Carol, 'O sisters two, how may we do' (fig. 7). Britannia's thigh wound and her resemblance to Athena suggest her defence of Troy-Novant (London). On the left a town is burning, evocative of Coventry. The alternative to war would be a sisterly embrace, paradoxically evoked by the embrace of war. This small picture (9 by 12 inches) has inspired considerable commentary by those detecting sadistic (why not incestuous, too?) lesbianism. One critic blames the picture for implying moral equivalence between antagonists.[25] Viewers for whom erotic, political, or moral implications preclude archetypal identification miss the meaning, which is the contemporary violation of archetypal sisterhood.

In 1939 Jones had met Barbara Moray, the Park Avenue American wife of Francis Stuart, Earl of Moray. Neither Catholic nor an intellectual, she was, he found, forthright, genuine, 'without an ounce of affectation', tough-minded, and 'extremely perceptive'. She liked his indifference to class and his liking Americans, a trait, she found, rare in the English. Feeling 'lifted up by being with him', she soon regarded him as 'a great man' – a discovery she shared with her best friend, the Queen. Barbara arranged their meeting for tea at her house at 1 Hans Place in Kensington in March 1941. Once or twice after that, she invited them together for drinks – in his pocket diary for 9 June 1943, he wrote 'Barbara's, drinks with the Queen'. He was 'perfectly at ease' with her, Barbara remembered. They talked about *In Parenthesis*, which the Queen admired. He thought her extremely intelligent. She found him unusual, intriguing, attractive, and was, Barbara said, 'rather taken with him'.[26]

* * *

For nearly a year, Burns had kept the Glebe Place flat solely for Jones's use but was letting it go at the end of March 1941. Arthur Pollen, a sculptor and an acquaintance since the early '30s, offered Jones a room in his house, his wife and children being away in the country. At the beginning of April, Jones moved to 57 Onslow Square in South Kensington, an immense Edwardian house with scagliola floors and pillars and a ballroom on the *piano nobile*. He brought with him books, Burns's record player, and his favourite records.* Pollen slept in the cellar, Jones in the third-floor nursery in a child's Chinese Chippendale four-poster bed, which he admired and, though he was too big, insisted on using. He refused to sleep downstairs, saying, 'I survived one war. I'm not going to be killed in this one.'[27]

8. Arthur Pollen, c. 1940

In Cheyne Walk on the Chelsea Embankment during a rare daytime raid, he was leaning on the parapet watching heavy bombing. A man running from upriver pointed backwards shouting to follow him. Ten minutes later he reappeared, running in the opposite direction, shouting to follow him. It was, Jones said, like something out of *Through the Looking-Glass*.[28]

Jones and Pollen (fig. 8) shared meals and talked far into the night about painters, painting, and mutual acquaintances. Jones confided his difficulty in getting money from Nan Kivell, who had that spring been paid in full for three of his pictures but refused to send a cheque. High-spirited with a wonderful sense of humour and real aesthetic sensitivity, Pollen was, in Jones's words, 'a golden man'.[29]

They visited galleries together, going in May to the National Gallery to see an exhibition of their mutual friend 'Harry' Moore, who had done, Jones thought, 'superb drawings of chaps in air-raid shelters'. Admiring the use of colour, he thought them Moore's best things: 'God be praised! They are somehow "romantic" in the true sense.'[30] †

Jones and Pollen worried about the equestrian statue of Charles I in Whitehall, which Jones considered the one '*absolutely* first rate, unquestionably great single statue in the round' in London. It was encased in sandbags but vulnerable to bombing, so, in a letter to *The Times*

---

* Plainchant, Welsh folk-songs, Palestrina, Monteverdi, 'Frankie and Johnny', 'Casey Jones', 'Water Boy', 'Ezechiel Saw the Wheel', 'My Lord What a Morning', 'Were You There When They Crucified My Lord', 'Joshua Fit the Battle of Jericho', and 'The Lady-killing Cowboy'. Most of the rest of the contents of the Glebe Place flat were put in storage and destroyed by bombing.

† He wrote to Ede: 'English artists are "Romantic" or nothing – I'm sure of that. Even old Ben [Nicholson] is really romantic in spite of the appearance of Benish "intelligence" – the old Frogs are really intelligent when they paint. We can't do it that way.'

(30 May 1941) co-signed by Pollen, he urged its removal to safety. Shortly after the letter was published the statue was removed.[31]

Jones began the second in a now projected series of four to six Malory paintings beginning with *Guinever*. Entitled *The Four Queens* (fig. 9), it depicts Morgan le Fay, with others contending for Lancelot's love, 'casting an enchantment on him as he sleeps' (Malory, VI, 3). The spikes of a loose spur insinuate a threat to his crotch as does the sharpened base of his standard, seeming to hover above it. His bare leg corresponds to that of Morgan, which parallels the menacing standard. Above his head is the fruit tree of the Fall. The contesting queens evoke the Judgement of Paris, but the visual model is Rubens's *The Three Graces*, of which Jones had made a preparatory study. The pavilion stabling the queens' horses is modelled on his Chippendale bed. Lancelot has affinity with the figure in the frontispiece of *In Parenthesis* (chapter 9, fig. 11), although Lancelot wears a German helmet and reflects memories of enemy dead in Mametz Wood. The intended meaning of the picture is romantic love resisting lustful enchantment. Balancing on the edge of chaos, form expresses the precariousness of Lancelot's situation. Because diaphanous shades contribute to opalescent iridescence, the picture is difficult to see and undergoes continual metamorphosis during viewing. John Rothenstein, the new director of the Tate (to whom Jones was introduced by the painter John Nash in April 1941), arranged for the Tate to buy it and *Guinever* for £120.[32]

In this, Rothenstein had the enthusiastic backing of Kenneth Clark, Director of the National Gallery. In the late 1920s, Ede had tried to interest Clark in Jones's pictures. Clark 'had no feeling for them at all,' Ede said, 'but two years later', after seeing them in galleries, he was saying that Jones was 'the best watercolourist since Blake'. In the winter of 1934, at Ede teas, Jones and Clark became friends, discovering during their first real conversation that they both regarded Turner as the best British painter. Now meeting at the National Gallery or the Tate, they often looked together at the Gainsboroughs and Constables – 'absolutely marvellous', Jones thought – then went into the cellars to see Turners. For Jones, Clark's public promotion of Turner would be his most important achievement.* In 1939, Jones read in Hartrick's autobiography, 'When Ruskin praised it was safe to follow . . . we could do with another Ruskin today', and wrote in the margin, 'We perhaps have in Kenneth Clark.' He would never drop the 'perhaps'. He thought Clark's *Landscape into Art* (1949) brilliant and 'inspired' but considered his *The Nude* (1956) a bad book. Nevertheless, Jones would write in 1962, 'I think he's by far

---

* Jones considered Turner the only English painter comparable to the great masters, a creative genius equivalent to Dante or Shakespeare – his only criticism being that Turner 'has no sense of locality'.

9. *The Four Queens*, 1941

the most perceptive of writers on the visual arts that this country has produced in recent times.'[33]

Clark's appreciation of Jones increased through the years. In 1936 he wrote that Jones was 'in many ways, the most gifted of all the younger English painters', his pre-breakdown work 'entirely original', his best watercolours having 'a poetical quality only surpassed by Blake'. By the late 1960s, Clark thought him the best living British painter, 'enormously underestimated in England ... absolutely unique, a remarkable genius'. (By then he had acquired three paintings by Jones.) He praised 'the very personal way in which he put down every line and every stroke. Not only was the whole very beautiful ... but the *ecriture* was extremely beautiful.' In Britain Jones benefited from Clark's ascendancy in the institutional art-scene. Having become chief buyer for the Contemporary Art Society in 1939, Clark had the Tate acquire Jones's work, and he bought it for Australian public galleries. As Director of the National Gallery, he included it in wartime and post-war exhibitions.[34]

The only serious limitation in Clark's appreciation of art, Jones thought, was his lack of religious experience, which precluded depth of sympathy with much Renaissance and most medieval art. Jones occasionally visited the Clarks until they moved to the country, then visited him sometimes for meals at his weekday set in Albany. He had reservations about Clark and would say to a friend, 'Kenneth is a funny chap, a funny chap' but would not elaborate.[35]*

Despite eye strain, Jones began working on a third Malory picture, of Sir Gareth with Lady Lyonesse (VII, 22), when 'rosy attacked just in the old way': panic, depression, insomnia. He was 'astounded'. He had thought he was 'rid of all that'. 'It is *so* absurd to be able to withstand bombing ... & be overcome with trying to paint a picture ... It is so embarrassing.' He stopped work on it, saw Dr Woods in early October, and acquired an (ineffectual) nerve tonic from Dr Lightwood.[36]

Jones was, he wrote to Burns, 'jolly sorry for the complete breakup of all the old Chelsea thing. *I can hardly bear it*'. Having learned that her husband had been killed, Prudence retreated to the family farm in Wales. The Plunket Greenes were in Wiltshire, the Grisewoods in a small house in Twickenham. (Jones visited 'but there is no longer the chance of lovely long heavenly discussions far into the night over old whisky & sandwiches'.)[37]

In July, Pollen joined the Air Force and announced the closing of his house – Jones had to move. Mary Gill told him of a woman letting rooms in a boarding house in Sheffield Terrace, off Kensington Church Street. On 23 September 1941, with Mary's help, he moved there. He had sprained his

* For a full account of Jones's friendship with Clark, see T. Dilworth, 'Letters from David Jones to Kenneth Clark', *Burlington Magazine*, 142 (April 2000), pp. 215–25.

ankle again, making the move difficult. With '*infernal* pain' and the aid of Pollen's gold-banded walking stick, he managed but was annoyed at being unable to walk at his usual quick pace, a way of keeping warm.[38]

No. 12 Sheffield Terrace was a tall whitewashed Georgian row house. Jones's room was 12 by 13 feet in a shallow basement at the east front of the building. The room was dark, the sill of its large triple window below ground (his head at pedestrian knee level), facing a low wall along the near side of the pavement – he kept a light on during the day. It was, he said, 'like being a fairly respectable prisoner in the Tower'. Meals were brought in on a tray, liberally seasoned with cumin, 'especially the soup, which one either had to get used to or somehow get rid of'. He made tea in a small saucepan on his open coal fire. He liked his Maltese landlady, Mary Muscat, but she could be a trial. When he complained about the food, she argued. She was sometimes angry and rude to his visitors.[39]

On 23 October he registered for Industrial Service but was excused, after Dr Woods wrote that he suffered from 'severe' 'Depressive Psychosis . . . marked by improvement with relapses' and was 'quite unfit for routine service in the military or in a civil capacity'.[40]

The darkness of his room discouraged painting, so Jones wrote. In September he finished an essay entitled 'Epoch, Church and Artist', which was published in the *Tablet* of 1 November. In reaction to a call for modern artists to serve the Church, he points out that the best modern painting is 'personal . . . intimate and private rather than public and corporate' and therefore not amenable to ecclesial use. He resumed writing poetry.[41]

After rereading *The Decline of the West*, in August 1941, he bought his own copy to read again and annotate. He liked Spengler's spatialising of time, especially his parallel between the late phases of Roman and modern Western civilisation. And he loved the richness of 'detail – like the biggest & most packed-with-juice-&-fruit type of cake you ever got your teeth into'. In February 1942, he saturated himself in it, often disagreeing with Spengler, who thought historical cycles separate. Dawson had shown Jones that they were continuous, forming a helix or spiral: conquerors always assimilated the defeated, even though continuings were transformational. Jones reread it again in 1943, marvelling at its perceptions, especially involving the arts. Of all modern writers, Spengler and Joyce were, he was sure, 'the two stars', and he wished he could hear them conversing 'in heaven, or wherever such things are possible'.[42] *The Anathemata* would partly be a response to *The Decline of the West*, continuing a dialogue begun in the margins of Jones's copy.

Visitors usually came singly to his little room, and Jones preferred speaking with one at a time. Once a month throughout the war, he invited Fr Richard Kehoe to visit. Summer or winter, Kehoe found him bundled up in a greatcoat, complaining of the draught. They conversed over whisky (brought by Kehoe) about the Roman Liturgy, the Mass, the Roman Empire, the Roman Army, von Hügel, Gill, Waugh, and other contemporaries. And with 'astounding knowledge & perception', Kehoe spoke at length about scripture – Jones had never experienced 'anything quite like it'. Their talks would have 'direct and immediate bearing' on *The Anathemata*. Kehoe later said that Jones 'made a deeper impression of goodness on me than anyone else I have ever known – except for a few lay-sisters'.[43]

Sundays Jones went to 11 o'clock Mass at the nearby Carmelite Church in Kensington Church Street, then to the Catherine Wheel, his principal neighbourhood pub. Attending Mass with him, a new friend, Peter Kelly, noticed how utterly absorbed in concentration he was, 'absolutely miles away – it was extraordinary'. Afterwards in the pub, Kelly watched him stare at a dog on the rug with the same long fixed concentration: 'He couldn't take his eyes off it – it was as though he was in a trance.' Jones's regular pub friends now included Mike Richey's seventy-two-year-old father, George, who had fought in India and South Africa in every conflict since the Bechuanaland Expedition (1884–5), rising no higher than colonel because he resigned whenever peace broke out. (About officers who served in peacetime he complained, 'They just don't like blood.') He fascinated Jones with war stories, one of them an account of fighting Bantus discharging with frightening accuracy showers of assegai (spears), which made 'very nasty' wounds – he showed where one had pierced his wrist – an account that would find its way into Jones's poetry (*SL* 98). 'What a bloke!' Jones later said. 'I loved that man.'[44]

Since the spring of 1937, on Friday nights, Jones occasionally joined a meeting of half-a-dozen culturally and politically engaged Welshmen, to whom he had been introduced by Will Griffith, whose Welsh bookshop off Charing Cross Road he had frequented since 1928. Meeting in a small restaurant nearby, they discussed Welsh affairs: 'heads together – gesticulations – rapid speech – rapped-out disagreements – partly in English, partly in Welsh', politely translated for his benefit. On the fringe, he occasionally illuminated a point with erudition that amazed them. In the winter of 1942, during a blackout, he went with them to Paddington to meet Aneirin Talfan Davies, a poet, broadcaster, publisher, and literary critic. In the lounge of the Paddington Hotel, Jones mentioned loving *Bryn Calfaria*, and spontaneously they sang it softly in three-part harmony, all conversation in the lounge ceasing, waiters stopped in their tracks. The Welshmen felt him 'one of us'. It was probably through them that, in 1940, he joined the Cymmrodorion Society. He became friends with Davies, a devout Anglican and 'one of the nicest persons' Jones knew – after love of Wales their chief bond being love of *Finnegans Wake*.[45]

In October 1941, Prudence came to town and stayed in his building. Her left side was numb and she was in pain. She told him, 'You could stick a pin in my bum and I wouldn't feel it.' That winter she was diagnosed with 'Disseminated Sclerosis', the incurable disease now called multiple sclerosis. In town again in March for (futile) treatment, she knew she was in for periods of paralysis ending in prolonged, undignified dying. In the summer, she rented a flat at 32 Dorset Square, where Jones often visited her. Paralysis moved to various parts of her body. When she was unable to walk, he shopped for her. She was always, he found, 'very cheerful' . . . & *tremendously* brave'. In the autumn, her paralysis worsened and, in extreme pain, she retreated to Mill House.[46]

*   *   *

Jones's writing involved continual research to verify accuracy of fact and nuance, usually confirming that he was 'right in the main'. Grisewood was borrowing books from the London Library for him including, in March, John Pinkerton's *A General Collection of the Best and Most Interesting Voyages and Travels* (1808). In it, he especially liked material on the Scilly Isles – which he would incorporate into *The Anathemata* (100). Other books were John Wilkes's *The Roman Army* and, at the end of May, books on the English language. In these and Ewart's *The French Language*, he discovered that *landa*, one of the few Old Celtic words surviving in French, became, in English, 'laund' and so 'lawn'. 'Next time I hear a lawn-mower clicking,' he wrote, 'I shall enjoy a wider vista.' He would use this Celtic survival when writing in 'The Hunt' of Arthur recklessly riding 'the close thicket as though it were an open launde' (*SL* 67).

He consulted classicists, chief among them Colin Hardie, a don at Magdalen College, Oxford, whom he met through the Walls.* Their correspondence would continue throughout the composition of *The Anathemata*. On 11 July 1945, Jones wrote to him, 'one does need really to know the hard facts'. If not,

> the 'magic' ceases to work – what a vast number of poetic cargoes have been wrecked on this rock . . . I feel that a whole lot of Spenser fails here – it's 'unreal' in consequence. One ceases to 'believe' it . . . No felicity of words makes up for it. It's the eternal 'Thou shalt not' of poetry – 'Thou shalt not bear false witness.'

A Welsh proverb and motto of the University of Wales meant a lot to him: 'The best muse is truth.' Contextualising his research was the churning up of relics of Roman London during the Blitz, an uncovering that would

---

* Others included Hague, Jones's cousin Ruth Daniels (who helped him with Greek), and A. H. Williams, headmaster of the county school in Ruthin, Denbighshire.

influence 'The Lady of the Pool' section of *The Anathemata*. (He especially liked a Roman tile on which a worker had written in Latin, 'Austalis goes off on his own for a week every day.')⁴⁷

Jones needed more access to books, so, in December 1943, Helen Sutherland bought him a library membership. He had difficulty at first with 'those bloody London Library indices etc.' but was soon taking out the limit of ten books and more. His dealings with the library involved a good deal of special pleading. At one point he had eight books above the limit, renewing some of them for years because, as he wrote to the secretary of the library, 'I am continuing to use them for a work on which I am engaged.'⁴⁸

About his writing, he told Grisewood, 'a certain amount gets done at great sweat & pressure & then nothing for weeks & a kind of nausea with what is done! . . . I walk round it, you know, . . . keep guard on it, turn it over, think about it, have a peep at it – rather like a patient!'⁴⁹

*   *   *

In May 1942, Jones dined with Dawson at his flat. They had both read John Cowper Powys's *Owen Glendower* and 'chuckled together about things in it'.* They spoke about the resurgence of 'torture, the police-state & Co', about Catholics becoming more institutional 'and mechanical', moving towards 'a belief in effecting things by organisation & formulas' – 'in short that "propaganda" is universally dominant in the Ch[urch] as outside it & once you yielded *internally* to the propagandist attitude y're sunk'. They lamented Vatican condemnation of Martin Luther's statement that burning heretics is offensive to the Holy Spirit – obviously true, they agreed, but condemned 'to justify Papal absurdity – all of which is a pity & *quite* irrelevant to the truths of the Cath. Religion'. Jones came away grateful for having talked 'to someone whose brain is the right *kind* – that's what one sighs for . . . the *temper* – . . . the *sort* of thing that a chap regards as *significant*'. Jones felt 'great affection' for Dawson, considered him 'one of the greatest Culture-historians of the West', and was 'astonished' at British failure to appreciate him. But he could see that this was 'partly' because he 'was shy & withdrawn & had none of those assertive qualities that seem to make people (in all professions) become regarded as figures of great importance' – qualities he realised that he also lacked. They met, though now infrequently, until Dawson took a chair at Harvard in 1958.⁵⁰

* Jones thought Powys's writing bad, full of padding, though he liked the content, later saying there was more of 'the real thing' of ancient Welsh literature and tradition in *Owen Glendower* and *Porius* than in any other Anglo-Welsh writing. The only new novels he now read concerned Wales.

Early in 1942, Clark had Helmut Ruhemann embark on radical restoration of paintings in the National Gallery by chemically removing old varnish. In May 1942, Jones saw newly cleaned El Greco's *Christ Driving the Money Changers from the Temple*: 'just a yellow drab mess before' but 'an absolute corker now . . . it looked about twice as "real" as the people walking about in front of it – I've *never* seen anything like it – for power & beauty – not for many years. It restores one's belief in the human race, – for a bit.' He asked Clark to keep it on display an extra week, and he did, enabling Jones to return repeatedly to see it. But, by removing tinted varnishes and subtle glazes, Ruhemann's restoration also spoiled paintings Jones loved: Gainsborough's portrait of his daughter, the Piero della Francescas, and Hogarth's *Shrimp Girl* (which he had spent an entire day looking at).[51] Only Ernst Gombrich publicly opposed this ruthless cleaning. Jones complained privately to Clark, who eventually lost confidence in Ruhemann's extreme methods, now universally discredited.

In 1942, Jones's revenue from sales of pictures had fallen to £20. He was mainly living off friends.* Unable to afford the amount of whisky he liked, he gave it up entirely. Having tried to quit smoking, but relapsing after a fortnight, he now rolled his own cigarettes. Eating poorly, he fantasised about food.[52]

Twice in 1942 he ran into Ben Nicholson on the street. At their second meeting, in July, they went together to see some of Nicholson's recent abstracts. Nicholson no longer insisted on art being abstract, and they found themselves once more in basic aesthetic agreement.[53]

In 1942, he encountered Douglas Cleverdon on the street. His Bristol bookstore destroyed by bombing, he was working as a producer in the Features Department of the BBC and living in a seedy club in Gloucester Walk near Sheffield Terrace. There Jones met his lover, Nest Lewis, twenty-one years old, short, pretty, vivacious, intelligent, also working at the BBC, and Welsh. He liked her immensely. They talked a good deal about food, a topic then on everyone's mind. She remembered him as pale, half-starved, worried, though prone to quiet laughter. They visited back and forth, and she taught him how to cook leeks on his coal fire.[54]

He made three pictures in his small dark room, one of a pregnant girl who several times passed before his window, drawn to get her out of his mind so he could resume writing. Another, *The Mother of the West*, of the Roman

---

* £4.10s. weekly from Helen Sutherland, £2 weekly from Tom Burns, and occasional gifts: in the previous year, £2 from his father, £13 from Prudence (Pelham) Branch, and £40 from Ralph and Manya Harari. For the years 1939/40 and 1940/41 he paid no income tax. In 41/42 he paid £3.5s.9d. In 42/43, he earned and received as gifts £289 and paid tax of £29.19s.0d.

10. *The Mother of the West*, 1942

wolf suckling the Lamb of God (fig. 10), expressed his hope that if the Nazis conquered, their imperium would eventually turn to Christianity.[55]

*   *   *

Writing brought on 'another bloody attack of Rosy', but he continued writing. Since 1939, he had drafted and redrafted seventy-seven pages concerning Crixus, a veteran, Oenomaus, a young conscript, and Brasso Olenius, a centurian who details them for the next day's crucifixion duty and delivers a chilling speech initiating them into required depersonalisation. Present here in embryo are all the Roman poems in *The Sleeping Lord*. At the beginning of 1943, depressed, Jones thought that 'only tiny bits here & there . . . come off. It is a bugger. But I think all the stuff done in the last year is not so bad.' Familiarity bred boredom, in response to which he revised. He wished the 'bloody book' a painting: 'the "ideas" in a painting are not so damned nailed down as in writing – words are buggers for that'.[56]

Since late 1942, Bernard Wall had been in charge of the Italian Department of the Foreign Office Research Department in London. (Pro-Franco during the Spanish Civil War, he had become bitterly anti-fascist.) Jones visited him often, sometimes at work, where the way to Wall's office – down halls, past checkpoints, around makeshift partitions – was a maze that would inform Jones's poetry (*SL* 38–9). They talked about Spengler, Dante, mutual friends, and Wall's acquaintances, including Ezra Pound, François Mauriac, and Alcide De Gasperi. They agreed that a new Dark

Age had begun, that language was becoming merely functional rather than symbolic, and talked of revitalising literary language by retrieving earlier styles.[57]*

Wall's wife, Barbara, and their children were in Oxford. Separated from Bernard by the war, she had fallen in love with Auberon Herbert, an Oxford undergraduate and brother-in-law of Evelyn Waugh. Auberon, she knew, 'loved' Jones, so she confided in him. Jones hated Bernard being hurt but, knowing marriage to him was difficult, was non-judgemental. He said to her, 'What absolute nonsense it is, this idea of having to be in the state of grace when you die or you're not going to go to heaven. It's just like when the mother and father come home and find that their children have made the most howling mess of the house. They're not going to love them any less.' Passion between Barbara and her undergraduate eventually cooled, and she stayed with Bernard, who, as a husband, remained emotionally absent (they would live in separate flats in the same road), and Jones felt sorry for her.[58]

Jones lunched with Robin Ironside, whom Clark had enlisted to edit a Penguin book on Jones after Kerrison Preston, the Blake collector and scholar, told him in January 1942 that Jones was like Blake as a painter-prophet of original imagination. Jones dreaded what Ironside might write – he disliked critics presuming 'to tamper with the arts & to "explain" them' – but liked him.[59]

Friendship with Barbara Moray warmed after her husband committed suicide (officially a 'hunting accident'), for which the new earl blamed her. Jones often lunched with her, and she visited him, usually bringing champagne. Among her aristocratic friends, she said, he loomed 'like a colossus' but seemed to her lonely and bereft, a sort of waif, and her affection for him was, to a degree, motherly. In a letter, she addressed him as 'my dear little David' and concluded, 'you are such a darling'.[60]

Now writing about Romans in Wales, Jones made and pinned to his wall a culture chart of Western myth and romance with arrows indicating directions of influence (20 by 24 inches, fig. 11), a time-map of the European mind including the main currents of imagination informing his writing.

While Jim Ede was visiting in early May 1943, Jones complained of an itchy rash on his back. Ede was staying with his former neighbour the psychoanalyst Dr Donald Winnicott and his family in Hampstead, took Jones there, and mentioned the rash. Winnicott had him remove his shirt and rubbed ointment on his back. Ede had not primed him about Jones's (Ede thought) fearing sex, but he subsequently told Ede that there was

---

* Jones and Wall would never lose connection, their conversations eventually taking place over the telephone. Jones would provide a drawing and an essay, entitled 'Art and Democracy' (EA 85–96), for the *Changing World* (1947–49), a review Wall co-edited with Manya Harari in 1947–9, dedicated to the union of religion and culture.

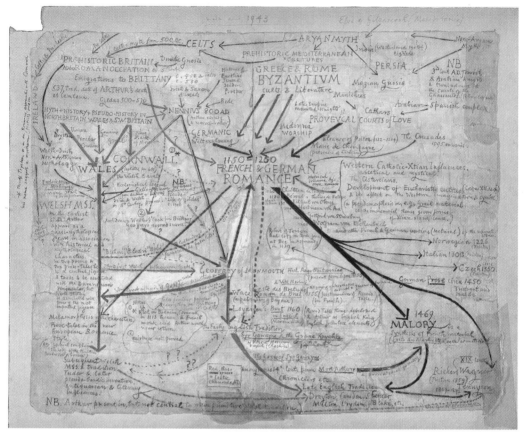

11. Culture chart, c. 1943

nothing physically wrong with Jones: 'All he needed was to be touched.' Winnicott later visited him at Sheffield Terrace with the placebo ointment, and Jones wrote to Ede, 'I *do* believe he has a magic touch (!) as no irritation since he examined it – most remarkable.'[61]

To Eliot, Jones mentioned working on a long essay about the aesthetics of war (*DG* 123–66). It concerned the 'abstract, difficult to posit, remote and removed' beauty that can be present in battle irrespective of practical or moral considerations. Eliot expressed interest, and, in early August 1943, after reading it, he advised expanding it into a book, then recasting it 'as separate *pensees*'. Doing neither, Jones would finish it in 1946, entitling it 'Art in Relation to War and Our Present Situation'. His argument is that all human activity is to some degree of '"man as artist" at play'.[62]

In the third week of May 1943, Clark had Eliot and Jones to dinner at his flat, and Jones expressed appreciation for Eliot's recently published 'Notes Towards a Definition of Culture'. He and Eliot agreed that, in Jones's words, '*in the end* you can't have the things the intelligentsia call "culture" unless you have a real "culture" underneath ... It is the *central* problem of our time ...

deeper than all else I think & the least understood.' The issue of 'real culture' would dominate his writing from now on. During meetings with Eliot – they had supper together at the Oxford and Cambridge Club on 26 April 1944 – Jones related his ideas about use and gratuity, civilisation and culture, and these would influence Eliot's culture-criticism published at the end of the war.[63]

Throughout the war, Hartrick occasionally visited, and Jones went to his house for lunch or tea. Together on the evening of 1 July 1943, they attended a slide lecture on Blake by Hartrick's former student, Tom Hennel. The magnification of Blake's illuminations on the screen was, for Jones, a revelation. 'I've always reckoned I liked Blake,' he wrote, 'but my God! – that size & with that luminosity they fair bowl you over – absolutely terrific. A certain tightness which sometimes, to me, mars Blake all disappears & the freedom of them becomes really overwhelming.' He was especially impressed by the illustration entitled *Cain* 'with the distraught Eve & Adam & the dead Abel' – 'unbelievable in its power'. He also liked the 'bloody good' illustrations of Gray's *Odes*. But he thought Blake's illuminated poems seriously hurt by the use of ordinary script instead of lettering that suits the pictures.[64]

* * *

Now forty-eight-years-old, Jones noticed in the mirror that his face was 'slipping down & getting large & loose on the bottom, a thing', he wrote to Dorothea Travis, 'I particularly hate'.[65]

He was visiting his eighty-four-year-old father in the Sydenham nursing home on the morning of 3 October 1943 when his father died, 'peacefully & happily . . . as he had lived'. That evening at supper with the Grays, Jones said, 'I never saw a man die before.' Basil said, 'But David, in the war, surely you saw men die.' 'That', he said, 'was different.'[66]

The value of his father's estate was £416.10s.10d., of which he inherited £149.0s.7d. The burial was in his mother's grave. He arranged for Michael Royde-Smith from Pigotts to add to Gill's inscription. After visiting the grave in April 1946, Jones would think the stone probably 'the only real art-work in Brockley'.[67]

Continuing civilian casualties depressed him. Pilotless winged V-1 buzz-bombs were now falling on London. He hated 'those awful doodlebugs . . . frightening things', particularly disliking the quiet between the shut-off of the motor and the explosion. A buzz-bomb killed his Aunt Alice Bradshaw in Croydon. Another landed in his sister's bed bending the iron frame, sticking in the box springs in Honor Oak Park. Late on Sunday evening, 20 February 1944, one hit the Carmelite church, leaving only 'the brickwork and bits left standing', 'a pathetic sight', which, to his surprise, gave the impression that it had been a beautiful building.[68]

Sometimes being turned away by the possessive landlady Muscat, Prudence had visited Jones often, giving him what money she could. In 1943, she fell in love with Robert Buhler, a painter, and moved into his flat without legally marrying – with her medical expenses, they could not afford to lose her widow's pension. She changed her surname to his by deed poll. Together they visited Jones, she reattaching his buttons and mending his socks as they talked. Buhler knew of his love for her but saw no signs of jealousy. Meeting and parting, Jones and she embraced but did not kiss.[69]

He 'took a great interest in my generation of painters,' Buhler said, 'and was most encouraging.' Buhler sent 'quite a number' of younger painters to see him, including Robert Colquhoun and Robert MacBryde, known as 'the Roberts'. They were Glasgow Scot nationalists, openly homosexual, interesting talkers, fine storytellers, warm and charming, but usually too drunk, Jones found, to converse with properly. Liking his pictures and finding in them encouragement for their own non-abstract work, 'they were', Buhler said, 'mad about him'.[70]

In the winter of 1943–44, Jones spent two months in bed with five bouts of flu – his worst winter ever for physical illness. But he wrote 'a good bit' until March, when, exhausted, his mind began going 'round & round'.[71]

That spring he moved from his tiny basement room to one on the ground floor, slightly larger (14 feet square) with a manteled fireplace. Facing a dishevelled garden with trees were two large French doors, which he hated – they let in the cold and 'the bloody damp'. But they gave the room 'a somewhat dim, mid-forest light', and he enjoyed watching the trees 'wrestling heavily in the wind'.[72]

With Clark's encouragement, in March 1944 the CEMA organised an exhibition of his work to tour Wales. Jones would not allow borrowing pictures from Helen Sutherland – they were safe with her. Twenty-seven paintings were assembled plus the *Deluge* and *Mariner* engravings. The opening was in Cardiff in April. He did not go.

The Grisewoods moved to Gatwick House in Essex near the village of Billericay. Sometimes visiting for the weekend, Jones fell ill and stayed for weeks, or, ill in London, went there to be looked after. During one visit, Margaret feared entering the larder in which she had seen a mouse. Jones drew her a picture (fig. 12), in which the chief of a number of rats is pierced with an arrow bearing a banner reading, 'Present from Margaret'. During a visit in the winter of 1944–45, he experienced anxiety and depression so severe that he went to bed for over a week, staying till well enough to travel. Such lengthening stays put a strain on the Grisewoods.[73]

When in London, Dorothea visited, sometimes with her twenty-year-old daughter, Beatrix, occasionally taking him for a meal at the Gourmet. Beatrix became a regular visitor. When she said she thought his room 'horrid', he said, 'I actually rather like it in a curious kind of way.' For her

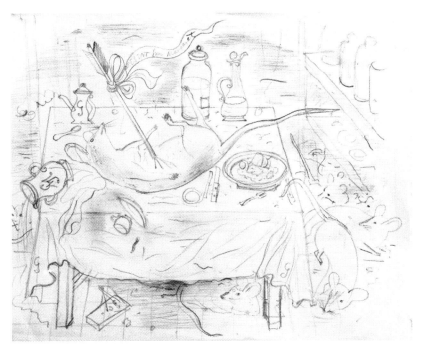

12. 'Present for Margaret', c. 1944

twenty-first birthday, in June 1945, she would take him to lunch at the Café Royal, where she told him, to his delight, a new way to spell 'birds': böds.[74]

Louis Bussell, a friend since 1924, often visited in the evenings. Earning a meagre living as a tutor, he was a woeful connoisseur of disaster. His wife had recently deserted him and their young son, and he was destitute, most adolescents having been evacuated from London. Cleverdon thought he 'inculcated gloom' and depressed Jones. Questioned years later, Burns thought this plausible; Grisewood and Mike Richey did not. And Jones later wrote that he and his 'melancholy friend' 'groused away together' quite happily.[75]

Through Morison, Jones tried unsuccessfully to get Bussell a job at *The Times* and, though poor himself, intermittently gave him money in varying amounts. (Cancelled cheques survive for one, five, and six pounds, gifts or loans that continued through 1946 and beyond.) Finding the littleness of Bussell's income incredible, Inland Revenue audited and harassed him. Desperate, he turned to Jones, who contacted Llewelyn Wyn Griffith, the author of *Up to Mametz* and a public relations officer for Inland Revenue. He interceded, and the persecution ceased. Bussell later wrote about Jones, 'No one is quicker to detect human suffering and to respect human dignity. One could weep in his presence without shame and I have done so.'[76]

On his way to the Catherine Wheel after Mass in the late autumn of 1944, Jones met Roy Campbell, the South African poet and Catholic convert, whom he had known before the war through Burns. Jones disliked

Campbell's poetry, which ridiculously, he thought, 'kept all the rules' of prosody, but liked him. They met regularly for a drink after Mass. Jones told him a favourite joke about a Welsh barmaid and a GI stationed in a Welsh village:

> The American says, 'Will you go out with me?'
> The barmaid says (in a Welsh accent), 'I'm too busy.'
> 'How about coffee in the morning?'
> 'I'm cleaning the pub.'
> 'How about after it closes?'
> 'I have m'lunch.'
> 'How about after it closes at night?'
> 'I go home to my mum.'
> 'Well, what d'you do about sex?'
> 'I have m'tea.'

In late 1945, Campbell would tell Jones that he wanted to visit Wyndham Lewis but heard he had become a Communist, and since he, Campbell, was a fascist, they might come to blows. Jones said, 'Oh go, for God's sake. This is not Russia. It doesn't matter what you believe here. Everyone is treated alike.' Campbell was, he said, 'a pugnacious chap but with a "heart of gold"' who, he felt, would have regarded him as a sissy had he not fought in the Great War.[77]

* * *

Jones was now poorer than he had ever been and undernourished. Lunch and supper were no longer served by 'the Muscat', and he was foraging for meals. Wheen brought him eggs and sometimes vegetables from a smallholding that he and his wife worked. Reduced weekly allowances from friends now totalled £2.5s.0d., while his weekly expenses were £6. Visiting in the spring of 1944, Ede had been appalled at his poverty and 'constant anxiety' about it. Convinced that Jones was 'one of the really important people in our country', he organised a fund to support him through anonymous donations from friends: Helen Sutherland increased her annual support from £54 to £63 and gave it anonymously through the fund; Grisewood contributed £25; Loulie Graham and her sister Anne Benthall, Australian admirers of his work, each contributed £10; Ede and Tom Burns each contributed £50; Clark £100.[78] (Jones never knew the extent of Clark's generosity to him.) With a continuing gift of £25 per year from the Hararis, his annual income leapt from £125 to £333.

In February 1945, working 'hard' at his writing precipitated a 'rather horrid return of neurasthenia'. Then he caught the flu and went to bed for seven weeks. In the papers and on a wireless inherited from his father, he followed the German offensive later called the Battle of the Bulge. It reminded him of the last great German push of March 1918. He admired the way the US Army 'held on so magnificently'. News of the Yalta Conference made him worry that the end of the war would be disastrous for Europe because Russia had conquered so much of it, and Russia 'is as totalitarian as Germany'.[79]

In March 1943, water pipes at 57 Onslow Square had frozen and burst, damaging some of his watercolours. Now, in March 1945, he learned, the house had been burglarised and 'any useful thing' of his taken along with his 1914–18 General Service Medal. He especially regretted the loss of Burns's portable record player and 'heavenly records', especially the one of Joyce reading from *Anna Livia Plurabelle*, which he would continue to miss until 'wonderful Dear Arthur Wheen' gave him a replacement in 1958.[80]

On 6 June 1945, Jones went to Pigotts for a week and stayed four months. High on its hill, Pigotts seemed to him 'curiously light' after his 'semi-subterranean back room'. Here he could eat, but kept getting his 'usual come-overs, a mixture of flu & nerves'.[81] It was hard to write separated from his books, but otherwise writing progressed well until Rosey erupted, making it 'next to impossible'. He later indicated what writing entailed for him emotionally:

> fear that accompanies any quite moderate and simple sorting or deciding or ordering or checking . . . the layers of disarray . . . not attending to things so that one complication piles on another. The muddle behind the muddles. Where to begin. The previous efforts of up-rooting and in spite of the effort – most unwise decisions and loss . . . Each procrastination making a further attempt more difficult. The sheer weight and complexity of material . . . muddle . . . even the simplest issue highly complex . . . crudeness of expression – a miss is as good as a mile when trying to express something.

Unwell all through the summer, on 6 October, feeling 'a bit better', he left for London after storing a large portfolio of pictures at Pigotts.[82]

On 16 October, he attended Eliot's inaugural lecture of the Virgil Society and, in the last week of November, went for lunch with Graham Greene.[83]

In November, Jones was able to resume writing, but 'struggling hard' with it in December ushered in Rosey again and with a vengeance. He was unable to work for a month, for a while unable even to read. Charles Burns told him that psychoanalysis would likely not help and that he had better stick with the neurologist, Dr Woods. Jones had hoped he was getting better and would soon be able to paint, so now he was near despair.[84] It was the worst time since his breakdown.

Like others, he had suspected early reports of the mass murder of Jews to be Allied propaganda of the worst sort, as in the previous war. But the destruction of the Warsaw ghetto in the autumn of 1944 appalled him. In April 1945, the Allied advance brought horrific revelations about the concentration camps. He was 'deeply shocked'. Later, he said, 'I just would not believe, about the Nazis, for ages . . . what they were doing . . . to the Jews. No, I couldn't believe it.' The nature and scale of the atrocity 'haunted' him. He was now convinced that the Germans, more than any other people, were afflicted with a split personality: 'It is a tragedy that so gifted, industrious, & outstandingly courageous a people should be *so ghastly* in other respects.' But he knew that they were not so unusual: he thought back to his service in Ireland and how 'certain types of men' behaved badly and, given official encouragement, could have been as bad as the Germans. But he 'had got the Nazi thing wrong', though he did not, then or later, change his view about the basic accuracy of Hitler's critique of Western cultural decadence.[85]

The end of war was, for Jones as for others, oddly anticlimactic and empty. Helen Sutherland's words, 'everything over and nothing done', perfectly expressed what he was 'in danger of feeling most of the time'.[86]

PART FIVE

RESURRECTIONS

CHAPTER 12: 1945–52

U ntil August 1946, Jones had worked in a spontaneous, unplanned way towards an epic-length poem. The writing begun in 1943 – concerning 'the Legions in Britain, especially in Wales' – grew to 143 pages, subsuming the earlier Roman writing of 1939–43. Again and again he revised, hoping unity would emerge, but it had not. He decided that his writing for the past seven years was worthless and abandoned it.[1]

In August 1946, Helen Sutherland was shocked by his sadness, malnourishment, and poverty – his trousers held up at the waist by safety pins – and had him accompany her to her new house, Cockley Moor, in the Lake District. It was an expanded, modernised farmhouse in the hamlet of High Row in Matterdale, above the village of Dockray – at 1,400 feet, the second highest house in Britain. Jones thought the east-facing view towards the peaks of Place Fell and, past Ullswater, High Dod 'staggering'.[2]

In April, while visiting the Grisewoods in Essex, he had managed to complete a painting he liked, *View from Gatwick House* (fig. 1). With a freedom and shimmering quality that would characterise his later paintings of trees and flowers-in-chalices, it was stylistically a new beginning. Encouraged by

1. *View from Gatwick House*, April 1946

2. *The Hogget*, Autumn 1946

having made it, now in Helen's house he painted the view from his bedroom window: 'hellish difficult' – 'picturesque' with 'Royal Academy pictures in all directions' – but 'incredibly beautiful & a new Turner sky each hour'. He was explosively prolific, in a month painting about ten good pictures, in which earth, hills, and cloudy sky consort in a unity of green and yellow tones – pictures largely of weather. One of the best he entitled *The Hogget* (fig. 2). Feeling 'unwell', on 3 September he returned to London. Back in Sheffield Terrace, he could not sleep. Nameless terror caused him to shake so much that his knees knocked.[3]

* * *

On 19 November Jones went to the newly married Cleverdons' basement flat at 49 Albany Street to hear the first radio broadcast of Douglas's adaptation of *In Parenthesis*, in which Emrys Jones played John Ball, Dylan Thomas delivered Dai Greatcoat's boast, and Richard Burton spoke the parts of four other figures. Jones was appalled. The actors falsely stressed words, exaggerated emotion. The musical interludes were ludicrous. For the repeat broadcast the next evening, he joined the Grisewoods in Essex and, while listening, exclaimed, 'Oh, no! Oh, no!' He hated it, broke down, and went to bed for a week. Harman suggested that he was reacting to hearing warfare made real in the acting and sound effects, but he objected that the realities of the Blitz had not distressed him. And his symptoms had begun in Cumberland. Too anxious and depressed to leave the Grisewoods, he stayed for a month before returning to London and his room.[4]

On 6 January 1947 a snowstorm inaugurated the worst winter in more than a century. Its extreme cold, to Jones like the return of the Ice Age, would underlie the image of apocalyptic cold in *The Anathemata* (68). From January through early March he recorded 'cold' and 'snow' in his pocket diary. After 6 March, its pages are blank. He could not sleep, could not read. When he spoke, it was in the weak, elderly, 'far-off voice' of severe depression. Tom Burns had returned from Spain and was living with his bride, Mabél, at 1 Victoria Square. Jones moved in with them. He 'really has been quite bad', Tom wrote Ede, 'really right *down* again in every way'. Tom and Jones's other friends were 'very worried'.[5]

In early March, Jones told Dr Woods that writing now made him ill. Woods advised him to stop. But he could not bear ending all creative activity. Tom suggested he see a psychiatrist, and Nicolete took him to Eric Strauss, now chief psychiatrist at St Bartholomew's. Strauss diagnosed him as schizophrenic (a more common diagnosis then) and prescribed electric shock treatment. Tom thought the diagnosis 'balls' and was adamant: 'On no account whatever should you have shock treatment. It might go wrong.' Jones did not want to return to Strauss because, he explained to Nicolete, while he had no objection to Strauss being Jewish, he (Jones) would feel obliged in kindness to dissimulate if anti-Jewish feelings ever came up in therapy.[6*]

Tom summoned his brother Charles, who consulted with Strauss but agreed that Jones must not be subjected to shock therapy, which would cause memory loss and disturb or even end his creative life. Before moving to Birmingham, Charles had worked at Bowden House Clinic in Harrow and knew and respected its practitioners. He thought that Jones should undergo treatment there, although the weekly fee was a staggering 16 guineas.

* Here I synthesise accounts by Nicolete Gray, who could not remember the psychiatrist's name and said he did not charge a fee, and Tom Burns, who named Strauss, who did charge a fee.

Charles made the arrangements and enlisted Helen Sutherland's financial help. She gave £50. The Burns brothers and other friends also contributed.[7] After three months of blank pages in his pocket diary, for 13 June 1947 Jones entered two words, 'Bowden House'.

*   *   *

Tom drove him there. It was a large late-Victorian blond brick house in ten acres of quiet, treed grounds on Sudbury Hill. The director was an elderly Scot named Hugh Crichton-Miller, the founder of the Tavistock Clinic in London. The other psychiatrists were Grace Nichol and Bill Stevenson – she a Jungian; he, like Crichton-Miller, eclectic. Jones concluded his first consultation by saying to Crichton-Miller, 'You're not going to make me normal, are you, because I don't want to be.'[8]

The first week at the clinic Jones was restricted to his room, on the first floor at the front, so he could experience his feelings with uninterrupted clarity. After a physical examination, he was injected with the truth-serum Pentothal, so he would talk freely about himself in response to questions. For psychotherapy he saw Stevenson for an hour each morning and sometimes briefly in the afternoon. The plan was to stay another week or two, have a holiday in Sidmouth, and resume treatment in London.[9] But it soon became apparent that he needed to stay longer, and he remained at the clinic for nearly half a year.

None of the Bowden House psychiatrists believed in electric shock therapy. Stevenson, in particular, opposed it. Dr Glyn Davies came to demonstrate it in 1948 but, according to Davies, who succeeded Crichton-Miller as director, shock therapy was never otherwise administered there. It has repeatedly been stated in print that Jones underwent electric shock therapy. He did not.[10] *

There were about a dozen patients – all, like Jones, voluntary admissions. After his week of solitude, he joined them (finding them congenial) in a daily routine that began with prayers and hymn singing, followed by breakfast, occupational therapy (weaving, pot-making, sculpting, spontaneous painting) and his private session with Stevenson. Then coffee, and the rest of the morning spent reading or walking in the grounds, followed by compulsory throwing of a ten-pound medicine ball – an exercise in group dynamics intended to reveal aggression. (Not knowing what the ball was called, he wrote to Grisewood, 'They call the game "Medicine Ball" – jolly embarrassing terms.') One of the patients was, Jones said, 'a medicine ball cannon'. At 1 p.m. they ate lunch, followed by organised sports, which included 'badmington' (sic), a game new to him that he liked, then group

* Tom Burns and Harman Grisewood confirmed this.

therapy with all patients, led by Stevenson or Nichol. Tea followed at 4, and a period of rest when they could see their psychiatrists again. Supper at 7, then they went either to the quiet lounge to read or to the other lounge to talk or listen to the radio or to hear one of their number play the piano. Then to their rooms and lights-out at 10.50.[11]

3. William A. H. Stevenson, c. 1965

Stevenson (fig. 3), a Scot, had trained at St Bartholomew's and served as a psychiatrist for the air force in India and Burma. He had read Philosophy at Oxford before studying medicine. A devout Anglican, he sometimes gave lay sermons in church. He was morally uncritical, had a good sense of humour, was interesting and spontaneous in conversation, and loved classical music and visual art.[12]

Trained as a Freudian, he diagnosed Jones as suffering from an unresolved Oedipus complex aggravated by war.[13] The Oedipal theory is basically that a young boy loves his mother but, fearful of paternal retaliation in the form of castration, represses sexual feeling towards her. He experiences this until about age five and again at puberty, after which he either outgrows the complex or represses his sexuality. At Stevenson's urging, Jones read *Totem and Taboo*, which largely concerns the Oedipus complex – he later bought a copy.

Jones found therapeutic sessions with Stevenson 'a strain' because he had 'to *think quite hard* in order to collaborate' in seeing his life in a Freudian light. In addition to agoraphobia, Jones feared dogs, horses, snakes, and germs (at Sheffield Terrace he took sponge baths in his sink rather than use the shared bath): underlying these phobias Stevenson saw displaced fear of sexual passion. According to Freud, phobias mask fear of castration. Whether or not spanking evokes castration, as Freud claimed (David's father spanked him at least twice), castration is certainly evoked by young David having his head stuck in a chair and (he thought) about to be sawed off at an event presided over by his father. Stevenson surely appreciated the trauma of David's circumcision at fourteen, after which, as David confided to Hague in the 1920s, he thought his penis would be 'unappealing' to a woman. (He had nightmares about his circumcision in his forties, when he was deeply in love with Prudence.) After his brother's death, when David was sixteen, his mother may have turned to him with increased affection, strengthening the Oedipal tie. It was then that he decided to forgo marriage for, he thought, the sake of art.[14]*

* In 1988, Petra inadvertently corroborated the Oedipal diagnosis when explaining Jones's lukewarmness during their engagement: he was 'a rather mixed up character because his mother fussed over him as a child. That's what David's sister said. He was a bit special to his mother.'

The Oedipus complex may explain his frequent and excessive illnesses. When young, sickness meant staying home with mother. Now, when unwell, he went to bed, a way of 'returning to the womb', which Freud called the 'substitute for copulation' for a man 'inhibited by the threat of castration'.[15]

Related to all this is Jones's refusal to assume a 'father figure' position. In notes for Stevenson, he wrote, 'I see how all my life I've avoided such a position in innumerable & subtle ways.' He had refused to take exams to qualify to teach art. He had declined to be commissioned as an officer. He wrote, 'I see how one repeats the pattern of one's life . . . I always had an inkling that this was so.' He had manifested what he calls 'my fear of sex' in making sexual advances to already attached women: Elsie Hancock and Dorothea de Halpert, both engaged to other men; Petra after her engagement to Tegetmeier; and Diana Creagh, in love with Tom Burns.

Stevenson inquired into Jones's blocked sexuality possibly finding homosexual expression. But Jones had always been certain about his sexual orientation. He once complained to Grisewood about affection for males being thought homosexual: 'It is absolutely natural to me to appreciate and enjoy the physical charm of my men friends and to love their features and their faces and so on. This is entirely natural to me and involves no implication of homosexuality. I should have thought that's simply part of being a sensitive and appreciative human being.'[16]*

He now attributed his neurosis partly to 'early family life'. Although none of his surviving notes for Stevenson concern sibling rivalry, a large part of his childhood involved struggle with his brother for their mother's affection. David had been winning and, in retaliation, Harold tormented him. How nine-year-old Harold must have resented having to share his room with 'little Benjamin'! Feelings towards siblings are seldom completely repressed, and David probably wished Harold dead. When he did die, David felt terrible guilt, which endured all his life. That is why he never spoke of his brother. It also accounts for a Freudian slip he made in 1953 when referring to the ghost of Marley, Scrooge's dead business partner, as 'the ghost of his brother'.[17]

Sharing a room with Harold for eleven years continued, in a sense, with platoon mates in huts, tents, bivouacs, and dugouts, their deaths cruelly multiplying Harold's death. Part of the deep underlying meaning of *In Parenthesis* involves re-enactment of that death, which was, for David

---

* Towards homosexuals he was unbiased. As a sometime resident of Chelsea and member of Ede's circle, he was familiar with them and had experienced their advances though only once to a distressing degree, when his own politeness and inclination to accommodate made discouraging an obdurate suitor painfully difficult. Jones later told a friend that he was 'driven mad' by it, adding, 'If you consider my nervous system, my so-called sensitivities, the way I live, what upsets me, what I like, I ought to be a homosexual but I'm not.'

emotionally fratricidal.* If, as seems likely, he felt survivor's guilt after the war, it was an extension of guilt over horrific success in Oedipal sibling rivalry. (It is now thought that what renders P.T.S.D. in adults a chronic rather than temporary condition is trauma experienced earlier, in childhood. In the death of Harold, David had experienced such trauma.)

Stevenson saw Jones's anxiety also as fear repressed in the trenches. There Jones had witnessed sexual mutilation and castration-like severing of limbs and heads. Far worse was the effect of repeated, prolonged enemy artillery fire. Even before therapy, writing to Charles Burns, Jones had said his continuous 'fear and distress' was to be endured 'like a "barrage"'.[18] His agoraphobia may well have its principal cause in artillery fire, from which he had huddled in dugouts – he regularly called his room his 'dugout'.

If Jones disclosed his feeling of walking two feet above the ground beside Petra in 1926, Stevenson would have interpreted it as phobic reaction to losing control. It may also be related to the feeling of unreality, absence, or depersonalisation during battle, since its analogue was his most frightening moment, about two feet above the ground on a plank bridge at Festubert in 1916.

Jones's new understanding gave him affinity with the figure of the Maimed King, alluded to in *In Parenthesis* (84, 162), and the wounded saviour-figure, the dying god – an affinity placing him imaginatively at the centre of Western culture. He would later say that the 'maimed king' who 'at any hour' visits to pray before the cross in *The Anathemata* (179) is Oedipus. Oedipal echoes would pervade that work.[19] †

On 16 July 1947, in his first letter from Bowden House, Jones told Grisewood that 'the *theory* of all this psychotherapy' is 'highly illuminating'. After fifteen years of not knowing why he suffered, it was

* Sentries perform 'brother-keeping' (*IP* 51, 69), a phrase evocative of Cain's question, 'Am I my brother's keeper?' In the poem's motif of Abel, every dead infantryman is innocent but implies a surviving guilty brother. Allusion to Malory's Balin and Balan (79) is to brothers who, their identities obscured, kill each other. The shared first syllable of their names is that of the surname of John Ball, the figure in the poem who physically represents Jones.

† In it Jones writes of Jesus and (as representative of mankind) Mary: 'He that was her son / is now her lover' (224), 'he her groom that is his mother' (235). During an erotic encounter, a stonemason admires his lover's breasts as 'Hills o' the Mother' (132), and a clerk from Oriel College confuses his lover with his mother (144). In 1970 Jones would write, 'I suppose my stuff has on the whole been centred round the Queen of Heaven & a cult-hero – son & spouse.' And the poem as a whole may have Oedipal associations. Freud saw art as mother-substitution, and writing was, for Jones, initially compensation for drawing and painting, activity originally associated with his mother. He habitually called this work by the short form *Ana* – he would write that reviewers 'think *Ana* is a very peculiar girl'. His mother's middle name was Ann.

'*something* to feel that'. He believed 'Freud really had it right, this father-mother relationship.' In notes for Stevenson he wrote, 'in some particulars in my own case the experience was indeed like pouring acid on an etching plate – there was the pattern quite clear . . . I see that *everything* one does is conditioned by one's psycho-pathology.'[20]

But in notes for Stevenson endorsing Freudian theory his tone is that of obediently repeating a lesson. He wrote more naturally when sceptical of Freud's simple-minded, reductive, 'part-for-the-whole' inclination:

> occasionally I have felt that the urgent & imperative demand for an answer coupled perhaps with a slight suggestion that such & such *must* be so has caused me to admit something which was only a half truth – even under narcotic I felt this. Perhaps it is all part of this same weakness in me of wanting to agree with what a person suggests, appearing to do so & worrying about it afterwards.

In later years, he would say of his Oedipal diagnosis, 'I just can't really believe it.' While remaining grateful to Crichton-Miller and Stevenson, he would recall some of what they said as nonsense and warn Grisewood against falling into the hands of 'trickcyclists' (army slang for psychiatrists).[21] To many of us now, Freud's terms seem crude, the Oedipus theory obscuring a more subtle dynamic of affection and fear.

How accurate is it to see Jones's 'Dad' as a threatening figure? It was 'Mother' who wielded the tickley-toe, which hung close-at-hand in the scullery – she who sang to her three progeny of three blind mice fleeing the wife with the knife. Her cool, abrupt, caustic disapproval was the primary early cause of her son's anxiety and repression. That disapproval was not castration (certainly not by the father) but withholding of love in all its awfulness, which, to a child so strongly attached to her, was tantamount to annihilation.

Underlying his love of women was fear. When writing about his nightmare of circumcision to Prudence, he drew the nurse who had presided. His mother had taken him there (his father having to work – and David was unconscious when the male doctor operated). With the Cleverdons, he would soon see a Harrow School production of *Macbeth* in which Lady Macbeth was played passionately in a way that was traumatic for Jones, who 'shook with emotion'. Afterwards, as the Cleverdons drove him home, he said, 'My God. What a bitch! What a *bloody* awful bitch! If that's what it's like give me a celibate life.'[22]

Guilt is the core of neurosis. Guilt over Harold's death explains a lot. But Jones was also generally prone to guilt. In the late 1920s, a remark such as 'Heavens! have you not read *Arabia Deserta*?' made him 'feel almost a criminal'. Christmas 'always' depressed him 'terribly', partly owing to guilt over not writing to people and sending gifts. He felt guilty about being no help to his aged parents. Dorothea's involvement in charitable works made him 'feel very guilty'. He would feel 'guilty' when Cleverdon became ill during a rehearsal for a new production of *In Parenthesis* in 1955. Unanswered letters weighed on his conscience. He apologised for not proofreading letters. A priest to whom he was confessing once told him to hurry up and not be so painstaking in enumerating his faults, which made him furious (another fault). One of his close friends later in life, Sarah Balme, said, 'I think he was always worried about his worthiness, not as a writer or artist – he had no doubt about that – but as a person.'[23]

Did Catholicism make him feel guilty, particularly about sex? Probably not. As a convert, he was untouched by Catholic-puritanical Jansenism, thanks largely to O'Connor, Gill, and John-Baptist Reeves. Along with the rest of the Chelsea Group, he thought Catholicism committed him to belief in the goodness of the body and sex.* Catholicism includes all the levels of psychological development: mythic, intellectual, and spiritual. Jones's faith was not limited to an immature narrative-mythic level, to which Freud reduces all religion. For Stevenson, as for Crichton-Miller, religion was psychologically toxic only when narrowly sectarian, ideologically or ritually obsessive, crudely fundamentalist, or prudishly repressive.[24] Jones's Catholicism was none of these.

Yet religion seems to have informed his neurosis. Since carrying a cross in the garden as a child, he had a devotion to the crucifixion. He once spoke to Grisewood about it, solemnly, barely able to speak, slowly drawing a cross as it actually looked in Roman times, indicating how the body hung in torment, the suffering inflicted being, to him, literally unspeakable. In the 1960s, he would wake from sleep to find that he had scratched a cross on his chest.[25] In a letter to the *Catholic Herald* of 15 August 1941, which opposed blaming Jews for killing Jesus, he expressed a belief in 'the general guilt of all . . . mankind' whereby 'you and I . . . drove in the nails & . . . spat upon the Victim' – a pietistic view that is guilt-instilling. The crucifixion understood as the Son's self-sacrificial obedience to the Father reflects the Oedipus complex and seems likely to intensify feelings of guilt in anyone who believes it happened for his or her sake.

Most psychologists today would ascribe Jones's neurosis simply to conditioning, in which his brother and mother played a part but only as contributory to the powerful effects of the 1914–18 war. Today he would be diagnosed as suffering from chronic post-traumatic stress disorder, symptoms of which include increased physical illnesses, dissociation

---

* For these reasons and because he had become a Catholic at twenty-six when psychologically fully formed, J. Miles and D. Shiel seem mistaken in repeatedly attributing his sexual reticence to Catholic prohibitions against extramarital sex (prohibited also to Anglicans) and what they call 'the forbidding nature of his adopted religion' (p. 243).

4. *Tree at Bowden House*, 1947

syndromes, and avoidance-withdrawal syndromes, making marriage difficult if not impossible.

Yet Freudian theory remains compelling. In *Totem and Taboo*, Jones read that repression takes on a life of its own so that, allowed to dominate in one area (sex), it tends to expand into another (art, in his case). Painting and writing sublimate sexuality. Any resurgence of the repressed libido in daring, prolific painting activates prohibition. He now realised that explosive artistic spontaneity in the summer of 1932 (resulting in scores of wonderful paintings and the new, open form of Part 7 of *In Parenthesis*) activated the repression reflex, as did his recent painting in Cumberland. Stevenson told him that, to combat such repression, he had to paint and write. He told Stevenson, 'I now see that like the imposers of the danegeld – the unconscious demands a higher & higher blackmail – less & less activity as a price so that the *only* way is to beat the unconscious in open war.' And since 'my *major* conflict displays itself in relation to painting . . . it *must* be fought out in that terrain'. In August 1947, Stevenson and Crichton-Miller restarted Jones drawing and painting. The old soldier was going to war again. He began taking back his creative life, and, for allowing him to do this, he would always respect Freud, while remaining wary of much of his theory.[26]*

* * *

Whether Jones felt like it or not and regardless of results, he was to paint. Forbidden to stop or tear up, he managed to finish a series of trees done in a style that is, like them, wild and free (fig. 4). The new drawing reflects

* To Charles Burns he said that he considered Freud 'something of an Aristotle . . . to Jung's Plato', believed 'Siggy Freud . . . more "Catholic"' than Jung, and felt Freud to be 'on surer ground & that in the end this is more "patient of baptism" than the more apparent "religiousness" of Jung'. In 1952 Jones would say with remarkable prescience about pre-theological thought, 'Freud will be the new Aristotle', the intellectual basis of Christianity. Two years later, reading the psychoanalyst-anthropologist Géza Róheim confirmed for him 'some aspects of this matter.'

'spontaneity', which he was discussing with Stevenson. A 'fundamental dictum' for Jones was the saying (by the poet Agathon, quoted in *Nicomachean Ethics*), 'Chance loves art and art loves chance.' Stevenson urged him to draw women he observed on his way to and from church and at Mass, and insisted that he resume writing and introduce women into his writing. Jones had Nicolete Gray bring him his long poetic manuscript.[27]

And so began the second spring of Jones's creative life. A few years later he would tell a young friend, Juliet Wood, that a thing is true only if broken and remade – an axiom for art reflecting his life experience.[28] Recovering from his second breaking, he would go on to produce nearly half his life's work.

In his therapy he made steady progress and, by the end of his stay, felt much better. Crichton-Miller told him, 'It is not just the theory of psychoanalysis that cures or alleviates an illness but the art of healing. There is no universal therapy, and Stevenson was not always successful with his patients, but he was just right for you.'[29]

Not a believer in the National Health Service (begun in 1946), Jones always paid, or neglected to pay, his doctor bills. He stayed at Bowden House five months and one week at a cost of £380 plus approximately £60 for personal expenses. His life savings of £103.2s.6d. vanished. The Artists' Benevolent Association contributed £130. (His father had paid since 1929, on his behalf, for a policy insuring him against illness.) That money plus donations from friends paid nearly half of what he owed the clinic. He would take a year to pay the rest.[30]

His treatment continued in weekly visits to Dr Stevenson that would enable him to fight depression with some success, but he '*never* returned', said Grisewood, 'to the David I first knew' and he remained agoraphobic. In 1969 Jones would say, 'One is never cured unless treated when young, but one is enabled to work.' In 1962, he said that his nervous breakdowns had cut his 'production in half'.[31]

* * *

Near the end of his stay, after finishing eight pictures, Jones began drawing three trees from his bedroom window: a huge cedar of Lebanon (with an unusual configuration in its topmost branches) flanked by a chestnut and a tall, bedraggled pine shorn of many of its branches. He made a number of drawings, the last becoming the painting *Vexilla Regis* (fig. 5), which takes its title from his favourite Good Friday hymn. In its early stages, he had tried to paint with only 'a slight adjustment' of the actual view, but 'the picture assumed a "view of trees at sunset" feeling … & dreaminess of technique became more & more offensive', so he introduced 'a number of' symbolic conceptions. There were several moments of crisis, during which he would

5. *Vexilla Regis*, 1948

have torn it up had he not promised Stevenson to destroy nothing without his permission, which Stevenson withheld. 'In a sense,' Jones wrote, Stevenson was the work's 'co-producer'.

Jones 'read' the painting to him. In the '"world forest"', the three foremost trees evoke the crucifixion. The central tree is symbolically multiple: the cross; the Tree of Life with a river flowing from its base 'for the healing of the nations' (Revelation 22:2); the paschal candle of Easter with five spikes of incense in diamond formation; and the Yggdrasil of Norse mythology – 'for all these things are one thing in some sense'. The historical setting is 'the collapse of the Roman world'. In the middle right is Stonehenge as he had seen it in 1915, to the right of it 'the Welsh hills'. The tree on the right of the central tree is that of the 'good thief' – in it nests the eucharistic pelican. To the left is the tree of 'the other thief'. Stevenson raised questions about this tree and guilt. Jones replied that 'far more pronounced' in his consciousness 'was 1) the imperial signum, 2) the lost standards of Varus in the Teutoburg Forest, the aquila' (Roman standard). 'It is also a . . . phallus, of course' and a 'may-pole' cross-wrapped with ribbons. As imperial standard and 'triumphal column', it is 'a power-symbol, . . . not rooted in the ground'. 'S. Augustine's remark that "empire is great robbery" influenced me here. It is *not* meant to be *bad* in itself but . . . proud and self-sufficient. Nevertheless it is shadowed by the spreading central Tree, and the dove, in fact, hovers over this tree of the truculent robber for somehow or other he is "redeemed" too!' Jones thought the picture 'special', not necessarily better than others or even as 'good'. Consisting of images, it was, he thought, 'a *bit* "literary"'.[32] It is a study for *The Anathemata*. He would consider using *Vexilla Regis* and *Aphrodite in Aulis* to illustrate *The Anathemata* though 'neither come off in [black and white] reproduction'.[33]

Stevenson and Crichton-Miller told him that returning to Sheffield Terrace would be a mistake. So he stayed with the Burnses, then the Hagues. He wanted to be near Bowden House, where he was seeing Stevenson as an outpatient, so in December 1947 he took a room in Northwick Lodge, a boarding house in Harrow, fifteen minutes walk from the clinic along High Street. Intending to stay 'for a month or two', he would stay for sixteen years.[34]

Northwick Lodge was, according to one visitor, 'a grotty old grey brick Victorian house where junior masters had squalid digs'. Dark-green linoleum covered the hallway floor. The wide creaking stairway smelled of damp plaster and cooked cabbage. Jones's room was at the back on the first floor. The house was built into the south-east slope of the hill, so his room was three stories above ground. A large 8- by 6-foot double window filled it with light. About twenty feet away grew a tall acacia, 'the tree of heaven'; and, beyond that, was a falling-away view through the tops of elms, over the Harrow playing fields, to central London and, on a very clear day, the Surrey Hills beyond. At night, the city lights were like a fallen constellation.[35] After Sheffield Terrace, Northwick Lodge was 'awfully nice' but, at £6 per week, 'expensive'.

Like the Brockley of his youth and like Sidmouth, Harrow was quasi-pastoral. Through his window, he watched boys playing rugby 'spotting the green of the field with red & white far away' and cows and sometimes ponies grazing in the adjacent school farm. Beyond was a derelict golf-course, whose bunkers reminded him 'of Passcendaele [sic] & burial mounds of chieftains'. North-east was a ploughed field. Looking at its waves of golden wheat, he sang 'John Barleycorn' to himself. He preferred the view in a light mist, which obscured the red-brick suburban sprawl beyond. In front of the house, Peterborough Hill Road resembled a country road but fell to the 'ghastly' new town, a district of commerce, heavy traffic, 'red brick & "Odeons" & seething multitudes of people'. What survived of old Harrow was 'an illusion of real country', but he enjoyed the illusion.[36]

Belonging to Harrow School, Northwick Lodge was run by Christopher Carlile, a retired mathematics master and bursar who was intelligent, courteous, and aristocratic in manner, lending the place an atmosphere of shabby gentility. Jones thought him 'remarkable', 'a heavenly old man', and, though agnostic, a 'saint'. Carlile came up to his room to ask, 'Will you have fish or some hare?' and Jones enjoyed the luxury of choosing. A bell summoned all to the communal dining room, which looked out on the back garden. Painting or writing, he could not easily break off, but Carlile did not mind his being late. On Hague's first visit, Carlile led him to Jones's room saying, 'A great man we think him, a very great man.' Cleaning was done by Mr Carol, kind, simple, and prone to depression – Jones felt affection for him. Mrs Carol, the cook, was lethargic, argumentative, bossy – he disliked her. When her cooking was unacceptable, he would eat grapefruit and a boiled egg in his room. On a small table there he kept a large jar of Nescafé, Lapsang Souchong tea, Bath Olivers, Gentleman's Relish, Oxo, and a loaf of bread.[37]

There were initially seven tenants, including two or three junior masters, two long-term residents, and the rest young men finishing professional studies. Jones enjoyed meals and tea with them. Dining there, the Cleverdons found the conversation 'general and jovial'. Long after supper, Jones and others would remain at table conversing. He was experiencing again the continuing fellowship he had liked in the army. His friends saw that he was becoming happier. It was the beginning of what Petra would remember as 'the happiest time of his life'. He was now seeing less of old friends and corresponding more with them. Each morning the post and The Times were left on a wicker hamper outside his door.[38]

Because Harrow was high, it was cold, and this house (draughty, without central heating) was, he wrote, 'the coldest house in it!' You could see your breath indoors. He heated his room with a coal fire and a gas ring, in winter wearing his greatcoat whenever not in bed. Evenings he spent hours on the unheated landing on the phone with friends. Later Carlile let him use the phone in his (heated) room.[39]

In spring the view from his window was 'jolly nice'. He loved the 'special fresh green' of trees 'that lasts only a few days'. 'Every conceivable bird . . . from blue tits to magpies' and 'heavenly' goldfinches appeared at his window. In the summer with the window open, their singing filled the room. On stormy nights, he enjoyed watching the lightning from his darkened high room. During the day he sometimes saw rainbows arching over the green receding landscape. He liked 'rainbows very greatly – one of the nicest of merely natural things'.[40]

*   *   *

Jones saw Stevenson each Tuesday, paying £5.5s. per visit. They also visited socially, at 'Steve's' home and Northwick Lodge. There Stevenson saw *Aphrodite in Aulis*, which he considered 'not psychologically balanced'. Jones responded, 'the balance between form & content is satisfactorily maintained – that is why I like it.' It was, he thought, his last painting 'to really *get there*'. He liked some of the recent tree-paintings 'quite genuinely' but did not see them 'as authentic & sure of direction or as pleasurable as the 1932 ones, . . . not as much "me"'.[41]

Within a week of moving in, he was painting the trees from his window and drawing 'large heads of imaginary people, mostly girls'. One of the best, done at Pentecost, is *Sunday Mass: In Homage to G. M. Hopkins S. J.* (fig. 6). A friend named Hilda Cochrane bought it for £150. He would visit her in 1960 to see it again, sitting silently for ten minutes, then asking, 'Do you like the bird?' To his astonishment, she asked, 'What bird?'[42] (There is a tiny bird in

6. *Sunday Mass: In Homage to G. M. Hopkins S. J.*, 1948

the far woman's hat looking like an ornament, as realistically it must be, but hinting at the descent of the Holy Spirit in the form of a dove.) Giving the picture vitality is its contrast between the monumental simplicity of the foremost face-and-neck and the frantic activity of hair, scarf, lace, dress, and background.

Jones now had enough pictures for an exhibition. Nan Kivell offered him one at the Redfern Gallery from 27 May to 26 June 1948, shared with Bryant Wynter and Derek Hill, or a solo exhibition in October. Jones chose the earlier date because he needed money. Thirty-three of his pictures were shown, and he went to the gallery 'nearly every other day' to meet people, enjoying reunions with many. One day he went with Nicolete, another with Prudence, who marked the occasion by giving him a copy of *Finnegans Wake*. They sat together on an inflated seat in the gallery, on which a fat woman then sat, raising their feet off the floor and giving them prolonged irrepressible 'giggles'. Clark said that he thought these paintings 'better work than before in many ways'. Jones wished not to part with two that he saw as 'related to' his writing: *The Lady* and *Vexilla Regis*, the former not for sale, the latter given the 'whacking price' of £500. Ralph Harari wanted it, but Jones explained that the price was so high to deter buyers, that if it sold he would prefer it to go to a national gallery, but, failing that, Harari could have it.[43]

Press coverage was minimal and tepid, but Herbert Read was impressed and chose a selection of Jones's pictures to go to the Venice Biennale along with works by Turner and Henry Moore. And the show was a commercial success. By 2 June, all pictures for sale except *Vexilla Regis* had sold, including three added after the opening. After expenses and taxes, Jones's share was £1,840.4s.0d., but he would receive only £400 this year. He pleaded repeatedly for more payments over the next few years, and Nan Kivell occasionally sent a cheque for £100.[44]

* * *

Through Carlile, Jones met Audrey and Edward Malan, a classicist and housemaster of 'The Knoll', across the road. Jones telephoned him with questions about Roman history and Latin, and he made quick academic house calls. Through the Malans, on 29 June 1948, he met other Harrow masters, including the senior Classics master and amateur cellist, E. V. Colin Plumtre, who became a close friend and resource for questions about classical antiquity. Another master was 'Ronnie' Watkins, who taught English and loved Shakespeare. A closer friend was Maurice Percival, the art master, a fellow lodger and Catholic convert, a melancholy bachelor who had lost an arm in an auto accident in which his fiancé died. Jones disliked his art and aesthetics but considered him 'a really *good* man', an 'admirable and dear man'. Percival introduced him to Len Walton, who taught modern languages and became his closest friend among the Harrow masters. Catholic, jovial, charming, an exacting scholar, formidable in argument, he was enthusiastic about Racine, Russian literature, and the religious philosopher Vladimir Solovyov, whom Jones came to admire. Walton and his wife, Peg, frequently had him to supper, always inviting him for Christmas Day.[45]

7. Stanley Honeyman, 1947

Among the lodgers, new friends included Julian Hall, a tall, tubercular, elegant, long-haired baronet and former major, currently a minor drama critic for *The Times*. He sometimes took Jones to dinner at the house of his friend Lady Sonia Melchett. Among the professional-student lodgers, Jones's closest friend was Stanley Honeyman (fig. 7), who arrived in the autumn of 1948, a lanky twenty-three-year-old Yorkshireman and former artillery captain working for an estate agent and studying evenings to qualify as a property surveyor. He remembered

> Being with David was like playing tennis with a better player. He brought from you insights, comments, knowledge that you didn't dream were there. He lifted you up. He always talked to the simplest person as an equal. I shouldn't think that he knew how to talk down to anyone. He had an original mind and a depth of mind that is rare, but you never heard big words from him or difficult constructions, high-falutin' approaches.

The originality of his mind was owing, Honeyman said, to 'lateral thinking'. Once after Honeyman praised some aspect of Western art, Jones said, 'you're like me, you've got the west wind in your face'. Jones regularly went, sometimes with him and Hall, for a pre-supper Guinness to the King's Head in the High Street, a dark, quiet, comfortable pub, the kind he liked.[46]

On 1 March 1949, Jones and Honeyman attended a lecture on architecture by John Betjeman in the Harrow School Speech Room. Betjeman showed slides of English buildings, including one of a church, saying, 'I'll give half-a-crown to anybody who knows where that is.' Jones whispered to Honeyman, 'St. Bartholomew the Great, Smithfield' and afterwards claimed his prize. Betjeman had praised in extravagant terms the Speech Room, a mock Gothic half-circle, and Jones remonstrated, 'John, if you use such adjectives of this place, what is left over for the Parthenon or Chartres?'[47]

Jones and Honeyman built up a repertory of phrases with private meanings. One or the other would say, 'Moses' beard', a reference in a joke to female pubic hair, to recall being caught between polite laughter at the joke and deference to Julian Carlile's (Chris's son) moral outrage at its crudeness. Or he would say, 'Keep your thumb on the blade and strike upward', advice on how to kill with a knife, given by a grateful bandit to the priest hearing his dying confession. Or, 'Thank Christ we've got Rose's', recalling the exclamation of a friend of Honeyman who believed that mixing gin with Rose's Lime Juice prevented hangovers.[48]

Jones became friendly with a lovely eighteen-year-old Glaswegian art student named Morag McLennan in the summer of 1948. In 1949–50, Morag lived in Harrow to help her elder sister, newly widowed with two small children, and visited Jones weekly. He talked with her about 'just anything', but when she tried to discuss Aubrey Beardsley, he said, 'I'm not interested in those decadent chaps.'[49]

He met her art-school friends, including Isabel Sharpe. She and Morag would bang on his door at midnight or one in the morning. Glad to see them, he gave them green olives, coffee, and whisky – teasing them, as he always did Scots, by turning a bottle of Scotch upside-down and shaking it before pouring. They chatted till 3 a.m. Isabel made him a cushion and a beautiful green-and-red bedspread and gave him a little red record player.

Jones got to know Morag's sister, May. She remarried in 1949 and lived in a house next to the Malans. Morag moved back to Glasgow but always visited him when visiting May. For Morag's twenty-first birthday, in 1951, he sent her the Penguin book about his art, published in 1949. (Although he disliked the inaccurate colour reproductions, he thought Ironside's essay, 'absolutely first class & *not embarrassing*'.) For her twenty-second birthday, he made her a drawing of a cat.[50]

Morag consulted him about suitors. He urged her to drop one she was 'terribly fond of', and, because she respected Jones, she did. (In retrospect, she thought he had tremendous good sense about matters of the heart.) Eventually she became interested in Richard Owens, a Harrow Classics master whom Jones knew and sometimes consulted. He encouraged her, and they married, living briefly in Harrow, leaving in the early 1950s when Richard became a stockbroker.

Thereafter, Jones would ring Morag up if worried about a spot, rash, or ailment; and she would dash to the chemist's for a remedy. He felt no compunction about her travelling thirty miles to bring it, after which he might ask her to go into central London to Rymans for the foolscap writing paper he liked. She mended clothes for him that she thought should be thrown out. When the barber, Mr Caddy, was unable to visit to cut his hair, she did it. She once took clothing to be cleaned and found in every available pocket of waistcoat and coat a folded pound note – put there, he explained, in case of emergency – but an issue no longer in circulation. When she told him that, he had no idea what to do. She went to the bank and exchanged them.[51]

Jones's youngest friend was Michael Rees, a sixth-former studying modern languages, whom Walton encouraged to visit. Rees was a native of Carmarthen, raised Anglican, but now 'convinced of the truth of the Catholic faith'. He left Harrow in 1949 for Jesus College, Cambridge. When Jones learned from his Christmas card in 1952 that he had entered the Catholic Church, he had a Mass said for him. Rees visited later that year, and Jones showed him 'with pride' his copy of the pocket Welsh Catholic missal, in which he had red-pencilled Latin crosses in the margins at the words of consecration.[52]

With Rees and many other visitors, increasingly now and at length, Jones recounted and interpreted Welsh history. Always he stressed the importance of Llywelyn's death in 1282; the Tudors making English the only official language of Wales, thereby splitting Welsh-speaking peasantry from the gentry; the Calvinism ('that most hateful of religions') of Welsh Methodism, severing the Welsh from their folk heritage and possibly altering the character of the people, who, in the Middle Ages, had been like the Irish; and the pressure of mass media now eliminating the Welsh language, 'the oldest living tradition in Britain'.[53]

Among old friends, Daphne and Arthur Pollen were now his most regular visitors, coming out to Harrow every few months. Jones frequently conducted hour-long telephone conversations with them, over time becoming closer to Daphne. Visiting them at Onslow Square, he noticed a small terracotta horse with a star on its belly, made by their daughter Lucy, for which he traded her two of his zoo pictures. He placed it on his mantel. A visitor asked why it had a star on its belly. He replied sharply, 'Because it bloody well couldn't be on top.'[54]

*　　*　　*

In July 1948, with a ticket John Betjeman couldn't use, Jones attended an Anglo-Catholic enactment of the third-century Mass of Hippolytus with commentary by Dom Gregory Dix, whose *Shape of the Liturgy* (1945) he was reading and finding 'full of exceedingly valuable stuff'. He agreed emphatically with its emphasis on the Eucharist as anamnesis, or re-presenting, meaning that it transcends time, making the faithful present at the Last Supper, the crucifixion, the resurrection, and the second coming. The notion of anamnesis, emphasised by Dix as earlier by de la Taille, would be essential to the meaning of *The Anathemata*. Their books and Louis Duchesne's *Christian Worship* (1903) had, he said, 'an incalculable effect' on him 'in all sorts of ways'.[55]

By the summer of 1948, he was seeing Dr Stevenson in London at 114 Harley Street, sometimes twice a week. Afterwards, he went to the BBC to see Grisewood who was running the newly established Third Programme. They often went for lunch to the Garrick Club, where Jones once noted, 'The lintels in the door are too big for the room.' Grisewood asked whether God is offended at this. Jones said, 'Yes. It is more important to him than to us. If God is the source of beauty and is himself beautiful, then he must disapprove of our offenses against beauty.' Occasionally he finished a day in London at the Burnses' house or the Grisewoods' flat in Tenby Mansions on Nottingham Street before wrapping himself in his long black greatcoat and going to Baker Street station for a late train to Harrow.[56]

From Hartrick he heard of a new technological wonder, a pen that 'makes a line always of one thickness'. He tried one, loved it, and recommended them to friends, pens 'called "Biros"'. He confided to his nephew, 'you can buy them in a little stationer's shop in Bond Street'. He once dispatched Peter Kelly to this shop, where they sold what Jones thought a very special make called 'BIC'. He came to rely on them exclusively for writing, liking the transparent shafts through which you can see how much ink remains. His supply grew because he seldom discarded those that ceased working. (Before writing he might try half a dozen.) During a visit by Joanna Hague, her young daughter, Rosalind, scribbled with one dry biro after another, getting the ink to flow, and he sent her a multi-coloured letter thanking her for reviving them.[57]

Ballpoint pens joined the clutter on his table. Newspapers accumulated in waist-high piles that also contained manuscript drafts, books, engravings, and articles of clothing. Searching for something often required archaeological digs down through the dated layers.[58]

*   *   *

He was now working on a picture entitled *A Latere Dextro*, in which a priest elevates the chalice at Mass (fig. 8). Like *Vexilla Regis*, it resembled an oil painting. For months Honeyman saw him struggling with it every evening as if 'fighting an animal'. He stopped in 1949 and regarded it as important but overworked, too tight, and 'realistic in a way that' is 'not quite my cup of tea'.[59] He intended never to exhibit it but showed it to visitors. A wonderful work, it involves multiple visual rhymings: pillars rise into curved vaulting as candles rise into curves of flame intensified at mid-picture by Pentecostal wind; flames of candles held by altar boys form with their shoulders and arms an oval of light. These rhyme with the circular candle rack, the circular base of the column, the rim of the bell a boy rings, the ghosted halos high above priest and chalice, and the small focal consecrated host on the altar. His 'windy Mass', as Jones called it, recalled the 'gusty' candle-flames at Mass

8. *A Latere Dextro*, 1949

seen near Ypres in 1917 and his discomfort in drafty churches. Is sculpted Mary coming alive? From the wound in the lamb (carved in relief on the right foreground side-altar) spills real water into a well, homage to St Trillo's and all sacred wells. Pentecostal (candle) fire, like water, comes from sacrificial dying. Flowers are everywhere, including fleur-de-lis in the priest's chasuble, which blends into the rest of the painting so that the priest and, by extension, the sacrament wears it all. Like *Vexilla Regis*, this picture visually anticipates *The Anathemata*. The abundance of detail, the result of working at it for so long, is overwhelming at first but rewards long and repeated viewing.

The previous spring, an 'enraptured' Helen Sutherland had praised *Vexilla Regis* to Jim Ede, saying she thought it worth £100. Subsequently, Ede told Jones that he wished to buy it unseen (based solely on the judgement of Helen, who, he knew, wanted it). The price of £500 was too steep for him, but he convinced his eighty-six-year-old mother to buy it. Jones liked the thought of the painting passing to Jim at her death, as he was told it would; so, Harari waiving his right of refusal, Jones sold it to Jim's mother. She loved it. Jim urged him to 'lend her or give her' the preliminary sketches – a suggestion typical of him, whose self-interest nearly equalled his generosity and helped explain Jones's slight reticence about him. Sutherland heard of the sale and, realising that Jim was procuring the painting for himself, was livid.[60] Three years later his mother died, and it was his.

Until the summer of 1949, Jones's room had the look of temporary digs. Most of his books and belongings remained in his room at Sheffield Terrace, which he would not relinquish even though imposing a financial strain – in the autumn of 1949, he owed seventeen weeks' back rent (£132.6s.). Then 12 Sheffield Terrace was sold, and stacks of books towered around his room in Northwick Lodge. This may have been when his cousin, Maurice Bradshaw, telephoning to propose a visit, was told, 'I don't know if you'll find a place to sit.' In December Jones had bookshelves made, clearing floor space. He stored some books and papers in a closet in May's house. He replaced the bed with his own, originally from Brockley, and moved in a few tables and chairs that had belonged to his father. There was no closet or wardrobe. He had little clothing – what did not fit in his dresser hung from hooks on the back of the door.[61]*

*   *   *

In 1940, Grisewood had sent Jones W. F. Jackson Knight's *Cumaean Gates* (1936), which he read with joyful astonishment, finding it 'very important . . . in every way exciting' and bearing 'very much on the thing

---

* His laundry lists indicate that he owned three shirts, three pairs of trousers, and three pairs of pyjamas.

I'm trying to write.' It 'verified and supported' what he 'instinctively felt' about primitive men and their art. More even than Dawson's *Age of the Gods*, it would inform *The Anathemata*. Three years later, he was surprised (because no great lover of Virgil) to be invited by Woodruff for tea on 12 April in Brown's Hotel to discuss the formation of a Virgil Society. Half a dozen were present. There were no introductions. To the man beside him Jones praised *Cumaean Gates* 'by a chap called Jackson Knight'. His listener rose to his feet, declaring, 'I am Jackson Knight.' Laughing, Jones introduced himself.[62]

They corresponded, Jones asking philological and factual questions. Knight read *In Parenthesis* and thought it 'tremendous,' a 'real grand epic'. Meeting for supper, they wowed each other in conversation. Jones loved his 'deeps of imaginative and acute scholarship'. To Helen Sutherland, he wrote that Knight was free of 'the donnish thing that mostly makes Classical scholars seem to not understand the very material that is theirs to deal with. It's "All alive-O" for J.K. & connected with "now".' Jones read Knight's *Roman Vergil* (1944), a *wonderful* book' with 'some grand things in it', particularly his psychoanalysis of Virgil. He associated Knight and Dawson as scholars 'singularly underrated' and would write to Knight in 1959, 'I owe you and Xristopher Dawson a very very very great deal.'[63]

After his 1948 exhibit, Jones concentrated exclusively on writing. He looked over his work since 1937 and, in January 1948, was determined to make 'a quite new start' – a book he decided to call *The Anathemata*, Greek for 'things dedicated to the gods' or 'significant things'. The title probably originated in a passage in Spengler that Jones marked, about 'festivals and Roman Catholic masses, blast furnaces and gladiatorial games, dervishes and Darwinians, railways and Roman roads, ... all ... equally signs and symbols' of the culture phases of their origin. He knew his title would put readers off and searched for another but always returned to it. He tested it on Knight, who liked it.[64]

In his new writing he wanted a 'much wider horizon' including the 'whole "Argosy of Mankind"' from prehistory to modern times. Instead of trying to weave a sequential whole, he decided on fragmented, open form after the fashion of *The Waste Land* and *Finnegans Wake*. In this he may have been influenced by Eliot's 1943 letter advising him to make 'Art in Relation to War' 'looser instead of tighter', which would involve 'separating & reshuffling' and be 'easier to add to'.* He separated and reshuffled much of what he had written and began writing new material, its rhythms modelled on those of *Piers Plowman*.[65]

---

* Suggesting this (as well as possible anxiety over influence) is Jones's saving it apart from his other letters from Eliot in an envelope marked 'Keep. *Private & Personal*'.

After several 'false starts & restarts', early in 1949, he chose a seven-page meditative fragment set during the consecration of the Mass. Written in 1945 and having as a tentative title 'The Mass', it began with the elevation of the host and ended with the elevation of the chalice. Dividing this text, he inserted between the halves a combination of selected, rewritten, and new material so that it grew from seven to twenty-four pages. This is the first foliation of *The Anathemata* (corresponding to pages 49–53, 241–3), which would frame all the rest and constitute a return-to-beginning, which reflects the natural shape of Jones's conversations. As a later friend, Peter Orr, remembered, 'He would appear to wander far and wide but wouldn't let you go until he had brought the thing back to its point of departure. It was a great circle.' Years later Jones would say that everything constituted a sort of circle – 'I need to think that everything is complete somewhere.'[66]

He divided this first foliation, expanding and in-filling, rewriting many passages more than a dozen (some over twenty) times. The second foliation ran to 259 foolscap pages, with a great deal of overlap, a new page often beginning with rewriting much of the previous page. Growing from a single-page insertion, the third foliation included a monologue by his maternal grandfather (one of his 'favourite bits') and a longer monologue by a late-medieval lavender-seller named Elen, who personifies London and symbolises Mother Earth (another of his favourite parts), her monologue ending at what is now its midpoint (156).[67] Finished in December 1949, this foliation was double the length of the second.

His material ranged through prehistory and history, but he believed that 'the "contactual", by whatever circuitous channel, *must come first*'. Ancient Aegean voyaging (84–97) and subsequent voyaging to Britain reflected hearing from Grisewood about sailing into Athens watching Greeks on board hail the Parthenon. Loquacious Elen is modelled on Medworth's Cockney grandmother ('Auntie' Mary) but also women Jones had known in childhood and, incongruously, Winston Churchill.* For help with nautical material he telephoned Mike Richey, who had served in the navy throughout the war and was the founding chief executive of the Institute of Navigation and founding editor of the *Journal of Navigation*. Richey later commented about the nautical passages, 'He got the whole thing absolutely right.'[68]

Although the text was far from complete, Jones sent it to Nest Cleverdon for typing, and retyping to get the spacing and layout right, a task later taken up by Ruth Winaver, Louise MacNeice's secretary who lodged with the Cleverdons, and then by Morag. With each, he insisted on precise line lengths and placings.[69]

---

* Later Jones said that for reading her part on the radio, 'Winston, in a certain mood, would be ideal for the job!'

Jones wrote four more series of drafts (using ballpoint pen for the first time). These included a universal world-ship (173–81), influenced by his memory of reading in the 1920s 'bits of' Gregory of Nyssa, Gregory of Nazianzus, and Clement of Alexandria. They also included a description of Arthur's queen, Gwenhwyfar, attending a fifth-century Christmas midnight Mass (194–221) – eight drafts, with eleven of a numinous description of her hair. He worried that it was a 'purple passage', but it was his favourite, a lyrical high-point in modern literature. He then adjusted geomorphic terminology earlier (61–74) to make her verbally redolent of the earth. Finally, he finished a conversation between medieval Welsh witches (206–15) – hard to write and the only part of the poem he had serious doubts about.[70]

By the time he had reached what is now the centre of Elen's monologue, in December 1949, he decided to expand the circularity of the framing Mass-text into a thoroughgoing chiasmic recession of parentheses or – since the containing act of consecration is brief and continuous – circles. Modelled on the chiasmic recessions of paired engravings in the *Deluge* and *Ancient Mariner*, these circles consist of breakings-off and resumptions of units of text. At what became the middle of Elen's monologue, he wrote a lyrical celebration of the paschal events (157), which the Eucharist sacramentally re-presents. This became the centre of the poem, symbolically identical with its Eucharistic circumference. Around this centre and inside the outer circumference he arranged eight split units of text to form circles-within-circles – lengths of text on either side of the centre being unequal, avoiding exact symmetry.* Original in modern literature, this structure is uniquely symbolic, implying that the Eucharist is sustained by and contains all human experience, thereby fulfilling the Chelsea Group's quest for a cultural unified-field theory. Jones hints at the chiasmic pattern of circle-within-circles in the epigraph of the poem, 'It was a dark and stormy night', adopted from the circle game of his childhood. He told Jackson Knight that the poem 'circles round [the] central theme' and, if it 'has a plot', it is as 'the dance round the may-pole plots itself out in patterns round the central arbor'.[71]

The subject of the poem is Western culture, which Jones thought, in all its complexity and variegation, the finest achievement of mankind. While writing it, the 'paramount question' haunting him was 'are we cut off

---

* The eight units of text broken off and resumed are: questions dating the paschal events (94/185), the account of a ship's arrival in ancient Greece (96/182), Elen calling her wares (125/168), her warning a Mediterranean captain about winter (125/168), her cataloging London churches (127/161), her recounting a tryst with a lover (130/160), her discussing her education by sea-captains (135/159), and her recounting a Syro-Phoenician's stories (155/158).

from our whole past'? If so, his writing was pointless; if not, it might carry the vitality of the past beyond the current Dark Age to a culturally vital future – like, but on a lesser scale than, Alcuin and Charlemagne restoring and preserving the inheritance of Classical culture. Other models were Gregory of Tours and Boethius, the latter nicknamed '"the Bridge" because he carried forward into an altogether metamorphosed world certain of the fading oracles which had sustained Antiquity'.* Jones hoped he was building such a bridge or, to retrieve a metaphor of twenty years back, an ark, out of which the core of Western cultural tradition might tumble safe. He felt his vocation was 'keeping the lines of communication open'.[72]

The first part of the poem, later entitled 'Rite and Fore-time', included an emphasis on geomorphology and evolutionary biology new to literature. (Jones found science 'incredibly "romantic" . . . & the more factual . . . the more moving'.) On 2 September 1950, he read in the *Tablet* the encyclical *Humani Generis*, in which Pope Pius XII reaffirms the 1906 condemnation of modernism and attacks the theory of evolution. Jones was furious. He visited Grisewood, and they went together to the Jesuit house in Farm Street, where Fr Vincent Turner reassured them that papal authority, like scriptural authority, is limited to faith and morals.[73] Doubting that it extended to morals, Jones returned to his writing. Concluding 'Rite and Fore-time', he celebrated 'the essential and labouring worm' (82), in homage to Darwin, whose last book was *The Formation of Vegetable Mould through the Action of Worms* (1881).

* * *

On 7 January 1949, Jones had received notice from the Prudential Assurance Company that a policy his father had taken out for him as a child had matured and asking him to complete forms in order to receive the amount payable. He ignored the notice, received another on 18 August, ignored that, and was visited the following winter by two men from Prudential. Later, a fellow lodger noticed that he was upset and asked what was wrong. He said, 'These two chaps arrived. I spoke to them over the banister. I wasn't prepared to go meet them. I could see that they were money people. These buggers had come to offer me *money*. I told them to go away, and they went. They seemed quite puzzled.'[74] It would not be until October 1961 that the ominous moneymen would succeed in giving him £276.7s.9d.

Once a month, he was seeing Dr Kenneth Bell, his physician, on Stevenson's recommendation. An Aberdeen-trained Scot, Bell was

---

* Other models for him were Malory, who conveyed for future ages the reality of medieval chivalry, and Cecil Sharp, 'only-just-in-time' to save Somersetshire folk-songs in the early twentieth century.

comforting, encouraging, and, though younger, almost a father figure for him. Bell made house calls, seldom to examine him, usually only to cheer him up. They shared war anecdotes, of which Bell had many, having been in the crack Fourth Armoured Brigade.* Once Jones mentioned an acquaintance, now a monsignor, who as an intelligence officer had wondered why arriving German prisoners were terrified of being interned in the south of England. Bell was able to tell him: at the end of the war, his brigade discovered in northern France large nerve-gas bombs and fifty-foot mortars, which, with V-5 rockets, had been intended to saturate the south of England with nerve gas, wiping out the entire population. The brigade was told never to mention this, and it was never made public.[75]

The Queen invited ('commanded') Jones to the Royal Garden Party in 1950. He told Barbara Moray that he wanted to go but was unwell and couldn't. She told him to write saying so, but he was not content with that and only calmed down when she agreed to go with him. Once there, he was fine. She took him to speak to the Queen, who drank tea with 'special chaps . . . with all the great mob of other chaps looking on' – it was, he thought, 'the last fading remnant of quasi-sacred personages being watched by the tribe'. When the king died in 1952, he wrote expressing sympathy, and the Queen replied thanking him. She invited him to subsequent Royal Garden Parties, but he only went once again, in 1953 with the Grisewoods. He felt out of place in suit and tie, the other men in 'morning clothes'.[76]

In the summer of 1949, he had read an announcement that the Tate had engaged the Ganymed Press to make a print of *The Four Queens* (chapter 11, fig. 9) as part of a series of works by him, Henry Moore, John Piper, and Graham Sutherland. Jones wrote to Rothenstein saying he was glad but that his permission should have been asked. After printing three monochrome proofs,[†] John Roberts at the press decided the picture was not colourful enough to generate sales and substituted *The Chapel in the Park* (chapter 8, fig. 8). Jones protested that *The Four Queens* is 'a so much more interesting' picture and 'of its kind . . . the best I've done, the other is not, of its kind, so successful.' But reluctantly he agreed to the switch, placated by the possibility of Ganymed later reproducing *The Four Queens*. The reproductions were so good that he could mistake them for the original from across a room. An American bought up most of them to

* For four years Bell had been a medical officer and section leader, 'shot at, shelled, and strafed a thousand times', in France, Belgium, Dunkirk, Palestine, Syria, North Africa, Italy, and Normandy. He had worked in an Arab hospital in Baalbek, a Greco-Roman city, and in his injections used tap water, which was sterile because the modern plumbing had been ripped out in favour of the original Roman plumbing. 'This', he said, 'was the sort of thing we talked about.'

† One of these, given to Ede, is now at Kettle's Yard, Cambridge.

put into motel rooms in the US – Jones was, a friend said, 'tickled pink about that'.[77]

In July 1950, a correspondent in the *Listener* attacked abstract painting as 'a fallacy and a hoax' and proclaimed that Victor Pasmore's latest paintings mean 'nothing'. Jones thought this 'offensive & . . . *stupid*' but wrote a letter 'tamely' in praise of Pasmore as 'an able and sincere artist' and saying that in all non-abstract art, 'it is an abstract *quality*, however hidden or devious, which determines real worth . . . This is true of Botticelli's Primavera, of the White Horse of Uffington, of the music of Monteverdi, of *Finnegans Wake*, of the "Alfred jewel", of the glass goblet I am now trying to draw, of the shape of a liturgy, of the shape of a tea-cup.' Abstraction is, moreover, characteristic of 'most of the vital works of our time'. His defence was published and elicited a letter of support from Herbert Read, to which Jones replied that it seemed odd that he, of all people, should be defending abstraction and in '1950 – not 1912'.[78]

At about this time, the coal fire in his room was replaced by an electric heater. 'They've taken away a living thing,' he said, and thought with dark irony of the words of an English song (slightly misremembered): 'Neither fire-light nor candle-light / Can ease my heart's despair.' Adding to his distress was his ineptitude with mechanical and electrical devices: 'If the electric lighting or heating gadgets go wrong I'm sunk – demoralized & wholly out of my depth – and sigh for candles or paraffin lamps . . . unless one knows at least how to replace a fuse or whatever the bloody thing's called one can do nothing – absolutely nothing without the assistance of someone or other familiar with all the gadgetry.' A visitor, William Blissett, observed him making tea: 'for quite a time he kept trying to get the element to heat, poking, shaking, thumping, quietly but firmly swearing, then finally, after many minutes, he saw that the switch was off at the wall plug'.[79]

Jones's visitors now included the painter Ray Howard-Jones (fig. 9), whom he had known as an art student in 1920, and her much younger lover, Raymond Moore, one of Britain's best photographers. David and she agreed about the importance of symbolism despite the contemporary fashion for abstraction. They complained about the lack of good draughtsmanship in so much current work and agreed that a painter should be true to himself or herself and not be swept up into an 'ism' – even though being in a clique enhances reputation because it allows for facile, general critical response.[80] At Jones's request, Moore photographed his pictures. He took scores of photographs of Jones himself, capturing his wide range of expression during conversation.

In 1951, Ray and Moore brought along Arthur Giardelli. (Jones met them at the house door and, after bringing them into his room, removed three overcoats.) Enthusiastic, spontaneous, intelligent, and genial, Giardelli was a forty-year-old South London painter, maker of relief constructions,

9. Jones and Ray Howard-Jones in Northwick Lodge, by Raymond Moore, c. 1950

and freelance lecturer. He had lectured on Jones's paintings during the 1944 touring exhibit and bought *Manawydan's Glass Door*. Having several times written to Jones without receiving a reply, Giardelli asked, 'Why didn't you answer my letters?' Jones said, 'I didn't know you would be like this.' (On the basis of his surname he had presumed him to be a mid-European intellectual.) They became friends. Giardelli having studied French literature and art history at Oxford, they spoke about the Arthurian legends in French romances. Hearing that he had written a thesis on Botticelli's illustrations of Dante, Jones expressed great admiration for them and astonishment that they were so little known and appreciated. Giardelli recited Villon's prayer to the Blessed Virgin, which instantly became a favourite of Jones. (From now on when Len Walton praised Racine, Jones said, 'I prefer Villon.') Giardelli loved Wales, and Jones told him he admired the paintings of Julius Caesar Ibbetson, which express a great sense of Welshness, and of Richard Wilson, a North Welsh eighteenth-century landscape painter. Giardelli later said about Jones, 'I've never known a man with a wider range of facial expression. He could look utterly dejected and then he could look seraphic.'[81] That is because he spoke with feeling.

On 22 February 1951, Jones received an offer of nomination to the Royal Academy.* Grisewood asked whether he would accept. Jones replied, 'It would be an absolutely disgusting betrayal of everything I ever believed

* In 1947 Robert Buhler had been elected to the R.A. and began conspiring with Rodrigo Moynihan, Ruskin Spear, James Fitton, and Edward La Bas to include better painters. Owing to them, David Jones, Robert Colquhoun, Robert MacBryde, Francis Bacon, and Lucien Freud were offered nominations.

in. I could no more have anything to do with the Royal Academy than I could fly.' On 26 February, in the shortest letter he ever wrote, he declined the nomination. Nine years later, Vincent Lines would invite him to be an honorary member of the Royal Watercolour Society, and he would accept.[82]

* * *

Jones was now painting unique still lifes. In June 1945 he had seen in a shop a large glass goblet 'very big & noble' but could not afford its price of twelve shillings. In 1948 he bought one like it, which had 'a light of its own' and inspired a return to painting still lifes. He put water in the goblet and wild flowers (never sweet peas, which he 'loathed') and set it on the table often on a white cloth, before his window, the landscape beyond being part of the picture. These paintings had what he liked most, 'light and movement'. Each 'painting of a bowl of flowers' was, he said, 'a *signum* of Flora Dea, but, unlike in *Vexilla Regis*, its symbolic meaning does not outweigh visuality'.[83]

In July 1949, he had made the first of these new still lifes, a 'whirling flower-piece'. The following spring, he painted *Flora in Calix-Light* (fig. 10), which Ede saw, loved, and bought. In it, the chalice and flanking goblets are redolent of the crucifixion scene informing *Vexilla Regis* but feminised – the glass vessels themselves flowerlike, the central '*calix*' (chalice) homonymous with calyx (the outer whorl of petals of a flower). Like flowers, each glass vessel has a stem – so does the tiny distant tree on the right. The picture explodes from its centre – the flanking goblets being empty to receive the outpouring. Iconographically, the thorns, the three vessels, and the large chalice suggest a union of crucifixion, Eucharist and overflowing springtime. Glass has affinity with water. Three waves on the water surface at the front of the chalice suggest water in lakes, rivers, and seas, and imply a breeze directly or indirectly making the waves so that air joins water and light. The ambiguous relationship between vivid flowers-and-background and the less distinct vessels has the effect of turning space inside out, suggesting a mystery of grace transcending space-time. Although concentrating on writing – Jones spent the summer correcting four typescripts of *The Anathemata* – he made at least ten glass-chalice pictures in 1951.[84]

They look as though painted with ease but were 'made "with fear & trembling"' for 'if one made a mess – too much here or too little of that there – one was bloody-well sunk'. In October 1952, a failed attempt prompted him to comment, 'It's always as though one had never drawn before. You can't see how to do it . . . When one is younger one is pleased with bits of "skill" . . . but when one is older there is *no point* unless one really can "say something". One tends to repeat one's old tricks, as it were, if one is not jolly careful.' His chief

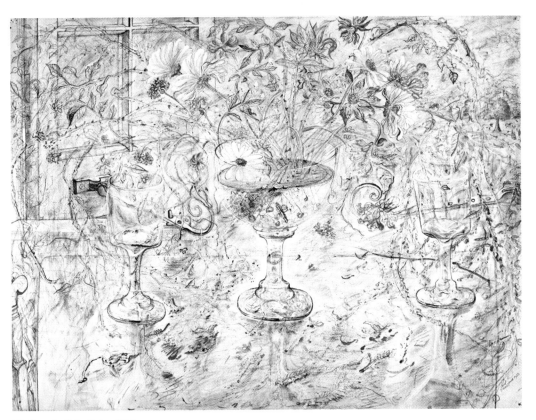

10. *Flora in Calix-Light*, 1950

consolation in life was 'getting one of these bloody works more or less right – that is, alive'.[85] They were such a challenge because each involves a precarious multiple balance: between beauty and incoherence, flatness and depth, colour and line, stasis and explosive movement.

Flowers for these pictures, which he made throughout the 1950s, initially came from the garden behind Northwick Lodge. He liked best wild roses (especially primroses), violets, aconite, forget-me-nots, and daisies. As the garden became increasingly overgrown, visitors supplied flowers. Audrey Malan brought roses, Canterbury bells, scented stocks, snapdragons, marigolds, asters, carnations, and lilies of the valley. The glass-chalice paintings took 'longer & longer to do' – flowers sometimes died 'four or five times' before he finished one. For St David's Day, a visitor brought daffodils, which he disliked and found 'absolute hell' to paint. Three 'heavenly bushes' of wild roses grew just below the house along a path to Northwick Park tube station, and in June he would go to look at them but he could not paint them because they died so soon after being cut.[86]

He was now painting as well as he had in 1932 though differently. It was, for him, a wonderful change, one he guarded, as if superstitiously, by continual complaint. He felt he was striving for a numinous quality that he never fully achieved and tended to see only 'the failure to arrive at the desired end'. But often he at least came close. In his final years he would like best of all his pictures these 'light "free" ones of bits of flowers & a view outside'. (After them his favourites would be some 1928–32 seascapes and animal drawings.) And he regarded them 'as belonging implicitly to the same world of commemoration and anamnesis as . . . *The Anathemata*'.[87]

* * *

On 22 September 1951, Jones wrote to T. S. Eliot, who had not previously seen any of it, to say that *The Anathemata* was nearly finished. Eliot had him to lunch on 8 October at the Garrick Club to hand over the typescript and talk about it. The next day, after his first quick inspection, Eliot wrote saying he was sure it would be published. He then read it carefully, 'in a state of excitement sustained to the end'. The poem is written in a richly allusive modernist style, and Eliot thought that its meaning could be grasped only on a third reading. But he repeatedly expressed enthusiasm for the preface, which suggests that he did not fully understand the poem. Years later Jones said, '*most* of my acquaintances . . . find [it] obscure, if not incomprehensible' and mentioned 'notable exceptions', including Edith Sitwell but not Eliot. Yet Eliot was keen to publish it; others in the firm were not. Jones would later say, 'without Tom, *The Anathemata* would probably not have been published', and Peter du Sautoy told me he was right. Only after a delay of three months was Eliot able to give verbal acceptance. Negotiating a contract with du Sautoy, Jones was refused an advance because, he was told, production would be expensive and readers few. He was offered only 10% royalties.[88]

He and Eliot had several more meetings before publication. 'He's a jolly nice bloke,' Jones wrote to Grisewood, '& I like him more the more I see of him.' He found him 'a withdrawn character . . . an astonishing fusion of something youthful & something immeasurably old & wise'. He was especially impressed at how 'incredibly hard' he worked at Faber. Their friendship was growing closer. He had addressed Eliot in letters as 'Tom E.' or 'T.S.E.' but from 4 October 1951 it was simply 'Tom'.[89] Eliot had addressed him as 'Davy', affectionately American, but Jones was no 'Davy' and politely told him so. Now it was 'David' and, as with closest friends, 'Dai'. They would remain good friends, although meeting after 1952 only about three times a year.

Jones considered Eliot '*really* a great chap' and a 'darling man, the soul of kindness and helpfulness'. He liked his beautiful grey eyes and thought him 'quite funny when he'd had a few drinks'. But he was irked by Eliot's tightness, his buttoned-up inability to achieve easy cordiality, and his 'puritanical streak'. Once during the war, Jones had proposed meeting in the evening to talk. Eliot declined because he was on fire-watcher duty on the Faber roof. 'So much the better,' Jones said. 'I don't mind where we talk.' 'No,' Eliot said, 'I have a system whereby I can get through several manuscripts while watching, and I make it a policy never to break with routine except for something extraordinary.' 'Well, this is extraordinary,' Jones said. 'We'll have a good talk about poetry.' 'No,' Eliot insisted. Once after lunch at the Garrick Club, Jones suggested taking a taxi to Faber so they could continue talking. Eliot said that he always took the Tube and 'didn't believe in spending money needlessly'. And Eliot sometimes cut him off sharply. When Jones introduced the topic of Robert Browning as the first to use colloquial language in poetry, Eliot turned to the waiter and said, 'Bring Mr. Jones another cup of coffee.' When Jones mentioned Chesterton's poetry as stylistically 'terrible' but with an often profound thought in every line, Eliot responded, 'Chesterton reminds me of a cabman beating himself to keep warm.' This sort of dismissal annoyed Jones, but he felt guilty criticising Eliot – both annoyance and guilt suggesting a degree of rivalry.[90]

Did Jones feel sibling rivalry towards Eliot, who was seven years his senior? The critic Harold Bloom writes that a poet living in the shadow of a 'strong' precursor escapes anxiety of influence by entering the other's great poem and rewriting it from within. It might be argued that formally Jones rewrote *The Waste Land* at the end of *In Parenthesis* and throughout *The Anathemata* – both being, to a degree, a writing through and beyond Eliot. But Jones never acknowledged the influence of *The Waste Land*, and said he thought it wrong to see Eliot as the source of widespread 'mythological & somewhat obscure "allusion-writing"', which is 'an inevitable trend' in 'this groping age'.[91] In general, he thought claims of influence reductive.

The University of Wales offered Jones an honorary doctorate. He wanted to refuse but 'had not the heart' to deny Wales. He was to receive it in the spring of 1951, bought his railway ticket, but, as the time approached, became increasingly anxious. The day before departure he developed stomach trouble. It was psychosomatic, he knew, 'but . . . somatic enough!' so he stayed home, telephoning his regrets.[92] The university deferred conferring the degree.

Ben Nicholson invited him to the opening of his new exhibition in 1952. Jones telephoned his regrets but went in the second week of May. He found the show 'very beautiful', being particularly impressed by a large picture called *Cromlech*, which had

astonishing serenity & also a *depth* which all of them have not got. He's streets ahead of any other English abstract painter, I think – a thousand times more sensitive for one thing – and never *boring* which is such a blessing. It's all within its own particular limits of course – & within those limits it seems to me to be of a wonderful perfection.[93]

Jones was 'dragged' in August to Burlington House by Grisewood to see the Ravenna Mosaics, which surprised him by their 'delicate & incredibly subtle & "gay" beauty'. Some were 'pretty rotten' but others overwhelmed him by 'sheer loveliness & delight and *freedom*'. This and the Nicholson show were the only exhibitions in recent years that he had liked very much.[94]

From February through mid-July 1952, he read proofs. His method was eccentric in one respect: if an error was obvious, he would not change it, since making a new plate to correct one frequently produced new errors.[95]

By 20 July, arrangements were made for illustrations to *The Anathemata*. He liked especially the seven inscriptions used, and made an inscription for the dust jacket (fig. 11), which Frank Morley said, and Eliot agreed, was 'the most beautiful jacket ever put out by F & F or anyone else in our times'.[96] They exhibited it at the National Book League.

During the writing of the third foliation, Jones had begun annotating *The Anathemata*. David Bland (working on production under de la Mare) and the printer wanted the notes at the back, but Jones insisted that they were 'a kind of running commentary & should go with the text' at the foot of pages and, where too extensive for that, on facing pages. When a page of notes faced a page of text, which 'looked so *beastly* typographically', he 'arranged the illustrations on purpose to cover 'em up'. To Ede he suggested that the best way to read *The Anathemata* was 'to take no notice of the notes except in the case of *pronunciation of Welsh words*'. And contradicting his insistence with Faber, he said, 'The notes are best consulted separately.' Subsequently vacillating between thinking them a necessary courtesy and a mistake because initially so off-putting, in the end he regretted them. Joyce had not annotated *Finnegans Wake* but had left the reader to discover allusions. Jones wished he had done that.[97]

He then added the subtitle, 'fragments of an attempted writing'. He explained, 'most of my work ... is an attempt ... and ... *necessarily* "fragmentary" *because*', owing to the complications of our civilisational phase,

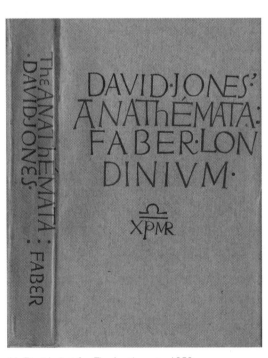

11. Dust jacket for *The Anathemata*, 1952

'*we surely tend to fragmented works.* Anyway, I *did not* mean to imply a lack of *artistic* wholeness.' And he added an epigraph, 'TESTE DAVID CVM SIBYLLA' (49), from the *Dies Irae*, symbolising 'the whole apperception of the Aramaean & Hellenistic cultures' and implying that he saw the poem as prophetic in the scriptural-Thomistic sense of announcing 'something *present* ... whose significance lies ultimately in eternity'.[98] Nearly the last thing he did was divide the text into eight numbered sections, giving each a title.

He thought the people at Faber '*jolly nice* chaps to deal with' and trying to meet all his 'complicated requirements in a most civilized way'. Their genuine affection for him was evident in their correspondence. Frank Morley, a director, was by now a real friend and, of all those at the firm, the greatest fan of *The Anathemata*, buying multiple copies to send to friends.[99]

Jones would increasingly believe *The Anathemata* 'a lot better than *In Parenthesis*', in later years describing it as 'worth fifty *In Parentheses*' and 'far the best thing I've tried to make at all.' In it he attempted, he wrote, 'to enclose "*a whole*" as far as it had come to me'. It is his poetic summa, a symbolic, multi-voiced anatomy of Western culture throughout time. Its thematic focus is on the making of gratuitous signs – an activity flourishing during vital culture phases and languishing during predominantly pragmatic periods. References to imperial Rome are also, by analogy, to Nazi and Soviet tyrannies. Although informed by his theory of culture, the work is not abstract or analytical. It progresses digressively, as interior and dramatic monologues (set in various historical periods) open to other monologues. Grisewood cannily called it 'a displaced epic', its displaced hero and heroine being man-the-maker and Mother Earth, who include Odysseus/Jesus and Penelope/Mary/mankind. Elen's monologue, entitled 'The Lady of the Pool' (124–68), is the most far-reaching poetic celebration of London in a single work of literature. The passages concerning ships and sailing make *The Anathemata* the great modern maritime poem. It is thematically unified paradoxically by antitheses – between culture and civilisation, country and city, love and greed, female and male – which make the work a complex wattle of continuous alterity. Owing to its chiasmic recession of circles, it is the only literary work to combine extensive (previously American) modernist 'open form' with structural unity. Its vocabulary is extraordinarily rich, greater in variety than all the poetry of Yeats, Eliot, William Carlos Williams, Wallace Stevens, and Larkin combined. In 1977, W. H. Auden said it is comparable to the inclusive, culturally authoritative long poems of Homer, Virgil, Dante, Chaucer, and Milton.[100]

While thinking that readers would find *The Anathemata* difficult, Jones was naïve about the capacities of the average reader. At lunch in Northwick Lodge, he expressed incredulity that the man 'who cleans my room says he can't understand it! It's as plain as a pikestaff.' He thought it required only a sense of humour, 'a bit of hard thought', and a sensitivity to 'what we call "poetry" – i.e. language at a heightened tension – a sense of form & shape, an exact & evocative use of *each* word'.[1]

Reviews were few and mostly, he thought, 'dim'. He was irked by those ascribing influences. One said it 'owes much to James Joyce', making him, Grisewood remembered, 'as near to cross as he could be'. Others noted the influence of Pound's *Cantos*, which Jones had not read. (So he looked at them in November 1952, saw the similarity, thought them '*marvellous*', but, fearing influence on his future poetry, read no more.) He was especially disappointed with reviewers calling the content odd, personal, and peculiar, since he dealt 'wholly & entirely with our common inherited myth' and history (including science). 'I know it's a bit of a bugger on the surface,' he wrote to Ede, 'but underneath it's pretty straight forward really, compared with most modern "personal experience" & "psychological" kinds of poetry.'[2]

Largely responsible for the poor reception was the publisher, which did not include him among its poets. Faber promoted *The Anathemata* among its 'Autobiographies and Memoirs'. Seeing it so classified in the *New Statesman*, Jones was amused: it was like calling '*Lear* a *Life of Shakespeare* or *The Origin of Species Darwin's Memoirs!*' Not until 1962 would he discover that the mistake was that of the Faber poetry editors – initially Eliot's, subsequently Charles Monteith's. Not until the summer of 1970 would the mistake be corrected – in response to complaints by Stuart Montgomery, of the Fulcrum Press, and William Cookson. Even then du Sautoy had trouble convincing Monteith, who was bothered by so much of the writing not being verse. And Faber would not include *In Parenthesis* in its poetry list until 1988. Generic misidentification postponed academic interpretation and, together with delay in finding a US publisher, kept Jones's long poems from the attention of the American 'New Critics', who analysed and canonised the other important achievements of literary modernism. About the genre of *The Anathemata*, Jones at least had no doubts: 'it is either poetry ... or *nothing at all*'.[3]

In the face of so much incomprehension and silence, he valued responses from friends, including praise from Desmond Chute, initiating a correspondence* in which Jones explicated *The Anathemata* in response to questions. His spirits were buoyed by Frank Morley, who had shipped on a whaler and written a book on whaling, saying that the parts to do with the sea and ships, which he especially liked, were authentic in every respect. Graham Greene wrote expressing 'a sense of excitement which makes one mark passage after passage on page after page'.[4]

Such responses strengthened Jones's patience. 'It's the kind of book', he wrote, 'that *if* it makes any impression *at all*, makes it very, very, slowly' like Hopkins's 'The Wreck of the Deutschland'. (Regarded in 1875 and 1918 as incomprehensible, Hopkins's poem was not securely in the literary canon till the mid-twentieth century.) At the end of his life Jones said that of all his work 'in painting or in writing', *The Anathemata* is 'the one that matters'.[5]

Its non-reception confirmed his sense of a broad rejection of modernism in the arts – a shift from objectivity to subjectivity and moralism. He complained, 'The important & true & vivifying principle' that 'an artwork' is 'a thing' and not an imitation or expression 'has been prostituted or forgotten'. The recent war was, he believed, the 'rubicon' of the century, ending a period of important intellectual and aesthetic achievement. Between the wars, he thought, the arts had transformed the 'decline of the west' into something splendid, as, on a larger scale, Arthurian romance had transformed the decline of the Celts from an epochal 'balls-up' to 'a kind of "Praise"'. In 1940, he had written Grisewood, 'Thank God Joyce did his stuff – *only just in time* it would seem', adding that when people in the future prefer their work to '"the Cézanne-appreciating-gin-&-lime & Jung & Doris-in-cellophane of the twenties" – I only hope that we don't capitulate to the moralists & deny the things perceived in those days.' What bothered him most was the assumption that modernism had not mattered – 'so that one & all can heave a sigh of relief, sink back, satisfied that nothing disturbing has happened – 3 cheers for the Royal Academy, Mr Eliot has said that Kipling is OK – splendid, that's what we always thought'.[6]

Jones was convinced that Eliot was caught up in the decline. He liked Eliot's early poems most and regarded *The Waste Land* as 'the best poem of all this period'. He thought *Four Quartets* 'very, very good' but 'East Coker' marred by subjectivity. (He positively disliked only the

---

* Published in *Inner Necessities*, ed. T. Dilworth (Toronto: Hugh Anson-Cartwright, 1984). Their correspondence enabled Chute to publish a review in *Downside Review* (*IN* 93–101), which Jones liked so much he sent it to Eliot. Chute ordered a copy of *The Anathemata* for his friend Ezra Pound, now in St Elizabeth's Hospital in Washington DC. Although it was also recommended by William Carlos Williams, Pound did not read it because, he later said, 'the Possum' (Eliot) had not told him about Jones.

1. *Vobiscum est*, 1953

'embarrassing' and 'awful poems about cats'.) He said, 'at *bottom* it's the trouble with Tom E. . . .. In fact, in one form or another, it holds the field. At base, I suppose it is this subjectivism that separates them *all* from Joyce.' He wrote to Grisewood with Eliot in mind: 'It could all be so different if just one or two chaps (I will not mention names) had refused to give an inch, had stood by the guns . . . Not that one doubts what one is trying to do, but it is a bit shaking when combined currents flow more & more against . . . [what] one feels to be the *only* direction that's worthwhile.'[7]

*   *   *

Jones had not seen Prudence since 1949 when worsening health forced her into a nursing home at a location undisclosed to her friends. She spent most of 1952 in a coma, dying on 13 October. Learning in December of her death, he could hardly take it in. She was, he said, 'of unique nobility & sensitivity & courage' 'and like no one else at all'. As a lament and a tribute he painted words from Propertius on the asbestos sheet on his fireplace (fig. 1). They are addressed to Persephone in Hades and translate: 'Iope is with you and snow-white Tyro too / And every Roman girl who was of their rank / Let one beautiful one abide on earth, if so it may be.' He painted it 'quite quickly one evening straight away'. It was one of his inscriptions that he liked best.[8] On 7 May 1953, he received the £1,000 she had bequeathed to him.

*   *   *

Months before its publication, Cleverdon had proposed a radio version of *The Anathemata*. Jones wanted 'a straight reading, not *necessarily* all in one go, though better so, with not a word left out'. Grisewood and Cleverdon persuaded him that it had to be dramatised and promised to consult him. At Cleverdon's request, he went through the book of music available to the BBC compiling a list of sixty-five titles: forty-seven pieces of liturgical chant, the rest carols, madrigals, and folk-songs – adding to the rich intertextuality of the poem.* He deliberately stayed away from rehearsals and declined to hear the programme in advance, knowing he would want changes.[9]

Listening to the broadcast on a borrowed radio on 5 May 1953, he thought the music 'most beautiful, as perfect as could be'. He liked the actresses performing Welsh witches – 'that was said almost exactly as I intended it' – and Dylan Thomas reading Gwenhwyfar's description was 'absolutely O.K.' Diana Maddox's rendition of Elen's monologue was only bad when 'she got excited & . . . coy' but conveyed nothing of the profound 'tutelary figure'. And he was upset at Norman Sherry's quick '"Gawd Blimey" Cockney' performance of his grandfather, who 'spoke with deliberation, rather slowly' and in a home county accent.[10]

But response to the programme was positive, and Jones was amused that 'people who regarded the book as totally unreadable lapped up this broadcast & were delighted'. After hearing subsequent broadcasts, he admitted that the production 'gets quite a bit across' and conveys an idea 'of the "mingled streams"' of the poem. But actors' misinterpretations, 'histrionics and exaggerated emphases' shook his confidence as a writer.[11] Broadcasts of his subsequent poetry would be solely him reading.

Alun Oldfield Davies had arranged for Elwyn Evans to produce for the Welsh Home Service a reading of Part VII of *The Anathemata*, 'Mabinog's Liturgy'. It was broadcast on the evening of 13 May as part of the Welsh contribution to coronation celebrations for Elizabeth II. Jones liked it, thought the actors (Arthur Phillips, Dilys Davies, Lorna Davies, Vera Mpazey) read sensitively, mostly with the right emphasis, and far preferred their 'straight reading' to Cleverdon's 'dramatized' version.[12]

On 30 March 1953, Jones had a long talk with Dylan Thomas in the Cleverdons' flat. They had met there twice before, but Thomas had been too drunk to converse. Now they talked for hours about medieval Welsh poetry, Jones doing most of the talking since Thomas knew little about it. Jones liked him, delighted in his antics, and admired him as a reader, especially after hearing Plumtre's 'marvellous gramophone records' of him reading poetry. Jones thought that he invigorated English through an underlying sense of Celtic language – like Joyce, though to a lesser degree.[13]

Dylan Thomas regarded Jones with 'great reverence', the Cleverdons remembered, and expressed huge admiration for him as a poet. During one of his American tours, his programme consisted entirely of readings from John Donne and *In Parenthesis*. After their third and final meeting, Thomas praised Jones to Grisewood for 'his holiness' and delicacy of mind, lack of both of which he lamented in himself. About Jones's

---

* See T. Dilworth, 'Music for *The Anathemata*', *Papers of the Bibliographical Society of America*, 85 (March 1991), pp. 27–47.

poetry, he said, 'I would like to have done anything as good as David Jones has done.' In November 1953, Jones was saddened by news of his death.[14]

In the year since the publication of *The Anathemata*, he had been unable to paint, partly because of a return of the feeling of emptiness that had followed the completion of *In Parenthesis*. But he did illustrate Eliot's 'The Cultivation of Christmas Trees', the first of a new series of Ariel Poems (fig. 2). Jones liked the drawing, but thought reproduction eliminated its feeling. When friends asked him to sign the reproduction, he refused.[15]

For Alun Oldfield Davies, he wrote a half-hour talk on 'Wales and the Crown' for Welsh radio. All talks were then broadcast live, but, frightened of that, he got the producer, Elwyn Evans, to pre-record it at Northwick Lodge – a 'nerve wracking' experience. Considering himself 'a very bad reader' he tried to speak 'slowly, deliberately & as clearly as possible'. Hearing the rebroadcast on the Third Programme on 29 November was a revelation. He read well.

2. Faber Ariel Christmas card, 1953

He would do three more pre-recorded radio talks in the next two years, and in the 1960s would record four new poems for broadcast, ultimately recording enough poetry to fill two-and-a-half long-playing records. People frequently told him that on the radio he sounded Churchillian, which he thought 'bloody funny' since 'I'm not exactly a Churchillian character!'[16]

He loathed television but, on 2 June 1953, at a neighbour's house, watched the coronation and was enthralled: 'the queen looked incredibly beautiful ... of immense dignity & *humility*, ... a real *anathéma*'. He was impressed by the splendour and historical continuity of the rite but appreciated 'something far deeper and more primal and quite ageless', the 'feeling of the gold-clad victim', which reminded him of Richard II in the Wilton Diptych. He attended the post-coronation garden party at Buckingham Palace and subsequently watched a newsreel of the coronation – his last visit to a cinema.[17]

From early November through mid-January 1954, he devoted most of his time to writing 'Art and Sacrament', his most important essay on aesthetics and culture (*EA* 143–79), a long, brilliant, meandering afterword to *The Anathemata*. It appeared in *Catholic Approaches*, edited by Elizabeth Pakenham (1955), a 'hotch-potch' book that he regarded as 'a mistake', finding the poor quality of some contributions embarrassing.[18]

* * *

Jones was in financial trouble. In January 1952, Ede's fund collapsed with Anne Benthall's death and Kenneth Clark no longer able to contribute. Jones's income after expenses for 1953 was £326, but that included a final gift from Clark of £125. Helen Sutherland continued sending £5 monthly. Ede suggested that Grisewood obtain a Civil List Pension for Jones. Having, with Tom Burns, attempted and failed at this years earlier, Grisewood now enlisted Hugh Fraser to operate behind the scenes and got Read, Clark, and Eliot to co-sign a letter of appeal. (Eliot had the letter expanded to say that illness limited Jones's output and prevented him from engaging in social self-promotion. Clark added more about Jones's 'really outstanding position as a painter'.) In 1954, Jones began receiving a Civil List Pension of £150, in quarterly instalments. From now on Grisewood acted as his liaison with Downing Street, giving detailed reports on his poverty and occasionally begging for an increase: in 1957 to £250, in 1958 to £350.[19]

Whenever Jones saw that one of his pictures in the Redfern had sold, he inquired of Nan Kivell (fig. 3), who only then might send partial payment – he treated all his artists this way. And he still owed Jones for sales from the 1948 exhibition. Since the autumn of 1950, when £1,223 was owed, Jones repeatedly telephoned and wrote the dealer. Cleverdon had lent Nan Kivell the plate of the dry-point pietà (finished in 1930 for

3. Rex Nan Kivell, by Ida Kar, 1953

the aborted *Morte D'Arthur* project) to make an edition of fifty prints to sell at £3 each entirely for Jones's benefit. All the prints had sold, but Jones received, and would receive, nothing. Writing on his behalf, Cleverdon got Nan Kivell to send £200 and a statement of account. Cleverdon then asked for the return of the plate. Nan Kivell replied that it was lost – a lie, since the gallery continued making and selling prints into the 1960s. In 1958, Jones would still be owed £283. Sir Rex (knighted in 1952) was a thief – he stole a Kit Wood and a number of Gaudier-Brzeskas from Ede and, during the war, had been jailed for stealing typewriters.[20]

Nan Kivell was also a fence for thieves. In 1954, someone brought to Jones for authentication pictures bought at the Redfern. One was by René Hague but initialled 'DJ' with a date. The others were authentic but had never been released for sale. Jones went to the gallery, saw more such pictures, and protested to Nan Kivell, who refused to disclose his source. Jones knew they were from the large portfolio he had stored during the war at Pigotts. It had contained watercolours and drawings that he wanted to keep 'as representative of various periods'. He became convinced that the thief was his own godson, twenty-two-year-old Michael Hague, a heavy drinker. Jones felt betrayed, but not wanting to upset René and Joanna, did not press charges and concocted a story for them about mistakenly leaving the portfolio in a taxi. The accidental death of their twenty-year-old son Richard in February 1955 strengthened his resolve to keep the secret. Only a few knew the identity of the thief, and they kept quiet. When asked in 1989 what he knew about the stolen portfolio, garrulous Michael Hague responded with uncharacteristic stony silence and, recovering his volubility, described its location (in the lumber room, behind the balcony above the stone-carving shop) and contents in self-incriminating detail. Many of the stolen pictures Jones considered unworthy of exhibition or sale and was angry that they were now in the public domain, hurting his reputation.* A second portfolio in storage disappeared, which he later referred to vaguely as '"lost" . . . by equal mischance . . . about the same time from a place elsewhere'.[21]

Oliver Brown of the Leicester Gallery asked him annually for the next decade to exhibit, but Nan Kivell's dishonesty was decisive. Jones would write in 1962, 'The whole affair has made me keep clear of dealers as far as possible.' In the early 1960s, Nan Kivell would hear that he was painting again and write asking to see the new paintings. Jones replied that he was too ill to receive visitors and asked for a statement of what yet remained owing from his 1948 exhibition and of sales of the dry-point pietà prints. Nan Kivell did not reply. Jones deleted the reference to his 1948 Redfern exhibition from his entry in *Who's Who*.[22]

*   *   *

On 26 June 1954, he was visited by the Welsh nationalist and author Saunders Lewis. They had known of each other since 1934, when Jones had read articles by him and Lewis had seen Jones's work at a Welsh Artists' Exhibition in Cardiff. (Augustus John had praised its beauty and urged him to look closely at the engravings.) In 1925 Lewis had co-founded the

---

* Jones was angry but also amused at paintings by René – with their dry, regular brushstrokes and stiff, uninteresting shapes – being attributed to him. When he discovered in the spring of 1957 that some of these were for sale at Christie's as his, he went to the director to have them withdrawn. Ten years later, one was donated to the Fitzwilliam Museum, Cambridge. A curator brought it to Jones, who declared it inauthentic.

Welsh Nationalist Party, *Plaid Cymru*, serving as its president for thirteen years. In 1936 he and two friends had burned a RAF bombing school in the Lleyn Peninsula in an attempt to stir the Welsh into demanding political rights. Lewis went to prison for nine months and lost his university post. Moved by his courage, Jones sent him a copy of *In Parenthesis*, and they began corresponding. During their first visit, in 1954, Jones told him of an Arts Council retrospective exhibition of his work to travel in the coming autumn to Swansea, Aberystwyth, Cardiff, Edinburgh, and London. Lewis wrote a short preface to the catalogue, which Jones liked for emphasising his painted inscriptions because, he wrote, 'they are . . . of special importance to me'. Four years later he would regard Lewis's foreword as 'the best thing written' about his work. They were, by then, close friends.[23]

They had a lot in common. Both had served in what they called 'our war' and were Catholic converts. Lewis was the only person Jones knew who fully shared his sense of Wales, a love mostly for the semi-tribal, aristocratic, medieval Catholic nation it had once been. Both felt an aversion for its modern, post-Methodist, petite bourgeoisie, twice removed from their medieval past. Because Catholic, Lewis was for him the great exception to Welsh narrowness, 'so very much more wide visioned than any other real Welsh Welshman that I have met. Centuries of Protestant nonconformity, *Calvinism in particular*, make most Welshmen impossible.'* He also loved Lewis's 'incisive, clear, quick . . . exact, "final"' thinking, his 'ability of seeing like a flash through a tangle of accidents', and his conciseness. He thought him intellectually comparable to Dawson. Lewis was also arrogant, vain, condescending, in his own mind the great Welshman, but none of this bothered Jones. Whenever Lewis was in London and could visit, he did. Never making the mistake of thinking Jones a Welshman, Lewis considered him 'a profoundly English writer' and would say so in print: 'the Welsh past . . . is a key to his work as English poet and painter'. (In November 1968, Jones would decline membership in the Welsh Academy partly because he considered himself 'a Londoner . . . outside and shy of these differing groups of Welshmen – in fact . . . in quite an anomalous position'.† The Anglo-Welsh poet Vernon Watkins – whom Jones knew through Eliot – had earlier asked him to participate in a broadcast conversation on the subject of being Welsh, and he had said no, explaining: 'You, yourself, and Dylan & others – R. S. Thomas, for example, although writing in English quite obviously

---

* 'In some ways & at times,' Jones told Lewis, '*we*, in so far as I can presume to include myself under that *we*, seem the most imperceptive, damned blockheaded of nations, fobbed-off by the most shallow vulgarities.'

† He also declined lest he endorse the liquidation of the Welsh language – the previous year, after consulting Lewis, he had signed a petition against relaxing the Welsh-only rule for literary submissions and performances at the National Eisteddfod.

write as *real Welshmen* – it comes out in all kinds of ways. But I am . . . totally English (indeed Cockney English), in upbringing, in environment, and in all kinds of ways.')[24]

In 1953, Jones had been elected to the Cymmrodorion Society and, in the spring of 1956, was elected vice president. This and his friendship with Lewis encouraged what was, for the next twenty years, an obsession with Wales.* About contemporary Wales Jones was pessimistic. He knew that the upland farming communities were doomed and there was not enough 'urban life of a decidedly Welsh character to even begin to cope with the thousand & one alien pressures'. In 1957, the discussion in parliament on the one day a year devoted to Wales convinced him that Wales, as 'the shadow of a living tradition', has '*had it*'. If his hope for Wales diminished, his love did not. He attended the annual St David's Day Mass of Welsh Roman Catholics of London.[25]

* * *

Silence from the US over *The Anathemata* was broken by explosive applause from W. H. Auden. He had read it carefully, fighting incomprehension, becoming increasingly impressed, reread it for ten months, and told Spender that it was astonishing. Spender urged him to review it in *Encounter*, and, in the February 1954 issue, Auden announced that *The Anathemata* is 'one of the most important poems of our times', and expressed surprise at its not being widely recognised as such.[26] Helen Sutherland told Jones of the review.

The following month, he received a letter notifying him that the US National Institute of Arts and Letters was giving him the Russell Loines Memorial Fund Award of $1,000. Auden had nominated him. Jones was pleased to learn that it was not an annual award but given only to especially deserving works, having been conferred only six times since its inception in 1924 and never before to a non-US citizen.[27]

Auden sent Jones a letter saying, 'Your work makes me feel very small and madly jealous.' In reply, Jones wrote that *The Poet's Tongue*, co-edited by Auden, 'has been one of my constant companions'. Grisewood arranged for them to meet over dinner at the end of July 1954

---

* On 25 March 1957, he subjected Grisewood to an eight-page foolscap letter on linguistic changes in Welsh from the fifth through the nineteenth centuries. In early 1966, he would spend most of two months writing a fifty-four-page foolscap letter to Grisewood on Llywelyn the Last and his place in Welsh history, and there are other lengthy letters on roughly the same subject. On any topic touching Wales, he would often begin writing a letter to the press – hundreds of fragmentary drafts survive – most of those finished, unpublished.

at Broadcasting House. Though realising that Auden was a celebrity, Jones was entirely natural, and Auden was respectful to him. Acting as host, Grisewood thought they got on well but without really connecting: there were 'gulfs between them'. Auden was English in a conventional way (fluent, refined, superficial) that Jones, Grisewood said, had long ago reacted against. Auden's interests were social, Jones's not. Auden wanted to talk about Catholicism; Jones did not.* And they were too far apart aesthetically to discuss literature. Dominating the conversation, Auden may not have realised any of this – according to Grisewood, he was much less sensitive. His sympathies being strongly homosexual, he may have hoped for a queer rapport. He suggested further meetings. Jones said, 'Oh no, I'm afraid I can't.' They did meet again, at a supper party at the Spenders' house in St John's Wood in June 1955. On this occasion, too, Auden dominated conversation, directing it again, as Jones had feared, to Catholicism. Jones noticed that when anyone else talked – the others being Osbert Sitwell, Elizabeth Glenconner, Francis Bacon, and Sonia Orwell – Auden did not listen but was preparing what to say next. After this second meeting, Jones told Grisewood that, while he was grateful for Auden's appreciation, he and Auden were utterly different and, sadly, had nothing artistically in common. They did not meet again. A literary social life would have advanced Jones professionally – in years past he could have mixed much more with Evelyn Waugh and Graham Greene – but he was not ambitious in that way.[28]

Spender, Jones realised, was inconsiderable as a poet and thinker, but he liked him. On a rare visit, Spender told him that he had bought two pictures that had belonged to Prudence, one of them entitled *The Tiger* (1941), of which Jones was particularly fond and asked for a photograph. Instead, Spender loaned him the painting for life. In gratitude, Jones would give him in 1962 a large, beautiful inscription (*Alma Mater*, 1960).[29]

He especially liked Spender's pianist wife, Natasha, and she loved him, admiring his childlike enjoyment of small things. Once when she began to say how Gregorian chant had influenced her, he became suddenly euphoric, saying, 'Do you love Gregorian chant? Well just wait a minute.' And from under his bed he brought out his little red gramophone and put on his favourite record, *The Early Renaissance* of Guillaume Du Fay's polyphony and plainchant including, he said, 'an

---

* Although caring deeply about 'the Catholic *res*', Jones found it difficult to talk about. The same was true of Welshness, the abstract in painting, sacrament in religion, 'the need for craftsmanship', and folk music. Asked about any of these, he would, he admitted, 'take evasive action', unable 'to say anything before clearing away a whole tangle of stuff'. Only with close friends who understood 'the Break' would he discuss these matters.

astoundingly beautiful canzone' and 'a marvellous setting to the antiphon *Alma Redemptoris Mater*' and his favourite hymn, *Vexilla Regis.** It was a recording that he often played for himself while alone in his room. Before playing it, he wiped it strenuously along and across the grooves with his pocket handkerchief. The record was so worn and the needle so dull that she could hear little more than its rasp in the groove, but he swayed gently to the obscured music, his face ecstatic. Afterwards she said, and he agreed, that listening to music is like praying.[30]

*   *   *

In March 1954 Jones was asked again to receive his honorary doctorate from Wales. Three times arrangements were made and he backed out, twice panicking only days before (and feeling guilty). He was invited yet again to receive it on 20 September 1954 in Cardiff. This was close to the opening ceremonies of his Arts Council exhibition there, which he had agreed to attend on the condition that his appearance be unpublicised. He planned to combine the two events with a trip to Ferryside to visit Laurie Cribb. Despite an anxiety attack that delayed departure, he did go to Cardiff. He stayed with Oldfield Davies, where Saunders Lewis and Aneirin Talfan Davies visited him. So did Professor T. J. Morgan, with whom he had a long conversation about Welsh etymology. Jones attended the opening of the exhibition in the National Museum. There Lewis took him to see the early Celtic and Romano-British artefacts, Jones paying particular attention to the casts of memorial inscriptions and being strongly affected by 'the feeling of them'. (Later he told Nicolete Gray that they influenced his painted inscriptions.) But his distress increased. A few days before the scheduled conferring of the degree, he panicked, mumbled apologies, and fled back to Harrow. He would never leave the London area again.[31]

As the exhibition travelled, reviews were ecstatic. It came to the Tate Gallery for the period from 17 December to 30 January 1955, Jones adding pictures, bringing the total to 131—74 watercolours, 17 drawings, 35 engravings, and 5 inscriptions. (He knew the owners of every one of these works; later, as they resold, he would be sad to lose track of them.)[32] Attending the late-afternoon private viewing on 16 December, he was surprised at how good they looked together, from now on regarding them as parts of a whole. He later advised friends to visit early in the day since the pictures 'look so *enormously* nicer by day-light. I, personally, *can't* see the *colour* at all by that horrible artificial light.' To him the Tate was 'a somewhat

* *Works, vocal. Selections* by Guillaume Dufay; Safford Cape; Pro Musica Antiqua (Brussels, Belgium) (1955); Archiv Produktion AMP 14019.

unsympathetic gallery' (he could not say why). It was jammed, and he was propelled about, seeing many old friends but unable to speak to anyone for long. It was an 'excruciatingly exhausting' day.[33]

After a fortnight in his room with fibrositis, he went three more times to the exhibition, accidentally meeting Kenneth Clark, Henry Moore, and Ben Nicholson. On 28 January, two days before the closing, he went a final time, to walk round the show with the Queen Mother. As they talked together, she said that she admired *The Anathemata*, demonstrated (he thought) a real understanding of art, and expressed special admiration for *Vexilla Regis*, which he interpreted for her.[34]

The English press was celebratory, and attendance reached 11,400. Boosting notoriety was a radio colloquium produced by Talfan Davies, broadcast over the Welsh Home Service on 29 October, involving an 'Autobiographical Talk' by Jones (*EA* 25–31) and talks on his work by Goronwy Rees, T. S. Eliot, Saunders Lewis, Nicolete Gray, and Gwyn A. Williams, all printed in *Dock Leaves* (Spring 1955). New fame generated unexpected sales of *The Anathemata* and *In Parenthesis* and a surge of letters, which, accumulating, he regarded with dread, guilt, and irritation, though he answered most of them.[35]

* * *

The Tate exhibition was his first to include painted inscriptions, an art form he invented and was perfecting. His earliest inscriptions, at Ditchling, had been private greetings, quickly done for feast days, saint's days, and birthdays. Sometimes he painted them in letters to friends. During the war he began making them as autonomous artworks. He tried drawing the letters and filling them in, but the result was unfree and boring, so he now kept preliminary planning to a minimum. With Nicolete Gray, who had become an expert on the subject, he looked at photographs of inscriptions and manuscripts and discussed kinds of lettering. In October 1948, she had given him her *The Palaeography of Latin Inscriptions in the Eighth, Ninth and Tenth Centuries in Italy* (1948), which he frequently consulted.[36]

He preferred for his inscriptions Latin, Welsh, or Greek as more economical than English with its visually unevocative prepositions, conjunctions, and articles. Non-English words also had the advantage of being seen rather than merely read.[37]

First he painted single quotations but in 1949, in *Exiit edictum* (fig. 4), in a modernist aesthetic, he began juxtaposing bits from different sources. He sometimes inscribed a second or third text up the left margin and across the top. His inscriptions combine (or bridge between) painting and poetry, as Saunders Lewis was the first to state in the 1955 Tate catalogue – Jones said, this is 'quite right'.[38]

Within an inscription, he varied the shape of letters in response to adjacent letters and spaces. Not mechanically aligned, placement is slightly wonky – words often crowding the right margin, letters tightening to fit, colours suiting meanings, and tone varying within a letter.

In *Exiit edictum*, he began applying Chinese White to portions of the background, emphasising it and giving letters 'incisiveness and lapidary feeling' and 'punch'. The letters hover in three-dimensional space.[39] In 1953 he began giving the entire paper a preliminary coating of Chinese White, allowing him to scrape or sponge out letters or entire lines and repaint. This left pastel ghosts in the white as background to the final letters. They consequently radiate into surrounding space in tones that are the visual/tactile analogue to acoustic resonance and linguistic connotation.

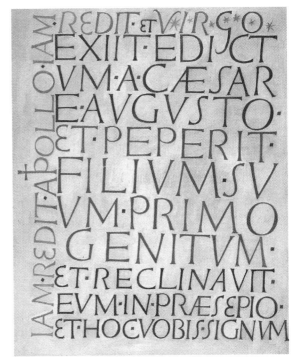

4. *Exiit edictum*, 1949

Now much of his effort in making inscriptions was to bring the surround into relationship with the lettering – something no one else had done. He found that generally inscriptions that required the most readjustment looked best. When they 'came off', they had 'an abstract quality' that gave him immense satisfaction.[40]

In May 1956 he received from Helen Sutherland his first commission to make an inscription, for £20. Till then he had never done one to sell. He worked on it for a month, combining Latin, Anglo-Saxon, and Greek texts, the first inscription he signed. He had it framed with clips, so it could easily be taken out to handle and look at closely.[41]

Also in 1956, Carmelite nuns at Presteigne, Wales, commissioned one for their chapel wall. It was his largest (23 by 31 inches), entitled *Pwy yw r gwr* (fig. 5) and consisting of Welsh (and Latin translation) from the fourteenth-century poet Gruffudd Gryg, divided horizontally by a white space that exerts a powerfully unifying force.* He maintained 'a slight entasis along the top . . . for "aesthetic" reasons' and . . . 'to get a bit of "celtic" curvature into the Latin rigidity'. The central space or 'as it were, *via*' he tried to keep 'as

---

* The Welsh and the Latin translation in English: 'Who is the man who has the crown? The white god with the wound under his breast. // A pure sacrifice, a holy sacrifice, an undefiled sacrifice.'

PWY·YW·R·GWR·PIAV·R·GORON
QVIS·EST·VIR·QVI·HABET·CORONAM
DVW·WYN·A·I·FRATH·DAN·EI·FRON
DEVS·CANDIDVS·VVLNERATVS·SVB·PECTORE

HOSTIAM+PVRAM·HOSTIAM+SANCTAM
ABERTH · PVR·ABERTH·GLAN
HOSTIAM+IMMACVLATAM
ABERTH· DI FRYCHEVLYD

5. *Pwy yw r gwr*, 1956

straight as possible but not mechanical or ruled, so that the letters seemed a bit like soldiers maintaining a dressing on an imagined line'. To counteract imbalances owing to differences in line length and number of letters, he reworked for fairly even distribution, the whole 'endlessly re-adjusted'. Upon delivery, the nuns rejected it as esoteric and he supplied, instead, a design for a chi-rho to be painted on a wall.[42] So he got to keep this marvellous inscription, which hung sometimes over his mantel, sometimes behind his work table – a masterpiece of living stillness.

Although it meant so much to Jones, Llywelyn's death in 1282 never became the subject of a picture (though he made one attempt) or poem. After many tries, in July 1959 he made an inscription concerning Llywelyn's death for the frontispiece of *Wales through the Ages*, commissioned by Aneirin Talfan Davies and beginning *Cara Wallia derelicta* (fig. 6). It mainly quotes Gruffudd's elegy for Llywelyn, in which, Jones said, 'line after line . . . seems to fall like hammer blows' so that it 'still has power to rend us'. Inclusion of a bit of the *Aeneid* evokes legendary British descent from Trojans and implies continuity between the Trojan ur-catastrophe and this man's death.*

* The principal combined texts translate: 'And then was cast down all Wales to the ground. It has come, the last day and ineluctable hour of Troy. A leader's head, a chief leader's head was on him, head of fair resolute Llywelyn, it shocks the world that an iron stake should pierce it. There is no counsel, no lock, no opening.'

The result is a heart-rending modernist poem-made-visible, its lines rumbling with irregular, barely contained emotion. Visually it is numinous – no reproduction captures its deep purples and shimmering golds. It was his favourite inscription, one of six he framed and hung in his room.[43]

The large later inscriptions are major works, taking weeks to complete, but not anxiety-provoking or exhausting like pictures. Jones never wondered whether an inscription was finished. Whenever painting pictures depressed or paralysed him, he could still easily paint inscriptions. 'I've got a "thing" about them,' he told a friend: 'I like doing them in a peculiar way', and he added, 'In some ways they mean more to me than most of my stuff.'[44] They solved his chief aesthetic problem: a desire to paint simply, without complication, as he had in 1929–32, while including the allusions that complicate his later 'symbols present' pictures. In his inscriptions the form is relatively simple, words making the allusions.

6. *Cara Wallia derelicta*, 1954

Jones would be recognised by many as the most important forerunner of lettering as a contemporary art form, including Ralph Beyer, the letter-carver for Coventry Cathedral, and David Kindersley, perhaps the foremost English stone-carver in the latter half of the twentieth century, who said that Jones 'reinvented the Roman alphabet' making it 'more primitive, and *so* beautiful'. But Jones's inscriptions are not mere forerunners. As the poet Michael Symmons Roberts said, they 'are like nothing else . . . in art or poetry. They are private and public, ancient and modern, formal and expressive.'[45]

*   *   *

Apart from the two long-term residents of Northwick Lodge (a female violin teacher and an old lady named Miss Evans, both of whom Jones liked), the lodgers had changed. They now included Miss Knott, an impoverished upper-class spinster; a diamond merchant from South Africa and Whitechapel; Mr Feakins, an automobile salesman who tried to sell motor cars to the others, including Jones; and a lobotomised salesman, who had to write orders down immediately before forgetting them and who told the story of his lobotomy again and again, adding, 'People say it has affected my memory but I think it's all right.' A woman who worked as a secretary and kept a bottle of sherry behind her mantelpiece mirror claimed to be engaged to the mayor of Monmouth. A young couple, Winifred and Raymond Durham, and their children stayed for a summer, she occasionally steaming white fish for Jones. But the residents were mostly single misfits. Colin Wilcockson, a young Oxford graduate staying for four months in 1955, recalled, 'There was a fair bit of gloom, actually, and David's reaction to these people was very tender and very sympathetic.' At meals 'he would cheerfully chatter away', beloved among them because gentle, kind, and 'very amusing'.[46]

He and Wilcockson often spoke and subsequently corresponded about medieval literature and their great shared enthusiasm, *Piers Plowman*.* Another young Oxford graduate staying temporarily was Geoffrey Treasure, with whom Jones talked about Arthur and the Middle Ages. Another student, staying for two years (1956-7), was a young Italian named Camillo Corvi Mora. He and Jones became 'great friends' and spoke 'for hours' about art and literature. Jones thought Mora's reading Dante aloud in Italian the most beautiful thing he had ever heard. Mora was, he said, 'one of the most intelligent persons I've ever met & jolly amusing', with a '*mind* as agile as a fish'. Jones was 'very sorry' when he left.[47] Since Mora was no correspondent, their friendship lapsed.

In the late winter of 1954–5, Jones was surprised by a letter from Edith Sitwell expressing admiration for *The Anathemata* as 'one of the … great poems of our time' and asking permission to include 'Rite and Fore-time' in her anthology, *The Atlantic Book of British and American Poetry* (1958). She had him to lunch at the Sesame Club on 21 June 1955. The party included Clark, Spender, Maurice Bowra, and her brother Osbert, whom Jones had known since the '30s and was fond of. Jones told them she had nearly got him killed in Sloane Square when, about to cross the road, he saw out of the corner of his eye what seemed a pillar box moving. Turning to look, he recognised from photographs six-foot-tall Edith dressed in red just as a bus crashed past within inches of his face. They spoke about King Canute, of whose historical reality he assured her, and Marilyn Monroe, whom she had recently met and liked. Edith invited him to other lunches and to tea parties. He found her 'very down-to-earth and straight forward'.[48]

In the summer of 1956, he asked one of his parish priests to remember Grisewood at Mass – he was suffering from painful rheumatoid arthritis. To Jones's surprise, the priest asked, 'Is he a Catholic?' Jones was dismayed that

---

* About Langland's B text, Jones wrote, '*What* a bloody good poem it is. Makes Chaucer, on the whole, lacking in *depth*, neither as "earthy" nor as "celestial".'

anyone's religion should be thought to have a bearing on whether he or she is remembered at Mass. Priests, he thought, 'what chaps they are!'[49]

Jones was corresponding with Vernon Watkins, who, in April 1955, had asked him to contribute to the Dylan Thomas memorial issue of *Poetry*. He had declined, but Watkins persisted, so he revisited material rejected from *The Anathemata*, eventually sending Watkins an eight-page handwritten poem entitled 'The Wall' (*SL* 10–15). It is an expression of existential unease by a Roman soldier in Jerusalem morally perturbed by the imperium he imposes. It is formally innovative: the temporal references in the poem mimic the spatial route of a triumphal march through Rome. It received the Harriet Monroe Prize of $100 for the best work published in *Poetry* in 1955. Watkins republished it for the Poetry Book Society.[50]

The Queen Mother's secretary phoned in late June 1955 to say that she wished to buy a picture. Jones said, 'I haven't any to sell', then, after a long silence, added, 'There might be one or two.' A meeting was arranged at Barbara Moray's house. Barbara asked him to bring several pictures, including one of trees that the Queen Mother was interested in (possibly *Cedar of Lebanon, Bowden House*, 1947). He said he might bring one but not that, which he considered 'a key picture' to which he wanted to refer while making others. 'But really, David,' Barbara said, 'you *can't* just take *one* to the Queen, you must give her some to choose from.' He replied, 'All right, I'll bring three, but this one, though I'll bring it, she can't have.' At their meeting on 4 July, he showed the three pictures like a conjurer, repeatedly hiding the one he wanted to keep by displaying the others in front of it, so that, to his relief, she chose an inferior one, *The Outward Walls* (1953), for which she paid £30. She probably noticed his stratagem. (Barbara certainly did and thought it improper.) On 2 August, the Queen Mother wrote thanking him for the picture and asking him to come to Clarence House to advise her on where to hang it and to bring 'the lovely picture of trees' to lend to her. There is no record of his going.[51]

On 22 November 1955, he gave his fourth radio broadcast, 'The *Viae*', a review of Ivan D. Margary's *Roman Roads in Britain* (*EA* 189–95). It was produced for the Third Programme by Anna (Neuta) Kallin, an extraordinary Russian Jew whose circle of friends included Manya Harari, Isaiah Berlin, and Vladimir Nabokov. At the urging of Grisewood, Director of the Spoken Word, Neuta had been asking Jones to broadcast at the BBC since 1947. Finally, because of growing affection for her, he agreed to do it – really, Grisewood said, to please her.[52]

Having no patience for his long phone calls, she used Hilary Reynolds as an intermediary. Hilary would ring up, 'Hello Mr Jones', and he would say, 'It's not Mr Jones; it's David.' One day he telephoned her saying,

'This is David David.' They became friends, and he gave her meals of grapefruit and a boiled egg, showing his paintings and discoursing on the Celts. She married the letter-carver Ralph Beyer, who twice visited him with her and saw his inscriptions.[53]

As a result of his 1954–5 exhibit and the Queen Mother's interest, Jones was appointed Commander of the Order of the British Empire. On the morning of 8 November 1955, he went to Buckingham Palace and joined other recipients of honours, feeling 'a bit odd' as though he 'had strayed by mistake into somebody else's party'. He was surprised at how large the anterooms were and wished he could see them with their chandeliers lit. Receiving his award, he told the Queen, 'I write the sort of books your mother reads.' (There was not much else to say: Elizabeth II, he later said, 'has the taste of a naval officer's wife'.) She seemed to him a bit wooden, with the beginning of Victoria's puffy cheeks. The proceedings lasted an hour-and-a-half, reminding him of the prize-giving ceremony at Brockley School. As an order 'of chivalry' one class below knighthood, the CBE meant so much to him that he ordered a copy of Burke's *Peerage*, in which he was now listed. But the medal was ugly, with a thick fleur-de-lis dangling by a point from a small crown – he told Grisewood, 'I'm not sure I'm going to keep the damn thing.'[54] It would not be among his personal effects at the time of his death.

* * *

Clarissa (née Spencer-Churchill) (fig. 7) was now the wife of the Prime Minister, Anthony Eden. In late March 1956, Jones sent them a print of *Chapel in the Park* and invited her to come for advice on how to frame it and to see some paintings. She visited several times. He sent her a copy of *In Parenthesis*, which Anthony read at night in bed. On 10 and 19 July, Jones went to tea at 10 Downing Street and enjoyed seeing Turners on the walls. He gave her a tiny (2 by 2 inches) painted copper-engraving of a rose (engraved in 1929, printed and painted in 1954), which he gave to beautiful women he felt attracted to (fig. 8).*

Their friendship warmed with the Suez crisis. On 26 July 1956, Gamal Abdel Nasser (Jones loved his name) nationalised the Anglo-French Suez Canal Company. Eden sent troops to seize the canal, thereby splitting his cabinet, dividing the public, alienating the US, and undermining the economy. Aware of the pressure on the Edens, in August Jones gave Clarissa an inscribed copy of *The Ancient Mariner*

7. Clarissa Eden, 1952

* Not listed in Cleverdon's *The Engravings of David Jones* and never previously reproduced.

and the inscription *Ex devina pulchritudine* (fig. 9), which surrounds Aquinas's Latin (translating, in part, 'From divine beauty is all being derived') with Chaucer's English by way of a tribute to her. 'Enchanted', she hung it beside her bed. On 27 August, he visited for tea and was glad to see it well framed. His lavish gifts indicate sympathy but also infatuation. When later asked if he had been in love with her, Clarissa replied, 'Maybe ... I mean obviously he liked me very much. Yes, in a way I suppose he was in love with me.'[55]

On 12 September, after hearing on the 6 p.m. news that Eden intended to govern the canal with France and the US, Jones wrote a short poem, entitled 'Isis', begging the goddess to save Egypt 'from / this new Antony / and his triumviri' of Eden, Dulles of the US, and Mollet of France.* He never

8. *Rose*, 1929

9. *Ex devina pulchritudine*, 1956

* Published by Oliver Bevington in 'This new Antony', *Times Literary Supplement* (22/3/2013), p. 14.

intended publication – it would have hurt Clarissa, and (he soon learned) the US wanted no such arrangement.

British bombing of Egypt appalled Jones. Through Grisewood and Hugh Fraser, now an MP and frequent visitor, he formed 'tentative notions about collusion' with France and Israel and Eden's deception of his cabinet and parliament. Nevertheless he loyally visited Clarissa, keeping his opinions to himself and allowing her to assume that he was 'pro Eden and pro Suez' – until he became so angry that he had to stop visiting. He now thought that 'from July on' 'dramatically foolish' decisions were 'rendering Britain no longer a major power'. When the Edens left London, Jones lost touch with them, although he would send Clarissa the Dent edition of Borrow's *Wild Wales* (with his preface) in 1958 and a copy of *Epoch and Artist* in 1959. In 1960, he would read 'old Anthony's boring Memoirs' and be 'aghast' at their success: 'he just says nothing that one did not know & takes evasive action over all the points . . . about Suez'.[56]

The Suez crisis paled in importance to the Hungarian uprising, occurring at the same time. 'Was there ever bravery to equal it,' Jones asked: 'it's terrific and something difficult to take in – this tremendous courage and nothing for them to hope for.' 'I never, during my whole life, felt so unhappy and disturbed about affairs.' He especially admired freedom fighters. During the Great War he had considered himself one, and they form a motif throughout his later poetry. On 9 November 1956, he first recorded poems for radio broadcast (over the Welsh Home Service): 'The Wall' and 'The Tutelar of the Place' both thematically anti-imperialist, the latter (*SL* 59–64), he would say in 1965, he liked 'perhaps best of my separate bits'. Reading them he may have had in mind the Soviet repression of Hungary.[57]*

* * *

Chris Carlile was declining rapidly. Once intelligent and witty, he was now seedy and sordid, answering the front door in dirty clothing, his shirt undone at the belt, smelling of alcohol, a cigarette dangling from his lip. He told Jones that he now slept in his clothes – 'oh, I take off my shoes' – and boasted that his bed did not need changing. His decline precipitated a power-struggle with Mrs Carol, which Jones regarded as 'an awful bore & all very very upsetting & unpleasant'. Sometimes there were no supplies or no bread.[58]

One day while cleaning, Mr Carol broke Jones's large glass chalice, kept on the windowsill. He was now, Jones realised, incompetent, owing to a lobotomy intended to cure depression, so Jones decided to clean his

---

* Later he would read a book which recorded that the Hungarians had put burning brushwood round Russian tanks. 'Very interesting,' he told Honeyman. 'In the 14th century at almost the very same place they used to do that to knights in armour.'

room himself. He subsequently claimed to 'spend most of the day trying to keep some sort of elementary order'. In the morning, this had long involved making his bed, onto which he moved books and papers from the floor (before retiring, moving them back to the floor). Now he cleaned and polished his sink-and-taps, finding that 'it looks quite nice' and was 'more of a thing than before – it gets more esse by being "loved"'. Occasionally he waxed the floor, 'a dreadful lot of work but it has to be done'. His cleaning was imperfect. A visitor years later, Juliet Wood, would notice on top of the bookshelves at ceiling-level a beer-foam of dust two inches thick.[59]

In August 1956, he had been visited several times by Jean Mambrino, a French Jesuit poet who had discovered him through a Sorbonne professor named Louis Bonnerot. Intending to lecture on *The Anathemata* in Metz, Mambrino had lots of questions. Jones thought him 'a sweet person and *extremely* intelligent but *so enthusiastic*' pacing 'the room and' shouting 'at the top of his voice and at an incredible speed. It's quite battering.' Mambrino read him one of his poems, entitled '*Le Coeur du Temps*', giving a literal translation, and Jones, in the course of eight drafts, translated it.[60]*

On 25 September 1956, Jones attended the wedding of Hugh Fraser to Antonia Pakenham, giving them an inscription. Early the following year they visited, asking to buy a picture as a wedding present for themselves. They picked *Calix and Necklace* (1954), paying £150. Once it was gone, it became his favourite. Though very busy as an MP and subsequently as Minister of the Air Force, Fraser often visited, bringing whisky. Once or twice a year he had Jones to lunch at his and Antonia's house in Campden Hill Square. On 3 June 1957, Jones became godfather to their daughter Rebecca Rose, for whom he made an inscription (he would make another for her first communion). On later visits, their children would often present him with drawings, which he took with appreciation and respect, keeping them with those by other children between pages of books. To Antonia he was 'always charming . . . whimsical, funny'. She bought one of his paintings of the garden at Pigotts, where, he told her, he had courted Petra – the only remembered indication by anyone, other than Petra in 1988, that he had pursued her after she had broken their engagement.[61]

He and Hugh reminisced about D'Arcy, Knox, and Martindale, and talked about the military (Fraser having been a paratrooper) and theology. But mostly they discussed current affairs, about which Fraser told him more than appeared in the papers. Jones was particularly interested in personalities, which he thought importantly shaped politics. Discussing French rule in Algeria, which he compared to the ill-fated 'Latin Kingdom of Jerusalem', he predicted that the 'the new Islamic nationalism' would be the major political factor in the coming years.[62]

---

* Published as 'The Heart of Time' in *Month* 226: 1211–12 (July–August 1968), p. 45, but without Jones's line breaks and placements.

To his surprise and that of the general public, in January 1957, T. S. Eliot married his secretary, Valerie, whose voice and 'beautiful hair' Jones had admired. He hoped that marriage would make Eliot more accessible, and it did. On 24 October, he invited Jones to lunch with them in their Kensington flat – the Eliots coming to the door holding hands. Infatuation made Tom happy in a sugary, cloying way that Jones was convinced ended his creative life: 'Finished!' he exclaimed to Honeyman after visiting them, 'Nothing there.' But Jones was glad for Tom's happiness. In 1961, Eliot would entrust him with their home phone number.[63]

Invited by Neville Braybrooke, Jones contributed an inscription (fig. 10) to a published symposium celebrating Eliot's seventieth birthday. Rereading much of Eliot's poetry looking for texts to use, he was 'more impressed *than ever* by his greatness'. He wrote Knight, 'there is a *validity* about his poetry which continues to set him very high indeed – also a most astonishing power of compression'. Owing to eye strain, Jones worked slowly on the inscription. When Braybrooke came to collect it, Jones had him kneel to view it flat on his bed, saying, 'Do you notice how the letters march across the page like columns of soldiers?' After printing, although considering it one of his best and 'hard to part with', he sent it to the Eliots as a belated wedding present. They hung it in their front hall. (Two years later, Tom would have him to lunch to sign it.) Invited to Tom's birthday party on 26 September 1958, Jones came down with 'some infection or chill or something' and, regretfully, was unable to go. Then he was immobilised by fibrositis at the base of his back.[64]

In November 1957, the Russians put into orbit a Sputnik containing a little dog named Laika. Jones found this very moving, and for years kept on his mantel a newspaper photograph of the dog.

For several years, Ede had sought to buy an inscription, any inscription. He was now founding a gallery called Kettle's Yard in Cambridge, paying for the renovations and donating his art together with himself as live-in custodian. He pleaded for an inscription for Kettle's Yard. Jones gave him one entitled *Quia per incarnati* (c. 1953).[65]

By the spring of 1958 Jones realised that the material written at Sheffield Terrace and excluded from *The Anathemata* would 'not be a "second part" of *The Ana*' as he had intended and not 'a continuous whole like *The Anathemata*, but . . . a sequence'. To his two already completed mid-length poems, 'The Wall' and 'The Tutelar of the Place', he added 'The Tribune's Visitation' (*SL* 59–64). Originating in memory of hearing an officer in the trenches criticising the General Staff, it is the candid monologue of a Roman tribune committed to imperialism out of a nihilistic conviction about necessity. Jones recorded it. It was broadcast and, to his surprise, published in the *Listener* (22 May 1958).[66]

Audrey Malan visited, bringing Reynolds Stone and his wife Janet, he an engraver Jones had met at Ditchling. Janet and Jones became close friends. Tall, blonde, attractive, affectionate, and, in her letters, gushy,

Aprilisthecruelstmthbreedīng Lilacs out of the dead land

NAM·SIBYLLAM
QVIDEM·CVMI S
EGO·IPSE·OCVLIS
ME I S·VIDI·IN
AMPVLLA·PENDERE
ET·CVM·ILLI·PVERI
DICERENT
ΣIBYΛΛΑTIΘEΛEIΣ
RESPONDEBAT·ILLA
AΠOΘANEIN·ΘEΛΩ.
LA·TERRE·GASTE·ETSOUTAINE
NAC·ANIVEIL·NA·MWGNA·DYN
ne·in·the·watir·no·fyssh·DauidmefecitThomae

10. *Nam Sibyllam*, 1957

she liked being the confidante of impressive men, and had now been, for six years, Kenneth Clark's lover. Jones and Clark were, she said, the two people whose company she most enjoyed. He was for her 'touchingly understanding' about her meetings with 'K' and the difficulties caused by K's alcoholic wife, his family obligations, and his busy professional life.[67] On a visit in August 1959, she photographed Jones and later sent the photographs c/o Benjamin Britten, although no account of his visit survives. Jones accepted her confidences sympathetically, without judgement.

Hilda Cochrane's son Malcolm brought to him a recent purchase, *The Jetsam Gatherer* (1936), an ink-and-chalk drawing by Jones of a Sidmouth beachcomber. Upset, he said that he had given it to Prudence with the understanding that 'it would possibly' come back to him. So Malcolm gave it to him. Jones stressed that it should never have been sold and spoke about a girl asking for a drawing – 'After all it is of me!' – forcing him to refuse and seem unkind. He mentioned the Pigotts portfolio and Nan Kivell as making him suspect people of trying to take pictures from him. But, at the end of the visit, he returned the picture saying, 'I can't imagine anybody that I'd like to have it better than yourself. By all means take it.'[68]

*   *   *

Grisewood had long urged Jones to publish selected essays to provide clarifying context for his poetry. But he was reluctant, saying his prose was laborious, 'old stuff ' was 'usually such a bore', essays were 'not' his 'real work', and the project would take time and effort. Having hit the Jonesian wall, Grisewood spoke to Eliot, who, after reading some of Jones's essays, in early April 1956, over lunch at the Garrick Club, urged Jones to undertake the project. Jones remained negative, but Eliot said, '*No*, it is a good idea and you *should* do it, and you'll be glad about it after.' Then he said that Grisewood could assemble and edit the material, and Jones relented. Grisewood collected the essays and reviews. Some were dropped, some Jones rewrote. Owing to Grisewood's persistence, Jones felt he was working, he said, 'with a luger in my back'. Writing the preface, he became optimistic. He thought 'chaps' will now 'have to say whether … my arguments' rest 'on a fallacy or not'. He supplied a frontispiece inscription and made a good many corrections and changes in proofs, at a charge against royalties of £67, which Eliot and Monteith lowered to £21, absorbed by Grisewood (whose editing fee was £50).[69]

Epoch and Artist was published on 8 May 1959, dedicated to Saunders Lewis. Jones thought that '*perhaps*' its 'key item' was the essay entitled 'Past & Present' because 'it puts what I feel in a nutshell'. But by far the most important essays are 'Art and Sacrament', which explains his theory of culture, and the rewritten 'Myth of Arthur', which discloses the historical, legendary, and mythic dimensions of the Arthurian tradition. These two essays convey much of the thought informing his poetry.[70]

The book confounded most reviewers. Jones concluded that either his 'somewhat involved way of putting ... questions did not register' or 'chaps didn't really *feel* the dilemmas that are, to me, central'. He wished it had caused debate. He would wonder to the end of his days how people 'had not the foggiest idea' what 'Art and Sacrament' was about.* He told Morag that he was considering signing his letters, 'The not understood, D.J.' But two reviews, by Kathleen Raine in *New Statesman* and (the 'most real') by Herbert Read in the *Listener*, encouraged him. Read saw affinity between Jones's 'philosophy' and Huizinga's theory of play and singled out his *Listener* letter on abstract art (*EA* 265–6) as settling 'the problem of definition with great intelligence'.[71] Clark's response also heartened him. Janet reported that Clark told her, 'I am GREATLY enjoying his book which is also helping me to think more truthfully.' Clark wrote to him, 'I don't know when I have had a book from which I have learnt as much' and it 'has been an immense help to me in clearing my mind . . . I would love to talk these things over' over lunch at the Albany.[72]

In February 1960, the Welsh section of the Arts Council gave Jones a £100 prize for *Epoch and Artist*. Surprised, he was delighted at 'it's coming from the Cymry'. But by the end of 1960 the book had sold only a few hundred copies. He worried about Faber suffering a financial loss but was glad that it was in print, because whenever someone wrote asking his views, he could recommend an essay in the book.[73]

* * *

On 2 June 1958, he had read a feature in *The Times* stating that Wales is a nation with its own language, literature, and values. Two days later, he read an approving letter by Valerie Price and sent a letter in support, which was published. He received a note from her inviting him to a party to raise money for *Plaid Cymru*. He declined by phone, promising to send a cheque and inviting her to visit. She came in mid-June with her boyfriend Michael Wynne-Williams, a law student. Jones liked them both but found her especially appealing. A native Welsh speaker, Valerie was twenty-five, dark-eyed, vivacious (fig. 11). She worked in the personnel department of a London chemical engineering firm, conducted interviews for her own weekly radio show

11. Valerie Price, 1959

* Jones would never know it, but this essay influenced Auden's later criticism. See 'Lame Shadows', *New York Review of Books*, 3/9/70.

in Cardiff and for Granada Television, worked for the magazine *Wales*, and sometimes modelled and acted.[74] By the end of their visit – like the professor in *The Blue Angel*, the Dietrich film he had liked so much – Jones was smitten.

Valerie continued to visit, sometimes weekly, usually with Michael. She found Jones 'marvellous' to be with, regarding him as simply a charming elderly man who agreed with her about Wales – until Keidric Rees, the editor of *Wales*, informed her about his eminence in the arts. Jones then showed her his paintings, finding her 'very perceptive about the visual arts'. On one of her visits, he boiled water for tea in his small saucepan, muttering apologetically, 'All so difficult, shops impossible, *can't* get out.' She left and returned shortly with a small kettle. On one visit, she wore a small wine-coloured jacket. To go with it, he thought she should have a golden torque like 'maidens . . . in "Kulhwch ac Olwen"'. In lieu of that, he bought her a gold chain, but eight months later he gave her a gold torque, saying, 'Welsh princesses wore torques.' Unable to find a Welsh equivalent for 'Valerie', he nicknamed her 'Elri', which at least sounded Welsh.[75] He felt privileged when with her. When they were apart, she preoccupied him. He fell asleep and awoke thinking of her. A moment's forgetting brought joy at remembering.

Valerie told him about contemporary Wales, its politics and culture, in which he had not previously been much interested. In November, at her request, he contributed again to *Plaid Cymru* and, at her urging, subscribed to its publication, *Welsh Nation*. Sometimes she translated Welsh for him. He liked hearing her speak it and had her read aloud the Welsh he was using in his writing to be sure of its sound. He loved 'the purity of her vowels especially when she got slightly excited'. He loved her hair, '*warm* black & glossy & vigorous and free' and told Hague he was strongly affected by her 'soft, clear-vowelled, capturing voice', adding, 'This *voice* thing is *terribly* potent . . . well, of course, the sirens & co.'[76]

Valerie gave a televised talk on his work for Granada on 21 January 1959. On the evening of the day before, she visited him with Philip Griffith who took photographs for the special (fig. 12). On 20 April 1959 Jones took her to meet Grisewood, and the next day wrote to her, 'You *did* make me feel *so* happy.' They sometimes met by arrangement at the London Library, in St James's Square, and went back together to Harrow. He would try to delay her leaving and then always walk her to the station – she usually had to catch the last train at eleven. As they had when she arrived, they hugged and kissed when she left.[77]

Through her he met more Welsh people than he had known since the Great War. These included Gwynfor Evans (the president of *Plaid Cymru*), Keidric Rees and his wife, Matti, the writer Caradog Prichard and his wife, Matti, and their 'dear little' daughter, Mari (who, unlike most children, did not frighten him) – he told the Prichards that he liked to think of Valerie as a Romano-British maiden. She introduced him to artists and actors, including Siân Phillips and Peter O'Toole.[78]

12. Jones and Valerie Price, by Philip Griffith, January 1959

Jones visited Valerie in her flat at 60 Pattison Road in Hampstead, which she shared with three young women, all ardent Welsh-speaking nationalists.[79] He usually came by taxi and spent hours with them, keeping the taxi waiting. They urged him to let it go – they would get him another – but he insisted, and they got used to this extravagance.

One evening, Valerie's flatmates being out, he reclined on the couch talking. She walked over and lay on him, embracing and kissing him passionately, inflaming his passion and subsequent anguish.[80] About this incident he confided only to Tom Burns and, doubtless, Stevenson.

Otherwise, he spoke candidly about his feelings for her to all his friends, prefacing his confidences with, 'Now, I'll tell you something that no one else is to know, ever.' He would do this for the next few years. According to Grisewood, he suffered more over Valerie than over Prudence: 'He was more deeply *physically* in love with Valerie – it was a very serious passion.' Nest agreed that the attraction was strongly physical. Hague thought it almost entirely so. Honeyman said, 'It was 90% sex, and he was just knocked sideways.' His psychosomatic rash returned, this time to his chest and arm – Dr Bell prescribed '*three* kinds of ointment' and had no idea what caused it. (The rashes continued through 1962, then became 'quiescent'.) Jones's letters to her are love letters, and he regularly sent her flowers – anemones, lilies, and on her birthday a dozen red roses – '*You* are,' he wrote, '*like a deep red rose* I *always think*.' Being unable to speak Welsh now had Freudian connotations: 'It's, for me, like having some essential part of one's self cut off – a deprivation at a very deep level.'[81] In June 1959, the Grisewoods had him and Valerie to supper. She arrived wearing her golden torque. He had looked forward to this for weeks but, during the meal, he was a neurotic mess, feeling 'horrible & weak & peculiar & frightened'.[82]

Valerie organised a meeting to promote the establishment of a Welsh-speaking TV channel in Wales, chaired by Megan Lloyd George. Invited, on 28 July 1959 at 6 p.m., Jones went to Committee Room 7 in the House of Commons. Few of those invited came, and he was unable to speak, even to object to 'red herrings'. Afterwards, he, Valerie, and the actor Clifford Evans dined together. He and Evans got on well, and Evans later visited him.[83] (There would be no Welsh-language TV channel until 1982.)

In mid-July 1959, Valerie had told him that she was marrying Michael. Jones's anguish was extreme. He confided to Janet Stone, 'I wish I could marry her. If only I could pull myself together.' Valerie was thirty-nine years younger, but Eliot had married his thirty-eight-years younger Valerie. Jones realised that his wish was 'unreal' but was 'surprised at the *intensity* and *ubiquitousness* of the distress'. He wrote to Janet: 'I expect I've been very stupid *about the whole thing* & expected things that cannot possibly be. Then one becomes united to the other . . . *in one's mind.*'[84]

When he and Valerie next met, he wept, declared his love, and grieved at the prospect of separation. She seemed coldly indifferent, so he told her that he would see her no more. But they met again, she assuring him of her affection, so he felt 'much more tranquil' and not tormented by 'that cut-off feeling'. In late July, he bravely went to the engagement party at her flat, for which he had lent her 'a couple of pictures to decorate the walls'.[85]

His love for her, he wrote Grisewood, was 'not really like anything I've ever before known about . . . everything else seems *relatively* unimportant'. To mitigate turmoil, he drank heavily. Friends rallied round. Hague visited on 28 June, and that evening Tom and Mabél Burns had him to dinner. He wrote to Grisewood, 'Damn this sex thing . . . from about 13 years onwards it's a bloody nuisance one way and other.' To Peter Kelly he said, 'The older you get the worse it gets.'[86] For about a year, he was in deep trouble, often unable to work or sleep.

Hague and other friends thought his infatuation foolish and cold-shouldered Valerie as an interloper and possible predator. She was not. Never did she ask for anything, although, Grisewood said, 'He would have given her whatever she wanted.' Over the years he would send her several inscriptions, paintings, and engravings – including his small engraved rose (fig. 8) – in all, about a dozen works. She was sympathetic, gentle, and honest, never, in Grisewood's view, exploitative.[87]

Jones wanted to make a portrait of her but found her elusive 'heavenly expression' hard to draw. Yet she inspired a painting, begun in early August 1959, of Aphrodite as a tall brunette reclining like the *Rokeby Venus* by Velázquez – Valerie as embodiment of the goddess. He began by sketching her sitting fully clothed in a chair. During a visit by Ray Howard-Jones and Raymond Moore, he mentioned wanting to sketch the naked female backside and asked her to pose. She stripped, leaned against his low mantel, and he quickly sketched her (fig. 13). He then turned the sketch on its side to match the reclining figure, though the painting would not resemble the drawing. At his request, Valerie sent a photo of her face, which he put in a small oval frame shaped like the mirror in the painting, in which the goddess gazes not at herself but the painter/viewer. The open window is his – within the picture she would be forever in his room. In February 1961, 'almost in desperation' he put in a 'pink bit of underblanket' which 'suddenly vastly improved' the picture.[88] He hung it over his bed. She was now, in a sense, sleeping with him.

Unified by pastel tones, its variety of shapes and colours give it magical vitality (fig. 14). Her upper body floats. Oversized window latches contribute to spatial indeterminacy, making her seem small. Gifts he had given Valerie lie on the

13. Study, 1959

bed. The realism and centrality of the goddess's bottom is in the tradition of Etty and of the English Parnassians of the previous century, whose nude and semi-nude goddesses were exercises in eroticism. Did sexual fixation distort

14. The Lee Shore, 1961

Jones's judgement, resulting in quasi-pornography? He told one young visitor that he was ashamed of the picture. He wanted it never to be exhibited. He thought it '*very* realistic in a funny sort of way – a bit Pre-Raphaelite', the technique not his. In the spring of 1960, he confided to Hague, 'In my heart of hearts I don't like' it – 'it's *too tight* & *fussed*. What I want to do is one full of all the complications & allusions executed with the freedom & directness that used to be in my still-lifes & landscapes – that's what I want to do before I die' – something he was currently doing in his inscriptions.

His working title was '*Gwener, Ceidwades Calonnau*' (Venus, Keeper of Hearts); then 'Love-lies-bleeding', after a flower evoking Aphrodite's dying lover, Adonis. The final title is *The Lee Shore*. He explained, 'all the ships are being driven relentlessly by the wind toward where Aphrodite is, . . . & the very term "Lee Shore" is always a bit of terror to sailors'. But with Valerie and others he continued calling it 'Gwener', and, for that reason, this is often mistakenly given as its title. In January 1962, he would tell Valerie that he wanted her to have it as a gift or legacy.[89]

For his birthday in 1959, Valerie and Michael had come for tea and seen the painting. She gave Jones a Victorian glass goblet 'with two little fighting-cocks engraved on it', which he hated, tried out of affection for her to keep on his mantel, but 'couldn't bear it'.[90]

In June 1958, he had written a book review entitled 'The Dying Gaul', a lyrical meditation on the Celts, 'one of the more satisfying' of his efforts, he thought (*DG* 50–8). On 9 April 1959, he went to the BBC to record it for broadcast on 24 April. It was published in the *Listener* (7 May). This essay joins 'The Myth of Arthur' and Jones's poetry in making an authentic contribution to the Arthurian tradition we call 'the Matter of Britain'.

15. William Cookson, 1960

Heartened by the success of 'The Wall', Jones decided, with the encouragement of Watkins, 'that kind good man', to send to *Poetry* 'The Tutelar of the Place'. But for two years he was unable to let it go because 'not quite' finished. In the spring of 1960, Watkins typed it for him, and it was published in the January 1961 issue, winning the Levinson Prize of $100 for the best poem examining technology within a broad context.[91]

Friends continued to visit, including twenty-year-old William Cookson (fig. 15). He had begun visiting four years earlier with Nicolete's son, Edmond – together they had given him a little Russian radio. Cookson was interested in modern poetry, his chief enthusiasm being Ezra Pound, whom he had visited for a week in 1958. Jones told Cookson that he liked poetry in Scots, he liked especially the work of Tom Scott, and Michael Alexander's translation of *The Battle of Maldon*. But, instead of reading contemporary poets, he reread his favourites. He felt slightly guilty about this, but there was too little time – he liked Baudelaire's having a handless clock with the words 'It's later than you think' written on its face. In May 1964, Morag would ask whether he had read Effie Ruskin's letters to Millet, and he said, 'No, I've hardly got to Lucretius yet.'[92]

In January 1959, with Pound's encouragement, Cookson founded the little magazine *Agenda*. Earning a living teaching English, he devoted weekends to editing it. Jones thought this 'heroic' and *Agenda* 'well worth supporting'.[93] On 28 July 1961, he contributed lettering for the title and contents page.

Other visitors included an 'extremely nice' Canadian English professor, Bill Blissett (a name Jones loved). In August 1959, he mentioned to Blissett that he intended to buy back his forty-two engraved blocks for *Gulliver's Travels* but had lent most of the money needed to an impoverished friend (Bussell). Blissett bought the blocks for £150 and gave them to him. Jones was astonished. After all, they were not old friends, and Blissett wasn't wealthy. This wonderful act seemed to Jones like something in a fairy tale and secured a transatlantic friendship that would involve nearly thirty visits and dozens of letters.[94]*

Other new friends were Sarah and Maurice Balme, he a Classics master, she a painter who had studied at the Chelsea Art School and in Paris. When she inquired about the food at Northwick Lodge, Jones said it was 'bloody awful' and asked to have a meal with them sometimes. So she occasionally had him to supper. He liked them both – Sarah, whom he thought 'terribly nice' and painted 'awfully well'; Maurice, 'a jolly nice chap' whom (unlike classicists 'interested only in the Augustan Age') he felt unafraid to ask about '5th Cent. blokes'. Plumtre having retired, Maurice was now his resident expert on Latin and the late Roman Empire. Jones more often saw Sarah, who asked him about Bloomsbury members, many of whom he had met and about whom he was 'slightly scathing', considering them affected and intellectually and artistically lightweight. He was seldom critical, she said, 'but pomposity brought him near to scoffing'. And he hated dishonesty. Paintings were then being brought for authentication to Bernard Beard, widely regarded as the foremost expert in Florentine Renaissance art. Jones had read him and told her, 'I don't trust that chap.' Twenty years later Beard, who conspired fraudulently with dealers, would be discredited.[95]

At Sarah's arrival and departure, Jones embraced and kissed her. 'He was tactile,' she remembered, 'and he liked to touch. When you began to leave, he would get up to see you to the door and rather hold on to you.' To her he seemed sexually inhibited but not frustrated or repressed, sentimental towards women, romantic, slightly idealistic, and speaking to them as equals, not condescendingly as other men of his generation did. Caught up in what

---

* For Jones's letters and Blissett's accounts of their visits, see W. Blissett, *The Long Conversation*, which Len Walton said accurately represents Jones as he knew him.

he was saying, he sometimes forgot he was with a young woman and used barracks-room language, like 'bugger', then vaguely recollected himself and temporarily reformed. She remembered that in repose his face was very sad. As he talked, he gently, sensually, not compulsively, touched his brushes, pencils, favourite stone (shaped like a Stanley knife), or, from his mother's kitchen, a knife in the handle of which he had carved '+STEPAULE'. Or he would hold a pencil, turning it over or drawing randomly on a scrap of paper. Another young visitor, Anne Beresford, once praised a big beautiful peach sitting on his table, and he said, 'Yes, I love the texture of them', and took it and stroked it 'as if it were a cat'.[96]

He appreciated how Sarah dressed in combinations of slight off-colours and was attentive to details of her clothing that, she thought, only a woman or dressmaker would notice. He would ask, 'Where did you get that?' and, feeling the material like a tailor, 'Is it linen?'

She asked whether he would ever sell any of the pictures in his portfolios. He replied, 'No, of course not. They're my children. They're like my family to me.'[97]

Northwick Lodge participated in Carlile's decline. In winter, there was no hot water, and the furnace was unlit in mid-December. In January 1959, the coin-box of the hall phone was full and the key lost, so Jones could receive but not make calls. On 11 October 1959, he was awakened by twenty inches of plaster ceiling-moulding falling, a small piece striking his head. Towards his current fellow lodgers, whom he called 'the old men', he remained polite, but they bored him, so he ate in his room. The cooking had become even more careless, the food greasy, sometimes burnt. When a meal was brought in, he politely accepted it, and ate, instead, cheese biscuits and Bath Olivers. Sarah occasionally brought soup.[98]

* * *

On 9 January 1960, Valerie married Michael Wynne-Williams. Knowing that Jones would be grief-stricken, the Prichards had him spend the day with them. He was gloomy, incommunicative. They resorted to television, on which a Western so intrigued him that he temporarily forgot his sorrow. He had sent Valerie a slender gold chain and a gold-lettered inscription, a brief marriage poem in Welsh of his own composing about rivers in the north and south joining to unite Wales. Though done quickly, it was, he thought, one of his best smaller inscriptions. (It arrived at her parents' house on the morning of the wedding in a cardboard tube, which, seemingly empty, was thrown out. He later made her a copy, but it was inferior to the original.) Now that she was gone, he missed 'her terribly'. He wrote to Hague, 'Last year when I was seeing Elri . . . I felt quite young again though it was only a bloody pain all the time – but now I feel useless & aged.'[99]

Valerie planned to come to him one Sunday in May 1960, or, failing that, Monday but arrived with her husband on Tuesday, when Hague was visiting. Having been disappointed for two days, Jones was 'irascible' and the visit sour – in his agitation he broke the lid of his teapot. She and Michael left, and she returned hours later with a new teapot as a 'peace-offering'. He 'could have *wept*' at her coming back, he wrote to Janet, 'it made up for everything'. Much later he would be moved to read in a letter from Valerie that she thought about him throughout the day.[100]

Before Christmas 1959, inspired by his aching, hopeless infatuation, he had begun another picture, one he had '*always* wanted to paint', of Tristan and Iseult immediately after drinking the fateful love potion aboard ship (Malory VIII, 24). Needing to know what an early medieval ship looked like, he consulted books, back issues of the *Journal of the Institute of Navigation* and *Mariner's Mirror* (having long subscribed to both), and Mike Richey, and George Naish, of the Maritime Museum in Greenwich. Jones decided to be 'noncommittal as to "period"', to accommodate the later romances that transmitted the story. Because he loved the look of a hull's ribs and because it improved the composition (they 'continue the sweeping line of Essyllt's figure & gown') he placed them on the outside of the hull as well as the inside – 'pure license …, a bit of "surrealism" if you like' (fig. 16). Wanting the temporal setting of the picture to be the feast of Saint Bridget, patroness of Iseult's native Ireland, he copied a star chart printed in *The Times* of 2 February. 'I didn't want to put in stars just where I thought they'd look nice,' he said. This decision has been criticised as 'pedanticism', a term having cogency only if beauty is sacrificed for factuality, and here the stars shimmer with exciting, wildly irregular loveliness. Imagining alone would have resulted in a tamer skyscape because, as Jones knew, imagination inclines to symmetry and harmony. (That is why he advised young artists, 'Look at what you've got, not at what you think it should be.')[101]

Sarah watched him work on the picture. He sat on his bed with his drawing board on his knee or against his pillow. His drawing arm out and around the paper, he held the pencil, very sharp, with the point inward like a tool, his hand hooked round, other sharpened pencils at the ready in the tray before him. He began erasing a line, and she said, 'Oh don't rub it out', explaining that her teachers forbade erasure. Surprised, he said, 'The way you draw and paint is up to you', adding, 'I know what lines I'm making, but I sometimes want to change them.' He drew unselfconsciously, slowly, sensually, looked a while, and drew again in silence. 'Then', she remembered,

> he would put his pencil down, look up at you with the most charm-
> ing smile and talk to you for a little. After drawing, he would
> touch the paper, moving his hand across it as though embracing
> it. Then he would see something that needed doing. It was an act
> of love – I mean he was loving the act of drawing. It was to him a

16. *Trystan ac Essyllt*, 1962

tremendous pleasure. He was feeling the emotions of his drawing. He was transferring himself into the picture. He was part of it. You could feel that.[102]

For the next two years, this picture was his chief artistic concern. It began on paper (bought decades ago in Paris) which deteriorated under repeated erasure. A new young friend, an artist named Peter Campbell, commented on its poor quality. Jones said, 'Yes, bloody awful, and they don't have the right paper in Harrow.' So Campbell went into London to an art-supply store for 400-pound hot-press Spotten paper at about £12 per sheet. In early March 1960, Jones transferred the picture, the first version becoming 'rather like the *natural scene* &' the new one 'the actual "art-work"'.[103]

He kept the first version behind his chest of drawers in a portfolio that, as he withdrew it, caught on a loose nail which, as he tugged, damaged several pictures, most severely this first version, tearing it in three pieces. In December 1965, watching in horror as he irritably tugged and pushed at the portfolio while complaining about the nail, Malcolm Cochrane reached in and easily pressed the nail back into the wood with a finger. He took the picture to the V&A Museum, whose experts repaired it. Jones was delighted, preferring it pasted together to its original wholeness. Stevenson wanted to buy it, but he would not part with it.[104]

Jones had 'never taken such a *monstrously long time*' on a picture. He wrote to Hague in February 1960, 'I take *weeks* now to do what I once would do in as many *hours* – everything gets more difficult & complex – there become more & more & more things to link up & I'm beginning to feel too old to deal with the bloody problems involved.' One of these was to keep it from 'looking like the death of Nelson'. Visiting on 5 July 1960, Kenneth Clark liked it (and bought one of the chalice pictures). In November, he visited again, and, while looking together at it, Jones said he was considering abandoning it.[105]

In February 1961, he felt it was nearly finished, 'like a gull . . . that can't *quite* take wing', but he was '*afraid* of *touching* it . . . because the balance of the colours and tones is so very close that one false step & I've had it!' With 'fear and trembling', he darkened the edges of the quarterdeck boards between the lovers' heads, and, to his relief, 'it pulled the whole design together'. He still considered the picture unfinished, and wished on that account that it not be exhibited.* It was, he wrote, 'the hardest thing I have tried to do'. It is also, surely, a masterpiece, precisely what he had failed to achieve with *The Lee Shore*, 'complications and allusions' combined with 'freedom and directness'. [106]

The lovers have been caught unawares, each with a shoe off, like Private Jones in October 1917, although here owing to dalliance below decks. The

---

* He did not want it hung in the Word and Image exhibition of 1972, but plans were fixed before he could intervene.

name Essyllt, he knew, means 'she who is to be gazed upon', and here she attracts the eye, exulting in her erotic power.[107] Blowing round to embrace Trystan's head, her golden hair evokes that of Botticelli's Venus. The mast behind her a cross, its base continuing visually to her forefoot – in an implied visual pun, the mast-cross's step, her step, she being Trystan's cross. The painting is, of course, autobiographical in depicting the smitten male like a Keatsian 'cloudy trophy hung'. From (and this seems significant) the waist down, he is an empty pencilled cipher, barely there. Fading into the background, he has a good deal in common with the infantryman in the frontispiece to *In Parenthesis* (chapter 9, fig. 10). About Trystan, Jones said, 'He's had it' – echoing the words he applied to himself if he made a mistake finishing the picture. In the upper right on the ship's pennant, a replica of the dancing bear he had drawn at age seven (chapter 1, fig. 4) stands upright, stressing that Trystan's fate is that of the artist. The ship's roll establishes the couple as occupying different realities – he stanced against the sway of the ship, perpendicular to gravity; she standing perpendicular to the ship, archetypally outside realistic space as she is outside time.

Cleaning glass-framed pictures and inscriptions in 1962, Jones was surprised 'at the thick coat of brown deposit of tobacco smoke removed' and the difference it made. He immediately had *Trystan ac Essyllt*, uncovered for so long on his easel, framed under glass.[108]

*   *   *

After not smoking for four years, in 1959 Jones had resumed 'like a fool'. He wrote, 'The worst of it is I work a lot better if I smoke, but it's an enslaving habit & very expensive, for I can't do it in much moderation. I think I *must* be immoderate by nature.' In 1960, he quit again and resumed again, smoking for the rest of his life.[109]

On Saturday 28 May 1960, Stanley Honeyman married Jacqueline Powell, to whom he had introduced Jones in 1957. The wedding was in St Margaret Lothbury, in the City. Jones came with flowers and, as a gift, the ninth *Deluge* print inscribed on the back, 'UBI CARITAS . . . IBI DEUS' ('Where charity is, there is God'). It was a very hot day, but he was wearing his greatcoat, which came down to his ankles. (With considerable indignation, he had recently heard from his tailor that he would repair it just once more.) Afterwards in the vestry, the vicar mentioned 'an Irish tramp' coming into the church just as the service was beginning. Stanley asked, 'How do you know he was Irish?' The vicar said, 'He crossed himself – I presume he was Catholic – and he was wearing a huge long coat as tramps do.' Stanley said, 'I think that might be our most eminent guest' (fig. 17). Not long after, Stanley gave Jones a Great War-vintage Lee-Enfield Rifle, which he kept in his room and brought out for children of visitors, but Stanley noticed, 'He took no pleasure in having it.'[110]

Stanley had once taken Jones to restaurants, where he ate morsels but at full prices, running up an impressive bill, which he never saw. The Honeymans now had him to their home in Chelsea for the sort of meal he liked: salad, fish or boiled chicken and rice, with prunes or stewed apple for desert. (They noticed that he was afraid of their Pekinese.) Behind the dining room was a small triangular walled garden. From inside, he admired a three-foot buttress to one wall and a beam of wood in another – 'That's accidental beauty,' he said. He loved being driven home by Stanley in the early hours of the morning at ninety miles an hour, passing all other cars. At a sign 'To South Wales,' he would say, 'Oh, let's go there.' Once, they got to Harrow in eleven minutes, Jones doing the timekeeping.[111]

17. The Honeymans and Jones, 28 May 1960

Throughout Stanley's skyrocketing career – he became Managing Director of the English Property Corporation and built Canary Wharf for the Reichmans – he and Jones visited weekly (Stanley often by himself on Saturday evenings) or spoke on the phone. Jones would ring at 11 p.m., and Stanley, who always had to end these conversations, later said, 'What a privilege they were.'[112]

* * *

Hilda Cochrane and her son Malcolm brought Jones a three-inch circular gilded frame with ornate curving floriations. She commissioned him to make a painting for it. He said, 'What in the world can I put in there?' Malcolm suggested, 'All your trademarks: your birds and your bows, the big toe split from the next toe, ponies, little shoes.' Jones asked, 'Are those my trademarks?' Malcolm said, 'Indeed they are. You always have something like that in your pictures.' Jones said, 'Well, I suppose I do.'[113] After two false starts, he made a large (13 by 8 inches) detailed drawing of a blonde dangling a foot in a stream, overarched by a tree with a fence in the background. He then zeroed in on the feet. Within the frame, a woman reaches to tie the laces of one pink shoe (fig. 18). The bird

18. Trademarks in frame, 1950

flying down across her left calf recalls the bird that Hilda had failed to see in the hat in *Sunday Mass* (chapter 12, fig. 6).

*   *   *

Yet again the University of Wales offered an honorary doctorate, at the convocation of 22 July 1960. Jones thought that now he could travel to receive it. He planned to stay with Valerie, a powerful inducement, but, as departure neared, anxiety mounted, and, to his relief, Dr Stevenson advised against going. Too late to find a replacement, the University sent his diploma by post, asking for a message to be read to the graduates and their families. He worked for a week and sent seven foolscap pages. In them he hopes that in spite of 'the increasingly urgent claims of technological studies', the University will 'conserve those studies which belong specifically to the mythos of Wales' as integral to 'our common Western deposit' involving Greece, Rome, and Christianity. And he concluded:

> the English have been with us for about a millennium and a half, so they can be regarded as naturalized by now. But they should, I think, if only in courtesy to what is anterior, pay respect to this vestigial tradition. For this thing belongs to the *mores* of all Britain and affords a living, direct, unbroken series of links with Antiquity and so with the formative period and the foundational things of this land.

He thought but did not say how comic it was that someone 'so uneducated and so unacademic' should be called a 'doctor of letters'.[114]*

* In 1964 St Andrews University would offer him an honorary doctorate but, he being unable to attend convocation, the offer was withdrawn. Later a proposal of an honorary doctorate from Oxford was blocked by Maurice Bowra, who remembered Jones's pre-war talk about the Germans and Hitler as treasonous.

PART SIX

ENDINGS

n early October 1960, two men brought forms for Jones's Old Age Pension, but he could not prove that he was Walter David Jones. And when he told them he worked '16 hours a day', they said he could only work 12 hours a week to qualify for a pension. In 1963 Grisewood would find a way to have him officially retired, owing to earning less than £100 a year. Even then, anxious about the tax ramifications of selling a work for a substantial sum, he declined to claim his pension. Not until January 1965, at age 69, would he begin receiving it, £262 per year.[1]

Turning sixty-five in 1960, he felt 'a great deal older'. Lack of energy '& loss of spirit' surprised him. He was suffering from haemorrhoids ('a ghastly word to spell'), reminding him of likewise-afflicted Alfred, 'the best king the English ever had'. He was also suffering from rheumatism, neuralgia, and fibrositis in his back, which, once aggravated, hurt for weeks.[2]

On Christmas day, the Eliots had him to lunch. He liked Valerie's mother (the only other guest) and admired Wyndham Lewis's portrait of Ezra Pound hanging on the wall. It was 'a peaceful and nice occasion'. He came away feeling 'deeply attached' to Tom and convinced that he was 'a really great man & a good one'.[3]

1. T. S. Eliot's elephant, 1961

1961 was a year of commissions. Eliot had Jones design a bookplate with a heraldic elephant's head, despite his protest that his lettering did not 'go with' his drawing and that he could not associate Eliot with elephants. The Eliots admired it (fig. 1), framed the original, and hung it in their front hall. Jones also did a drawing and inscription for the 1961 Faber Christmas card (fig. 2) and designed an emblem with lettering for the cover of *Taliesin, A Journal for the 'Welsh Academy'*. And in the spring, he painted *The Wife of the Count of the Saxon-Shore* for Jonathan Scott, a history student at Balliol, whom he had first known at Harrow in 1958, when they used to talk about Arthurian and Celtic literature.[4]

In February 1961, Jones read and found 'exceedingly moving' Pierre Teilhard de Chardin's *The Divine Milieu* (tr. Bernard Wall), the work of 'a great & truly religious mind' by a 'man of tremendous qualities and

2. Faber Christmas card, 1961

transparent & evident goodness & holiness'. In 1962 he read *The Phenomenon of Man* and was reminded of 'Rite and Fore-time' in *The Anathemata*, where evolution has its purpose and fulfilment in the Incarnation. He felt 'a compelling sympathy' with Teilhard, while noting his failure to see that with technological advances 'the notion of *signa*, or "sacrament", becomes more and more alien' to people. He thought Teilhard's idea of evolution towards union with God naïve – like any belief in general progress. In art, for example, 'Picasso is no improvement over Lascaux.'[5]

In the spring of 1961, to his poetic sequence of 'separate (more or less) fragments', Jones added 'The Dream of Private Clitus' (*SL* 15–23), a celebration of friendship as antithetical to empire. For radio broadcast, he refused to allow performance by an actor and read it himself. Recording on the evenings of 5 and 7 May at Broadcasting House, he was irritated and nervous, disliking 'those blasted sound-proof cubicles' and unable to hear it replayed. Listening to the broadcast on 31 August, he was happily surprised and wondered whether irritation had improved his reading. In September 1963, he gave the poem to Sonia Orwell for publication in *Art and Literature*, where it appeared the following March, to his disappointment without an accompanying photograph of Mother Earth in the *Ara Pacis*.[6]

* * *

Eliot was concerned about Jones's poverty, his lodgings, and his health. A few days before Christmas 1961, as they lunched together, Jones mentioned taking Nembutal. This troubled Eliot, having himself overcome a Nembutal addiction. He urged Grisewood to speak to Jones's doctor, but Grisewood thought it proper to speak to Jones, who appreciated Eliot's concern but deferred to Dr Stevenson's judgement. Grisewood now considered Jones drug-addicted.[7]

Prior to 1960, Stevenson's treatment of Jones had been predominantly psychotherapy. Then psychiatry became pharmacological, and Stevenson prescribed the new barbiturates and amphetamines. Barbiturates were especially dangerous because addictive and require increased doses for effect. They depressed his central nervous system to help him sleep but dulled his mental faculties. He was now sleeping twelve hours a day but never woke rested.[*] Throughout the 1960s, he would complain to friends

* By the spring of 1962, when suffering 'a return of the old nerve trouble', he was taking: Benzedrine (an amphetamine) in the morning, Phenobarbitone (a mild sedative), Lithium (a mood-stabilising antidepressant) four times daily; and, at night, Nembutal, the worst of the barbiturates, which he would take for at least three years. Surviving prescriptions include one for Parnate (9 July 1962), a dangerous antidepressant, which he disliked because of side effects (increased anxiety, insomnia, drowsiness). Dr Bell

that 'the endless "drugs"' made him feel 'groggy and slow' until 3.30 in the afternoon, when he began to feel 'human' but 'terribly tired almost all the time', like a 'plane that is running on one engine instead of six!' He complained to Stevenson, and to Bell, who told him he was better even if he did not feel it. Taking five different pills in 1965, Jones complained to Hilary Beyer about them and, when she asked what they were, showed her a grapefruit and laughed.[8]

Drugs all but ended his creative life. On 15 September 1960, he had confided to Clark about 'a dull, stupid feeling of absolute futility . . . which I can't seem to throw off'. On 11 March 1962, he complained to Kathleen Raine of 'fatigue and inertia' and said, 'I'm as dry as a bloody dead bone, confused and uncertain, both in drawing & in writing.' This would be his refrain for the next ten years.

*   *   *

At long last there was to be an American edition of *In Parenthesis*. The former president of CBS Television, Louis G. Cowan founded Chilmark Press and, influenced by Auden and Spender, wanted his first title to be *In Parenthesis* and planned to publish Jones's other books. Jones wrote to him that in a quarter century *In Parenthesis* had sold only 3,000 copies. 'There is *something* . . . about *In Paren* that is under suspicion or something. They don't really like it.' *The Anathemata*, 'which I think a far better book', would, he warned, have even fewer readers. Cowan was undeterred. Eliot wrote 'A Note of Introduction' in which he elevates Jones to the status of Pound, Joyce, and himself (Eliot). (Initially, in his 'Note', Eliot had referred to Jones as 'a Welshman', a mistake Jones had him correct to 'a Londoner of Welsh and English descent'.) An edition of 1,500 copies was printed with 300 extra for a limited Faber issue. About the limited edition, which Eliot and Jones signed, he (in his financial innocence) 'never *quite* knew why it was made'.[9]

Cowan visited him several times, and they became friends. Cowan was fifty-six, soft-spoken, and extremely rich. Jones thought him 'the nicest kind

---

knew it was dangerous, so it was replaced by Drinamyl (17 July), taken in the morning, a mixture of amphetamine (stimulant) and phenobarb (depressant) intended to balance each other. Jones also took Nardil (26 July), an antidepressant that inhibits phobic anxiety, replaced in December by Tofranil (four, then five, then six tablets daily), an antidepressant with many severe adverse effects (confusion, anxiety, blurred vision). He began taking Diazepam twice daily to alleviate acute anxiety. It reduces alertness and physical coordination – he wrote to Valerie, 'I fall over very easily.' It also produces drowsiness and is addictive. Much of this time he also took Lithium. He was subsequently prescribed the barbiturate Phenobarbital.

of cultivated American' and, indicating how much he liked him, allowed him
to buy a picture. With a son in Israel, he was very Jewish, and Jones talked
with him about the Israeli army being the best since the German army, and
that the best since the Roman army.[10]

By early August 1962, *In Parenthesis* sold 1,100 copies in the United
States and was receiving ecstatic reviews, which expressed dismay that
it had taken so long to find US publication. Auden wrote that in it Jones
did 'for the British and the Germans what Homer did for the Greeks and
the Trojans'. In the *New York Times*, Spender insightfully pointed out that
it 'challenges the view that' modernism 'has to be ironical'. In the *Herald
Tribune*, Winfield Scott prophesied that Jones would be seen 'as one of the
central, seminal writers' and praised especially the impact of his immediate
language: 'What it does supremely is re-create', its language surpassing 'in
its feeling of massive necessity' even 'the richest, most allusive passages of
the *Cantos*' – Jones thought this the best of the reviews.[11]

And after a quarter century of neglect, the first academic interpretation
of *In Parenthesis* appeared: John H. Johnston's 'David Jones, the Heroic
Vision' in the *Review of Politics* in January 1962. Jones thought it 'accurate'
and 'remarkable', 'the *only* decent scholarly thing written' about the poem
– although he objected theologically to Johnston identifying 'the sacrifices
etc. of soldiers with the Sacrifice of the Cross' and regretted his not seeing
how, as a visual artist, his writing differed from that of other poets.[12]

Len Walton visited and opined that Jones's paintings were more
important than his poetry. Jones mulled this over for a week and, when
they next met, strongly objected. In 1962, he told Richard Wald of the
Herald Tribune that he suspected his writing was better than his painting,
even though he continued to regard himself as primarily a painter.[13]

* * *

The British Council wanted him to record his poetry for its collection,
held in common with the Poetry Room of Lamont Library, Harvard
College. On 28 August 1961, John Lincoln (Jack) Sweeney, curator of the
Poetry Room, and his wife Moira visited. Jones liked them 'very much'
– 'they are both absolutely charming' – and found himself in agreement
with them 'about practically everything'. For Sweeney he would record
'The Wall', 'The Tutelar', and 'The Dream of Private Clitus'. Jack visited
several times and by October 1962, was 'a great friend'.[14]

In 1962, Cowan published 1,500 copies of *The Anathemata*. The
American reviews showed, Jones thought, 'a far greater sense of its nature'
than had the British. In the *Mid-Century*, Auden called it 'very probably the
finest long poem written in English in this century'. By mid-September
1962, over a thousand copies had been sold, and 'very appreciative'

letters began arriving, many from students of Fr William T. Noon at a Jesuit seminary in Scrub Oaks, New York, 'their remarks or questions . . . absolutely on the spot'. In responding, Jones was prodigal, in gratitude for finally being understood. In 1967, Noon would publish *Poetry and Prayer*, including, Jones thought, 'the best analysis of what it's all about'. The American Trappist Thomas Merton read *The Anathemata* just before his final journey to the East and, as a token of enthusiasm, sent his translation of *A Prayer of Cassiodorus* (1967) and promised a letter to follow. (He died before he could write it.) Positive American reception encouraged Jones to bring his recent poetry to book publication.[15]

Cowan also published *Epoch and Artist*, but only 500 copies. Expecting little response, Jones was surprised to find it reviewed at length and brilliantly by the American art critic Harold Rosenberg in the *New Yorker* in August 1964. Appreciating the originality of Jones's theory of culture, Rosenberg praises him as 'an arch-vanguardist' with remarkable 'breadth of . . . insights', who has here produced 'some of the most acutely relevant writing on contemporary form and value to have appeared in years' and has, in fact, 'formulated the axiomatic precondition for understanding contemporary creation'. This was, Jones thought, 'the only proper critique' of the book, and a huge relief – its essays were capable of communicating after all.[16]

Prompted by Cowan's success, Faber published *In Parenthesis* in paperback, minus the illustrations – Jones arguing in vain for inclusion of at least the frontispiece, which he considered 'integral'. In Britain *In Parenthesis* had been selling 25 to 50 copies a year. Between publication of the paperback on 13 November and 31 December 1963, sales jumped to 56 copies in hardback and 976 in paperback. Faber had printed four separate impressions since 1937 without correcting the text – after the first printing, Jones had supplied a list of errors. These were corrected in the Chilmark edition and the new Faber paperback. But he was aghast to see all the old mistakes in a new Viking paperback, though it contained all the illustrations. How, he asked, could 'the Yanks . . . include the pictures in a paperback costing no more than the British paperback'? And the difficult-to-read typesetting persisted. Grisewood urged him to change publishers, but he would not, he said, because of his friendship with Eliot.[17]

* * *

On 23 November 1961, Jones met Valerie Wynne-Williams for lunch at the Paddington Hotel. They were 'like two children out on a Sunday-school Treat having a bit of a lark', he thought. 'It was easy & relaxed.' He wrote to Janet, 'Sometimes I've cried & cried in this 'ere room when

I thought V. didn't care a damn, and then I drank too much.' Now 'I feel nearer to her than ever I did before.'

> I feel that it's just as real to her [as] it has always been to me. It all seems so *totally* other from what chaps talk about when they speak of a 'passion' or of 'being in love' with someone . . . there is no feeling of wanting to possess anything, or of jealousy, or even of desire (although, I know, of course, it's partly physical) – it seems more like a kind of dumb . . . *mutual* compassion between two people *wholly remote* from each other in most respects . . . and yet, underneath, the wholly unaccountable feeling that makes me weep so often.[18]

He wrote to Valerie frequently and at length, often pleading for a note. Her replies were few and brief. He told Grisewood, 'I've not heard from her for weeks & that is a considerable misery.' Worrying, he fantasised about her having terrible accidents and telephoned or sent registered letters. When she did write, he was '*greatly* relieved' and deeply touched. He wrote her 139 letters totalling 369 foolscap pages. She sent 59 short letters and 4 postcards, which he kept in a special case lined with red silk.[19]

He resorted increasingly to telephoning, speaking with her at great length. Sometimes she visited unannounced, to his joyful astonishment. Valerie later recalled, 'there was so much laughter in our meetings'.[20] She was the best tonic for depression, but sometimes after seeing her, he suffered a recurrence of his symptom of sexual repression, entering in his pocket diary the single word 'rash'.

Their Welshness did not much coincide. She urged him to send money to *Plaid Cymru*, but now he would not, a disinclination sharpened by Lewis objecting to the party as currently a 'nest of Aldermaston Anglo-Welsh socialists' opposing the government instead of promoting the language. (Since 1961 Jones contributed 'all' he 'could afford' – in May 1962, £15.15s.od. – to a private fee-paying Welsh Language school at Eglwys Dewi Sant, Paddington.) In vain Valerie urged him to join the party. In November 1963, he was asked to be president of the London branch and declined, saying he was not a member '& quite useless in political matters'.[21]

* * *

He seldom went out. In the evenings he telephoned friends, each for an hour or more. After Morag visited, he often phoned to add something and continued talking. When Hague tried to end a phone conversation, Jones would say, 'No, don't hang up. I might think of something else in a minute or two.' Many found him difficult to hear. Hague often said, 'For heaven's sake, speak into the mouthpiece.' Jones replied, 'I can't hold this damn thing too close – it's full of germs.'[22]

Two or three visits per week are recorded in Jones's pocket diary. Unrecorded are weekly visits by Bussell, Honeyman, and Walton, and by others who phoned and then came. During the war, visits had lasted two hours; now they lasted five or six, most beginning with forty-five minutes of desultory talk as he emerged from the doldrums until, as Honeyman put it, 'David came back', speaking warmly and freely. The warm-up was briefer with women, instantaneous with Valerie, unless she had someone with her.[23]

New visitors included the children of friends and, since the mid-1950s, Richard Shirley-Smith and his soon-to-be wife, Juliet Wood, 'an artist to her very finger tips' and 'a remarkable character'; since 1959, Teleri Hughes, the vivacious daughter of a Bogota millionaire gangster, whom Jones liked ('a *real* bloke – tough as a 16th century buccaneer but with a heart of gold and an unbounded love of Wales'); since 1959, Stuart Piggott, a professor of Prehistoric Archaeology at Edinburgh, whom Jones consulted and greatly admired; since 1959, Peter and Kate Campbell; and in the early 1960s, Catherine Ivainer (later Rousseau – she married during the period when she visited him), writing her Sorbonne thesis on *The Anathemata*.[24]

* * *

In the winter of 1961, for Grisewood and Anna Kallin, Jones wrote a talk entitled 'Use and Sign', an 'unequivocal, emphatic defence of the extra-utile'. Broadcast on 26 April 1962, published in the *Listener* in May, it is the most concise, clear, and powerful of his essays, the shortest and easiest introduction to his thoughts on culture (*DG* 177–85).[25]

* * *

In August 1962 he began the last of his important paintings, *Annunciation in a Welsh Hill Setting*, also called *Y Cyfarchiad I Fair* (fig. 3). In it Mary subsumes the Welsh mother-goddess Rhiannon and her romance type Olwen. Enclosing her is a wattle fence like one that had ringed the garden at Capel-y-ffin. In style and content, the picture is writerly, and Jones interpreted it as he might a text. The vividly realistic animals are chiefly from *The Mabinogion*, where Kilhwch is aided by an ousel, stag, owl, eagle, and salmon. The Roman wolf at her feet is Mary's counterpart because both nursed divinely fathered sons. Gabriel/Mercury (with Holy Spirit-evoking birds at head and heels) presents the sword of suffering that will pierce her soul (Luke 2:35). The second Eve, she holds an apple redolent of Eden (and Newton gravitation, punning on the fall of man) and the *orbis* of Roman empire, itself soon to fall. This the fall-reversing

3. *Annunciation in a Welsh Hill Setting*, 1963

moment of conception: birds penetrate her circular enclosure as a sperm does an ovum.

*   *   *

Jones wanted to stay in Northwick Lodge despite the 'damned stupidity & inefficiency' now making it 'sometimes *nearly beyond endurance*'. The winter of 1962–3 was too cold for him to make or receive phone calls. There was no hot water in the house. He left his gas fire on all night, its flames three inches high, crouching over it during the day, appalled at how 'ravenously' the 'bloody meter eats up shillings'. He was unable to make a Christmas inscription because his room was too cold, because of the effect of drugs, and because he had hiccups for eight days, during most of which he breathed into a cellophane bag. Two days after Christmas the hiccups stopped, leaving him 'pretty shaken'. On 3 January 1963 'two black crows rested for a while' on the 'white-laden boughs' of the acacia, cawed, then 'winged away', scattering snow. He would have drawn them but his room was too cold.[26]

*   *   *

One afternoon in late May 1963, he was summoned to the phone and heard, 'I'm calling on behalf of Igor Stravinsky.' Jones said, 'You can't mean me – you must have the wrong number.' The voice said, 'Oh no, Stravinsky wants to meet you.' Astonished, he said that he didn't go out much but would come into London to see him. The voice said, 'He wants to visit you at home and see some of your pictures.' After setting a date and time, he hung up, suspecting a prank. But on Saturday afternoon 1 June 1963, Stravinsky arrived in a black limousine with his wife, his secretary (who had telephoned), and Stephen Spender. For a visit to England sponsored by the Arts Council, Stravinsky had requested to meet with four people: Isaiah Berlin, Kenneth Clark, Henry Moore, and chiefly David Jones, whom he regarded as 'a writer of genius'. Initially shy, Jones gradually relaxed and found the Stravinskys 'absolutely sweet, both of them, straight forward, . . . amusing & relaxed'. He apologised for music being outside his sphere but said that plainsong and early polyphony, folk and primitive music had meant much to him for many years. Stravinsky mentioned sharing with Pope John XXIII a love of sixteenth-century music.* Jones seldom played music on his ancient record player, he said, but pulled out 'The Early Renaissance', to

---

* This news of the Pope's sensitivity to the arts increased Jones's admiration for him. On 3 June, when the Pope died, Jones was '*deeply* upset'. He told Clark that history receives such a pope no more than 'once in about 500 years'.

which they listened. Stravinsky proposed that he and Jones write an opera together, Jones supplying the libretto. Without declining, but disliking operas, he sidestepped the proposition by showing his pictures. Stravinsky liked best *Annunciation in a Welsh Hill Setting*, which Jones said seemed complete and might, if worked on further, become too complex, though he wanted to add a bit more colour 'if, at the same time, I can keep it a drawing. Of course, I don't much like anything I do.' Stravinsky said, 'I would like to buy it.' Jones said, 'I don't sell my pictures.' Admiring the inscription over his mantel, *Pwy yw r gwr* (chapter 13, fig. 5), Mme Stravinsky said it would make a wonderful embroidered tapestry, convincing Jones that she appreciated the feeling of it. He explained that it had been commissioned by nuns in Wales who returned it saying, 'No one has any use for Welsh in Wales any more', adding with a fading smile, 'Evidently even fewer people have any use for Latin.' She asked his astrological sign. He closed his eyes and counted on his fingers in an effort to determine whether he was a Capricorn or a Scorpio. He offered to make tea, but seeing how difficult that would be for so many, they made excuses to go. As they drove away, Stravinsky said that it had seemed 'like visiting a holy man in his cell'. And, dropping Spender at his house, he told Natasha, 'I have been in the presence of a holy man.' Jones later told Clark that he 'liked them *tremendously* . . . absolutely "real" & direct & appreciative'.[27]

When John. F. Kennedy was assassinated at the end of November, Jones felt a sense of loss that left him 'without words . . . it seemed the taking away of someone absolutely necessary'. But he realised that such people were scarcely missed when dead: 'Look at all these chaps' listed in *Who's Who* and *The Book of Rome*, 'they all thought they were important and they disappeared without trace and without it mattering at all. In fifty years ninety-nine percent of the world's "important" people will have gone, and it will not have mattered a damn.'[28]

* * *

Having sold Pigotts, in August 1963 the Hagues and Tegetmeiers were preparing to move. At Jones's request, René brought his 1923 carving of St Dominic (fig. 6 below). The Hagues moved to Shanagarry, near Cork in Ireland. René's departure was hard on Jones. René had visited often and had been within telephoning distance. One of Jones's 'chief miseries' was separation from close friends. He also particularly missed Grisewood, fully occupied at the BBC and unable to visit often owing to crippling rheumatoid arthritis.[29]

Jones would do all he could to detain a visiting friend about to leave. Remarkable in his openness to people and readiness, depth, and durability of affection, he was also emotionally dependent. Grisewood said, 'He always wanted more from the people around him than they could give – from Tom, me, René, half-a-dozen perhaps. And when they left or were doing something else, though he understood, it was nothing other than a grief to him and a deprivation.'[30]

*   *   *

Cleverdon and Cowan decided to republish the illustrated *Ancient Mariner*, for which Jones began writing an introduction in June 1963, confining himself to what he 'felt personally about the poem'. Completed in August, it filled fifty-two foolscap pages. Owing to a limited supply of commissioned paper, only the first six pages could be published, which, happily, formed a unit. The new edition appeared in 1965: ninety copies in Britain (at £25 each), 180 for the Chilmark Press in the US (£12.10s.). Jones received a fee of £100 plus £50 for his introduction and subsequently £112.13s.11d. in royalties.[31]

Cowan gave Nest Cleverdon $25 to buy Jones a new radio for his birthday. Jones told her, 'I don't want a bloody *machine*.' She asked him to choose something else. Months later, he rang up to say, 'I'd rather like a gold cup – I've always wondered what it was like to be King Arthur drinking from a gold cup.' Nest said, 'Don't be silly, Dai, $25 won't buy a gold cup.' He was crestfallen. Weeks later he phoned again: 'I used to have a marvellous Jaeger dressing gown and some bloody woman said it wanted washing, took it away, and she said it fell to pieces in the wash.' A Jaeger dressing gown cost £200, but $25 bought enough camel-hair wool cloth for a dressing gown. She made one, which, she said, he 'practically lived in' for the next decade.[32]

*   *   *

Convinced that Jones was a genius and his poetry of permanent value, Louis Bonnerot, the editor of *Étude Anglaise*, while on sabbatical in London in 1964, visited often. Energetic, passionate, and demonstrative, he had an exceptional sense of poetry and deep religious faith – both unusual, Jones knew, for an academic. Apropos of the rape of Ilia in *The Anathemata* (86–7), Bonnerot mentioned Yeats's 'Leda and the Swan', which, to his surprise, Jones had not read. Before one scheduled visit, Jones phoned him at three in the morning asking him to buy and bring Agarol for piles. Another time he phoned after midnight requesting cigarettes and, after Bonnerot went back to sleep, phoned again to say he preferred cork tips. Bonnerot, a scholar of great literary-critical sophistication, would publish one of the first insightful articles on *The Anathemata** and be the first French translator of Jones's poetry.[33]

* * *

When Robert Speaight's biography of Gill appeared in 1966, Jones refused three requests to review it. Replying to Frank Kermode at *Encounter*, he objected in general to '*any* biography', which necessarily fails 'to capture contradictory, or anyway, complex quiddities & haecceities of the chap'. But his chief reason was to avoid hurting Speaight, a serial biographer who worked quickly and lacked intellectual and emotional depth. Jones told a friend, 'I don't like a person' writing 'more than one biography in a lifetime. He cannot have researched the man properly', which requires living into the subject. Jones also disliked Speaight's biography for being too much about ideas, too little 'about chaps'.[34]

* * *

In 1960, Jones had received the Bollingen Prize for Poetry – Auden, Clark, D'Arcy, Dawson, Eliot, Raine, Read, Sitwell, and Spender having sponsored the application. The award was $3,000 (£2,084) a year for three years beginning in January 1961, requiring suspension of his Civil List Pension. The prize made a big difference to his finances. From 1944 to 1956 he had in the bank an average of £105; in 1964 this rose to £2,075.15s.11d. In August 1962, he was informed that the Head Office Inspector of Taxes wanted to tax the grant. This was a blow. No previous recipient had paid tax on it, but each case was decided by a different inspector. He wanted not to appeal lest an adverse judgement affect earlier recipients, especially Kathleen Raine, who had little money, but Clark and Read urged him to do it for the sake of future recipients, and Ethel Watts insisted. Jones was pessimistic, but allowed her to launch an appeal. It came before the Special Commissions of Income Tax at Turnstile House in High Holborn on 6 June 1963. Auden, Read, Clark, and Eliot sent letters in support, Eliot noting that Jones was, in his opinion, 'one of the most interesting artists, and one of the most distinguished writers, of my generation', someone of 'very high literary eminence'. This and the other letters were disallowed because the writers were not present for cross-examination. Raine and Spender were present and cross-examined. The proceedings lasted five hours, the tug-of-war by lawyers striking Jones as so ludicrous that he laughed out loud and was called to order. Taking the stand, he tried to distinguish between

* 'David Jones, down the traversed history-paths', *Agenda*, 5: 1–3 (Summer–Spring 1967), pp. 124–34.

initiating an application and completing a form sent on the initiative of the granting body, a statement ruled 'not germane'. The appeal was turned down, based on the precedent of a judgement on a gift by Lord Bute to a winning jockey. Jones drew £400 from his savings to pay tax. With the encouragement and financial backing of Faber and the Society of Authors, to which he had recently been elected, Ethel Watts planned a new appeal but died in November 1963, and he let the matter drop.[35]

In compensation for this defeat, for his birthday in 1964, Janet Stone gave him £200 – half from Clark, the rest from her and 'a lot of your friends'. Six days later she gave him an additional £35 'to help keep wolves away'.[36]

* * *

In March 1963, Chris Carlile died, and Northwick Lodge was scheduled for demolition. Jones had to find somewhere else to live. After all other residents moved, he enjoyed living there alone – it was 'gloriously peaceful'. The front door permanently locked, he entered and left through the back cellar-door, which was broken open by tramps. Maurice Balme padlocked it and gave him a key. Sarah brought him food, and he regularly joined them for lunch.[37]

His friends looked for digs for him. Ede and Wheen offered rooms, but he would not leave London. Janet found a large, inexpensive room in the maids' quarters of the Cavendish Hotel. He went with her to look, liked it, but couldn't bring himself to take it. He 'very nearly moved' into a two-room flat in Kathleen Raine's house in Chelsea – on 23 April, sending her £100 to reserve it. But 'at the last moment, the arrangement fell through', probably because he disliked the prospect of having her as live-in landlady. She was formidable, dominant, and revered him – he told Grisewood he found her 'suffocating'.[38]*

Dr Bell suggested a residential hotel in lower Harrow called Monksdene, which the proprietor, Peter Heath, had created by joining together several houses (fig. 4). A ground-floor room was coming vacant. Jones hated this part of town and disliked the room being smaller than his present room, its being on the ground floor, its draughty north-facing French doors, and its darkness; but he thought it would do temporarily. Until it became vacant, he had to move into a smaller room on the floor above and put much of his furniture into storage. He was unwilling to discard his stacks of newspapers (mixed with other papers), so Barbara Moray stored 'eight or ten tea chests' of them in her basement, Honeyman storing the rest at his house.[39]

* Jones admired her Blake scholarship, was silent about her poetry except to tell Helen Sutherland that he liked 'very much' some of the poems in *The Pythoness*.

4. Monksdene Residential Hotel

The move took place on Monday, 23 March 1964, Morag helping. Before she left, Jones gave her a book, inscribing it, 'For Morag on the day of the,' asking, 'How do you spell "trek"?' Ten days later, on 2 April, all his possessions were moved again, into the ground-floor room. The double move left him muddled. Before bookshelves could be built in mid-May, he wandered through a maze of stacked packing cases and, for months after, had trouble finding whatever he needed, including books and working drafts.[40]

Jones's room was six inches longer than that on the hill but two feet narrower. He arranged things as they had been there, but where a clear space had been in the middle now was none. The accumulation on his bed increased, now taking an hour to remove at bedtime. When too tired for that, he slept in his armchair. Daylight from the French doors failed to reach the opposite end of the room. He sometimes carried writing to the windows to read and kept the ceiling light on during the day. (The ceiling was fibreboard and sagged.) Partly because of the darkness, he would never paint a picture here and would make only a few, mostly minor inscriptions. Janet would remember it as 'the most dreadful place, very dark'. He referred to it as his 'cave' or 'dugout', and wrote to Charles Burns that he wished he 'could build a barrier of sand-bags half way up' the French doors – he soon blocked them to the doorknobs with books. It was noisy on weekends: at night when people came to the hotel to drink and during the day 'especially if it's sunny' because 'people sit about on deck chairs' in the garden and 'children, & girls in trousers, disport themselves' on a swing. He feared that in July it would be 'like Palm Beach or Capri'. But he liked the view: remnants of an orchard with 'fruit-trees & a reasonably un-tidied-up area of grass & a rather nice weathered fence of palings at the back'. He wanted to draw it 'before they doll it up & before there are too many leaves on the trees', but darkness and weariness owing to drugs precluded that.[41]

The room was equipped with an electric fire, a gas ring, and a washbasin, at which he washed nightly – lifting one foot into the sink, then the other. One night he caught his toe in the drain and stubbed it so badly that he had difficulty walking for days.[42]

Most residents being transient, there was no sense of fellowship, so, instead of eating in the dining room, he took meals (dinner on weekdays and lunch on the weekend) in his room. Breakfast was also provided, but he woke too late for that and fixed his own – a boiled egg, half a grapefruit, and Earl Gray tea, consumed in bed, where he read *The Times* and the post. Then he dressed and made his bed, piling onto it the papers and books relegated to the floor the night before. Later in the day he had his favourite tea, Lapsang Souchong, with Bath Olivers, which he stored in old biscuit tins sealed with Sellotape that he had to rip off to open. Otherwise, he thought, mice got to them.[43]

Vermin* had easy access to his room owing to a corner gap in outside walls where you could see daylight. This also meant that his first winter was frigid – even visitors kept their overcoats on. Yet when the Malans and Waltons invited him for Christmas supper he preferred to sit in his room alone in his greatcoat with a blanket round his shoulders, 'jolly nice, like being in the trenches'. Honeyman had two brick-lined gas heaters installed. Barbara Moray and Joy Finzi (the composer's widow who met Jones through her son, a Harrow student) bought him electric heaters.[44]

The entrance to the building was a reception area with cheap chandeliers, painted wrought iron, and a front desk where Mr Heath greeted you eagerly, hoping you were staying the night. When you asked to see Mr Jones, he escorted you past the dining room and down a narrow corridor on the left with dark-red flock wallpaper, purple carpeting, and fluorescent lights. Many visitors wondered how Jones could live here. Upon first seeing it, Sarah Balme exclaimed, 'But, David, the wall paper!' 'I *know*,' he said, 'it's like a bloody Turkish brothel.' But it was clean and well run and the managers kind – he liked the landlady.[45]

The neighbourhood combined urban heavy traffic with suburban sprawl. The shops he liked were far away. Going to Mass involved crossing a busy intersection and passing along traffic-congested Gayton Road, so he took a taxi. He went out less, walked less, was more reclusive, more reliant on friends to shop for him. Cheques went uncashed, and, although there was a pillar box nearby, bills went unpaid. He no longer accompanied departing women visitors to the Underground station. Going out in summer, he wore his ankle-length greatcoat, 'not because of the cold,' he told Grisewood, 'but I feel naked without it'.[46]

---

* Years later, while moving boxes to clean for him, Jacqueline Honeyman found a dead rat, which Stanley silently disposed of.

Northwick Lodge was demolished and the rubble burned in December 1964. He walked several times to the spot where it had been 'taken out like a tooth'. The acacia, he was glad, remained. He wrote to Valerie, 'I loved that house and old CC.' Ill-kept, disorderly, it seemed, in retrospect, 'creaturely'. He missed his high room. He would consider it the last place he 'could paint or write with ease'.[47]

* * *

Charles Burns, who had last visited two years before, died on 8 June 1964 at the age of 69. Jones could not imagine the world without him.[48]

* * *

On 15 July 1964, he went for lunch in the Old Stables of Kensington Palace with Barbara Moray, Sir Alan Lascelles (the Queen's private secretary) and his wife, and Siegfried Sassoon. Afterwards, Lascelles invited them into the garden, and Jones said, 'If you don't mind, I'd prefer to stay in this room as I loathe sitting in gardens', so they left him and Sassoon to talk. Wearing dentures, Sassoon spoke without opening his mouth much, and Jones, deaf in his left ear, had trouble hearing him. Nevertheless, they spoke about Prudence, whom Sassoon had known through Miriam Rothschild, and about Blunden and Graves and the Welch Fusiliers at Mametz and Limerick. Sassoon said that however much he tried he could not get the Great War out of his system and this was true also for Blunden. Jones said it was true for him, too. Sassoon invited him to stay with him in Wiltshire. Jones thought that he *'couldn't* have been more friendly and agreeable' but was disappointed at not being able to 'make much contact . . . about *poiesis'*.[49]

* * *

On 2 March 1962, David Pryce-Jones and his wife, Clarissa, had introduced him to Peter Levi, a thirty-year-old Jesuit seminarian who subsequently visited on his own. He was learned, enthusiastic about art and archaeology, and seemed to know 'everybody'. Jones thought him 'of extraordinary apperception & intelligence' with 'a most lovable disposition' and also 'a jolly good poet'. (He told Cookson that he liked Levi's poem entitled 'Christmas Sermon'.) In the spring of 1964, Levi asked him to make an inscription for his ordination card. On 7 May, Jones began, working large (22½ by 16¼ inches) since lettering reduced perfectly. 'A brute to get right', it was the last of his great inscriptions (fig. 5). Levi's family wanted to pay him, but he insisted on it being an ordination gift. Ecstatic about it,

Levi had it reproduced in its original size. Shortly after making it, Jones changed his mind about Levi. He was disappointed in him as a person – he would not say why, but this was the impression friends had.[50]

In the spring of 1961, Grisewood had given Jones *The Epic of Gilgamesh*, translated by N. K. Sanders. He found it 'truly astounding' – 'It's got *everything* & is as fresh as the morning . . . although it's awe-inspiring in its barbaric primitivity, yet it shows extraordinary & touching awarenesses of all sorts. A huge feeling of the tragedy of the human condition . . . The translation seems to me *in every way admirable* – perfectly straight modern English, but not losing the *poiesis*.'[51] He added the words 'Epic of Gilgamesh (Mesopotamia)' to the top of his culture chart, made in 1943 (chapter 11, fig.11).

In the summer of 1964 he praised it to Levi, who suggested to

5. *Extensis manibus*, 1964

Audrey Malan that she arrange for Jones to meet the translator, Nancy Sanders. Audrey had the two of them to lunch, during which, not realising who she was, he spoke 'in a rather formal, polite way'. Nancy was an archaeologist, so they talked on that subject. As lunch was ending, he mentioned the 'marvellous' *Epic of Gilgamesh*, and she declared herself its translator. He took her directly to Monksdene, where he relaxed, and they spent the afternoon talking enthusiastically about Mesopotamia and ancient myths.[52]

A private scholar who went on archaeological digs in the Middle East, Nancy was, he thought, 'wonderful' – he felt 'greatly privileged' to know her. She had the best historical mind he had encountered since Dawson and 'that rare combination of great and exact scholarship' with a strong aesthetic sensibility. Also 'a jolly nice sense of humour'. They talked about the Roman Army, the central European homeland of the Celts, the Picts, *The Tain*, articles in the *Journal of Celtic Studies*, and Celtic marvellousness versus the 'repellent ice-cold beastliness that seems already "Nazi"' in Teutonic and Nordic sources. He told her of his love for the work of the great historical illustrator Alan Sorrell. On aesthetic matters they agreed. Both found Wagner 'insufferable'. Jones told her, 'I expect, as you say, it is partly the *heldentenor* and all the stage setup, but, also there is, I think, an essential *vulgarity* however great the genius in Wagner.' Jones loved when she visited, every two or three months.[53]

* * *

He also 'enormously' enjoyed visits by Arthur Giardelli, who was exhibiting relief panels made of debris, so Jones called him 'Arthur Brass-Taps', after the Welsh manner of identifying by profession. Having convinced the Welsh Arts Council to commission Jones to make an inscription commemorating the installation of the Prince of Wales, Giardelli asked him. Jones emphatically said 'No' without explanation. Back in Aberystwyth, Giardelli recounted this to the cultural anthropologist Alwyn Rees, who said, 'Of course he said no – the last prince of Wales died in 1282.'[54]

Early in 1965 Giardelli gave him a large abstract relief composed of rows of small pieces of wood in various shapes (fig. 6). It was wired to hang vertically, but Jones rewired it to hang horizontally. In 1967 he would belatedly give in exchange a study for *Trystan ac Essyllt* (marked 6B, indicating that there were at least seven preliminary sketches). He and Giardelli shared a fascination with the Tristan story in all of its versions and often talked about it.[55]

Through Giardelli and the Welsh Arts Council, Jones lent art to the National Eisteddfod in the summer of 1964. One Saturday at 9 a.m., he was called from bed to the telephone in the hall. It was Vernon Watkins with

6. Jones with St Dominic and Giardelli's abstract relief, by Raymond Moore, c. 1965

news that he had won an Eisteddfod gold medal. He said he couldn't go to receive it and asked that it be posted to him. Watkins tried to persuade him: 'Dai, we meet before dawn beneath the dripping trees and we wait for the sun to rise through the mists as the cool winds blow. Dai, Dai, it's like Paradise!' Jones said, 'It sounds like hell.'[56]

The painter Ceri Richards and his wife, Frances, visited on 18 October 1964. A visit from Ceri was rare, for he was shy and looked upon Jones as a great man. His wife had sought Jones out and introduced them. When Ceri received the CBE in 1960, Jones phoned him, and when he won the Eisteddfod gold medal in August 1961, sent congratulations. He thought him 'an *awfully good & imaginative* artist' but diminished by the influence of Picasso. (He also said, 'my friend Graham Sutherland was a more interesting, less self-conscious artist before he became quite so influenced by Picasso. I think of Milton and of how his huge genius buggered-up English poetry for centuries.') During their visit, Jones showed him the Levi inscription and *Trystan ac Essyllt* and was '*delighted*' that he liked them. They talked about Wales. (The greatest grief of both was not speaking Welsh.) They spoke of Tintoretto, whom both admired – Jones saying, *Susanna and the Elders* had a great 'effect upon me for some many years' – and agreed about Bonnard being 'the top' of the French post-Impressionists. Jones wrote to Ceri about their meeting, 'It's a long time since I've enjoyed anything as much.'[57]

*   *   *

In 1964 Jones was several times visited by Solange Dayras, a Sorbonne professor co-authoring a book to be entitled *Le Catholicisme en Angleterre.* She asked him what Catholicism meant to him. He pulled his hair, she remembered, 'like a little boy' and muttered that it was difficult to say but 'It is just everything to me.' He confided that his poetry after *In Parenthesis* was and would be about the Eucharist as the real presence of Christ. 'I'm continually saying the same thing – I know I do.' He said, 'My faith is simple, non-intellectual.' He told her that he loved the Latin Mass, its poetic language, its theology, its action, and considered it 'the highest achievement of the human spirit'.[58] But its importance to him was now an occasion of suffering.

Liturgical 'reforms' distressed him. They had begun in 1955 with the introduction on Good Friday of Mass with distribution of Communion and the dropping of the *Vexilla Regis.* This sixth-century hymn he thought 'axial' in content, a bridge that had spanned the Dark Ages, now broken. In 1961, the Christmas Preface was removed from the Mass of Corpus Christi, where it had illuminated the conceptual rhyme between the Incarnation and the Eucharist, which is thematically fundamental to *The Anathemata.* And now, in 1965, the Second Vatican Council replaced liturgical Latin with vernacular languages, ending linguistic continuity with Classical times and replacing numinously beautiful plainchant with painfully banal hymns. Worse, the language of the consecration now implied its being merely a memorial – with 'Do this in remembrance of me' rather than what he would have preferred, 'Do this to make me present.'[59]

Apart from its sweeping away many of the 'reference points' of *The Anathemata*, he thought the renewal calamitous, informed by utilitarian principles, diminishing sacramental *poiesis*. He 'wasted hours & hours & days & days writing & destroying letters . . . to *The Tablet*', over a hundred abandoned because he realised 'the futility of yet another layman airing his opinions'.[60] In the spring of 1965 he signed an open letter (and in March 1971, he would sign a petition) to the Pope requesting the preservation of the Tridentine Mass.

The liturgical renewal was the most painful protracted event of Jones's later years, analogous to the linguistic/cultural decline of Wales but worse. What had been for nearly two millennia a continuous and sustaining numinous tradition, his spiritual home as an adult, was being demolished. A visitor in 1966 asked him whether he went to Mass. He replied, 'Oh, yes', adding, 'I used to look forward to going all week but no longer.'[61]

* * *

Jones regularly declined requests for interviews and disliked television. In April 1964, receiving a letter inviting him to take part in a 'Writer's World' TV programme, he would have declined but was won over by Anthony Powell's son Tristram. A fledgling producer, soft-spoken and gentle, Powell explained that the show would involve Jones giving a talk. Instead, Jones wanted to be interviewed by Saunders Lewis.[62]

On an early spring morning in 1965 in his room, Jones and Lewis were filmed conversing for two hours. Forgetting 'completely' the presence of technicians and equipment, though lowering his head in the glare of the lights, Jones spoke naturally. The two-hour conversation was cut to twenty minutes. He watched it with the Balmes on 15 March 1965, on the edge of his seat, moving his lips to what his televised image was saying and wringing his hands with delight. He was glad 'that the salient argument' about the arts being essentially sacramental 'came across very well'.[63]

The interview has survived. In it Jones is marvellous: humble, natural, charmingly tentative, sincere. Mary Crozier writing in the *Guardian* praised it, 'intensely interesting and really moving', a 'model of how television . . . can on occasion give us an unspoilt view of a great man . . . everything comes straight from him and everything is original and all of a piece'. In the *Listener*, Anthony Burgess lamented the general failure to recognise Jones's greatness despite 'the brilliance' of his long poems and said that the interview conveyed the impression 'of ... great coherence, towering intellectual dignity'. Kenneth Adam, the Director of Television, wrote to Powell that it was one of the most remarkably authentic pieces of television he had seen. Near the end of his career, Powell considered it the most successful programme he had produced.[64]

* * *

Cookson had asked for something to publish in *Agenda*, so in 1961 Jones had set to work on a five-page poem entitled 'The Hunt' (*SL* 65–9), concerning Arthur and his men chasing the land-wasting Great Boar (*Twrch Trwyth*) in the tale 'Culhwch and Olwen'. It originated in a series of questions written around 1950. In the four years he worked on the poem, its muse was Valerie, who was raised near the River Twrch, which has legendary associations with the hunt. She told him the Welsh names of neighbouring farms resonating with the story and together they traced the track taken by the boar on an Ordnance Survey map. In 1965 he gave the poem to Cookson, modestly asking whether it was all right.[65] Lyrically musical and highly visual, it is one of the great modern English lyric poems. Among Jones's most immediately appealing works, it is the first poem that anyone should read by him but, unanthologised, it is virtually unknown. His wish that Valerie like it accounts in large part for it being so accessible.

On 24 August 1965 he recorded it for the British Council along with selections from *In Parenthesis* and *The Anathemata* for release on vinyl disk (Argo PLP 1093), making an inscription to be used on its jacket. The record validated, he thought, his having written for the ear.* His recording of 'The Hunt' is one of the best of a poem by its author. He recorded it again in October 1965 for BBC Wales. After its broadcast, Lewis phoned to say, 'it was the best thing' he had 'ever read on the radio' and later wrote, 'I very seriously thought your poem and your delivery of it magnificent. It was big stuff – worthy of the Palestrina that followed it ... the impact was tremendous, major poetry ... There was grandeur in your performance.' Jones was delighted to learn from Valerie that she heard and liked it.[66]

* * *

On 4 January 1965, he turned on the radio for the late news summary and heard a familiar voice concluding a tribute to someone. Then the announcer said, 'That was Mr Auden speaking of Mr Eliot who died today.' Jones was

---

* He now considered buying a tape recorder to help him hear how his writing sounded; he acquired brochures, liked the look of one model, but could not imagine how it worked, so gave up the idea.

shaken. He had recently received the Eliots' Christmas card and had been about to reply. Half of the next day he spent drafting a letter of condolence to Valerie Eliot. Two days later, he wrote to Hague, 'It was an awful blow to me.' To Grisewood he said, 'It is the end of an era.'[67] In the weeks and months to come, he increasingly felt the loss.

* * *

On 27 March 1965, Heath began constructing an addition to Monksdene and turning rooms adjacent to Jones's into a lounge. The construction was noisy, and in May, amid a clutter of packing cases, he was forced into the dark half of his room 'with only a curtain & a bit of cardboard for one wall' and the ceiling light on the other side. It was 'dark as the inside of a cow'. When the noise became unendurable, he moved into the former lounge. In all this discord, he was writing a reminiscence of the 1930s for *London Magazine*, wanting to because Ben Nicholson and Victor Pasmore were also contributing reminiscences.[68]

On 9 June, Jones returned to his room – now sealed against the outdoors and widened at the outer wall by an alcove. The *Trystan* and *Annunciation* paintings looked 'rather nice' on the walls, newly painted light grey. 'One can somehow *see* them as they were *meant* to be', no longer propped against the bed or on a chair but 'flat ... & also isolated – hence concentrated' so that you can 'see them whole'. New nylon curtains admitted light but no air, so the room was stuffy. On clear days he watched the sun play on the apple tree and the pear tree just outside his window.[69]

During his displacement, he had begun finishing an eighteen-page poem (a process that would take six months) called 'The Fatigue' (*SL* 24–42), a crucifixion-centred triptych beginning with two legionary friends (good thieves) and ending with Sejanus and Tiberius (bad thieves). He sent Cleverdon the only copy, a manuscript largely in pencil. Cleverdon typed it for him, and Jones recorded it. He was glad it was broadcast on 'the right day', Good Friday, 1965, and that it was followed by Palestrina's setting of the *Stabat Mater* and *Vexilla Regis*. Giardelli delighted him by saying that his Irish maid 'liked the lilt of it'.[70]

In 1965 in advance of Jones's seventieth birthday, Kathleen Raine called a meeting of some of his friends to consider using the occasion for his benefit. They agreed to Cleverdon's proposal to publish a limited edition of one of his poems for subscribers. Jones chose 'The Fatigue'. Cleverdon compiled a list of subscribers to pay £3.5s. each, the profit (after expenses) to go to Jones. The prospectus went out under the patronage of Auden, Clark, Stravinsky, and the Queen Mother. Faber, Auden, and Cowan each contributed £50. The subscription amounted to £1,100 for an edition of 225 numbered copies, 50 for Jones. A new friend, Peter Orr, helped him correct galleys. Jones thought the poem beautifully printed, by Sebastian Carter, especially liking the addition of a concluding star *. It went out to subscribers in December 1965.[71]

Earlier, on Jones's birthday, the Cleverdons had a small party at their new house at 27 Barnsbury Square at which he was given a cheque for £800. He was fascinated by the house being on the site of the Roman general Suetonius's camp the night before descending on Boudicca's forces in AD 50. He shared this fascination with John Betjeman, whom he subsequently met here on several occasions. (According to Nest Cleverdon, they 'loved each another'.)[72]

Jones now had half the mid-length poems he needed for a book. He had hoped by now to have more 'but . . . I've had so many things interfering with settling down & also a blank & confused mind & a sense of futility'. Evidence of the effect of drugs is his composing in November thirteen drafts of a letter thanking Bernard Bergonzi for publishing a chapter on *In Parenthesis* in *Heroes' Twilight* (1965). He also tired himself out answering nearly every letter he received, always writing more fully than the correspondent had.[73]

* * *

Jones had first met Peter Orr on 15 October 1964. Orr was Herbert Read's nephew, a devout Anglican, energetic, rambunctious, mentally aggressive, well-spoken and precise, a marvellous conversationalist, and quick to argue. He had recorded Jones's readings for the British Council. Now visiting weekly, he became Jones's factotum as well as friend, bringing him supplies, passing on his copy of the *TLS*, and driving him to the dentist. Their first such trip was on 17 May 1966 when, having a tooth drilled, Jones refused anaesthetic because, he explained to Orr, 'We didn't [use it] in the First War, you see, and then it doesn't hurt afterwards.'[74] He was, Orr noticed, interested in the various instruments and chemical preparations, discussing them with the dentist as one craftsman to another.

One evening Jones asked Orr whether he had 'any of those . . . ?' Orr began trying to supply the word: 'tissues? matches?' Jones: 'No, no.' Further guesses failing, Jones muttered sheepishly, 'You know, those pound-note things.' He needed £5 cash but was embarrassed to mention money. Orr gave it to him, and Jones began writing a cheque for the amount but paused. It seemed ungracious to write 'five pounds *only*'. He was unable to proceed until Orr suggested '*exactly*'.[75]

* * *

In late 1965 'the lineup' for the Monksdene telephone was so 'awful' that Jones was not even phoning Valerie. So in early December, he had a

7. Douglas Cleverdon, Harman Grisewood, Alun Oldfield Davies, Saunders Lewis, Jones, Aneirin Talfan Davies (left to right), 1 March 1966

telephone installed in his room. In one of his first calls, he delivered to Grisewood an hour-long disquisition on fifth-century Welsh missionary monks. He then wrote a sixteen-page foolscap 'confirmation' of what he had said. Grisewood was more interested than usual because he was delivering the annual St David's Day radio lecture in 1966, on 'David Jones: Writer and Artist'. Oldfield Davies invited Jones to Broadcasting House to hear the talk and have dinner afterwards with other guests.[76] A photograph was taken (fig. 7).

For Helen Sutherland's eightieth birthday, in 1961, Jones had spent two weeks working on a large inscription, as a present partly from him, partly from mutual friends who paid for it. He had also allowed Nicolete to buy a flower painting to give to her. Now Helen was in a nursing home in Stoke Poges, fifteen miles south-west of Harrow. She asked him to visit, but he said he was unwell. Audrey Malan, on her way to see her, asked him to come along. He declined. In April, Nicolete told him that Helen, now in hospital with stomach cancer, wished him to visit or at least write. He may have written or phoned but did not go. She died on 29 April 1966 without seeing him again – his refusal owing, of course, to agoraphobia. In Edward Hodgkin's opinion, Jones was 'the person who owed most to her, and who, taking all things into consideration, gave most to her'.[77]

She bequeathed to him her father's ship's chronometer, which became a prominent addition to his room, and £6,000. But he was 'hurt and disappointed' that she hadn't left him his pictures, which all went to Nicolete, who refused to lend him any. From now on he would say of his pictures, 'Of course, you know, Nicky's got the best.'[78]

He hoped now to live off the interest from Helen's bequest plus his Civil List Pension in addition to fees and royalties: £725 annually. He could now pay the £546 for room and board plus the cost of utilities and telephone, but only just. As late as 1969, he seriously contemplated supporting himself by running a boarding house as Chris Carlile had done.[79]

* * *

In 1965 Jones and Sarah Balme looked together at reproductions of paintings by Bonnard, who was, he said, 'a bloody magician. You can't see *where*, by, or *how* the "poetry" is there but my God it's *there*.' He disliked the landscapes 'with blue green "decorative" ships & trees' but loved 'the ones of tables laid for a meal' and 'the *stupendous* one of the refracted figure of a girl in . . . bath' at the Tate. He mentioned the 355 Bonnards coming to Burlington House in early January. Sarah offered to take him. He delayed till the exhibition was drawing to a close, then she fetched him by car. It was a summery March day, but he wore his hat, his greatcoat extending to his ankles, and a long muffler round his neck. She left him in the foyer of the Royal Academy and went to park the car. 'No. No, don't leave me,' he appealed. When she returned, he was in the midst of a panic attack, reached out, and physically clung to her. An attendant asked her, 'Do you know anything about this tramp? He won't part with his coat.' The coat over his arm, he began viewing the pictures. His anxiety vanished and he was transported.* But if she moved away, he called out, 'Sarah, Sarah, where are you?' Acquaintances approached him, renewing his anxiety because he disliked making introductions. Afterwards, the car hiccupped up Piccadilly. He asked, 'What's the matter?' At each traffic signal it stalled, then commenced a series of jerks. He clutched the dashboard and door handle. '*What's the matter?*' Finally it juddered to a halt. He was frantic. A lorry driver stopped and fixed the motor sufficiently to allow Sarah to drive to a garage where it was repaired. Jones was late for an appointment with Dr Bell and told her, 'I'll never go out again.'[80]

But he did, to his sister's fiftieth wedding anniversary party on 14 April 1967 at her home in Honor Oak Park. He had visited her, usually briefly, about twice a year ('just to say hello', his sister said), always on her birthday (never Christmas), always coming the entire way by taxi, which he kept waiting with the meter running in case, he said, he couldn't get another. He had visited in 1961 for her seventieth birthday and stayed hours, all the while keeping a taxi waiting. Having no inkling of his agoraphobia, his relatives thought this extravagantly eccentric. At the wedding anniversary, he stayed an hour. His grandniece, Sarah Hyne, remembered him there, 'very impressive in hat and long black coat, like a bird of paradise in a colony of sparrows'.[81]

* His favourites, marked in his copy of the catalogue, were *L'Effet de Neige près de Chambéry, Fenêtre ouverte à Uriage, Siesta*, and *The Road to Nantes*.

One Saturday afternoon, he took a taxi to his parish church to go to confession, a sacrament of which he now seldom availed himself. He began according to formula, 'Bless me Father for I have sinned. It has been two and a half years since my last confession' and mentioned missing Sunday Mass, then considered a mortal sin. The young priest admonished, 'What would have happened if you had slipped and hit your head and died? You might have gone straight to hell!' Jones replied, 'Look, Father, the immortal soul is not like a watch that you drop down the lavatory and it's gone forever. It doesn't happen accidentally.' The priest continued to remonstrate, and Jones said, 'While no one relishes a long theological discussion more than I, if it is all the same to you, I would prefer to postpone it since I have a taxi ticking away outside.'[82] Absolution was given with the meter running.

* * *

In the autumn of 1966, while walking barefoot in his room, he bashed his left big toe 'against some hard object'. The accident made him furious. The intensity of his fury astonished him. Astonishment gave way to admiration of the marvellous black and blue colour of the bruised toe.[83]

* * *

Cookson had decided in the autumn of 1966 to combine three issues of *Agenda* into a special issue on Jones, to contain all the mid-length poems so far completed, except 'The Tribune's Visitation', intended for separate publication. In November, Jones began writing a poem entitled 'The Sleeping Lord' for inclusion if he could finish it in time. He worked on it for five months, 'to the neglect of all else' including correspondence, sometimes till four in the morning. At twenty-seven pages, this may be the foremost ecological poem of the century. Informing it is the despoliation of South Wales and novels he had read about it.* It also derives felt intensity from the view from his window. In the late winter of 1966, soon after the green shoots on the trees in the garden began delighting him, workers with bulldozers arrived and, to his horror, turned it into a macadamised car park. The 'ghastly' change was symbolic for him of 'the whole of this island ... becoming virtually a car-park'. The loss of this rural remnant underlies the grief that pervades 'The Sleeping Lord' (*SL* 70–96) – twice he was forced to suspend work on the poem by noise made by the garden

* Among these were Richard Llewellyn's 'amazing' *How Green Was My Valley*, which Jones reviewed anonymously for the *TLS* (7/10/39), and Alexander Cordell's 'terrifying' *Rape of the Fair Country* (1961).

8. Jones in his room (with view) at Monksdene, c. 1967

destroyers.[84] The subsequent view of parked cars (fig. 8) forced him to retreat into the dark end of the room.

His writing 'The Fatigue' and 'The Sleeping Lord' suggests that he was, at intervals, secretly not taking his pills. To prevent this, Dr Bell was giving only the prescribed number for two weeks so that he would know when Jones ran out. But Jones outsmarted him by depositing the pills daily into a large paper bag, which eventually filled up with thousands of tablets and capsules, discovered after his death.[85] One way or another, these poems invite wonder as to what he might have achieved during this largely lost decade were he not – for the most part – drugged.

Cookson and he met to decide on artwork to reproduce in the special issue and on contributors to ask for essays. Jones 'insisted' on the inclusion of 'A Note' by Aneirin Talfan Davies on his poetry and *Finnegans Wake* being 'similar in . . . synthesizing quality' – 'just', Jones said, 'what I wanted someone to say'. The special issue, in June 1967, turned out '*far* better' than he 'dared to hope'. Of contributions by others, he thought the best were by Nancy Sanders and (best of all) Stuart Piggott, 'a relief from all this blasted "art" & "literary" criticism'. The special issue brought him new prominence. On 27 October 1967, he received a fan letter from the American poet W. S. Merwin, who had twice reread *In Parenthesis* and, having just read *The Anathemata*, considered him 'one of the greatest twentieth century poets in English'. Anthony Powell sent a letter praising the special issue and recalling their meeting in 1937, saying that he had since developed an interest in his own Welsh background.[86]

*   *   *

On 4 June 1968, two men at Jones's door presented him with a letter bearing the arms of the City of London. 'Good God,' he said, 'am I for the Tower or what?' He opened the envelope and read that he was to receive the first City of London Midsummer Prize, valued at £1,500, for a Londoner practising one or more of the arts who has made 'an outstanding contribution to Britain's culture'. Unable to go to the Mansion House banquet for the ceremony – he explained, because of his 'nervous breakdown' – he received the prize in absentia on 22 June.[87]

*   *   *

'The Tribune's Visitation' was published as a small book by Fulcrum Press in 1968. In 1969 Orr came to record Jones reading it for the British Council, Harvard College, and Argo Records. He had Jones improvise a short introduction and record without rehearsal. When Jones later played the record, he was astonished at how good the reading sounded.[88]

In 1969, playing it for visitors, he would place his gramophone on a chair seat and kneel or sit on the floor, applying with his finger just the right pressure on the head to keep the disk turning at the proper speed. Later, he managed this by taping a two-shilling bit to the top of the head. Cookson took the machine to be repaired and was told it was unfixable. In July 1971, at Jones's request, Orr's secretary, Cathie Hunt, found him a new one, simple to operate and, at £12, he thought 'pleasantly inexpensive'. The new machine revealed how badly scratched his 'Tribune' disk was, so she brought him a replacement, which made 'all the difference in the world'. Listening to it, he came to regard the poem as 'probably the best of all the separate' (mid-length) 'pieces'. 'Almost every word tells . . . It's the "whole works" in brief space.' He liked it so much 'partly because it states quite simply the situation of to-day'.[89] Now it was the recording he most often played for visitors.

*   *   *

Only a few poets had visited: Ned O'Gorman from New York; Elizabeth Jennings, who considered Jones 'the supreme example of the Christian artist'; and John Heath-Stubbs, the nearly blind poet, who was the first to call In Parenthesis Jones's Iliad and The Anathemata his Odyssey. He visited three times (in 1959, 19 October 1963, and June 1965), saying to Noel

White after his second visit that he felt as though he had been in the presence of William Blake. Owing largely to US publication and the *Agenda* special issue, other poets now came. One was Louis Zukofsky, who had read *The Anathemata* with great interest and admiration, as the markings in his copy indicate. On 29 May 1969, Cookson brought him and his wife, Celia. It was a good visit. Jones had not read his work, but they liked each other. Jones was rereading Theodora Kroeber's *Ishi in Two Worlds* (1961), a moving account of the last of a tribe of California Indians. He described and praised it, and they talked at length about the mistreatment of Native Americans. Jones recounted that, when asked whether he believed in God, Ishi replied, 'Sure, Mike.' While shaking hands in parting, he and Zukofsky simultaneously said, 'Sure, Mike.' Basil Bunting visited probably in the spring of 1969. He thought Jones one of the best poets of the century and, while finding Catholicism repugnant, was impressed at how, in *The Anathemata,* he 'made the Mass a complex of symbols capable of ordering and interpreting pretty well the whole history of the world and the whole order of nature'. In 1968 Allen Ginsberg asked to visit, but, feeling unwell, Jones declined.[90]

In 1969 the Irish poet John Montague and his wife visited, and Jones reminisced about his time in Ireland. He spoke of disliking Graves's *Goodbye to All That* as 'too clever' and too much 'about himself' and expressed reservations about *The White Goddess,* many of its assertions being, Jones knew, silly.[91] About the White Goddess herself, he said, 'Imagine meeting her on a dark night or praying to her when you're cast down. She'd gobble you up, bones and everything.' He said that Graves forgets the suffering of wives and mothers, their never-ending tasks, the pain of childbirth. 'I see her as softer, more maternal, vulnerable, mother of Rome, mother of God, mother of us all.' He asked, 'You know that lovely old ballad, "In green wood she lies slain?"' – and, sitting erect, he sang it. He then moved on to the Celtic view of love and showed them *Trystan ac Essyllt.*

Montague visited yearly. In 1971, he mentioned to Geoffrey Hill that he was on his way to see Jones, and Hill told him that he admired David Jones above all other poets, that he owed a lot to his example, and that 'of course, he's the main influence on *Mercian Hymns*'. On one visit Montague came with Gareth Brown, who tried in vain to sign Jones to a recording contract – Brown wearing lace ruffs at his wrists, which, Montague could see, intrigued Jones. They brought with them Paddy Moloney of 'The Chieftains', who played the tin whistle, beginning with slow airs and moving into a jig – Jones enjoyed that. On one visit, Montague and Jones generated a fantasy airplane flight, Jones describing and giving legendary associations to places beneath them in Wales, Montague taking over once they crossed the Irish Sea. They agreed that Ireland could be included in the term 'the British Isles' because the British were not the English but the early Celtic *Pritani* – so that the term had pre-imperialistic validity. Together they regretted English ignorance of what 'British' really means. As for England, Jones said, 'there was an England once, but you can no longer see it. There are few of the wild places left, on the edge of an arterial road.'[92]

In 1971 Cookson brought the poet Anne Beresford, who subsequently visited, and Jones loved seeing her. It was the era of Laura Ashley romanticism, which he liked – the maxi was in – and, always noticing what she wore, he said his mother had had a coat like hers. He played his recordings for her, and she noticed his own pleasure listening as 'almost childlike'. On one visit he took out the dressing gown Nest had made him, showing where a button was missing and a seam had opened. She offered to mend it, and he explained gratefully, 'I can't thread needles easily anymore.' She remembered him laughing in amazement at what his pictures now sold for.[93]

Other young visitors included: beginning in 1963, Philip (Rod) Lowery, a silversmith and former protégé of Hague; beginning in 1966, Pat and Tony Stoneburner, he a Methodist minister and initially a graduate student at Michigan, 'an extraordinary chap . . . of much perception', who intended to write a critical biography of Jones; also in 1966, David Blamires, a lecturer at Manchester, 'a jolly nice chap' who wrote, Jones thought, 'the best & most concise critique' of *The Anathemata* and an 'introductory' book on his work;* in 1968, Paul Hills, a Cambridge and then Courtauld student, 'awfully aware & sensitive', who published a long 'extremely good' essay on Jones's visual art;† in 1969, Colin Hughes, who was writing a history of the 38th Welsh Division during the Great War – a visit from him was 'a great treat' – Jones gave him his Argo record inscription; in 1970, Thomas Whitaker, an English professor at Iowa; in 1971–72, I accompanied Blissett, whose student I had been; and, in 1972, Jeremy Hooker, whose critical writing Jones admired, considering him 'someone to watch'.[94]

In autumn 1972, a special issue of *Poetry Wales* was devoted to Jones, in which he thought Giardelli's essay 'awfully well done' and Lewis's essay on the inscriptions 'the best in the collection'. He also particularly liked Hooker's essay, 'The Poetry of David Jones'.[95]

Among current political figures, Jones admired Dag Hammarskjöld for combining great diplomatic skill with scholarship and artistic understanding 'at least of contemporary literature'. He admired Enoch Powell as a classicist, historian, and poet, thinking him 'the most intelligent man in public life'. He agreed with Powell's wish to limit immigration from Asia and Africa to a

---

* D. Blamires, 'The Ordered World', *Review of English Literature*, 7: 2 (April 1966), pp. 75–86, revised for *Agenda*, 5:1–3 (Spring–Summer 1967), pp. 101–11; D. Blamires, *David Jones, Artist and Writer* (1971). In response to this book, Stoneburner stopped working on his biography. Jones thought this unfortunate, since Stoneburner's expression and thinking were 'so different' and he understood Jones's work 'from the inside'.

† 'The Romantic Tradition in David Jones,' *Malahat Review*, 27 (1973), pp. 39–80.

number that could be assimilated, preserving British cultural identity. Like Powell, he thought most Conservative Party politicians lacked the courage to be thoroughly to the right, and, like him, Jones disliked the European Economic Community – 'by instinct I distrust it' as being 'about nothing but money'. He also greatly admired Bernadette Devlin, the twenty-two-year-old MP for Northern Ireland who had been imprisoned for inciting a riot. In 1970 he kept her photograph on his table.[96]

* * *

From mid-March 1970, he felt slightly 'off colour'. Visiting on 19 March, Morag noticed that one side of his mouth was sagging. Dr Bell was consulted and told him that he had had a slight stroke. He began feeling better, but two days later, on Palm Sunday morning, when nearly finished piling onto his bed its mound of books and papers, he tripped on a rip in the carpet and crashed to the floor. The pain was excruciating. He could not move his left leg. Determined to escape 'the appalling draught' from under the door, he hoisted himself to the edge of the bed, where he sat, the pain precipitating double vision (which would last several days). A cleaning woman discovered him, and he was taken by ambulance to Harrow Hospital. While being carried to a public ward on a balcony, he was jostled, experiencing explosive pain. 'CHRIST ALMIGHTY,' he shouted. The matron scolded, 'None of that language here.' Jones replied, 'I'll bloody well remember that in future.' X-rays showed he had broken off the ball of his femur – the doctor was astonished that he had not lost consciousness. On 23 March he was operated on, the broken ball replaced with a metal insert, his pain now especially bad when urinating and defecating – 'I know what suffering is,' he said, and he also knew that he was 'a coward, a bloody awful coward'. It was Passion Week, and he had, he thought, new appreciation of the suffering of Jesus, although his own was less, and of Odin, 'nine nights on the windy tree'.[97]

The ward was 'hell' because its television, ten feet from Jones's bed, was on at high volume from noon to midnight – 'distracting. You can never think.' Honeyman telephoned Bell, who had him moved to a private room – one he could not afford. So Honeyman undertook to establish a fund and solicited contributions for his hospital and medical fees.[98]

Jones was impressed by the generosity and patience of the Irish and Jamaican nurses, whose duties were, he thought, inexorable. He told Honeyman he had always admired 'rather grand' women, but these working-class nurses, white and black, were the most impressive women he had ever known.[99]

The painkillers kept him 'weary, dull witted & half-asleep' during the day, 'but, damn & blast it, awake like anything during the night'.

He practised walking down the corridor using a steel frame – 'damned exhausting'. Visiting while this was taking place, Edward Hodgkin heard the matron say, 'Come on, Mr Jones, you mustn't give in. Use your *will*', and Jones answer, 'For God's sake don't talk about will to me.' What he most disliked was 'this water-works, bed-pan stuff. It's far, far more ignominious, embarrassing etc. than I had remembered.' In the hospital he began meditating on 'all the trials, pains, and miseries of the human race' and concluded that the more mundane required the most courage: 'that's why one has always thought of women as more "brave" than men'.[100]

After eight days in hospital, he went to Bethany Nursing Home in Highgate, run by Augustinian nuns. Kenneth Clark suggested it, and Valerie and her husband got him a room there. He liked it, partly for the 'marvellous view ... across a garden & tall trees' to London. He also liked having a telephone on his bedside table and phoning friends.[101]

Clark, who was absorbing much of the cost of Jones's stay, telephoned in the first week of April to say he was coming to visit. The nuns insisted that Jones change into fresh pyjamas (he did) and shave (he refused: 'If you think I'm shaving for Kenneth Clark, I am not!'). Visiting again on 13 April, Clark found him 'extremely talkative and ... enjoying a stream of visitors (three others beside myself)'. Visiting three days later, Clark and Janet Stone found the room full of visitors and Jones 'in amazing lively form – even shuffling around walking with a prop'.[102]

Bethany Nursing Home was unaffordable. Barbara Moray proposed as an alternative Calvary Nursing Home on Sudbury Hill, run by the Little Company of Mary, 'the Blue Nuns'. On 6 June he moved there, a sprawling Victorian red-brick house surrounded by large grounds. The initial cost was £27 per week, with extra for physiotherapy. He moved into Room 1 (right at the main entrance, down a spotless, polished, red-tiled corridor, past the public telephone and left down a second corridor). The room was fifteen feet long, ten feet wide, with a large north-facing window overlooking the grounds. Thinking the polished floors dangerous, he suggested to a young nun that they put down sawdust as in pubs, adding, 'but then I suppose you have never been in a pub'.[103]

He was awakened for breakfast at 5.30 – it was like being called to stand-to. Visiting hours ended at 7 p.m., so weekday visitors could not stay long. Jones confided to Hodgkin, 'It's not just one thing; it's everything.' Especially bad was the distance from the telephone. To take or make a call he had to hobble forty yards. Long phone calls were a thing of the past. Initially hating the place, calling it 'Sodbury' Hill, he eventually ceased complaining and appreciated the nuns as 'awfully kind & considerate'. And they liked him. One remembered him as 'gracious to everyone, unassuming, simple, self-effacing, one of the nicest patients'.[104]

He initially disliked (and discarded some of) the food but eventually ate whatever 'rations' they brought – 'strange sorts of food that he'd never eaten before'. Daphne Pollen arranged for grapefruit to be delivered, but he issued a frantic plea to stop because he did not want to hurt the nuns' feelings.[105]

Not having his books was 'a constant curse' partly because he needed them 'to lick into shape' his new volume of poetry. He also missed his paintings, but when Honeyman offered to fetch one, he declined, since that would imply permanent residence. For the same reason he refused Clark's offered loan of *Petra im Rosenhag*. Many proposed that he have a private telephone installed, some offering to pay for it. He refused for the same reason.[106]

Jones retained his room at Monksdene. If he was late receiving the bill for its rent, he fantasised about its contents being emptied onto the curb and sent Orr to ask if there was a problem. He fixated on airing the bed, now so long covered with papers and books. And he wanted to retrieve his old black greatcoat and tweed hat. He had Jacqueline Honeyman fetch *The Lee Shore* and give it to Valerie, whom he lent the key to take other things she liked that he wanted her to have, including a small pencil drawing of a lion and an inscription.[107]

He wanted to leave his money to his sister, the Welsh Language Society, the Welsh school in Paddington, and possibly the Welsh League of Youth, and the Cymmrodorion Society. His books and papers were to go to the National Library of Wales, his pictures to the National Museum of Wales. It was important to him that the pictures stay together; otherwise inferior work, which should be available only to students of his development, would be exhibited and sold and hurt his reputation.[108]

Cleverdon estimated the pictures and manuscripts to be worth between £30,000 and £40,000. Honeyman urged selling his pictures to the National Museum now with the proviso that he keep them till his death, and Jones agreed, but the Museum offered only £2,000–£3,000 for all existing and future pictures, manuscripts, and books, exclusive of individual bequests to be stipulated immediately. Honeyman (rightly) advised against this. Then Hugh Fraser convinced Jones to retain ownership of the pictures as a hedge against inflation.[109]

Saunders Lewis was advising Jones, all the while negotiating behind his back. In December 1970, he convinced David Jenkins of the National Library to buy the manuscripts, papers, and books for £5,000, a fraction of their value. Jones declined but only because he was 'ashamed' of the *In Parenthesis* manuscript being 'full of spelling mistakes'. On 10 March 1972, the Library offered money now for his papers and books after his death. Lewis urged him to accept, but Jones said that deciding 'is a thing I've *never* been able to do' except in making a painting or poem. In September, Lewis again urged him to accept, but that would mean strangers coming to sort out his stuff. The Museum was now willing to offer £20,000 for posthumous possession of his paintings, an offer that Lewis urged its director to halve.[110] Unaware of Lewis's petty treachery, Jones continued to procrastinate.

In June 1971, Honeyman urged him to have the pictures and manuscripts removed to a bank vault. He resisted until Honeyman mentioned the danger of fire, which was real to Jones. There are in his drawings, manuscripts, and letters hundreds of cigarette burns, the degree of charring in some indicating small fires extinguished. On Honeyman's next visit, Jones handed him the key, saying, 'If you'd like to go in – nobody else – and take all the pictures to the bank, I'd be pleased.' Honeyman rented a vault in the main branch of Coutts Bank, in Lombard Street. Jacqueline, her friend Charlotte Gere, Cookson, and Nancy Sanders wrapped the pictures and portfolios for shipment, most of the manuscripts going in tea chests to the Honeymans' basement. The move was finished by the summer of 1972, and a document drawn up listing four framed inscriptions, twenty-one framed watercolours, eight portfolios containing 123 watercolours, twenty-three inscriptions, and hundreds of drawings. Some of these drawings Jones wanted burned but could not, from the list, tell precisely which.[111] The management at Monksdene wanted his room and provided him with another, in an annex, and his friends moved his books, furniture, and newspapers there.

* * *

Bill Stevenson had visited Jones in the hospital and Bethany Nursing Home, saying he would come again but didn't – Jones assumed he was too busy. Then Dr Bell informed him that Stevenson, who was fifty-eight, died on 7 May 1971. Jones was distraught. Stevenson had been a close friend and mainstay, making possible, as he wrote, 'the major part of *The Anathemata*', the new writing in *Epoch and Artist*, 'the large inscriptions & the water-colours' of flowers in glass chalices, and the mid-length poems accumulating towards a third book of poetry. Now, whenever he felt depressed or anxious, he would say, 'I wish to God he hadn't died.'[112]

* * *

In collusion with Grisewood, Honeyman was soliciting funds to provide an annuity in which capital gains would be largely tax-free. An appeal for donations went out. Cheques came in, including $1,000 from Jack Sweeney, requesting anonymity. Some refused to contribute on the grounds that Jones could sell paintings if he needed money. Separately Honeyman, Grisewood, and Barbara Moray urged him to do this, but he explained that they were a hedge against inflation.[113]

Through a friend of Elizabeth Taylor, Honeyman contacted Richard Burton, who had acted in the second radio production of *In Parenthesis* and considered it the finest thing he had ever performed in.* Four days later, on 19 October 1971, Honeyman received a cheque for £1,000. Jones was grateful, but, not having met Burton, declined to write thanking them – Honeyman did it, giving as an excuse Jones's poor health.[114]

A total of £1,500 was added to Jones's life savings of £7,000, and, with this, Honeyman purchased an annuity, to be paid in quarterly instalments of £417.25, beginning in February 1972. This plus Jones's old age pension of £250 and his Civil List pension exceeded the nursing-home cost, which had risen to £35 a week. Honeyman and Grisewood also established a backup fund of £250, in case Jones needed an operation.[115]

* * *

Jones's work was selected for the 1972 Word and Image Exhibition, beginning in London and touring Wales. Now in retirement, Cleverdon agreed to organise it. Jones allowed him to go to the vault with Jacqueline Honeyman to select pictures. He wrote the catalogue, Jones correcting and expanding entries. When it was published, Jones disliked the 'horrible' egg-yolk cover, the photographs done without removing glass from pictures, and the plethora of inaccuracies, which he laboriously corrected in several copies. Consisting of 170 works, the exhibition was opened on 7 February by Kenneth Clark. Jones was too unwell to go. The *TLS* reviewer wrote that his 'polymorphous talent is one of the great original forces in art and letters of our time', and Guy Manners in the *Investors Chronicle* praised him as 'the greatest British poet of the century and one of the finest watercolourists'.[116]

Cleverdon had proposed publishing Jones's complete introduction to the *Ancient Mariner* to coincide with the exhibition. Jones had agreed but wanted to complete an appendix about classical influence on early Welsh literature, which, despite a year's work and a thousand draft pages, he was finding elusive. Only when the essay was in press did he finally abandon the appendix as 'a foolish and temerarious thing to attempt'. Signing copy after copy of the *Introduction to the Rime of the Ancient Mariner* in the spring of 1972, he felt unreal and empty, so he began inscribing each book differently, but that merely increased his feeling of insubstantiality. He was disappointed in the few reviews and their praising it solely as an

---

* Burton told Cleverdon, 'The highest point in my acting career was the part of *In Parenthesis* when the men are going over the top.' Burton told Cowan that he wanted to record Dai's boast and was an avid admirer of Jones's poetry.

example of poetic imagination. He wanted them to address whether its assertions were 'true or . . . damned nonsense'.[117]

In the spring of 1966, Giardelli had suggested reprinting *The Deluge* and had secured funding from the Welsh Committee of the Arts Council. But Jones had waffled over the value of 'old stuff'. Now, in 1972, Cleverdon renewed the proposal. Jones agreed and asked Jacqueline and Morag to fetch the ten woodblocks, in cases in his Monksdene bookshelves. They found only eight. To avoid causing him anguish, Cleverdon kept this from him and quietly dropped the scheme.[118]*

In July 1972, Jones was 'amazed' to be mentioned in *The Times* leader along with Betjeman and MacDiarmid as likely candidates for poet laureate. He thought the article 'probably right' about Betjeman, who received the appointment.[119]

* * *

In late July 1972 Jones suffered an 'atrocious tooth-ache'. In July and August Orr drove him, 'feeble and confused', to the dentist seven times. Cathie Hunt sometimes attended him while Orr parked the car. One sweltering August day, emerging from the car in his greatcoat, hat, and muffler, he noticed people looking at him and asked, 'Do I look odd, Cathie?' Arriving home, extricating himself from the car with much gasping and groaning, grasping the car door, he heaved himself to his feet, exclaiming triumphantly, 'I made it!' A nun said, 'Yes, but Mr Jones, your legs are crossed.'[120]

In early 1970 Honeyman had advised Jones to make a will, and David had met with Ben Jones of Linklaters and Paines, chairman of the Cymmrodorion Society and recommended by Valerie. Ben Jones went on holiday, and she retained a London solicitor to draw up a will, but David would not sign it. In May 1970 Ben Jones drew one up. But, certain only that he wanted Grisewood to be executor and trustee, David vacillated. Ben Jones suggested that a list of possible beneficiaries be drawn up for Grisewood's discretion as executor, and Honeyman made one. David wouldn't sign it. (He had a fear of all legal documents, hating, for example, signing income tax returns.) In 1973, Honeyman pressed him again to make a will, and Ben Jones was once more summoned but he paralysed David by pointing out every hypothetical difficulty with each possible decision. David said to Grisewood, 'I want to leave some money to the Welsh Language Society but it's been pointed out to me that by the time I'm dead left-wingers might be in charge, and I'm not going

---

* When Jones had lent Valerie his room key, she had taken two blocks. Cleverdon later traced them to her, procured them, and reprinted *The Deluge* (1977). All the blocks subsequently went to the National Museum of Wales.

to give money to Communists.' Grisewood said, 'All right, if you don't sign a will, at least appoint a literary executor.' Jones said, 'I, I don't know. I don't think I really want to talk about it.' Grisewood gave up. Honeyman persisted but in vain.[121]

*   *   *

Released from dependency on Dr Stevenson, in the spring of 1972 Jones visited Edward McClellan, a Harley Street consultant-surgeon and friend of Grisewood, who made the appointment. McClellan told Jones that the combination of drugs he was taking was 'mistaken', took him off barbiturates, and gave him a new prescription. He immediately improved. Swelling in his ankles disappeared. He was 'more alert' and 'able to work without falling asleep'. When asked how he felt, he now said, 'Not bad' instead of 'Pretty mouldy.' McClellan further adjusted his medication on 2 January 1973.[122]

Freed from debilitating drugs, Jones was able to produce his third book of poetry, towards which he had received two Arts Council grants. While visiting on 20 July 1971, Cookson had suggested that the new volume consist solely of the already published Roman and Celtic poems, and Jones liked the idea. At about 100 pages, the new book would serve as an introduction for readers unfamiliar with the long poems. In 1972 he also wanted to include three or four essays, but Cookson and Peter du Sautoy discouraged this, proposing instead a second book of four essays.* In September 1972 du Sautoy received from Cookson most of the material for the volume of poetry to be entitled *The Sleeping Lord and Other Fragments*, and Jones signed a contract. He would receive royalties of 12½% on the first 3,000 copies and 15% on a limited signed edition of 150 copies, with an advance of £200 upon signing.[123]

In December 1973, he suffered a return of what he called 'my old nerve thing'. It felt like what he had suffered forty years before but without insomnia. Any work, even writing letters, was extremely difficult. He could not motivate himself to see Dr McClellan again. Visiting, Audrey Malan found him entirely unresponsive to her remarks and questions, literally speechless. After five months of severe depression, in April he felt better.[124]

He decided to include two more poems in his new book. One was a section from the end of 'The Book of Balaam's Ass' manuscript, tentatively entitled 'Assault on the Mill', largely the memory of an attack at Passchendaele by an ex-serviceman who explicitly refutes the notion that

---

* These were to be an 'autobiographical fragment', 'The Dying Gaul', 'Use and Sign', and 'An Introduction to the Rime of the Ancient Mariner', later published with other essays in *The Dying Gaul*.

alluding to romance glorifies war (an ill-considered criticism that had been and would again be levelled at *In Parenthesis*). Grimly humorous, 'Balaam's Ass' (*SL* 97–111) discerns spiritual meaning in (and despite) physical calamity. The final typescript shows substantial reworking to increase resonance with the earlier Roman and Celtic poems, unifying the collection as a sequence. He also wanted to include 'The Kensington Mass' but could not finish it in time.[125]

For the proposed book of essays, Jones had begun work on an autobiographical piece. In 1973, with du Sautoy's encouragement, he began expanding it to a full autobiography, towards which Orr volunteered to tape his reminiscences.[126] (On the tapes Jones's voice is high and thin as he struggles to remember, strains for the right word, lapses into silence; Orr sometimes losing his temper, becomes sharp, dictatorial, Jones, doing his best to comply, never loses patience.) After barely beginning, Jones set aside this project to work on 'The Kensington Mass', finishing the initial part in time for its inclusion in an issue of *Agenda* scheduled to coincide with the publication of *The Sleeping Lord*.

In mid-January 1974, he fell on his left hip and was bedridden, in great pain from bruised groin muscles. Eye trouble made reading and writing difficult. On 7 February, he received word that his sister had died. The nuns noticed that he took it 'quite badly'.[127]

At du Sautoy's request, he made an inscription for the dust jacket of *The Sleeping Lord* but it was 'rather rough' because his eyes were bad and his hands 'not really firm'. He wanted to illustrate both 'The Hunt' and 'The Sleeping Lord' with a half-tone reproduction of *Tir y Blaenau* (chapter 6 fig. 3) – it was included in the page proofs but subsequently dropped, to his chagrin, though retained for a limited, signed edition. *The Sleeping Lord* was published on 25 March 1974:[128] 2,500 copies were printed, 750 to be sold by Chilmark Press in an American edition.

The poems of *The Sleeping Lord* are wonderful and no doubt benefit from the prolonged consideration given them. But it had taken twenty years to achieve what should have taken, at most, seven. In addition to eruptions of his 'old nerve thing', the delay was owing to enervating lethargy induced by barbiturates. In these circumstances, this book of poetry is in many respects a remarkable achievement.

The best review 'by far' was in the *Spectator* by Seamus Heaney, who praised Jones as 'an extraordinary writer' who has 'returned to the origin and brought something back, something to enrich not only the language but people's consciousness of who they have been and who they consequently are'. Decades later W. S. Merwin would call these poems 'some of his great splendours'.[129] More than any other collection or sequence in English, they test traditional values in the face of modern mechanised war, technological pragmatism, and political totalitarianism.

Jones told Honeyman, 'I have such masses of things I want to make that I fear now won't get made.' With a sense of urgency, he pressed on with 'The Kensington Mass'. It had begun as 'The Mass' in a draft of 1945 but was now entirely new, meandering 'off into a quite different' and longer 'shape' (RQ 87–96). Writing it, he felt constantly the need for books still at Monksdene. Without his Cruden's Concordance, he resorted to 'endless futile' searches 'in the O.T. that takes hours & hours'.[130]

This, his last poem, was never completed, largely because of a painstaking, year-long, time-consuming correspondence explicating *The Anathemata* for a commentary Hague was writing. In reply to his questions, Jones wrote hundreds of foolscap pages, from which Hague would quote extensively in his book.* In one of his last letters to Hague, Jones urges a recess in the correspondence so that he can work on his poem, which he says will likely not be finished till 'the spring of 1975'.[131]

In mid-April 1974, Cleverdon brought Hague to London to take part in a David Jones evening at the Mermaid Theatre. Hague visited Jones twice before the event, 'a great treat' for him. Petra visited on her way to the theatre – in the dim light of his room he failed to recognise her, but knew her when she spoke, and 'it was such a surprise'. At the theatre, before a small audience, Cleverdon and Hague talked, and actors read from the poetry. Friends later reported that Hague's contribution was wonderful. Kathleen Raine said that Bernard Wall, whom she had accompanied, 'was so moved that he wept'. Hague and Wall visited Jones afterwards.[132]

Two weeks later, Bernard Wall died. The news cast Jones into gloom for weeks. He grieved deeply for 'dear, very dear, Bernard'. Three months later, he still could not 'take it in' or 'believe' it.[133]

Shortly after, he learned of the death of Louis Bonnerot, 'a delightful man & friend.' He had introduced Jones's work to France, publishing translations of 'The Dream of Private Clitus', 'Rite and Fore-time', and, in 1973, 'The Tribune's Visitation' – a translation Jones believed 'better than the original'.[134]

* * *

On 14 May 1974, Jones was notified that he would receive the rank of Companion of Honour, the highest British award after the Order of Merit and limited to sixty-five people. When the badge arrived, he was, to his surprise, delighted, and enjoyed sending a receipt to the Central Chancery of the Order of Knighthood, St James's Palace. After the public announcement, he was inundated with letters and telegrams. The only one he replied to

* R. Hague, *A Commentary on 'The Anathemata' of David Jones* (Wellingborough: Skelton, 1977).

was from Margaret Grisewood, whom Harman had left – Jones thought her letter 'expressly kind as she was obviously still in much distress'.[135] For all the others, he published a brief note of thanks in *The Times*. He showed the medallion to visitors, several of whom described his delight as childlike. On 2 June 1974, Grisewood visited, 'a marvellous happiness' for Jones, 'a most affectionate meeting' though brief – Harman did not speak of his break with Margaret.[136]

On 1 October, George Johnston, a Canadian poet and Old Norse scholar, visited, and they conversed about the Norse King Olaf Tryggvason, the sea god Aegir, feudalism, and Geoffrey of Monmouth. 'The talk was not tiring him,' Johnston recalled. 'It was making him stronger' and 'what wonderful talk it was'.* Later that month, Paul Hills visited, and they discussed rugby football, Jones enthusing over the beauty of the drop-kick and the running formation. Peter Orr visited on Friday 25 October, finding him lively, in good humour, lying on his bed in the camel-hair dressing gown.[137]

The next day, Jones received news he had been dreading, that he would be moved to a room upstairs. On Sunday morning, he attended Mass in the chapel. That night just before midnight, a nun looked in to suggest he turn off the light, and he said, 'I will. Let me work just a little longer' – he was redrafting and expanding 'The Kensington Mass'. The next morning at 6.15, three days before his seventy-ninth birthday, a nun looked in and phoned her superior, saying, 'Mr Jones is gone.'[138] He had died in his sleep of degenerative heart failure.

The funeral was on 5 November, a bitterly cold day. The Mass (arranged by Louis Bussell) was at St Mary Magdalen's in Brockley, close to the house of his birth. Present were his nieces and nephew and their spouses, Bussell, the Honeymans, Morag and her husband, Tom Burns, Harman Grisewood (looking much distressed) leaning on the arm of Leslie (Mrs Alexander) Hope, William Cookson with Anne Beresford, Rod Lowery, Peter Kelly and his wife, Maurice Percival, Cecil Gill (looking eerily like his brother Eric), and Valerie Wynne-Williams. It was a Latin low Mass, with no music, but a choir nearby was rehearsing a particularly lovely hymn. The priest, who had not known Jones, spoke gently of how those present, through the merits of Christ, were helping 'our brother David' to be received in paradise. He recited the *Dies Irae*, which includes the words '*teste David cum Sibylla*'. The mourners drove to the south-west quadrant of the Ladywell and Brockley Cemetery, where the body was buried in the grave of his parents and sister, within sight of the Hilly Fields where he had played as a boy. Jacqueline Honeyman placed anemones on the grave. The Kellys placed holly. Valerie quietly wept.[139]

---

* Two weeks later, on 19 October, at a poetry reading in London, Johnston heard Hugh MacDiarmid call Jones 'the greatest native British poet of the century'.

Tom Burns arranged a memorial service on 13 December in Westminster Cathedral. To the surprise of most present, the enormous nave was full, largely of Jones's friends and acquaintances, many unknown to one another. The Introit, Offertory verse, and Communion antiphon were Gregorian chant. The *Dies Irae* was sung as was music by the sixteenth-century composer John Shepherd and, at communion, Palestrina's *Alma Redemptoris Mater*. Fr Peter Levi delivered the sermon and eulogy. A reception followed at the Goring Hotel for Jones's forty-two closest and/or most famous friends. A woman there, unrecognised by any of the rest, announced that nobody had been closer to him than she (probably Ray Howard-Jones).[140]

The conversation among those leaving the cathedral and at the hotel may be imagined from what some of them later said. Henry Moore: 'I admire his writing, as also his painting and drawing. I think he is a great poet, and I respond deeply to his work.' Harman Grisewood: 'He was a holy person' whose 'outstanding characteristic was humility'. Malcolm Cochrane: 'the most saintly man I ever met'. Tom Burns: he 'always made me believe in truth and beauty', and 'I doubt if any other mortal soul has been such a counsellor, such a kind comrade.' Tristram Powell: 'He was one of the most remarkable people I have met.' The architect Philip Jebb: 'Visits with him were the privilege of a lifetime.' Cathie Hunt: he was 'so sweet and gentle. You just couldn't help loving him.' Peter Orr: 'He did more for me than I ever did for him.' Stanley Honeyman: 'The debt is from me to him.' Barbara Moray: 'He was a genius' and 'repaid friendship a thousand fold'. Philip Hagreen: 'How blessed we are in having known him! He was as unlike other men of his generation as Blake was in his day.'[141]

The insurance company providing Jones's annuity got most of his life savings. His nieces and nephew inherited his property.[142] They sold his books and manuscripts to the National Library of Wales and many of his paintings and drawings to the National Museum of Wales.

*   *   *

A brilliant visual artist, the best modern native British poet, and the author of an original and convincing theory of culture, David Jones may be the foremost native British modernist. He created so much intelligent beauty during so many decades of psychological distress, that his creative life is probably the greatest existential achievement of international modernism.

✻

Acknowledgements

Without attempting to influence or have editorial licence, two generations of the trustees of David Jones's estate have generously given me full access to all his unpublished writing and permission to quote from it and reproduce his art. My most important living sources were Jones's close friends: Tom Burns, Jim Ede, Harman Grisewood, Philip Hagreen, Stanley Honeyman, and Petra Tegetmeier. Others who shared memories or gave access to letters or pictures were Mary Adams, Julian Asquith, Josie Bacon, Sarah and Maurice Balme, Kenneth Bell, Hilary Beyer, Fabian Binyon OSB, David Blamires, William Blissett – he introduced me to Jones's poetry and then to Jones, with whom we shared four long visits – John Bodley, Luce Bonnerot, Robert Buhler, Morag Bulbrook, Vincent Bywater SJ, Douglas and Nest Cleverdon, Malcolm and John Cochrane, Cathie Collins, William Cookson, Kevin Cribb, Glyn Davies, Solange Dayras, Pamela Donner, Polly Drysdale, Bee Dufort, Clarissa Eden, Valerie Eliot, Mollie Elkin, Nick Elkin, Rosalind Erangey, Elwyn Evans, Susan Falkner, Joy Finzi, Antonia Fraser, Arthur Giardelli, Rita M. Gibbs, Nicolete, Basil, Edmund, and Sophie Gray, Margaret Grisewood, Michael Hague, Ernest Hawkins, Paul Hills, Dorothy Hodgkin, Edward Hodgkin, Edgar Holloway, Jeremy Hooker, Cecile and Edmund Howard, Ray Howard-Jones, Colin Hughes, Tony Hyne, Vicky Ingrams, Lucy and Philip Jebb, Ian Jennings, Peter Kelly, Jenny Kilbride, David Kindersley, Peter Levi, Kathleen Lockitt, Diana Lodge, Philip and Angela Lowery, Audrey Malan, Jean Mambrino SJ, Anthony Meredith SJ, John Montague, Barbara Moray, Joseph Munitz SJ, E. Q. Nicholson, Peter and Kay Orr, Conrad Pepler OP, Tristram Powell, Kathleen Raine, Michael Rees, Michael Richey, Catherine Rousseau, John Ryan, Nancy Sanders, Peter du Sautoy, Christina Scott, Jonathan Scott, Rupert Shepherd, Sydney Shepherd, Walter Shewring, Richard Shirley-Smith, Elizabeth and Christopher Skelton, John Skelton, Diana Smith, Stephen Spender, Janet Stone, Tony Stoneburner (who showed me his letters from Jones, and his notes on conversations with Jones and his friends), Elizabeth Swan, Vincent Turner SJ, Barbara Wall, Len Walton, Ronald Watkins, Colin Wilcockson, Sarah Williams, Juliet Wood, Stella Wright, and Valerie Wynne-Williams.

I received information and photographs from Donald Allchin, Hugh Anson-Cartwright, Jonathan Barker at the British Council, Jay Bosanquet, Paul Burns, Peter Chasseaud, Margaret Cookson, Valerie H. Corbett, Beryl Dixon, Hildebrand Flint OSB, Fiona MacCarthy, Patricia McCarthy, Jonathan Miles, Mary Cooper Moore, Roland Murphy OCD, June Penn, Stephen Petrovik, Menna Phillips, David Poulter, Miriam Rothschild, and

Derek Shiel. The poet John Matthias gave encouragement. I benefited from the expertise of Glyn Davies and Irene Fast (psychoanalytic), Byron Rourke (neuropsychological), and Brian Burke (psychiatric-pharmacological). Huw Ceiriog Jones helped me in many ways, as did Daniel Huws and Philip Davies, then of the National Library of Wales, which houses most of Jones's poetry manuscripts and personal library. His letters to Jim Ede are at Kettle's Yard, Cambridge; those to Harman Grisewood at the Beinecke Library, Yale; those to René Hague at the University of Toronto Library; those to Peter Levi and Janet Stone at the Bodleian, Oxford; and those to Herbert Read at the McPherson Library, University of Victoria. The letters to Kenneth Clark, Nicolete Gray, and Helen Sutherland are in the Tate Gallery Archives; Faber and Faber correspondence is in the Faber archives; and the letters to W. H. Auden, Bernard Bergonzi, Desmond Chute, T. S. Eliot, Philip Hagreen, Stanley Honeyman, Stuart Pigott, Kathleen Raine, Nancy Sanders, Richard Shirley-Smith, and Tony Stoneburner are at the National Library of Wales – though I had access to them when in private hands. The largest number of good colour reproductions of Jones's visual art appear in Ariane Banks and Paul Hills, *The Art of David Jones, Vision and Memory* (2015).

The most important published sources are René Hague's *Dai Greatcoat* (1980) and William Blissett's *The Long Conversation* (1981). The most complete collection of Jones's visual art is Jonathan Miles and Derek Shiel's *David Jones, The Maker Unmade* (1995). These three books are predominantly the sources of Keith Aldritt's *David Jones, Writer and Artist* (2003), a short biography that repeats all their errors, which I correct, for the most part, silently. Information from Blissett's visits to Jones that I shared comes, unless otherwise specified, from my memory of them, which sometimes differs from his.

The Social Science and Humanities Research Council of Canada generously funded my research as did a Killam Research Fellowship and a University of Windsor Humanities Research Fellowship. By being a wonderful mother to our daughters, Kate Connors freed me to do much of my research. Encouraging, patient, discerning, Robin Robertson made this biography his first commission, in 1987, and has since been the best of editors. Dougles Cleverdon brought us together in what was the last of his many enablings of collaboration.

The present biography is a condensation of a much longer document, which will eventually be a public website.

1985–2016

Abbreviations for works by David Jones

A   *The Anathemata* (London: Faber and Faber, 1972).

DG   *The Dying Gaul*, ed. Harman Grisewood (London: Faber and Faber, 1978).

DGC   *Dai Greatcoat*, ed. René Hague (London: Faber and Faber, 1980).

EA   *Epoch and Artist*, ed. Harman Grisewood (London: Faber and Faber, 1959).

IN   *Inner Necessities*, ed. Thomas Dilworth (Toronto: Anson-Cartwright, 1984).

IP   *In Parenthesis* (London: Faber and Faber, 1978).

LF   *Letters to a Friend*, ed. Aneirin Talfan Davies (Swansea: Christopher Davies, 1980).

LVW   *Letters to Vernon Watkins*, ed. Ruth Pryor (Cardiff: University of Wales, 1976).

RQ   *The Roman Quarry*, ed. Harman Grisewood and René Hague (London: Agenda Editions, 1981).

SL   *The Sleeping Lord* (London: Faber and Faber, 1974).

WP   *Wedding Poems*, ed. Thomas Dilworth (London: Enitharmon, 2002).

List of Illustrations

Ownership and/or location of images:
HSC Helen Sutherland Collection
IWM Imperial War Museum, London
KY Kettle's Yard, Cambridge
NLW National Library of Wales, Aberystwyth
NMW National Museum of Wales, Cardiff
NPG National Portrait Gallery, London
SBL St Bride Library, London
TA Tate Archive, London
TEDJ Trustees of the Estate of David Jones
TG Tate Gallery, London

The trustees own copyright for all reproductions of David Jones's art.
Every effort has been made to identify photographers.

Chapter 1

1. Arabin Road. By author.
2. Jim, Harold, Cissy, David, Alice Ann Jones, 1899. NLW.
3. *Tiger and Leopard*, 1901. TA.
4. *The Bear*, 1903. Private Collection.
5. Sketches, *Daily News*, 19 October 1903. Original lost.
6. Christmas card, 1904. NLW. Original lost.
7. *Wolf in Snow*, 1906. Robin Ironside, ed., *David Jones* (Penguin, 1948), plate 4. Original lost.
8. David Jones reclining; behind him Effie Tozer and parents; back right, Harold and Cissy, *c*. 1910. TEDJ.
9. St Trillo's Chapel, *c*. 1900. NLW.
10. Ruined manor house on *Bryn Euryn*. By author.

Chapter 2

1. *Lions*, 1910. TA.
2. *Soldier and Old Man*, 1914. NLW.
3. *The Skipper*, *c*. 1913. TEDJ.
4. Jones as Friar, *c*. 1912. NLW.
5. Jones as Bard, *c*. 1912. NLW.
6. Jones and Medworth (left), Hawkins (right), March 1913. NLW.

Chapter 3

1. Private David Jones, 1915. TEDJ.
2. 'Pro Patria', *Graphic*, 11 December 1915. Original lost.
3. 'shrapnel burst, 1916 Givenchy, supports', 1916. TEDJ.
4. 'Front line 1916 – why not fixed bayonette?', 1916. TEDJ.
5. 'Yours ever Elsie', 1916. NLW.
6. *Lancelot and Guinevere*, 1916. TEDJ.
7. 'Close Quarters', *Graphic*, 9 September 1916. Original lost.
8. Equipment, 1917. TEDJ.
9. *Breilen Aug 18, 1917, N. W. of Ypres Mark I or Mark IV Tank?* TEDJ.
10. 'Germany and Peace', *Graphic*, 20 January 1917. Original lost.
11. Leslie Poulter, *c.* 1917. David Poulter.
12. *The Quest*, New Year, 1918. NLW. Original lost.
13. 'Civilisation bound by the Black Knight of Prussia', *Graphic*, 13 July 1918. Original lost.

Chapter 4

1. Hillcrest, 115 Howson Road, 1934. NLW.
2. *The Betrayal*, 1921. TA.
3. *The Military*, 1919. TA.
4. '1920–1 West[minster]', 1921. TA.
5. Dorothea de Halpert, *c.* 1920. Beatrix Dufort.
6. Jones, possibly by Dorothea de Halpert or Frank Medworth, *c.* 1920. NLW.
7. John O'Connor, *c.* 1925. Kelly Library, St Michael's College, Toronto.
8. *North Downs*, 1921. Private Collection.
9. *Our Lady of the Hills*, 1921. Private Collection.
10. Desmond Chute, 1919. F. MacCarthy, *Eric Gill* (Faber, 1989).
11. Hilary Pepler, 1921. MacCarthy, *Eric Gill*.

Chapter 5

1. *Entry into Jerusalem*, or *Cum Floribus et Palmis*, 1923. Sorrowful Mysteries, Ditchling Common.
2. *Sancta Helena*, 18 August 1922. Private Collection.
3. Jones and Eric Gill, Bristol, by G. Methven Brownlee, 1926. NLW.
4. Martin D'Arcy, by Howard Coster, 1938. NLW.
5. Jones engraving, 1923. Ernest Hawkins.
6. Woodcutters and family, 1923. D. Cleverdon. *The Engravings of David Jones* (Cloves Hill Edition, 1981). Cleverdon estate.
7. *Mater Castissima*, back, 1924. Private Collection.

8. 'The Presentation', *A Child's Rosary Book*, 1924. Cleverdon, *Engravings*. Cleverdon estate.
9. Cover, *Libellus Lapidum*, 1924. Ditchling: Pepler, 1924. NLW.
10. *The Garden Enclosed*, 1924. TG.
11. Cover, *The Townchilds Alphabet*, 1924. E. Farjeon, *The Town Child's Alphabet* (Poetry Bookshop, 1924). NLW.

Chapter 6

1. The monastery at Capel-y-ffin. By author.
2. *By the Mystery of thy Holy Incarnation*, 1924. Cleverdon, *Engravings*. Cleverdon estate.
3. *Tir y Blaenau*, December 1924–January 1925. NLW.
4. Mural, Capel-y-ffin, 1925. Monastery, Capel-y-ffin. TEDJ.
5. Jones by Dom Theodore Bailey, 1927. NLW.
6. *Ship off Ynys Byr*, 1925. Ashmoleum Museum, Oxford.
7. *Gulliver's Travels* illustration 35, 1925. Cleverdon, *Engravings*. Cleverdon estate.
8. *St Helena*, 1925. Private Collection.
9. René Hague, *c.* 1925. Estate of René Hague.
10. *Y Twmpa, Nant Honddu*, 1926. Private Collection.
11. *The Town Garden*, 1926. Loftus Collection.
12. *The Book of Jonah* illustration 13, 1926. Golden Cockerel Press, 1926. Cleverdon estate.
13. Douglas Cleverdon, by G. Methven Brownlee, 1924. SBL.
14. Jones, by Brownlee, 1926. NLW.
15. Petra Gill, by Brownlee, 1926. NLW.
16. Stanley Morison, 1933. James Moran, *Stanley Morison: his typographic achievement* (Hastings House, 1971).
17. *Seven Fables of Aesop* illustration 1, 1928. (Lanston Monotype Corporation, 1928). Cleverdon, *Engravings*. Cleverdon estate.
18. *Llyfr y Pregeth-wr*, 1927. Cleverdon, *Engravings*. Cleverdon estate.
19. *Deluge 6, The Chester Play of the Deluge*, 1927. Reprinted Clever Hill Editions, 1977. Cleverdon estate.
20. *Deluge 9, The Chester Play of the Deluge*, 1927. Reprinted Clever Hill Editions, Cleverdon estate.
21. *Self-portrait*, 1928. Art Gallery of New South Wales.

Chapter 7

1. Hove Seaside Villas, *c.* 1927. Number 5 is the third from foremost. Private Collection.
2. Jim Ede, *c.* 1936. NLW.

3. Jones passport photograph, 1928. NLW.
4. *Licq-Athérey*, 1928. NLW.
5. *Montes et Omnes Colles*, 1928. Whitworth Art Gallery, Manchester.
6. *The Rime of the Ancient Mariner 6*, 1929. Samuel Taylor Coleridge, *The Rime of the Ancient Mariner* (Douglas Cleverdon, 1929). Cleverdon estate.
7. *The Rime of the Ancient Mariner 8*, 1929. Coleridge, *The Rime of the Ancient Mariner*. Cleverdon estate.
8. *The Artist's Worktable*, 1929. HSC.
9. Tom Burns, *c.*1928. NLW.
10. *Nude* (Enid Furminger), 1929. Private Collection.
11. *Nude*, for Diana Lodge, *c.*1930. Private Collection.
12. Denis and Petra Tegetmeier and Joanna Gill, 7 January 1930. NLW.
13. *The Bride*, 1930. KY.
14. Pigotts farmyard from Jones's bedroom window. By author.
15. *Pigotts Farmyard*, 1930. HSC.
16. *Lady Prudence Pelham*, 1930. Stoke-on-Trent City Museum and Art Gallery.
17. Harman Grisewood *c.* 1935. Harman Grisewood.
18. *Order*, 1929. Tom Burns.
19. Charles Burns, *c.* 1936. Paul Burns.
20. Cover illustration, *The Gum Trees*, 1929. NLW.

Chapter 8

1. *Merlin Land*, 1930–32. Private Collection.
2. Christopher Dawson, *c.* 1935. NLW.
3. *Agag*, 1930. Private Collection.
4. *Curtained Outlook*, 1931. British Council, London.
5. Jones's pocket calendar, August 1931. NLW.
6. *Petra im Rosenhag*, 1931. Private Collection.
7. Rock Hall, *c.* 1935. Postcard. NLW.
8. *The Chapel in the Park*, 1931. TG.
9. Helen Sutherland, *c.* 1950. Val Corbett.
10. Michael Sadler, Walter Sickert, Jones, and Nicolete Binyon, *Oxford Mail*, 14 June 1930. N. Binyon.
11. *He Frees the Waters in Helyon*, 1932. Cleverdon, *Engravings*. Cleverdon estate.
12. *Human Being*, 1931. HSC.
13. *Calypso's Seaward Prospect*, 1931. Private Collection.
14. *Portrait of a Maker*, 1932. Private Collection.
15. *Briar Cup*, 1932. HSC.
16. *The Translator of the Chanson de Roland*, 1932. NMW.
17. *July Change, Flowers on a Table*, 1932. Pallant House, Chichester.
18. *The Seated Mother*, 1932. HSC.
19. Christmas card, 1933. NLW.

Chapter 9

1. Jones in his 'little coat' on the *Malaja*, 1934. NLW.
2. Dhows, 26 April 1934. Letter to Petra Tegetmeier.
3. Buffalo, ass, pyramids, 26 April 1934. Letter to Petra Tegetmeier.
4. Zozer pyramid, 1934. NLW.
5. View from Jones's room at the Austrian Hospice [1993]. By author.
6. The Fort Hotel, Sidmouth. By author.
7. Otho de Grandisson, Ottery St Mary. By author.
8. Ex Libris Prudence Mary Pelham, 1938. Private Collection.
9. Prudence Pelham, *c.* 1935. NLW.
10. Jones revising, *c.* 1935. TEDJ.
11. Frontispiece, *In Parenthesis*, 1936. NMW.
12. *Window at Rock*, 1936. HSC.

Chapter 10

1. *The Farm Door*, 1937. Private Collection.
2. Study for *Guinever*, 1938. TA.
3. *Guinever*, 1940. TG.
4. *Mells Church*, 1939. Private Collection.

Chapter 11

1. Margaret Bailey, *c.* 1938. Margaret Grisewood.
2. Douglas Woodruff, *c.* 1940. Tom Burns.
3. *Air-raid Warden*, *c.* 1940. Private Collection.
4. *Aphrodite in Aulis*, 1941. TG.
5. *Margaret's Hands*, 1940. Private Collection.
6. *Aphrodite* 'for Harman', 1940. Private Collection.
7. *Germania and Britannia*, 'Epiphany', 1941. IWM.
8. Arthur Pollen, *c.* 1940. Lucy Jebb.
9. *The Four Queens*, 1941. TG.
10. *The Mother of the West*, 1942. Laing Art Gallery, Newcastle.
11. Culture chart, *c.* 1943. TA.
12. 'Present for Margaret', *c.* 1944. Private Collection.

Chapter 12

1. *View from Gatwick House*, April 1946. Private Collection.
2. *The Hogget*, Autumn 1946. HSC.
3. William A. H. Stevenson, *c.* 1965. E. D. P., 'W. A. H. Stevenson', *British Medical Journal*, 2 (21 May 1971). Fox photo.
4. *Tree at Bowden House*, 1947. Private Collection.

5. *Vexilla Regis*, 1948. KY.

6. *Sunday Mass: In Homage to G. M. Hopkins S. J.*, 1948. Private Collection.

7. Stanley Honeyman, 1947. Jacqueline and Stanley Honeyman.

8. *A Latere Dextro*, 1949. NMW.

9. Jones and Ray Howard-Jones in Northwick Lodge, by Raymond Moore, *c*. 1950. Estate of Raymond Moore.

10. *Flora in Calix-Light*, 1950. KY.

11. Dust jacket for *The Anathemata*, 1952. Private Collection.

Chapter 13

1. *Vobiscum est*, 1953. Wolseley Fine Art. Private Collection.

2. Faber Ariel Christmas card, 1953. TEDJ.

3. Rex Nan Kivell, by Ida Kar, 1953. NPG 125521.

4. *Exiit edictum*, 1949. TG.

5. *Pwy yw r gwr*, 1956. NLW.

6. *Cara Wallia derelicta*, 1954. NLW.

7. Clarissa Eden, 1952. Leamington History Group. Alan Griffin.

8. *Rose*, 1929. Private Collection.

9. *Ex devina pulchritudine*, 1956. Countess of Avon.

10. *Nam Sibyllam*, 1957. Estate of Valerie Eliot.

11. Valerie Price, 1959. NLW.

12. Jones and Valerie Price, by Philip Griffith, January 1959. Derek Shiel.

13. Study, 1959. TA.

14. *The Lee Shore*, 1961. Private Collection.

15. William Cookson, 1960. Margaret Cookson.

16. *Trystan ac Essyllt*, 1962. NMW.

17. The Honeymans and Jones, 28 May 1960. Jacqueline and Stanley Honeyman.

18. Trademarks in frame, 1950. Private Collection.

Chapter 14

1. T. S. Eliot's elephant, 1961. Estate of Valerie Eliot.

2. Faber Christmas card, 1961. Private Collection.

3. *Annunciation in a Welsh Hill Setting*, 1963. NMW.

4. Monksdene Residential Hotel. By author.

5. *Extensis manibus*, 1964. Estate of Peter Levi.

6. Jones with St Dominic and Giardelli's abstract relief, by Raymond Moore, *c*. 1965. Estate of Raymond Moore.

7. Douglas Cleverdon, Harman Grisewood, Alun Oldfield Davies, Saunders Lewis, Jones, Aneirin Talfan Davies (left to right), 1 March 1966. Harman Grisewood.

8. Jones in his room (with view) at Monksdene, *c*. 1967. Derek Shiel.

Citations

To economise, I gather citations in a single endnote for each paragraph or series of related paragraphs, listing citations in sequence but eliminating repeat citations within a note and citations to unaddressed manuscript fragments that cannot be dated. Letters from Jones are cited solely by the name of the recipient and the date. Unless indicated, Jones's spelling has been corrected. Size of visual art is given in main text when pertinent. Years in which the century is not indicated are twentieth century. Dates are not included for undated Durrant clippings and undated letters from Prudence Pelham. Since I give full bibliographical data in the first citation of a source, no bibliography is appended. People cited by first initial and surname can be identified in the Acknowledgements. Full first names are given for those with the same first initial and surname. Citations for footnotes are in the endnotes to the paragraphs of main text. I conducted all interviews not attributed to another interviewer by name.

Shortened titles are used after first citation of published works. The following abbreviations are used:

DJ = David Jones
au. = author
c. w. = in conversation with
frag. = fragment
int. = interviewed
Ms = manuscript
Ts = typescript

Notes

Epigraph

1. To H. Grisewood, 31/5/38.

Preface

1. K. Clark to J. Stone to au. 2/10/87.
2. Eric Gill, 'David Jones', ms, 7/9/28; Kenneth Clark quoted by J. Stone int. 2/10/87; T. S. Eliot, 'A Note of Introduction', *In Parenthesis* (London: Faber 1961), p. vii; W. H. Auden, 'A Contemporary Epic', *Encounter* (2/64), p. 65; Michael Howard, *The Lessons of History* (New Haven: Yale, 1997) p. 185; Adam Thorpe, 'Distressed perspectives', *Poetry Review* 86 (Spring 1996) p. 56; Graham Greene, *Ways of Escape* (Toronto: Lester & Orpen Dennys, 1980), p. 28; Herbert Read, 'War and the Spirit,' *Times Literary Supplement* (19/6/37), p. 457; W.H. Auden, *A Certain World* (New York: Viking, 1970) p. 373; Seamus Heaney, 'Now and in England', *Spectator*, 4/4/74, p. 547; T. S. Eliot to Bollingen Foundation, quoted by H. Grisewood to J. F. Hewitt 16/12/63; Igor Stravinsky, quoted by Robert Craft, *Stravinsky: Chronicle of Friendship 1948–1972* (New York: Knopf, 1972), pp. 227–8; Dylan Thomas to Harman Grisewood, int. 4/10/87; Hugh MacDiarmid, poetry reading, Central London Polytechnic, 19/9/74; W. S. Merwin, to author (7/4/08); Harold Rosenberg, 'Aesthetics of Crisis', *New Yorker* (22/8/64), pp. 114, 115, 122; Guy Davenport, 'In Love with All Things Made', *New York Times Book Review* (17/9/82), p. 9.

Chapter 1

1. To V. Wynne-Williams 3/11/59; DJ int. by P. Orr early 1970s; DJ, 'A Letter from David Jones', *Poetry Wales*, 8 (Winter 1972), p. 6; Alice Ann Jones to DJ to V. Wynne-Williams 10/6/59; *Kentish Mercury*, 12/7/40, with emendations by James Jones.
2. DJ int. by T. Stoneburner 5/5/66; DJ, 'A Letter from David Jones', p. 6; to V. Wynne-Williams 10/6/59; *Kentish Mercury*, 12/7/40, with emendations by James Jones.
3. To R. Hague 27/9/74; S. Wright int. 19/6/88, 21/6/89; Maurice Bradshaw int. by T. Stoneburner 1975; T. Hyne int. 6/85; to V. Wynne-Williams 7/2/74; to Saunders Lewis 9/4/70; S. Wright int. 26/6/86.
4. To V. Wynne-Williams 23/2/61; M. Elkin int. 21/4/95.

5. Cissy (Jones) Hyne c. w. S. Wright int. 21/6/89, 2/5/93; K. Lockitt and S. Wright int. 21/6/89; DJ, 'Fragments of an Attempted Autobiographical Writing', *Agenda*, 12:4–13:1 (Winter–Spring 1975), p. 99.

6. Petra (Gill) Tegetmeier int. 18/6/88; *A* draft ms note.

7. M. Elkin int. 6/85; T. Hyne int. 24/6/86; DJ int. by T. Stoneburner 26/5/69; S. Wright int. 19/6/88, 21/6/89.

8. W. Blissett, *The Long Conversation* (Oxford: Oxford University Press, 1981); J. Miles and D. Shiel, *David Jones, The Maker Unmade* (Bridgend, Wales: Seren, 1995); to Denis Tegetmeier 29/12/60; to V. Wynne-Williams 12/8/59, 24/9/62; M. Elkin int. 6/85.

9. To V. Wynne-Williams frag. n.d.; M. Bradshaw to S. Wright 20/8/76; DJ to W. Blissett, *Long*, p. 69; to R. Hague 27/9/74.

10. To P. Donner 8/5/62; Angela Gloria Donati Dorenkamp, *'In the Order of Signs', An Introduction to the Poetry of David Jones* (PhD, University of Connecticut, 1974), p. 7.

11. DJ ms draft [*c*. 1970]; DJ int. by P. Orr early 1970s; DJ to W. Blissett, *Long*, p. 121; DJ, 'Fragments of an Attempted Autobiographical Writing', p. 99.

12. DJ int. by T. Stoneburner 26/5/69.

13. To H. Grisewood 6/10/72; to J. Stone 15/3/65; to H. Grisewood 9/10/61.

14. DJ recorded by A. Giardelli 1965; 'Sign of the bear, David Jones talks to Nesta Roberts', *Guardian* 17/2/64, p. 12; DJ, 'Fragments of an Attempted Autobiographical Writing', p. 104.

15. 'David Jones – Maker of Signs' (BBC/British Council), script broadcast on Radio 3, 6/11/75.

16. S. Wright to R. Hague 1/3/79; to S. Lewis 9/4/70; to D. Blamires 9/7/66; to J. Stone 18/4/65; Maurice Percival to D. Cleverdon 1/10/77.

17. To Mr Rates draft n.d.; DJ ms draft [*c*. 1970]; to T. Stoneburner 30/7/69; to V. Wynne-Williams 25/11/64; P. Tegetmeier int. 12/6/86.

18. To H. Grisewood 14/10/70; DJ int. by T. Stoneburner 5/5/66.

19. S. Wright int. 11/10/87; DJ quoted by Richard Wald, 'I Don't Think I'm Modern', *New York Herald Tribune Books*, 8/7/62, p. 11; S. Wright int. 19/6/88.

20. To H. Grisewood 14/8/51; to J. Stone 7/3/65.

21. To H. Grisewood 22/5/62; 'DJ life for Jim Ede' (5/9/35), second correction of TS 3/5/43; R. Hague, *David Jones* (Cardiff: University of Wales Press, 1975), p. 45.

22. P. Hills int. 11/6/91.

23. T. Hyne int. 6/85; P. Tegetmeier int. 3/10/87; *IP* ms; obituary of James Jones, *Christian Herald*, 21/10/43; to T. Stoneburner 5/8/69; P. Hagreen int. 27/6/86; DJ c. w. T. Stoneburner 5/5/66.

24. To R. Hague 9–15/7/73; to P. Donner 11/5/74; DJ to W. Blissett, *Long*, p. 126.

25. To D. Blamires 7/6/66; DJ c. w. T. Stoneburner 9/6/66; DJ to D. Allchin int. 23/9/95.

26. V. Wynne-Williams int. 22/9/95; 'DJ life for Jim Ede' (5/9/35), second correction of TS 3/5/43; DJ int. by P. Orr early 1970s.

27. To H. Sutherland 2/4/58; to S. Lewis 9/4/70.

28. DJ int. by P. Orr Summer 1972; to J. Stone 16/10/70.

29. 'DJ life for Jim Ede' (5/9/35), second correction of TS 3/5/43; 'Sign of the bear'.

30. DJ int. by P. Orr, TS 1973.

31. To John H. Johnston 16/5/64; H. Grisewood int. 23/6/86.

32. To R. Hague 29/2/60; to *The Times* 22/2/61; DJ to W. Blissett, *Long*, p. 110.

33. To H. Grisewood 15–24/4/72; *IP* ms.

34. To S. Lewis 9/4/70; to H. Grisewood 1/2/71; DJ int. by T. Stoneburner 26/5/69; to Jackson Knight 11/10/52.

35. C. Wilcockson int. 22/6/88; DJ int. by P. Orr early 1970s; to R. Hague 19/6/74.

36. To A. Giardelli 9–11/8/73.

37. DJ int. by Jon Silkin 1965.

38. To Mr Revell [c. 1972]; to T. Stoneburner 20/10/64.

39. To V. Wynne-Williams 26/12/64.

40. DJ c. w. au. 31/8/72.

41. K. Lockitt int. 21/6/89; to V. Wynne-Williams 5/4/62.

42. Archibald Standish Hartrick, *A Painter's Pilgrimage Through Fifty Years* (Cambridge: Cambridge University Press, 1939), p. 7.

43. S. Wright int. 19/6/88; Alice Jones to DJ 28/3/37; M. Elkin int. 6/85.

44. P. Tegetmeier int. 3/10/87; M. Bradshaw int. by T. Stoneburner 1975; Cissy (Jones) Hyne to Petra Gill 3/8/31; to R. Hague 18/2/36.

45. To J. Knight 11/10/52; DJ c. w. au. 9/9/72; to Frank Morley unposted 1/53; to W. H. Auden 24/2/54; DJ c. w. au. 9/9/72.

46. DJ int. by J. Silkin, TS 1971; to T. Stoneburner 15/3/68.

47. To V. Wynne-Williams 11/12/72; S. Williams to au. 21/11/11.

48. DJ, 'A Letter from David Jones', pp. 8–9; Alice A. Jones to DJ 11/3/37; to H. Grisewood 1/1/64.

49. T. Hyne int. 6/85; to V. Wynne-Williams 5/4/62.

50. To Valerie Price 11/8/59; to T. Hyne 18/5/72; Richard Baddeley, *The Borough of Conwyn Handbook* (Borough of Conwyn, n.d.), p. 63.

51. To T. Hyne 18/5/72; to S. Lewis 3/7/54.

52. To Gwladys Toser 26/10/48; *EA* 27.

53. To H. Grisewood 28/3/61, 25/7/35; to R. Hague 27/9/74; DJ c. w. T. Stoneburner 9/6/66; to V. Wynne-Williams, unposted

5/4/62; to Vernon Watkins 20/4/62; James Jones to DJ 24/9/21; to V. Wynne-Williams 5/2/61.

54. To J. Hooker 8/5/70; to H. Grisewood 1/1/64; to P. Levi 29/1/65.
55. To J. Hooker 8/5/70; DJ, 'A Letter from David Jones', p. 6; to S. Lewis 22/7/48, 6/7/60; DJ c. w. T. Stoneburner 9/6/66, 26/5/69; to S. Lewis 4/71; to V. Wynne-Williams 4/2/59; *RQ* 11.
56. H. Grisewood int. 8/83; to D. Tegetmeier 18/3/74; to S. Lewis 14/6/72.
57. DJ, notes for his psychotherapist [1948]; G. Davies int. 8/10/89; R. Hague int. by P. Orr 15/2/77; DJ to S. Honeyman int. 24/11/2013; Prudence Pelham to DJ [1936]; DJ to R. Hague int. 1976.

Chapter 2

1. DJ in margin of A. S. Hartrick, *Painter's Pilgrimage*, p. 206; E. Hawkins to au. 26/1/88; DJ c. w. T. Stoneburner 7/6/69.
2. E. Hawkins int. 15/6/88; to Aneirin Talfan Davies 27/11/62; DJ int. by J. Silkin 1971.
3. To H. Grisewood 12/12/66; DJ c. w. au. 24/8/72; DJ c. w. T. Stoneburner 9/6/66; to T. Stoneburner 5/8/69.
4. S. Wright to au. 3/10/83; M. Elkin int. 6/85; H. Grisewood int. 5/10/87, 16/6/89.
5. S. Wright int. 26/6/86; M. Bradshaw int. by T. Stoneburner 1975; K. Lockitt int. 21/6/89; M. Bradshaw to S. Wright 20/8/76.
6. Camberwell School minutes of 27/1/11; DJ marginal note in A. S. Hartrick, *Painter's Pilgrimage*, p. 223.
7. To N. Gray 4/4/61; E. Hawkins int. 15/6/88.
8. To R. Hague 22/12/33, 5/1/35; Camberwell School Catalogue, 1910–11; to P. Hagreen 1/7/38; E. Hawkins int. 15/6/88; DJ, ms draft note to *Paintings, Engravings and Writings of David Jones* (London: Word and Image Catalogue, 1972); to J. Ede 15/4/43; to R. Hague Easter 1936.
9. A. S. Hartrick's obituary, *The Times* 2/2/50.
10. A. S. Hartrick, *Drawing* (London: Pitman, 1921), pp. 54–7, *Painter's Pilgrimage*, pp. 8, 37, 95; DJ c. w. au. 24/8/72; A. S. Hartrick, *Drawing*, pp. 38–41, 5; A. S. Hartrick, *Painter's Pilgrimage*, pp. 233–4.
11. S. Balme int. 17/6/90; to V. Wynne-Williams 12/5/74, 5/4/72; DJ to W. Blissett, *Long*, p. 44.
12. DJ in margin of A. S. Hartrick, *Painter's Pilgrimage*, p. 209.
13. DJ int. by P. Orr early 1970s; A. S. Hartrick, *Painter's Pilgrimage*, p. 215.
14. T. Hyne int. 23/6/91; T. Hyne to au. 24/4/96.
15. A. S. Hartrick, *Painter's Pilgrimage*, pp. 145, 84, 56, underlined by DJ.
16. DJ int. by P. Orr early 1970s; 'DJ life for Jim Ede' TS 5/9/35; to S. Lewis 4/71.

17. DJ, ms note in A. S. Hartrick, *Painter's Pilgrimage*, p. 222; DJ, 'Looking Back at the Thirties', *London Magazine*, 5 (April 1965), p. 48; A. S. Hartrick, *Painter's Pilgrimage*, pp. 224, 221.

18. A. S. Hartrick, *Painter's Pilgrimage*, p. 98; DJ c. w. au. 1972; to J. Stone 18/4/65.

19. A. S. Hartrick, *Drawing*, p. 60; P. Hills int. 11/6/91; to W. Blissett, *Long*, p. 56; to R. Hague 9–15/7/73; A. S. Hartrick, *Drawing*, pp. 68–78; to H. Grisewood 17/12/70; A. S. Hartrick, *Drawing*, p. 95.

20. To Kenneth Clark 3/8/60; to *The Times* draft [1947]; DJ, 'Note on Ms' [*c.* 1942].

21. E. Hawkins int. 1/8/87, 1/9/87.

22. E. Hawkins int. 15/6/88; to H. Sutherland 17/10/43.

23. DJ int. by P. Orr early 1970s; DJ to W. Blissett, *Long*, p. 41.

24. To R. Hague 9–15/7/73; to T. Stoneburner 30/8/63; to R. Hague 22/12/33; to J. H. Johnston 2/5/62; to H. Sutherland 29/9/58; to K. Raine frag. n.d.; to T. Stoneburner 25/6/67; to T. Burns 17/10/71; to H. Grisewood 7/5/64; *DG* 186.

25. To H. Grisewood 18/5/56; to A. T. Davies 17–18/2/59; to V. Watkins 5/4/62; to Mr Emlyn-Davies 19/6/64; to R. Hague 27/9/63, 11/8/74; to Meic Stephens draft 27/2/73.

26. Joanna (Gill) Hague int. 20/6/89; 'Sign of the bear'; DJ ms frag. n.d.; J. Hooker int. 20/6/89.

27. E. Hawkins int. 15/6/88; S. Wright int. 21/6/89; to H. Grisewood 1/9/56; K. Lockitt int. 21/6/89.

28. *LF* 11 12; T. Hyne int. 20/6/90; T. Hyne to au. 23/4/96; DJ quoted, *Western Mail* 26/10/84; DJ to V. Wynne-Williams 22/8/60; Newsletter, Acquisitions Dept of Pictures and Maps, National Library of Wales 1984.

29. To V. Wynne-Williams 22/10/60.

30. To N. Sanders 12/10/70; *LF* 12–13.

31. To J. Stone 18/4/65; to N. Sanders 10/12/70; biographical note for the British Council n.d. [*c.* 1970]; *LF* 14; to S. Lewis 4/71.

32. To R. Hague 9–15/7/73; DJ to W. Blissett, *Long*, p. 126.

33. To R. Hague 9–15/7/73, 11/8/74; M. Bradshaw int. by T. Stoneburner 1975.

34. E. Hawkins int. 1/9/87; David Lawson, 'A bit on David Jones, R.I.P.' TS, *c.* 1975.

35. E. Hawkins to au. 26/1/88; E. Hawkins int. 1/9/87; H. Grisewood int. 5/6/86.

36. To H. Grisewood 24/8/56; Hawkins int. 1/9/87; D. Lawson, 'A bit on David Jones, R.I.P.' TS.

37. 'DJ life for Jim Ede', TS 5/9/35; Eileen Chanin and Steven Miller, *The Art and Life of Weaver Hawkins* (Roseville, New South Wales: Craftsman House, 1995), p. 20; to R. Hague 21/10/63.

Chapter 3

1. To H. Grisewood, 4/8/62; David Lloyd George, *Through Terror to Triumph* (London: Hodder and Stoughton, 1915), p. 13; DJ to W. Blissett, *Long*, pp. 116–17; Certified Notice of Attestation 12/11/14; *DGC* 26.

2. DJ c. w. au. 5/6/71; Chris Williams to au. 30/7/2014; to V. Wynne-Williams 6/8/62.

3. To P. Levi 29/10/63; J. E. Munby, ed., *A History of the 38th (Welsh) Division by the G.S.O.'s I of the Division* (London: Hugh Rees, 1920), dated by DJ July 1929, p. 13.

4. To S. Lewis 4/71. For most of the details of the movements of the battalion in this chapter, I rely on the battalion war diary (National Archives); to John Roberts of Ganymed Press frag. [1961].

5. To V. Wynne-Williams 5/4/63; 1928 passport; *IP* 6; DJ c.w. au. 24/8/72.

6. DJ c. w. au. 31/8/72.

7. Anthony Bailley, 'The Front Line', TS 2/73; to S. Lewis 27/4/74; DJ int. by J. Silkin 1971; DJ int. by P. Orr early 1970s; P. Orr int. 2/6/86.

8. To V. Wynne-Williams 3/11/62.

9. DJ, 'Somewhere in France', TS, May 1917; Bernard Wall to T. Stoneburner 5/5/66.

10. To P. Levi 29/10/63; to H. Sutherland 9/2/48.

11. To T. Stoneburner 20/12/64; to H. Grisewood 9/10/71.

12. DJ to W. Blissett, *Long*, pp. 133, 81; Arthur Pritchard-Williams to DJ 15/11/44.

13. DJ c. w. au. 31/8/72.

14. To J. Silkin 13/10/59; DJ int. by P. Orr early 1970s; DJ quoted in A. Dorenkamp, *In the Order*, p. 19; to R. Hague 9–15/7/73.

15. DJ int. by J. Silkin 1971; DJ to W. Blissett, *Long*, p. 95.

16. Llewelyn Wyn Griffith, *Up to Mametz and Beyond* (London: Faber and Faber, 1931), p. 63; DJ to W. Blissett, *Long*, p. 122.

17. DJ int. by P. Orr early 1970s; to P. Levi 29/10/63; to J. H. Johnston 23/3/62, 30/9/63.

18. DJ, annotation to J. E. Munby, *38th (Welsh) Division*, p. 16; to J. Knight 28/4/59; DJ int. by J. Silkin 1971; DJ c. w. au. 4/6/71.

19. To Dorothea Travis 18/3/74; DJ int. by P. Orr early 1970s; DJ to W. Blissett, *Long*, p. 77; DJ int. by J. Silkin 1971.

20. To T. Burns 2/7/71; *IP* ms; A. Bailley, 'The Front Line', TS 2/73.

21. To R. Hague 2/7/35; to D. Blamires 6/11/66; Malory X, 29; DJ, annotations to J. E. Munby, *38th (Welsh) Division*, p. 16.

22. To N. Sanders 11/7/72; to R. Hague 27/9/74; DJ int. by J. Silkin 1971. Cf. *IP* 160, 166; DJ c. w. au. 31/8/72.

23. *IP* 163; to R. Hague 27/9/74.

24. *IP* 167. For personal details, such as this, I rely on *IP* – whenever I asked DJ whether an experience of its John Ball happened to him, he said that it had.

25. *IP* 168; to R. Hague 14/6/70; *IP* 170; to H. Grisewood 31/12/71.

26. Colin Hughes, *David Jones, The Man Who Was on the Field. 'In Parenthesis' as Straight Reporting* (Manchester: David Jones Society, 1979), p. 21; DJ, annotation to A. S. Hartrick, *Painter's Pilgrimage*, p. 7; *IP* 172; to T. Burns 2/7/71; *IP* 175.

27. To R. Hague 10/7/35; 27/9/74; DJ, annotation to A. S. Hartrick, *Painter's Pilgrimage*, p. 7; to R. Hague 10/7/35.

28. DJ, annotation to J. E. Munby, *38th (Welsh) Division*, p. 19; to H. Grisewood 14/2/38; Alex Hamilton, 'From David Jones' Locker', *Manchester Guardian* 26/2/72, p. 21; P. Hagreen to au. 9/10/85; T. Hyne int. 6/85.

29. To Allan Lascelles 27/6/64; *DGC* 175; to T. Burns, 2/7/71.

30. DJ int. by P. Orr Summer 1972; to J. Stone 7–8/7/72; *DGC* 258; to H. Grisewood 30/6/72; to J. Stone 7–8/7/72.

31. A. S. Hartrick, *Painter's Pilgrimage*, pp. 233–4.

32. DJ to W. Blissett, *Long*, p. 122.

33. *DGC* 243; to R. Hague 14/12/73; *DGC* 251.

34. To Miss [Jane] Carver 29–30/6/72; to D. Blamires 9/7/66.

35. To S. Lewis 27/4/74.

36. Peter Chasseaud to au. 8/7/93; P. Chasseaud, 'David Jones and the Survey', *David Jones, Artist and Poet*, ed. P. Hills (Scolar Press: Aldershot, 1997), pp. 18–30; to J. Asquith 13/11/39.

37. *DGC* 242–3; A. Dorenkamp, *In the Order*, p. 7.

38. *IP* 207 n. 37; to R. Hague 11/8/74; to S. Lewis 19/11/54.

39. To T. Hyne 19/6/74.

40. To R. Hague 1/1/73; to T. Hyne 19/6/74; D. Poulter int. 11/6/90.

41. DJ quoted by R. Hague in *David Jones*, p. 58; *DGC* 248; to R. Hague, 9–15/7/73; DJ c. w. T. Stoneburner 5/5/66.

42. DJ to W. Blissett, *Long*, p. 64; DJ int. by P. Orr 1972; to R. Hague 9–15/7/73.

43. To Mr [Thomas] Whitaker draft 1970; DJ c. w. au. 4/6/71; DJ to W. Blissett, *Long*, p. 66.

44. To T. Stoneburner 30/7/69; to Miss [J.] Carver 5/7/72.

45. To Sister Mary Ursula draft n.d.

46. To T. Burns 14/9/40.

47. To H. Grisewood 21/5/40, 2/10/64.

48. To D. Blamires 6/11/66; DJ, annotation to J. E. Munby, *38th (Welsh) Division*, p. 25.

49. *DGC* 234; to H. Grisewood 9/10/71; DJ to W. Blissett, *Long*, p. 134; DJ c. w. au. 4/6/71.

50. DJ, annotation to J. E. Munby, *38th (Welsh) Division*, p. 29; *DGC* 203; to S. Lewis 27/4/74; D. Blamires, 'The Medieval Inspiration of David Jones', *David Jones: Eight Essays*, ed. Roland Mathias (Llandysul: Gomer Press, 1976), p. 18.

51. To S. Lewis 27/4/74; DJ *Word and Image,* compiled by D. Cleverdon (1972), p. 50; DJ to W. Blissett, *Long*, p. 140.

52. DJ c. w. au. 31/8/72; DJ, 'For the Front', *Tablet* 13/1/40; DJ c. w. W. Blissett, *Long*, p. 107.

53. To M. Wilkinson 30/7/65; to P. Levi 29/1/65; DJ int. by J. Silkin 1971; DJ to W. Blissett, *Long*, p. 127; DJ, annotation to J. E. Munby, *38th (Welsh) Division*, p. 21.

54. To Sister M. Ursula draft n.d.; DJ c. w. W. Blissett 6/73.

55. D. Poulter to au. 9/2/90; D. Poulter int. 11/6/90; DJ, 'A Soldier's Memories', *Tablet* (16/9/38), p. 506.

56. J. E. Munby, *38th (Welsh) Division*, pp. 46–7; DJ to W. Blissett, *Long*, p. 122; 'Sign of the bear'.

57. DJ annotation to J. E. Munby, *38th (Welsh) Division*, p. 31; to Catherine Ivainer 13/3/61.

58. DJ quoted by A. Bailley, 'The Front Line', TS 2/73.

59. To H. Grisewood 12/12/66; R. Hague int. by P. Orr 15/2/77; R. Hague to Jane Carter 3/7/80.

60. DJ in 1970 to J. Montague int. 9/9/89; DJ c. w. T. Stoneburner 26/5/69.

61. To D. Travis 26/12/48; DJ to W. Blissett, *Long*, p. 129; to R. Hague 1/55; to H. Grisewood 12/12/66; *RQ* 101.

62. To S. Lewis 4/71; DJ to W. Blissett, *Long*, p. 129; S. Honeyman int. 6/86.

63. J. Ede int. 6/85; A. Hamilton, 'From David Jones', p. 21.

Chapter 4

1. DJ int. by P. Orr early 1970s; to J. Stone 7–8/7/72.

2. Anne Beresford, 'A Friendship with David Jones – a personal account', TS n.d.; D. Poulter to au. 9/2/90; DJ to W. Blissett, *Long*, p. 133; Harold Stanley Ede, 'David Jones', *Horizon*, 8 (August 1940), p. 126.

3. To S. Lewis draft 15/1/63; DJ to P. Hills int. 11/6/91.

4. E. Hawkins to au. 29/4/88; Diana MacCartney-Filgate to au. 18/4/91; E. Hawkins int. 1/8/87.

5. E. Hawkins int. 15/6/88; DJ c. w. au. 9/9/72; D. MacCartney-Filgate to au. 24/1/91, 23/9/2013; birth certificate of Charles Joseph Medworth, born 11/11/1863.

6. E. Hawkins int. 15/6/88; to R. Hague 27/9/74; DJ c. w. T. Stoneburner 7/6/69.

7. DJ, 'Autobiographical details given to D. Cleverdon 3 July 1970'; E. Hawkins int. 15/6/88.

8. Walter Bayes, 'The Grammar of Drawing II', *Architectural Review*, 55 (Feb. 1924), pp. 54–5; E. Hawkins int. 1/9/87.

9. To P. Gill 17/6/23; 'D.J. life for Jim Ede' 3/5/43; DJ to W. Blissett, *Long*, p. 4. Paul Hills, *The Art of David Jones, Vision and Memory* (London: Lund Humphries, 2015), p. 119.

10. E. Hawkins int. 1/8 /87; P. G. Konody, *Sunday Observer* 9/11/19.

11. E. Hawkins int. 1/8/87, 15/6/88; 'DJ life for Jim Ede', TS 5/9/35.

12. To Mr McCormic 8/1/65; to S. Lewis 4/71; *LF* 15; E. Hawkins int. 7/9/87.

13. To *Tablet* draft 20/12/45; to S. Lewis 3/12/67.

14. To *Tablet* draft 20/12/45; DJ c. w. au. 31/8/72.

15. 'D.J. life for Jim Ede' 3/5/43; A. Giardelli int. 8/6/86.

16. R. Hague int. by P. Orr 15/2/77; DJ c. w. T. Stoneburner 5/5/66; E. Hawkins int. 15/6/88; S. Honeyman int. 1/9/87.

17. DJ ms draft n.d.; W. Blissett, *Long*, p. 11.

18. To H. Grisewood 15/2/57; B. Dufort to au. 23/9/86; to R. Hague 9–15/7/73; to Jacqueline and S. Honeyman 29/7/62.

19. To D. Tegetmeier 25/8/43, 20/2/43, 26/12/48.

20. DJ c. w. au. 4/6/71, see W. Blissett, *Long*, p. 74.

21. B. Dufort to au. 23/9/86; R. Hague int. by P. Orr 15/2/77; H. Grisewood int. 22/6/86; B. Dufort's diary 27/2/29 (thanks to her granddaughter Beatrix [Travis] Dufort for permission to quote).

22. DJ c. w. au. 4/6/71; to William T. Noon SJ 7/10/65; to P. Levi 3/11/67; to R. Hague Holy Saturday 1932.

23. To H. Grisewood 12/12/66, 26/11/70.

24. To D. Blamires 6/11/61; Frank Wall int. by T. Stoneburner 7/6/69; to T. Stoneburner 31/3/65; DJ, 'Autobiographical details given to D. Cleverdon 3 July 1970'; to H. Grisewood 26/7/61; R. Hague int. by P. Orr 15/2/77; S. Honeyman int. 6/86.

25. To T. Stoneburner 31/3/65; to H. Grisewood 31/12/71; to R. Hague 18/5/74; to H. Grisewood 15–17/1/68, 23/12/65.

26. P. Tegetmeier int. 12/6/86; to N. Gray 4/4/61; A. Dorenkamp, *In the Order*, p. 7.

27. To T. Hyne 25/5/71, 25/6/71; DJ c. w. T. Stoneburner 19/6/69; DJ quoted by R. Wald, 'I Don't Think', p. 3.

28. DJ c. w. au. 1971 or 1972; Robert Speaight, *The Life of Eric Gill* (London: Methuen, 1966), p. 111; Fiona MacCarthy, *Eric Gill* (London: Faber, 1989), p. 152.

29. To Eric Gill 26/7/21; to P. Levi 24/4/64; to N. Gray 15/1/63.

30. To N. Gray 14/4/61; DJ to A. Dorenkamp, *In the Order*, p. 13.

31. To D. Allchin draft 14/1/70.

32. P. Hagreen int. 27/6/86.

33. Donald Attwater, *A Cell of Good Living* (London: Chapman, 1969), p. 80; to H. Grisewood 9/10/71.
34. To R. Hague 26/2/74; to S. Lewis 27/4/74.
35. To T. Stoneburner 31/3/65; to S. Lewis 27/4/74; to R. Hague 9–11/6/74; John O'Connor to W. Shewring int. 24/6/88.
36. To H. Grisewood 10/6/64.
37. To R. Shirley-Smith 13/11/61; DJ to *The Times* unpublished n.d.
38. To T. Stoneburner draft n.d.; to H. Grisewood 9/10/71, 3/10/71.
39. John Rothenstein, *Modern English Painters*, Vol. II (London: Eyre & Spottiswoode, 1952), p. 215; Walter Sickert, 'The Teaching of Art and Development of the Artist', *English Review*, 11 (July 1912), pp. 314–15.
40. Here as elsewhere when Eric Gill is present, I take information from his diary.
41. To R. Hague 9/9/74; to H. Grisewood 1/1/64; to R. Hague 13/12/63.

Chapter 5

1. DJ int. by P. Orr early 1970s; John Ginger, 'A Brother's Life: Reginald Lawson, 1891–1985', TS; DJ c. w. T. Stoneburner 26/5/69.
2. P. Hagreen int. 27/6/86; S. Falkner, *A Ditchling Childhood: 1916–1936* (Bures: Iceni, 1994), pp. 26, 15; to R. Hague 22/12/33; C. Pepler, 'In Diebus Illis: Some Memories of Ditchling', *Chesterton Review*, 7 (Nov. 1982), p. 346; to Bernard Wall 30/1/43.
3. To H. Grisewood 29/12/72; to V. Wynne-Williams 18/10/62; DJ to W. Blissett, *Long*, p. 22; Eric Gill to D. Chute 12/1/24; Fr Benedict Wallis to au. 23/4/86, 8/5/86; to T. Stoneburner 13/1/70, 28/9/67; P. Hagreen to au. 19/10/85; to H. Grisewood 1/1/64.
4. H. Grisewood int. 16/6/89; DJ c. w. au. 4/6/71; H. Grisewood int. 5/6/86; to H. Grisewood 5/12/44, 10/6/64.
5. P. Tegetmeier int. 18/6/88; J. Ginger, 'A Brother's Life', TS.
6. To Joanna Gill (Hague), 6/11/23; P. Hagreen to DJ 12/40.
7. Eric Gill's diary 25/8/23; P. Tegetmeier int. 3/10/87; J. Ginger, 'A Brother's Life', TS; D. Attwater, *Cell*, p. 76; C. Pepler int. 11/6/89.
8. To T. Stoneburner 24–25/10/69; DJ c. w. T. Stoneburner 26/5/69.
9. P. Hagreen int. by D. Cleverdon 1982; P. Tegetmeier int. 18/6/88.
10. P. Hagreen to R. Hague 17/2/78; P. Hagreen int. 27/6/86, 2/6/86.
11. K. Lockitt int. 21/6/89; P. Tegetmeier int. 18/6/88.
12. DJ c. w. au. 4/6/71; to H. Grisewood 29/12/72.
13. To V. Wynne-Williams [1966]; to R. Hague 5/11/64.
14. P. Tegetmeier int. 12/6/86, 18/6/88; P. Pelham remembered by Stuart Hampshire int. 22/1/89; P. Hagreen int. 27/6/86; P. Hagreen to R. Hague 2/78.

15. To Ray Howard-Jones int. 11/9/89; DJ c. w. T. Stoneburner 20/6/72; DJ to T. Stoneburner 30/8/72.
16. H. Grisewood int. 19/6/90; to *Catholic Herald* draft 1/2/48.
17. P. Hagreen to au. 4/11/85; to J. H. Johnston 24/8/62; to Frank Kermode 12/7/66.
18. 'DJ life for Jim Ede', TS 5/9/35; to J. Ede 11/4/39; to H. Grisewood 22/5/62; E. Hawkins int. 1/9/87; J. Ede int. 31/5/85.
19. Martin D'Arcy to T. Stoneburner 12/4/60; to T. Stoneburner 20/12/64; H. Grisewood int. 8/83, 5/10/87.
20. DJ c. w. T. Stoneburner 5/5/66; DJ to Reginald Lawson 4/11/23; P. Tegetmeier int. 3/10/87; B. Dufort int. 9/6/86; E. Hawkins int. 1/9/87.
21. D. Cleverdon int. 6/85.
22. P. Hagreen to T. Stoneburner 1/9/69; R. Hague, *David Jones*, p. 151.
23. P. Hagreen int. 27/6/86; P. Hagreen to au. 4/11/85; P. Hagreen to R. Hague 27/2/78; P. Hagreen to au. 9/10/85; P. Hagreen int. 2/6/86, 11/10/87.
24. P. Hagreen to au. 4/11/85; P. Hagreen to R. Hague 30/4/78.
25. P. Tegetmeier int. 3/10/87, 18/6/88, 9/8/92, 22/6/90.
26. DJ c. w. T. Stoneburner 30/8/72; P. Hagreen to au. 23/11/85.
27. P. Hagreen to au. 5/9/85; P. Hagreen int. 27/6/86; T. Burns int. 13/6/88; P. Tegetmeier int. 22/6/90; P. Hagreen int. 10/87; P. Tegetmeier int. 18/6/88, 12/6/86; DJ, notes for his psychotherapist [1948]; T. Burns int. 14/6/89; Eric Gill's diary 12/1/20; Merlin James, *David Jones 1895–1974: A Map of the Artist's Mind* (London: Lund Humphries, 1995).
28. P. Hagreen int. by D. Cleverdon 1982; P. Hagreen to R. Hague 14/7/78.
29. P. Tegetmeier int. 12/6/86.
30. *DGC* 30; F. MacCarthy, *Eric Gill*, p. 148, confuses the date of his profession as a postulant with that of his profession as a tertiary; to T. Stoneburner 7/10/64.
31. Eric Gill to D. Chute 8/6/24; to Evan Gill 8/8/61; DJ, 'Autobiographical details given to D. Cleverdon 3 July 1970'; D. Cleverdon int. 6/85; to T. Stoneburner 16/11/56; DJ c. w. T. Stoneburner 5/5/66; to D. Chute 13/8/24.
32. P. Hagreen to au. 30/11/85, 13/1/86; P. Hagreen int. 27/6/86.
33. P. Tegetmeier int. 3/10/87; to H. Grisewood 12/8/56; A. Dorenkamp, '*In the Order*', p. 72; to Juliet Shirley-Smith 4/8/61; 'DJ life for Jim Ede', TS 5/9/35; E. Hawkins int. 15/6/88; P. Tegetmeier int. 3/10/87.
34. P. Tegetmeier int. 22/6/90, 9/8/92, 12/6/86, 18/6/88, 3/10/87.
35. Eric Gill to D. Chute 19/10/24.

Chapter 6

1. A. Dorenkamp, *'In the Order'*, p. 15; D. Attwater, *Cell*, p. 89; R. Hague to T. Stoneburner 21/10/n.y./, 8/1/63.
2. P. Tegetmeier int. 3/10/87, 22/6/90.
3. To T. Stoneburner 29/6/65; P. Tegetmeier int. 6/88.
4. P. Tegetmeier int. 18/6/88, 12/6/86; to J. Stone 20/11/63; J. Hague int. by W. Blissett 8/77; to V.Wynne-Williams 22/8/60.
5. DJ int. by S. Lewis 1965, in Michael Alexander, 'David Jones', BBC Radio 2 programme, 1977; P. Hagreen to au. 10/4/86.
6. To N. Gray 14/4/61.
7. To A. Giardelli 29/9/66.
8. To P. Hagreen 26/3/25; Dyfrig Rushton and Alban Léotaud int. 11/6/86.
9. To P. Hagreen 26/3/25; to Alun Oldfield Davies 21/12/60; to H. Grisewood 23/3/32.
10. DJ to W. Blissett, *Long*, pp. 71, 56.
11. Eric Gill to D. Chute 23/5/25.
12. DJ, ms note on invitation to Leslie Poulter's wedding on 26/7/24; J. Ede int. 25/6/86, 31/5/86; P. Tegetmeier int. 3/10/87.
13. P. Tegetmeier int. 18/6/88, 9/8/92.
14. P. Tegetmeier int. 18/6/88, 3/10/87, 9/8/92.
15. DJ c. w. T. Stoneburner 20/6/72; to V. Watkins 2/2/63; to R. Hague 18/5/65, 2/5/74; to Eric Gill 14/6/36.
16. R. Erangey int. 28/6/88; M. Hague int. 10/9/89; P. Tegetmeier int. 18/6/88; to R. Hague 19/1/73.
17. P. Tegetmeier int. 18/6/88; to T. Stoneburner frag. [c. 1964]; thanks to Petra Tegetmeier for permission to publish her father's writing; D. Cleverdon, *The Engravings of David Jones* (London: Clover Hill, 1981), p. 11.
18. To P. Hagreen 2nd Sunday in Lent 1927; *IN* 50; DJ int. by P. Orr early 1970s.
19. D. and N. Cleverdon int. 28/6/86; H. Grisewood to au. 31/10/90.
20. P. Tegetmeier int. 18/6/88; E. Hawkins int. 15/6/88; DJ c. w. au. 24/8/72; P. Hagreen to au. 1/3/86.
21. D. Lodge int. 20/6/88; P. Tegetmeier int. 9/8/92, 22/6/90.
22. Eric Gill to Romney Green 20/3/34; to *Universe* 7/12/34.
23. DJ to W. Blissett, *Long*, p. 10.
24. D. Cleverdon int. 6/85; to T. Stoneburner 8/9/65; N. Cleverdon int. 6/6/90.
25. To R. Hague 13/12/63; to D. Cleverdon 20/10/26, 6/85; *DG* 214, 187; to D. Cleverdon 22/6/27.
26. DJ to W. Blissett, *Long*, p. 134; D. Cleverdon, *Engravings*, p. 15; DJ quoted by R. Wald, 'I Don't Think', p. 11.

27. To Roger Billcliffe of the Walker Gallery 21/5/68; to Mr Allsop draft 6/12/44; D. Cleverdon, *Engravings*, p. 13; to D. Cleverdon 22/6/27.

28. J. Ede int. 6/85; DJ c. w. T. Stoneburner 19/6/69.

29. J. Ginger, 'A Brother's Life'.

30. R. Hague to W. Blissett 24/11/79; Robert Gibbings to Henry Bergen 31/12/27; to B. Gray 3/2/43; DJ quoted by Cleverdon, *Engravings*, p. 14; to J. Ede 29/10/35, 2/10/27, 4/11/27.

31. To D. Cleverdon 27/11/28.

32. J. Ede int. 6/85; to J. Ede 2/10/27; J. Ede int. 31/5/85; to H. Grisewood 12/12/66; Eric Gill to DJ 11/4/27; 'DJ life for Jim Ede' (5/9/35), second correction of TS 3/5/43.

33. Edward Marsh to DJ 10/5/[1927]; D. Blamires, 'An Honest Patron: A Tribute to Sir Edward Marsh', *David Jones Newsletter*, 3 (July 1976), p. 1.

34. J. Ede int. 31/5/85; J. Ede's pocket diary; J. Ede int. 27/6/88, 25/6/86; to J. Ede 12/2/36; J. Ede to R. Hague 15/11/77.

35. J. Ede int. 6/85, 31/5/85.

36. DJ quoted by R. Wald, 'I Don't Think', p. 11; J. Ede int. 25/6/86.

37. P. Tegetmeier int. 3/10/87; F. MacCarthy, 'Gibbings and Gill: Arcady in Berkshire', *Matrix,* 9 (Winter 1989), p. 30; P. Tegetmeier int. 18/6/88; R. Hague int. by P. Orr 15/2/77; D. Cleverdon int. 6/85.

38. R. Hague int. by P. Orr 15/2/77; P. Tegetmeier int. 12/6/86, 18/6/88; P. Hagreen int. 2/6/86, 27/6/86.

39. DJ quoted by R. Wald, 'I Don't Think', p. 11; to T. Stoneburner 31/3/65; DJ c. w. T. Stoneburner 19/6/69.

40. P. Tegetmeier int. 3/10/87, 18/6/88, 9/8/92, 12/6/86, 22/6/90.

41. To J. Ede 10/27, 4/11/27; Benedictine visitors' book for Caldey Island, Prinknash Archive.

42. P. Tegetmeier int. 9/8/92.

43. Thanks to P. Tegetmeier for permission to quote from this previously unpublished letter.

44. P. Tegetmeier int. 12/6/86, 18/6/88; Monica McHardy int. 13/1/86; J. Miles and D. Shiel, *Maker Unmade*, pp. 9, 248.

45. P. Hagreen int. 2/6/86, 27/6/86; P. Tegetmeier int. 18/6/88; D. Rushton int. 11/6/86.

46. To P. Hagreen 2nd Sunday in Lent 1927; to J. Ede 4/11/27; DJ c. w. au. 4/6/71; P. Tegetmeier int. 18/6/86.

47. Eric Gill diary; J. Ede int. 31/5/86, 25/6/86; Eric Gill to DJ 5/5/27; J. Ede to DJ 'Tuesday' [1927]; DJ c. w. T. Stoneburner 26/5/69.

Chapter 7

1. DJ to A. Dorenkamp, '*In the Order*', p. 17; DJ int. by P. Orr 1973; to J. Ede 4/11/27; *DG* 140–1; to S. Lewis 18/1/62; to D. Cleverdon 16/12/27.

2. DJ int. by P. Orr Summer 1972; *DGC* 198.

3. E. Hodgkin int. 5/8/87; J. Ede int. 31/5/85, 25/6/86.

4. J. Ede int. 6/85; to J. Ede 24/10/29; to P. Tegetmeier 3/10/31; to J. Ede 29/8/28; M. Adams int. 13/6/86.

5. To J. Ede 12/2/36; J. Ede int. 31/5/85; to J. Ede 16/9/63; M. Adams int. 13/6/86; E. Swan int. 24/6/86; J. Ede int. 6/85.

6. DJ c. w. T. Stoneburner 7/6/69; to J. Ede 21/2/70; to T. Stoneburner 12–16/8/68; H. S. Ede, *A Way of Life* (Cambridge: Cambridge University Press, 1984), p. 58; to K. Raine 28/3/62; to P. Tegetmeier 9/3/30; J. Ede pocket diary; DJ to W. Blissett, *Long*, p. 58.

7. J. Ede int. 31/5/85; H. Sutherland to J. Ede 9/1/27; K. Raine int. 6/85.

8. J. Ede int. 25/6/86; to D. Blamires 9/7/70; Minute book of the 7 & 5 Society.

9. H. Grisewood int. 4/10/87; to P. Tegetmeier 21/4/31; to H. Grisewood 18/2/60; DJ int. by J. Silkin 1965; DJ quoted by R. Wald, 'I Don't Think', p. 11; to K. Raine draft [1972]; to H. Sutherland 6/12/57; to J. H. Johnston 2/5/62; to R. Hague 9–15/7/73; DJ int. by Glyn Roberts, *Western Mail* 23/6/37; to R. Hague 14/6/70; 'Sign of the bear'; to P. Hagreen 22/7/37; to R. Hague 28/7/31.

10. 'Sign of the bear' p. 12; to *Tablet* 2/10/61.

11. To D. Cleverdon 17/6/28; DJ int. by Peter Orr early 1970s; DJ c. w. T. Stoneburner 7/6/69; P. Hagreen int. 27/6/86.

12. DJ c. w. T. Stoneburner 26/4/69; DJ to W. Blissett, *Long*, p. 17; to V. Wynne-Williams 2/8/61.

13. P. Hagreen to T. Stoneburner n.d.; to R. Hague 11/8/74.

14. P. Hagreen to DJ 27/3/72; to J. Ede 21/5/28.

15. To J. Ede 21/5/28; P. Hagreen to R. Hague 27/3/78.

16. To J. Ede 21/5/28; DJ int. by P. Orr 1973; P. Hagreen to S. Wright 28/1/78.

17. P. Hagreen int. 7/6/86; P. Hagreen to R. Hague 29/5/78, 18/7/78; P. Hagreen to au. 29/6/86.

18. To T. Stoneburner 9/9/69; J. Ede int. 25/6/86; to Len Walton 8/5/67.

19. To P. Tegetmeier 3/10/30; to Evan Gill 26/11/51; to H. Sutherland 26/11/63; to Miss Barber unposted 4/9/64.

20. To D. Cleverdon 16/9/27.

21. To A. Giardelli 11/8/73; *DG* 188.

22. To D. Cleverdon 30/8/28.

23. D. Cleverdon to S. Morison 7/9/28; to D. Cleverdon 9/1/29; N. Cleverdon to au. 4/8/96.

24. To D. Cleverdon 12/1/28, 26/1/28, 14/2/29.

25. To D. Cleverdon 30/8/28; Philip James, *English Book Illustration since 1800* (London: C.E.M. A., 1943–44), p. 26; D. Cleverdon, *Engravings*, pp. 17–18.

26. To D. Cleverdon 16/5/29.

27. Simon Brett, 'Seeing and Showing,' *David Jones*, ed. P. Hills, pp. 65–78.

28. To D. Cleverdon 26/9/28, 13/5/29; Hildebrand Flint int. 11/6/86; Alban Léotaud int. 11/6/86; to Fr Michael Hanbury 30/3/63; to S. Lewis 22/7/60; to Fr Sylvester 4/4/73.

29. T. Burns, *The Use of Memory* (London: Sheed & Ward, 1993), pp. 36–72; T. Burns to R. Hague 12/8/78; T. Burns int. 13/6/88.

30. T Burns int. 13/6/88; T. Burns, *Use*, pp. 5, 16, 24–5, 43; H. Grisewood int. 6/91; J. Ede to R. Hague 26/9/78.

31. T. Burns int. 14/6/89, 20/6/86; V. Ingrams int. 14/6/88.

32. To P. Tegetmeier 3/10/30; R. Hague, *David Jones*, pp. 6–7; H. Grisewood int. 5/10/87; to Nicolette Binyon 27/6/32; to J. Stone 20/11/63; R. Hague, *David Jones*, p. 5.

33. D. Lodge int. 20/6/88; D. Cleverdon int. 2/6/86.

34. D. Lodge int. 20/6/88.

35. P. Tegetmeier int. 18/6/88.

36. To R. Hague n.d.; DJ c. w. au. 4/6/71; DJ int. by P. Orr Summer 1972; DJ quoted by Brian North Lee, *Richard Shirley-Smith* (Oxford: Ashmolean, 1981), p. 2.

37. R. and J. Hague int. 8/77; to R. Hague 3/10/30.

38. F. MacCarthy, *Eric Gill*, p. 241; R. and J. Hague int. by T. Stoneburner 11/6/69.

39. M. Rothschild int. 15/12/88; J. Bacon int. 5/10/87; T. Burns int. 13/6/88.

40. To T. Stoneburner 26/8/68; R. Hague to DJ 21/5/n.y.; to Harry Whiteman draft n.d.

41. J. Ede pocket diary 1927; J. Ede int. 6/85; N. Gray, *Helen Sutherland Collection* (London: Arts Council, 1970), pp. 15–16, 26, 22; H. Sutherland to J. Ede 25/3/29; to H. Sutherland 7/10/29; K. Raine int. 26/6/86; H. Sutherland to N. Gray int. 17/6/84.

42. To D. Travis 29/12/60; H. Grisewood int. 6/91.

43. To Mr [Thomas] Whitaker draft n.d. [1970]; DJ quoted in A. Dorenkamp, *In the Order*, p. 17; *DGC* 83; to J. Ede 24/10/29; J. Rothenstein, *Modern English Painters*, Vol. II, p. 218.

44. H. Grisewood int. 19/6/90; J. Ede int. 31/5/85.

45. To H. Grisewood 6/2/51; Friedrich von Hügel, *Letters to a Niece* (Chicago: Henry Regnery, 1955), pp. 119, 115.

46. T. Burns, *Use*, p. 49; to R. Hague 10/10/63; to Francis Harlow frag n.d.; to T. Burns 1/11/41; H. Grisewood int. 19/6/90, 4/10/87, 8/83; F. Howard int. 16/6/90; H. Grisewood int. 16/6/89; T. Burns int. 14/6/88; T. Burns, *Use*, p. 41; J. Bacon int. 22/6/88.

47. K. Raine int. 26/6/86; D. Cleverdon int. 28/6/86; to T. Stoneburner 16/12/65.

48. To P. Tegetmeier 3/10/30; DJ int. by P. Orr early 1970s; W. Blissett, *Long*, p. 61; T. Burns, *Use*, p. 42; Barbara Wall, p. 20.

49. T. Burns to DJ 9/1/28; H. Grisewood int. 19/6/90.

50. H. Grisewood int. 5/10/87; Christopher Dawson, *Christianity and Sex* (London: Faber and Faber, 1930), pp. 33, 35, passages marked by DJ; Edward Ingram Watkin, *The Bow in the Clouds* (London: Sheed & Ward, 1931), pp. 110–18; *Tablet* 13/3/51; to H. Grisewood 12/4/51; to J. H. Johnston 16/5/62; DJ c. w. au. 4/6/71; H. Grisewood int. 21/7/96.

51. To J. H. Johnston 16/5/62; to S. Lewis 4/71; DJ c. w. au. 24/8/72.

52. R. Hague, *David Jones*, p. 39; to T. Stoneburner 30/8/63; H. Grisewood int. 8/85, 4/10/87; to H. Grisewood 14/4/39; P. Orr, *The Poet Speaks* (London: Routledge, 1966), p. 103.

53. H. Grisewood int. 23/6/86; E. I. Watkin, *Bow*, pp. 55–8.

54. DJ c. w. au. 24/8/72; to J. Knight 16/1/44; C. Dawson, *Progress*, pp. 233, 158, 4, passages marked by DJ; H. Grisewood int. 8/83; see C. Wilcockson, 'David Jones and "The Break"', *Agenda* 15:2–3 (1977), pp. 130–1; to H. Grisewood 15/2/57.

55. H. Grisewood int. 5/6/86; T. Burns int. 20/6/86.

56. T. Burns int. 14/6/89; H. Grisewood int. 19/6/90.

57. E. I. Watkin, *Bow*, pp. 131–7; to H. Grisewood 23/3/32; DJ c. w. au. 4/6/71.

58. T. Burns int. 14/6/89; to H. Grisewood 5/10/48.

59. To D. Travis 14/1/35; to H. Grisewood 23/3/32.

60. H. Grisewood int. 16/6/89; to H. Grisewood 9/10/71; H. Grisewood int. 4/10/87.

61. H. Grisewood int. 22/6/86.

62. T. Burns int. 13/6/88, 20/6/86; DJ c. w. T. Stoneburner 30/8/72; Charles Burns, 'Psychology and Catholics', *Blackfriars*, 31 (March 1950), pp. 120, 122; to C. Burns 20/10/52.

63. T. Burns int. 14/6/89; DJ int. by J. Silkin, 1965; to P. Tegetmeier 9/3/30; to L. W. Griffith 12/9/64; DJ quoted in Anon., 'Words Gone to War', *Time Magazine* 6/4/62, p. 100; to J. H. Johnston 2/5/62.

64. To R. Hague 9–15/7/73; to J. H. Johnston frag. unposted 27/4/62; DJ, 'Looking Back at the Thirties', p. 52; to H. Grisewood 20/1/72.

65. H. Grisewood int. 15/9/96, 5/10/87; to H. Grisewood 30/3/35; H. Grisewood int. 16/6/89, 4/10/87; DJ c. w. au. 5/6/71.

66. H. Grisewood int. 5/10/87; to Laurence Binyon 13/7/37; to J. H. Johnston 24/8/62.

67. H. Grisewood int. 16/6/89; to J. H. Johnston 24/8/62; to D. Travis 29/12/60; DJ c. w. au. 4/6/71; to K. Raine 28/3/62.

68. To T. Stoneburner 30/8/63; to J. H. Johnston 3/3/63; to J. Ede 9/12/49.

69. To R. Hague 2/12/35.

70. To T. Stoneburner 16/12/65; E. Hodgkin int. 6/8/87; 'Sign of the bear'; DJ quoted by S. Honeyman 20/6/86.

71. H. Grisewood int. 3/6/86; J. Ede int. 25/6/86; DJ int. by J. Silkin 1965.

72. R. Hague to J. Ede 3/6/65; to H. Grisewood 4th Sunday after Easter 1966; H. Grisewood int. 5/10 87; to H. Grisewood 9/10/71; H. Grisewood int. 23/6/86; to V. Wynne-Williams 11/8/62; to K. Clark 16/11/60, 3/8/60; DJ c. w. P. Hills int. 11/6/91; Ariane Bankes, P. Hills, *The Art of David Jones, Vision and Memory* (London: Lund Humphries, 2015).

73. H. Grisewood int. 16/6/89; to J. Knight 16/1/44; to N. Binyon 10/6/32.

74. B. Dixon int. 17/6/89; to V. Wynne-Williams 11/2/63; T. Burns int. 20/6/86.

75. Arthur Wheen to DJ 18/2/64; S. Honeyman int. 20/6/86.

76. H. Grisewood int. 5/10/87; P. Tegetmeier int. 18/6/88; T. Burns int. 14/6/89; DJ int. by P. Orr early 1970s; vision scientist James M. Hillis c. w. au. 28/9/2002.

77. E. Hawkins int. 15/6/88; D. MacCartney-Filgate to E. Skelton 18/4/80; to F. Wall 27/6/44.

78. Eve Clark int. 17/2/91; T. Burns int. 14/6/88; E. Q. Nicholson int. 7/6/90.

79. H. Grisewood to au. 16/2/90; DJ c. w. au. 4/6/71; to P. Tegetmeier 3/10/30.

80. To Helen Ede 13/8/28; to S. Lewis 14/6/72.

81. To P. Tegetmeier 1/11/30.

82. To P. Tegetmeier 3/10/30; to E. Hodgkin 25/10/30; to P. Tegetmeier 21/10/30, 23/12/30; to H. Grisewood 25/12/30.

83. H. S. Ede, 'David Jones', p. 129; to J. Ede 24/10/29.

Chapter 8

1. To D. Cleverdon 30/8/28, 16/5/29, 13/5/29; *EA* 280; to N. Binyon 9/6/32; to H. Read 21/9/64.

2. T. Burns int. 14/6/89; to H. Grisewood 12/8/56; Louis Bussell to T. Stoneburner 21/8/69; C. Scott int. 15/6/90.

3. To H. Ede 30/4/30; DJ int. by P. Orr Summer 1972; to Mr Allsop draft unposted 6/12/44; Guy Davenport to au. 1/96.

4. P. Hagreen int. by D. Cleverdon, TS 1982.

5. M. Hague int. 10/9/89; E. Montague int. 9/9/89.

6. To N. Binyon 8/7/31; to H. Grisewood 5/8/52.

7. To R. and J. Shirley-Smith 11/2/61.

8. P. Tegetmeier int.18/6/88; K. Clark int. by M. Alexander.

9. To P. Tegetmeier 3/10/31; to T. Stoneburner 6/3/65, 12–16/8/68.

10. H. Grisewood int. 16/6/89, 5/10/87, 5/6/86.

11. To H. Sutherland 29/10/31.

12. To P. Tegetmeier 3/8/31; E. Hodgkin to au. 19/5/96.

13. E. Hodgkin int. 5/8/87; to E. Hodgkin 14/9/38.

14. S. Balme int. 24/6/88.

15. To R. Hague 2/8/35; to H. Grisewood 12–14/1/68; to H. Sutherland 7/10/29; *IP* 180.

16. To H. Grisewood 3/10/38, 4/10/38; M. Adams int. 13/6/86; to H. Grisewood 5/8/31; E. Hodgkin, 'Some Memories', TS n.d.

17. To R. Hague 17/9/35; K. Raine, *The Land Unknown* (London: Hamish Hamilton, 1975), p. 135; K. Raine int. 26/6/86.

18. K. Raine int. 6/85; J. Ede int. 6/85; H. Sutherland to J. Ede n.d.; N. Gray int. 17/6/86.

19. E. Hodgkin int. 5/8/87.

20. To J. Stone 15/3/65; to R. Hague 5/11/64, 2/6/55.

21. To J. Stone 15/3/65; to H. Grisewood 1–16/2/66, 20/7/35; H. Grisewood int. 6/91, 4/10/87, 8/83.

22. E. Hodgkin int. 5/8/87, 16/3/98; D. Hodgkin int. 19/6/89.

23. E. Hodgkin int. 5/8/87; E. Hodgkin, 'Some Memories'.

24. S. Honeyman int. 20/6/86; Barbara Wall int. by T. Stoneburner n.d.; to R. Hague 10/11/34; to J. Stone 4/4/63.

25. To R. Hague 18/10/34; E. Hodgkin int. 5/8/87.

26. E. Hodgkin int. 5/8/87; to P. Tegetmeier 2/5/33; to R. Hague 27/9/63; to E. Hodgkin 14/9/38.

27. To R. Hague 4/5/74; to J. Stone 30/3/65; to S. Lewis 13/7/72; to H. Grisewood 7/7/71.

28. To J. Stone 15/3/65; to S. Honeyman 14/11/71; to T. Hyne 19/6/74; E. Hodgkin int. 5/8/87.

29. To E. Evans 14/11/53; to T. Hodgkin 23/11/73; to S. Wright 6/12/72; E. Hodgkin to au. 17/9/97.

30. H. Sutherland to J. Ede 3/6/32; H. Sutherland to DJ 28/10/52; E. Hodgkin int. 5/8/87.

31. R. Hague int. by P. Orr 15/2/77; DJ int. by P. Orr Summer 1972; DJ c. w. au. 4/6/71.

32. DJ int. by P. Orr 1973.

33. P. Hills int. 11/6/91.

34. H. Grisewood int. 19/6/90, 4/10/91, 6/91, 5/10/87; H. Grisewood, *One Thing at a Time* (London: Hutchinson, 1968), pp. 72, 75.

35. A. Giardelli int. 8/6/86; A. Hamilton, 'From David Jones', p.21.

36. To N. Binyon 16/2/32; DJ int. by P. Orr 1973; to *Catholic Herald* 22/8/52.

37. To R. Hague 27/9/74.

38. To Dom Michael draft n.d.; H. Grisewood int. 19/6/90.

39. H. Grisewood to au. 16/2/90; DJ, 'Further Note on the Great Divorce', unpublished TS intended as a note to 'Art and Sacrament' in *Catholic Approaches*.

40. To H. Grisewood 1/1/64, 14/2/38, 8/10/35; H. Grisewood int. 4/10/87; S. Honeyman int. 9/10/87.

41. V. Ingrams int. 1/5/93.

42. H. Grisewood int. 23/6/86.

43. To J. H. Johnston 24/8/62; T.Burns int. 20/6/86.

44. To T. Stoneburner 12–16/8/68.

45. T. Burns int. 14/6/88; V. Wynne-Williams 18/10/62.

46. To H. Sutherland 8/4/32; to N. Binyon 9/6/32.

47. J. Ede, 'David Jones', *Horizon*, 7:44 (August 1943), p. 130; S. Brett, 'Seeing', p. 72.

48. To *Tablet* 2/10/61, 1/7/66.

49. R. Hague to H. Grisewood 29/1/76.

50. *IP* ms note; *EA* 248.

51. J. Ede to Richard de la Mare 10/11/38; R. de la Mare to DJ 17/10/32; to R. de la Mare 20/10/32.

52. To N. Binyon 11/7/32.

53. To R. Hague 1/1/73.

54. DJ to W. Blissett, *Long*, p. 13; N. Gray, *The Paintings of David Jones* (Hatfield: J.Taylor/Tate Gallery, 1989), p. 34; to J. Ede 19/8/43.

55. K. Raine int. 26/6/86; K. Raine, *Land*, p. 132.

56. To J. Ede 15/4/43; to Miss Hirst n.d.; to S. Lewis 18/9/70; to P. Tegetmeier 3/10/30; to N. Binyon 11/7/32; R. Hague int. by T. Stoneburner 11/6/69; R. Hague int. by W. Blissett 8/77; P. Pelham to M. Rothschild to au. 9/8/88.

57. To J. Asquith 21/3/39; to K. Raine 20/6/59; to H. Grisewood 20/1/72.

58. DJ to W. Blissett, *Long*, p. 67; DJ c. w. au. 4/6/71; DJ c. w. T. Stoneburner 19/6/69; Dr James Wood to the National Service 20/11/41.

59. N. Gray int. 17/6/88; to H. Grisewood 31/3/72; S. Wright int. 26/6/86; DJ to P. Pelham n.d.

60. To C. Burns 29/5/40; T. Burns int. 14/6/88.

61. H. Grisewood int. 8/83, 16/6/89, 23/6/86; to T. Stoneburner 12–16/8/68.

Chapter 9

1. To P. Tegetmeier 8/2/33; to R. Hague 22/11/34.
2. To P. Tegetmeier Good Friday 1934; T. Burns int. 14/6/88; to D. Tegetmeier 14/1/35; to P. Tegetmeier 17/4/34; DJ c. w. au. 4/6/71.
3. T. Burns int. 14/6/89, 2/6/86.
4. To S. Piggott 20/11/59; to P. Tegetmeier 2-3/5/34.
5. To H. Grisewood 4/3/60; to Victoria Reid 3/5/34; to P. Tegetmeier 2-3/5/34; to Ruth Daniels unposted 1/45.
6. H. Grisewood int. 4/10/87.
7. Thomas Hodgkin, *Letters from Palestine 1932-36*, ed. E. C. Hodgkin (London, New York: Quartet Books, 1986), p. 38; Eric Gill, *From the Palestine Diary* (London: Harvill Press, 1949), p. 69; to T. Stoneburner 30/7/69.
8. T. Hodgkin, *Palestine*, p. 60; to V. Reid 3/5-11/6/34; to R. Hague 23/9/35; T. Hodgkin, *Palestine*, p. 57.
9. To V. Reid 3/5-11/6/34.
10. Eric Gill diary; DJ to W. Blissett, *Long*, p. 144.
11. DJ c. w. T. Stoneburner 19/6/69.
12. T. Hodgkin, *Palestine*, pp. 60, 65.
13. To S. Lewis 4/71.
14. P. Pelham to E. Hodgkin 1/6/36; T. Hodgkin, *Palestine*, pp. 64, 66, 67, 60; P. Pelham to DJ 22/11/ [36].
15. To V. Reid 3/5-11/6/34.
16. To S. Lewis 4/71; DJ int. by P. Orr [c. 1969]; to Clarissa Churchill 14/11/40; DJ c. w. au. 4/6/71.
17. T. Hodgkin, *Palestine*, p. 71; to S. Lewis 4/71.
18. Eric Gill, *Palestine*, p. 34; to P. Tegetmeier 7/7/34.
19. To H. Grisewood 8/7/34; E. Hodgkin int. 5/8/87; DJ c. w. T. Stoneburner 19/6/69; to P. Tegetmeier 7/7/34.
20. T. Burns int. 13/6/88, 14/6/89; H. Grisewood to au. 24/9/86; H. Grisewood int. 8/85.
21. D. Smith int. 30/1/88; P. Burns to au. 19/9/90; T. Burns to R. Hague 12/8/78; T. Burns int. 14/6/88, 20/6/86; to T. Burns 30/7/40; S. Honeyman int. 6/86.
22. Richard Kehoe to T. Stoneburner [1972].
23. D. Poulter int. 11/6/90.
24. To R. Hague 4/10/34; S. and M. Balme int. 17/6/90.
25. To R. Hague 4/10/34; E. Hodgkin, 'Some Memories'.
26. To V. Eliot draft [5/1/65]; DJ c. w. T. Stoneburner 9/6/66.
27. To H. Sutherland 1/11/34.

28. To H. Sutherland 1/11/34; to R. Hague 17/9/35; to H. Sutherland 15/1/35.

29. To J. Stone 4/4/63; to R. Hague 22/11/34; S. Honeyman int. 14/6/91.

30. To R. Hague 22/11/34; to T. Stoneburner 18/7/72; S. Honeyman int. 1/9/87.

31. H. Grisewood int. 16/6/89, 4/10/87; DJ pocket diary.

32. To R. Hague 5/1/35, 18/2/36; to Eric Gill 21/2/35; to H. Grisewood 1/1/64; to J. Ede 7/3/35, 5/2/35; to H. Sutherland 3/1/39; to N. Gray 10–11/1/35; to R. Hague 14/12/73, 18/2/36.

33. DJ c. w. T. Stoneburner 7/6/69; to R. Hague 18/1[sic]/35, 28/4/35; to J. Ede 11/3/35; P. Pelham to DJ 29/11/35; to H. Grisewood 13/4/40, 17/5/72; to R. Hague 3/6/35.

34. To J. Ede 18/11/34; to R. Hague 17/9/35; to H. Ede 5/2/35.

35. To D. Tegetmeier 9/1/35; to P. Tegetmeier 17/2/36; to N. Gray 24/6/36.

36. To R. Hague 3/6/35; to H. Grisewood 30/3/35; C. Scott int. 26/6/86.

37. To R. Hague 18/1[sic]/35.

38. To H. Grisewood 30/3/35; DJ to M. Elkin int. 23/4/95; to H. Grisewood 30/3/35.

39. To J. Ede 11/3/35; to R. Hague 2/4/35, 5/3/35; P. Pelham to DJ 5/4/35.

40. To R. Hague 29/4/35.

41. P. Pelham to DJ 29/11/35; Robert Buhler int. 6/85; H. Grisewood int. 5/10/87.

42. M. Richey int. 15/12/88; E. Hodgkin int. 5/8/87, 6/8/87; to R. Hague 24/8/35.

43. E. Hodgkin int. 5/8/87; P. Pelham to DJ n.d. (from here on, her undated letters to him are uncited); M. Richey int. 15/12/88; P. Pelham to DJ 29/11/35; to R. Hague 27/9/63.

44. R. Buhler int. 16/6/88.

45. P. Pelham to DJ 8/4/37; M. Richey int. 15/12/88; R. Buhler int. 15/6/88; J. Miles and D. Shiel, Maker Unmade, p. 253; H. Grisewood int. 19/6/90.

46. R. Buhler int. 6/85; M. Richey int. 15/12/88.

47. P. Pelham to DJ 22/11/[35]; to J. Ede 11/4/37; P. Pelham to DJ 8/4/37.

48. To R. Hague 29/4/35, 16/5/35.

49. To R. Hague 23/6/35; to J. Ede 11/3/35.

50. To R. Hague 2/8/35, 3/6/35.

51. To J. Ede 11/3/35; prescription filled 22/8/35 at Alnwick.

52. To P. Tegetmeier 29/6/35; to N. Gray 3/10/36.

53. To R. Hague 10/7/35; to H. Grisewood 20/7/35.

54. To H. Grisewood 20/7/35, 25/7/35; Julian Trevelyan, *Indigo Days* (Aldershot: Scolar, 1996), p. 92.

55. To J. Hague 17/9/35.

56. To R. Hague 2/8/35; S. Honeyman int. 20/6/86; DJ to K. Raine 1946; P. Pelham to R. and J. Hague 16/8/35.

57. To R. Hague 10/7/35; to H. Grisewood 20/7/35; to R. Hague 2/8/35.

58. To H. Grisewood 8/10/35; R. Shepherd int. 28/6/89.

59. To H. Sutherland 27/1/41; S. Honeyman int. 9/10/87; to R. Hague 29/4/66; *IN* 76.

60. To H. Grisewood 18/5/56; to R. Hague Holy Saturday 1932; *IN* 50.

61. To S. Lewis 18/9/70; to A. Giardelli 9–11/8/73; to H. Grisewood 8/8/42.

62. To H. Grisewood 10/8/53, 30/3/35; to R. Hague 2/5/74; to S. Lewis 18/9/70; H. Grisewood int. 16/6/89.

63. DJ c. w. au. 24/8/72; to J. Ede 7/3/35, 6/6/43; to T. Burns 28/8/40; to R. Hague 14/6/70; DJ c. w. au. 4/6/71; to R. Hague 27/9/63.

64. To J. Hague 2/5/62; to H. Grisewood 14/4/39, 29/2/60.

65. *LF* 80–1; *EA* 239; to J. Ede 15/4/43.

66. To V. Watkins 17/4/62; to J. Ede 15/4/43, 18/1/34, 15/4/43.

67. *EA* 239.

68. To H. Grisewood 12/8/57; to S. Lewis 22/7/48.

69. To H. Grisewood 8/10/35; to R. Hague 24/8/35.

70. To L. Binyon 13/7/37; to R. Hague 7/11/35, 12/12/35, Easter 1936.

71. To J. Ede 8/2/36, 29/3/37; to R. Hague 5/2/36.

72. To R. Hague 5/3/36.

73. To J. Ede 20/3/36; C. Scott int. 26/6/86; to R. Hague 23/3/36; to J. Ede 25/7/36.

74. DJ ms note 5/51; to R. Hague 1/3/36; *IP* 54.

75. To J. Ede 8/2/36.

76. To J. Ede 3/4/36, 20/3/36; to R. Hague Easter 1936; to J. Ede 29/3/37.

77. To C. Churchill 7/2/40; to J. Ede 20/3/36, 2/7/36.

78. To J. Ede 3/4/36; *EA* 266.

79. To J. Ede 22/6/36; J. Ede to DJ 6/6/36; J. Ede int. 31/5/85; to J. Ede 3/4/36, 8/2/36.

80. To F. Wall 27/6/44; C. Scott int. 26/6/86.

81. To R. Hague 11/2/36; to H. Sutherland 28/11/39; R. Hague int. by W. Blissett 8/77.

82. To J. Ede 8/2/36, 2/7/36.

83. DJ, 'David Jones Artist and Writer', a taped commentary on his paintings; H. Sutherland to E. Hodgkin n.d.

84. T. Hodgkin, *Palestine*, p. 168; to R. Hague 1/3/36, 5/2/36; P. Pelham to DJ 3 or 4/8/[36].

85. To N. Gray 3/10/36; R. de la Mare to DJ 1/10/36, 13/10/36; R. de la Mare to John Easton 5/11/36; R. de la Mare to DJ 20/1/37.

86. To H. Grisewood 7/3/41; Dora Griffin to Kevin Cecil quoted by D. Blamires, 'David Jones at Sidmouth', *David Jones Newsletter* 13 (May 1978), p. 4; to H. Grisewood 8/8/42; Col. Hastings to DJ 16/1/40; to R. Hague 12/12/35, 25/2/36; to H. Grisewood 7/3/41; H. Grisewood int. 8/83, 19/6/90.

87. T. Burns int. 14/6/89; H. Grisewood int. 8/83; T. Burns, *Use*, p. 74; P. Pelham to E. Hodgkin n.d.

88. To V. Wynne-Williams 20/6/1961; H. Grisewood int. 8/83; H. Grisewood *One Thing*, pp. 102–5; to H. Grisewood 17/5/72; to *The Times* draft [6/72]; to H. Grisewood 17/5/72, 1–16/2/66; to T. Stoneburner 30/7/69; DJ c. w. au. 4/6/71; to J. Ede 6/3/37; to H. Grisewood 18/6/40; to T. Stoneburner 12–16/8/68.

89. To Anthony Powell 10–11/7/67; A. Powell to au. 17/1/90.

90. J. Ede int. 31/5/85; to J. Ede 8/2/36, 25/11/36.

91. To J. Ede 25/11/36, 6/3/37; to R. de la Mare 5/5/37; to J. Ede 11/4/37; R. Hague to H. Grisewood 29/1/76.

92. P. Pelham to DJ 8/2/37.

93. To P. Tegetmeier 17/2/36; Martha Sprackland to au. 6/4/2016.

94. To L. Binyon 13/7/37; thanks to N. Gray for permission to quote from her father's letter; to H. Sutherland 11/7/37.

95. H. Read, 'War and the Spirit', *TLS*, 19/6/37, p. 457; DJ int. by P. Orr early 1970s; H. Grisewood int. 5/10/87; to J. H. Johnston [1/65], 17/4/62, 2/5/62; K. Raine int. 26/6/86.

96. To J. Ede 29/3/37; to Beryl de Zoete frag. unposted 20/10/38.

97. To E. Hodgkin 18/11/36; DJ c. w. au. 9/9/72, 31/8/72.

98. T. S. Eliot, 'A Note of Introduction', *In Parenthesis* (London: Faber, 1961), p. vii; W. H. Auden, 'The Geste Says This and the Man Who was on the Field', *Mid-Century Review*, 39 (March 1962), pp. 12, 1, 3; Graham Greene, *Ways of Escape* (London: Bodley Head, 1980), p. 28; Michael Howard, *The Lessons of History* (New Haven: Yale, 1991), p. 185; Adam Thorpe, 'Distressed perspectives', *Poetry Review*, 86 (Spring 1996), p. 56; to H. Grisewood 14/2/38.

Chapter 10

1. To H. Sutherland 11/7/37; DJ c. w. au. 24/8/72; to J. H. Johnston 16/5/64.

2. To H. Sutherland 11/7/37; DJ to P. Kelly int. 9/6/86.

3. To H. Grisewood 5/4/73.

4. H. Grisewood int. 4/10/87; M. Richey int. 7/6/86, 18/6/89;
P. Tegetmeier int. 22/6/90; M. Hague int. 10/9/89.

5. DJ to W. Blissett, *Long*, p. 123; to J. Ede 5/10/43; P. Pelham to
E. Hodgkin [23/9/37]; W. Blissett, *Long*, p. 36; to H. Grisewood
14/2/38.

6. To J. Ede 19/10/37; to Gladys Evans unposted n.d.; to V. Wynne-
Williams 22/10/60.

7. T. Hyne int. 6/85, 24/6/86; to S. Lewis 10/72.

8. To T. Stoneburner 12–16/8/68; Joseph Jones to DJ 19/1/48; *Chester
Chronicle* 2/7/38.

9. To H. Sutherland 22/5/37; to J. Ede 5/11/37; to P. Tegetmeier
4/11/37; T. Burns int. 20/6/86.

10. To P. Donner 5/7/62; to T. Burns 4–9/8/63; to H. Grisewood
9/5/41; to V. Wynne-Williams 9/8/59.

11. D. Smith (neé Creagh) to au. 1/10/92; D. Smith int. 30/1/88.

12. D. Smith int. 30/6/88; D. Smith to au. 19/3/88; to D. Smith draft
24/3/62; D. Smith to au. 22/9/86.

13. DJ, 'Fragments of an Attempted Autobiographical Writing', p. 101; to
H. Grisewood 12/4/51.

14. H. Grisewood int. 5/10/87, 8/83.

15. W. Blissett, *Long*, p. 21.

16. P. Pelham to DJ 22/12/36; to E. Hodgkin 18/11/36.

17. P. Pelham to E. Hodgkin n.d.; E. Hodgkin int. 6/8/87.

18. D. Cleverdon int. 28/6/86; N. Cleverdon int. 25/6/90; to
H. Grisewood 14/2/38; to J. Ede 27/6/38.

19. To A. Giardelli 9–11/8/73; D. Cleverdon, *Engravings*, p. 22; to
H. Grisewood 14/2/38.

20. To H. Grisewood 9/6/46; DJ, notes for the Tate Gallery 10/58.

21. To A. Giardelli 11/8/73.

22. To J. Ede 27/6/38; N. White to au. 12/2/96.

23. To H. Grisewood 31/5/38.

24. To P. Hagreen 1/7/38; DJ quoted by Correspondent, 'The
Hawthornden Prize: 1938', *Tablet* 2/7/38, p. 19: to H. Grisewood
31/5/38; to J. Ede 16/6/38, 27/6/38.

25. To T. Stoneburner 12–16/8/68.

26. S. Honeyman to H. Grisewood 25/9/84; to L. Bussell 30/9/39; to
J. Ede 11/4/39; S. Honeyman int. 1/9/87.

27. T. Burns int. 14/6/89; H. Grisewood int. 8/83; M. Richey to au.
3/7/89; M. Richey int. 18/6/89.

28. T. Burns int. 14/6/89; D. Smith to au. 23/11/86, 5/7/86; to
L. Bussell 30/9/39.

29. D. Smith to au. 10/1/87; to H. Grisewood 24/4/39; H. Grisewood int. 8/83; S. Honeyman to H. Grisewood 25/9/84.

30. DJ to S. Honeyman int. 20/6/86, 10/87; DJ int. by J. Silkin 1965; to R. Hague 11/8/74.

31. S. Honeyman to H. Grisewood 25/9/84; to R. Hague 11/8/74.

32. H. Grisewood to au. 10/8/84; C. Dawson, *Beyond Politics* (London: Sheed & Ward, 1939), p. 83.

33. H. Grisewood int. 23/6/86; M. Richey int. 18/6/89.

34. C. Dawson, *Understanding Europe* (London: Sheed & Ward, 1952), p. 240, passage marked with three marginal lines by DJ; David Jones, 'Poetry and Anarchy', *Tablet* 16/7/38, p. 77; to T. Hodgkin 12/11/35; T. Burns int. 2/6/86.

35. T. Burns int. 2/6/86, 14/6/88; H. Grisewood 16/6/89; J. Roggendorf, *Between Two Cultures* (Folkstone: Global Oriental, 2004), pp. 5, 23, 25, 27, 42.

36. S. Honeyman int. 6/86.

37. To H. Sutherland 3/1/39; to C. Churchill 14/11/40.

38. To H. Grisewood 3/10/38, 24/9/38; to T. Stoneburner 30/7/69; to B. de Zoete frag. unposted 20/10/38; DJ c. w au. 9/9/72.

39. Katharine Asquith to DJ 7/8/37.

40. To T. Stoneburner 20/12/64.

41. To C. Churchill 16/5/40; S. Hampshire int. 22/1/89.

42. To H. Grisewood 17/1/39, 14/4/39; to J. Ede 11/4/39; to D. Attwater 10/12/44.

43. To J. Ede 11/4/39; to J. Asquith 21/3/39.

44. P. Pelham to DJ 21/5/39; to J. Asquith 21/3/39; to J. Ede 11/4/39; Markby, Steward & Wadesons to Elizabeth Pelham 3/12/52; to J. Ede 11/4/39; to H. Grisewood 23/6/39.

45. P. Levi int. 17/2/91; to T. Stoneburner 20/12/64; to H. Grisewood 23/6/39; V. Turner int. 10/87.

46. To T. Stoneburner 16/12/65; *EA* 257; to H. Grisewood 4/10/87; V. Turner int. 10/87; Maurice Collis, *Stanley Spencer* (London: Harvill Press, 1962), pp. 157–9.

47. Stanley Spencer, *Letters and Writings*, ed. Adrian Glew (London: Tate, 2001), p. 193; V. Turner int. 10/87; R. Buhler int. 15/6/88; to T. Stoneburner 16/12/65; S. Honeyman int. 1/9/87.

48. To H. Sutherland 28/7/52.

49. To V. Wynne-Williams 12/6/64; DJ ms draft [c. 1970]; to T. Stoneburner 30/7/69; to J. Asquith 5/3/40; to K. Asquith 3/8/39.

50. To K. Asquith 3/8/39.

51. To J. Asquith 3/8/39.

52. To C. Churchill 29/9/39; *DGC* 175; to J. Asquith 8/7/39.

53. J. Asquith int. 20/6/89; to K. Asquith 3/8/39, 21/9/39.
54. To K. Asquith 3/8/39.

Chapter 11

1. To H. Grisewood 13/4/40; H. Grisewood int. 4/10/87.
2. To J. Asquith 4/10/39; H. Grisewood to au. 29/7/84; T. Burns int. 14/6/89.
3. *The Times* 10/1/40; to P. Tegetmeier 27/1/40.
4. To H. Sutherland 6/9/40; DJ's 1944 pocket diary.
5. To P. Tegetmeier 27/1/40; to Valerie Price 7/2/60.
6. To H. Grisewood, 19/3/40.
7. To H. Grisewood, 19/3/40, 13/4/40.
8. To C. Burns 29/5/40; to H. Grisewood 16/5/40; DJ draft frag. 3/6/40.
9. To C. Burns 29/5/40; to H. Grisewood draft 6/6/40.
10. To H. Grisewood 18/6/40; M. Grisewood int. 21/6/97.
11. To H. Grisewood 18/6/40, 7/3/41; to T. Burns 29/1/41, 28/8/40; to T. Stoneburner 19/9/64; T. Burns int. 14/6/89.
12. To H. Grisewood 21/5/40; to T. Burns 4/9/40; *DG* 100; to T. Burns 28/8/40.
13. To T. Burns 4/9/40; to H. Sutherland 6/9/40; to T. Burns 28/8/40; DJ c. w. au. 9/9/72; Ann (Bowes-Lyon) D'Abreu int. 1/5/95; H. Grisewood int. 4/10/87.
14. To T. Burns 14/8/40, 27/11/40.
15. To C. Churchill 14/11/40; to H. Grisewood 5/2/68; to J. Ede 29–30/8/42; to T. Burns 4/9/40; to H. Sutherland 6/9/40; H. Grisewood int. 8/83; N. Gray int. 17/6/86.
16. H. Grisewood int. 8/83, 4/10/87.
17. To H. and M. Grisewood 14/12/65; to H. Sutherland 16/9/40; to T. Burns 14/8/40.
18. To R. Hague 9/9/74.
19. To J. Ede 29–30/8/42; M. Grisewood int. 26/9/89, 24/6/89, 8/6/90.
20. To T. Burns 14/8/40; to H. Sutherland 6/9/40.
21. To T. Burns 28/8/40, 29/1/41.
22. *WP* 26–30.
23. To P. Hagreen 12/12/40; DJ quoted in A. Hamilton, 'From David Jones', p.21; to T. Stoneburner 15/5/67; to Will Carter 16/9/65.
24. To C. Churchill 14/11/40; to T. Burns 29/1/41.
25. James, *A Map of the Artist's Mind*, p. 46; Julian Bell, 'Moon Behind Clouds', *TLS* 5/4/96, p. 10; J. Miles and D. Shiel, *Maker Unmade*, p. 258.
26. B. Moray int. 6/85.

27. L. Jebb and Cecilia Hall int. 12/6/91; to T. Burns 15/4/41.

28. Daphne Pollen to T. Stoneburner 21/10/75.

29. Arthur Pollen to D. Pollen [Spring 1941]; D. Pollen to T. Stoneburner 21/10/75.

30. To J. Ede 29–30/8/42.

31. To T. Burns 21/6/41.

32. DJ *Word and Image*, p. 51; DJ to the Tate Gallery 10/58; J. Rothenstein to DJ 10/6/41, 8/12/41.

33. J. Ede int. 6/85, 31/5/86, 25/6/86; K. Clark to J. Ede 28/8/36; DJ to P. Hills int. 11/6/91; DJ int. by P. Orr late 1960s; S. Honeyman int. 20/6/86; to J. Stone 1962; A. S. Hartrick *Painter's Pilgrimage*, p. 9 (DJ's copy).

34. K. Clark to T. Stoneburner 1/7/77; K. Clark to J. Ede 29/8/36; K. Clark to H. Grisewood 17/8/53; K. Clark quoted by J. Stone int. 2/10/87; K. Clark int. by M. Alexander, 'David Jones'.

35. H. Grisewood int. 8/83; to K. Clark 11/3/54; K. Clark to DJ 9/2/61; S. Balme int. 17/6/90.

36. D. Pollen to T. Stoneburner 21/10/75; to T. Burns 21/6/41.

37. To T. Burns 21/9/41; to J. Ede 15/1/45.

38. P. Tegetmeier int. 18/6/88; to T. Burns 21/9/41; to P. Tegetmeier 3/11/41.

39. To H. Grisewood Whitsun 1946; H. Grisewood int. 16/6/89, 6/91.

40. To H. Sutherland 25/11/41; James Woods for DJ 20/11/41.

41. To T. Burns 1/11/41. 'Epoch, Church and Artist' reprinted as 'Religion and the Muses' (*EA* 97–106).

42. To *TLS* draft n.d; to H. Grisewood 26/2/42.

43. R. Kehoe to T. Stoneburner [1972]; *A* 38–9.

44. P. Kelly int. 9/6/86; to N. Sanders 7/4/66; M. Richey to au. 23/4/86; to H. Grisewood 14/7/71; M. Richey int. 7/6/86; DJ c. w. au. 24/8/72.

45. To R. Hague 5/11/64; to A. T. Davies 26/7/59; *LF* 7; to V. Wynne-Williams 11/2/63; S. Honeyman int. 9/10/87; to A. Oldfield Davies 20/10/61.

46. Prudence (Pelham) Buhler to DJ 24/2/45; W. Blissett, *Long*, p. 143; to T. Burns 15/3/42, 2/6/42, 5/10/42.

47. To H. Grisewood 5/4/73; to J. Knight 21/1/47; to H. Grisewood 21/2/42.

48. To H. Grisewood 13/2/43; to Secretary, London Library 29/12/45.

49. To H. Grisewood 21/2/42.

50. To T. Burns 6/5/43; to H. Grisewood 1/6/42; to P. Donner 16/6/61; to R. Matthias draft n.d.

51. To T. Burns 16/5/42; D. Pollen to T. Stoneburner 21/10/75; W. Blissett, *Long*, p. 19; to *Observer* draft n.d.

52. To T. Burns 21/9/41, 5/10/42; to D. Travis 25/8/n.y.

53. To J. Ede 29–30/8/42.

54. To P. Tegetmeier 9/11/43; N. Cleverdon, in M. James, *David Jones*, p. 59; N. Cleverdon, 'A Handshake with the Past', *David Jones Journal* (Summer 1997), p. 30.

55. A. Giardelli, in M. James, *David Jones*, p. 58.

56. To T. Burns 16/5/42; to H. Grisewood 13/2/43; to J. Ede 15/4/43, 19/8/43.

57. Bernard Wall, *Headlong into Change* (London: Harvill, 1969), pp. 120, 111–13, 114–15; W. Blissett, *Long*, p. 141.

58. Barbara Wall int. 27/6/86; H. Grisewood int. 5/10/87.

59. K. Clark to DJ 27/7/42; to H. Grisewood 13/2/43.

60. H. Grisewood int. 5/6/86; B. Moray int. 6/85; B. Moray to DJ 26/11/45.

61. To T. Burns 6/5/43; J. Ede to R. Hague 26/9/78; J. Ede int. 31/5/86, 25/6/86; to J. Ede 17/5/43.

62. T. S. Eliot to DJ 10/9/43; to H. Grisewood 13/2/43; *DG* 140–1.

63. To H. Sutherland 14/11/39, 14/5/43.

64. To K. Clark 20/1/44; to J. Ede 3/7/43; DJ c. w. au. 24/8/72; to H. Grisewood 14/8/51.

65. To D. Travis 25/8/43.

66. To D. Travis 25/8/43; to J. Ede 3/7/43; N. and Basil Gray int. 17/6/86.

67. Last Will and Testament of James Jones 10/41; to H. Grisewood 28/8/45; to R. Hague 23/4/46.

68. To H. Grisewood 23/3/44; E. Hodgkin 'Some Memories'; Ronan Murphy to au. 24/12/93; to J. Ede 13/3/44; S. Williams to au. 29/3/2016.

69. To J. Stone 12/2/63; R. Buhler int. 16/6/88.

70. R. Buhler int. 15/6/88, 6/85.

71. To J. Ede 13/3/44.

72. To D. Travis 14/2/45: to H. Sutherland 19/6/45; P. Orr int. 2/6/86.

73. To H. Sutherland 31/12/45; M. Grisewood int. 26/9/89; to D. Travis 14/2/45.

74. To H. Grisewood 19/2/45; B. Dufort int. 9/6/86; to H. Grisewood 25/6/45.

75. D. Cleverdon int. 28/6/86; Cleverdon, *Engravings*, p. 22; T. Burns int. 20/8/86; M. Richey int. 18/6/89; H. Grisewood int. 4/10/87, 16/6/89; to R. Hague 15/8/67.

76. L. Bussell to T. Stoneburner 12/8/69.

77. DJ c. w. au. 24/8/72, 4/6/71.

78. H. Sutherland to DJ 1/9/45; H. Sutherland to J. Ede 7/7/44; T. Burns to J. Ede 8/8/44; J. Ede to K. Clark 24/11/44; H. Sutherland to J. Ede 7/7/44; J. Ede to K. Clark 23/7/44; J. Ede int. 25/6/86; J. Ede's annotations to DJ's letter to him 3/12/45; to J. Ede 10/8/45; J. Ede to K. Clark 12/10/44.

79. To D. Travis 14/2/45; to J. H. Johnston [1/65]; to H. Grisewood 19/2/45.
80. H. Grisewood int. 4/10/87; to L. Bussell 14/3/45; to H. Grisewood 11/7/58.
81. To B. Travis 20/5/45.
82. To H. Grisewood 25/6/45; DJ ms note for Dr William Stevenson discovered by Lauren J. Jefferson 'A Kind of Space Between', MA thesis, University of York, September 2000, p. 10; P. Tegetmeier int. 18/6/88.
83. To D. Travis 14/2/45; to C. Burns 7/1/46.
84. To H. Grisewood 5/12/44; to J. Ede 15/1/45.
85. P. Buhler to DJ 22/4/45; to H. Grisewood 6/9/44; H. Grisewood to au. 20/9/85; to S. Honeyman 5/11/63; S. Honeyman to H. Grisewood 25/9/84; DJ int. by J. Silkin 1965; S. Honeyman to H. Grisewood 25/9/84.
86. To H. Sutherland 14/8/50.

Chapter 12

1. DJ, poetry mss; H. Grisewood int. 5/10/87.
2. To L. Bussell 20/8/46; E. Hodgkin, 'Helen Sutherland', TS n.d.
3. To J. Ede 23/7/46; to L. Bussell 28/8/46.
4. D. Cleverdon, 'David Jones and Broadcasting', *Poetry Wales*, 8 (Winter 1972), pp. 73–4; D. Cleverdon int. 6/85; H. Grisewood int. 8/83.
5. T. Burns int. 13/6/88; T. Burns to J. Ede 25/3/47.
6. N. Gray int. 17/6/86; T. Burns int. 20/8/86, 14/6/88.
7. T. Burns to J. Ede 25/3/47; T. Burns int. 13/6/88; T. Burns to J. Ede 8/11/47.
8. H. Grisewood int. 19/6/90.
9. G. Davies int. 8/10/89; to H. Sutherland 18/7/47; C. Burns to H. Sutherland 19/7/47.
10. K. Bell int. 12/6/86; G. Davies int. 19/6/90, 8/10/89. The source of the error is Alex Hamilton, 'From David Jones's Locker', *Manchester Guardian* (11/2/72). It is repeated by J. Miles and D. Shiel, *Maker Unmade*, p. 263 and K. Alldritt, *David Jones, Writer and Artist* (London: Constable, 2003), p. 137.
11. G. Davies int. 8/10/87; to H. Grisewood 24/8/47.

12. E. D. P., 'W. A. H. Stevenson', *British Medical Journal*, 2 (22/5/71), p. 472; G. Davies int. 8/10/89; K. Bell int. 12/6/86.

13. DJ to C. Wilcockson int. 18/6/90.

14. To H. Sutherland 18/7/47; P. Orr int. 2/6/86; Richard S. Hallam, *Anxiety: Psychological Perspectives on Panic and Agoraphobia* (London: Academic Press, 1985), p. 135; Sigmund Freud, *Inhibitions, Symptoms and Anxiety*, tr. Alix Strachey (London: Hogarth, 1926), p. 55; Hallam, *Anxiety*, p. 28; to H. Grisewood, 16/7/47; P. Tegetmeier int. 18/6/88.

15. S. Freud, *Inhibitions*, p. 65.

16. H. Grisewood int. 8/83; S. Honeyman int. 20/6/86.

17. DJ, Application to the Artists' Benevolent Fund, draft [1947]; *IN* 54.

18. To C. Burns 29/5/40.

19. To D. Blamires 26/1/72.

20. *DGC* 131.

21. C. Wilcockson int. 22/6/88, 18/6/90; H. Grisewood int. 8/83.

22. N. Cleverdon, 'Handshake', p. 31.

23. To W. Blissett, *Long*, p. 41; to R. Shirley-Smith 16/12/60; to D. Travis 29/12/60; to D. Cleverdon 18/1/55; DJ to S. Honeyman int. 17/9/98; S. Balme int. 24/6/88; J. Miles and D. Shiel, *Maker Unmade*, p. 243.

24. DJ, notes for William Stevenson [1948]; G. Davies on universal guilt over masturbation, int. 8/10/87; Hugh Crichton-Miller, *Psycho-Analysis and its Derivatives* (London: Butterworth, 1933), p. 136.

25. H. Grisewood int. 8/83; J. Stone to J. Miles and D. Shiel, *Maker Unmade*, p. 9.

26. S. Freud, *Totem and Taboo* (Harmondsworth: Penguin, 1940), p. 30; to H. Grisewood 24/8/47; to C. Burns 26/3/53; DJ c. w. au. 4/6/71; to C. Burns, 20/10/52.

27. To H. Grisewood 24/8/47; to H. Sutherland 15/7/48; DJ, notes for W. Stevenson [1947]; N. Gray to R. Hague 24/11/78.

28. DJ to J. Wood to S. Brett int. 21/4/95.

29. DJ c. w. T. Stoneburner 30/8/72.

30. T. Burns to J. Ede 8/11/47; Artists' General Benevolent Association to DJ 10/10/47; H. Crichton-Miller to DJ 2/10/48.

31. H. Grisewood int. 8/83; DJ c. w. T. Stoneburner 19/6/69; DJ to R. Wald, 'I Don't Think', p. 11.

32. DJ, note for W. Stevenson [1948]; to Mildred Ede 28/8/49.

33. To J. Ede 31/8/49.

34. T. Burns to J. Ede 8/11/47; to T. Stoneburner 19/9/64.

35. J. Scott int. 16/6/88; to T. Stoneburner 30/7/69; A. Malan int. 22/6/89; S. and M. Balme int. 17/6/90, 24/6/88.

36. To V. Wynne-Williams 9/60, 4/6/65, 4/3/61, 28/8/62; to T. Stoneburner 30/7/69; to H. Sutherland 9/10/50; to Elwyn Evans 23/5/53; to D. Travis 26/12/48; to J. Ede 9/12/49.

37. S. and M. Balme int. 17/6/90, R. Hague to DJ 21/5/n.y.; to B. Travis 26/4/48; to H. Sutherland 19/1/48, 7/12/49.

38. C. Wilcockson int. 22/6/88; to D. Travis 26/12/48; A. Malan int. 22/6/89; S. Honeyman int. 6/91; N. Cleverdon, 'David Jones Remembered', in M. James, *A Map of the Artist's Mind*, p. 59; C. Skelton int. 22/6/88; S. Honeyman, int. 10/87; Frances Richards, *Remembering David Jones* (Privately Printed, Wellingborough: Skelton's Press, 1980), pp. 1-2; P. Tegetmeier int.18/6/88; to J. Stone 12/2/63.

39. To D. Travis 26/12/48; to J. Ede 3/2/63; to S. Lewis 25/12/56; M. Bulbrook int. 28/6/88; Frances Richards, *Remembering David Jones*, p. 4; C. Wilcockson int. 22/6/88.

40. To P. Donner 8/4/62; to N. Sanders 7/4/66; to R. Hague 2/5/70; to H. Grisewood Tues/8/52, 8/8/54.

41. DJ, notes for W. Stevenson [1948].

42. M. Cochrane int. 20/6/88.

43. To J. Ede 23/5/48; to B. Travis 7/48; to C. Burns 29/6/48; to H. Sutherland 15/7/48.

44. Elizabeth Davison to DJ 16/9/48; to H. Sutherland 15/7/48; J. Miles and D. Shiel, *Maker Unmade*, p. 202.

45. A. Malan int. 22/6/89; S. and M. Balme int. 24/6/88, 17/6/90; to H. Grisewood 15–24/4/72; to S. Lewis 18/9/70; L. Walton int. 22/6/88; to H. Grisewood 12/4/51.

46. To H. Grisewood 14/2/50; L. Walton int. 13/6/88; S. Honeyman int. 9/10/87.

47. S. Honeyman int. 29/6/86; to H. Grisewood 20/1/72.

48. S. Honeyman int. 1/9/87; 14/6/91.

49. S. Honeyman int. 6/2009; to R. Hague 27/9/63.

50. S. Honeyman int. 14/6/91; to S. Honeyman 14/11/71; to H. Sutherland 25/3/49.

51. M. Balme int. 28/6/88.

52. M. Rees to au. 12/6/99; M. Rees to DJ 4/2/52.

53. To H. Grisewood 1/1/64, 4/8/62; to S. Lewis 10/72.

54. To H. Sutherland 13/11/52; L. Jebb int. 15/6/90; D. Pollen to T. Stoneburner 21/10/75.

55. To H. Sutherland 15/7/48; H. Grisewood int. 4/10/87.

56. To V. Wynne-Williams 5/2/61; T. Burns int. 20/8/86.

57. To H. Sutherland 7/12/49; T. Hyne c. w. au. 19/9/99; P. Orr int. 2/6/86; Rosalind Erangey int. 28/6/88.

58. Witnessed by au. 31/8/72.

59. S. Honeyman int. 6/86; to J. Knight 8/8/51.

60. N. Gray int. 17/6/88; K. Raine int. 26/6/86; J. Ede to DJ 30/8/49.

61. To H. Sutherland 10/1/59; M. Bradshaw int. by T. Stoneburner 1975; V. Wynne-Williams int. 25/9/89; Hilary Beyer int. 23/6/89.

62. To H. Grisewood 13/4/40, 21/5/40; to J. Knight 5/5/58.

63. To H. Sutherland 28/11/48; to J. Knight 1/11/48, 28/4/59. Thanks to Valerie Eliot for permission to quote from this and other letters from T. S. Eliot.

64. To P. Levi 10/5/66, 3/11/67; Oswald Spengler, *Decline of the West*, tr. Charles F. Atkinson (Allen & Unwin, 1926), I, p. 160; to J. Knight 15/8/52.

65. To T. Stoneburner 19/9/64; to S. Piggott 20/11/59; to N. Gray 16/12/52.

66. P. Orr int. 2/6/86. Others who noticed this pattern include Arthur and Bim Giardelli, R. Hague, S. Dayras, W. Blissett, and au.

67. To J. Knight 31/7/51; to H. Grisewood 16/10/52.

68. To F. Morley unposted 1/53; to H. Grisewood 22/5/62; H. Grisewood, *One Thing*, p. 63; To H. Grisewood 15/10/52; M. Richey int. 18/6/89, 7/6/86.

69. N. Cleverdon, 'Handshake', p. 31; N. Cleverdon to au. 15/7/92.

70. To T. Stoneburner 2/67; to H. Grisewood 15–24/4/72; to H. Sutherland 26/11/63; to N. Saunders 27/8/71; to H. Sutherland 13/11/52.

71. DJ int. by J. Silkin 1965; to J. Knight 13/10/52.

72. DJ, Bollingen Prize application 12/8/59; to E. Evans 14/11/53; to T. Stoneburner 2/8/68.

73. To J. Ede 27/3/43; V. Turner int. 7/9/87.

74. J. Ryan int. 6/8/87.

75. K. Bell int. 12/6/86; to J. Ede 21/2/70.

76. B. Moray int. 6/85; to V. Wynne-Williams 6/8/62.

77. John Roberts to DJ 26/2/51; to J. Rothenstein 4/2/50; J. Roberts to DJ 14/3/51, 27/6/51; V. Wynne Williams int. 25/9/89.

78. To H. Sutherland 24/8/51; *EA* 265; to H. Read 22/8/50; to H. Sutherland 24/8/51.

79. To unidentified recipient, draft frag. n.d.; W. Blissett, *Long*, p. 50.

80. R. Hague int. 11/9/89; DJ, 'Ray Howard-Jones: An Introduction', *Anglo-Welsh Review*, 17 (Summer 1968), p. 53.

81. A. Giardelli int. 8/6/86; to A. Giardelli 4/9/64.

82. R. Buhler int. 16/6/88; H. Grisewood int. 8/83; to H. Grisewood 15/11/60.

83. To H. Grisewood 25/6/45; to H. Sutherland 24/8/51; to J. Ede 15/1/52.

84. To J. Ede 31/7/49; P. Hills, *David Jones* (London: Tate Gallery, 1981), p. 119; to H. Sutherland 24/8/51.

85. To J. Stone 6–7/9/60; to R. and J. Shirley-Smith 11/2/61; to J. Knight 6/10/52.

86. A. Malan to au. 28/1/93; to H. Read 22/8/50; to J. Stone 15/3/65; to K. Raine 17/6/59.

87. DJ int. by P. Orr Summer 1972; to T. Stoneburner 28/9/67.

88. T. S. Eliot, blurb for *A*, Faber catalogue (1952); to T. Stoneburner 6/11/51; to Louis Bonnerot draft frag. 4/1/60; P. du Sautoy int. 23/6/88; DJ c. w. au. 24/8/72; to J. Knight 23/12/51; P. du Sautoy to DJ 13/12/51; to P. du Sautoy 17/12/51.

89. To H. Sutherland 11/9/52; to H. Grisewood 5/8/52.

90. To T. Burns 6/5/43; DJ c. w. au. 24/8/71, 29/9/72; H. Grisewood int. 4/10/87.

91. Harold Bloom, *The Anxiety of Influence* (New York: Oxford University Press, 1997), p. 80; to H. Sutherland 25/11/41.

92. To C. Burns 4/8/54.

93. To H. Sutherland 15/5/52.

94. To H. Sutherland 11/9/52.

95. DJ c. w. T. Stoneburner 5/5/66.

96. To J. Ede 1/10/52; F. Morley to DJ 12/1/52.

97. David Bland to James Shand 17/12/51; to W. H. Auden 24/2/54; to J. Ede 16/11/52; DJ int. by P. Orr n.d.

98. To T. Stoneburner 24/2/59; Victor White, *God and the Unconscious* (London: Harvill Press, 1952), passage marked by DJ, pp. 131–2.

99. To H. Sutherland 11/9/52; B. Dufort int. 17/6/89; P. du Sautoy int. 23/6/88.

100. To J. Knight 8/8/51; to H. Grisewood 22/5/62; to H. Read 21/9/64; to J. Hooker 8/5/70; W. H. Auden, 'The Geste Says This', p. 13.

Chapter 13

1. To C. Burns 20/10/52; J. Ryan int. 6/8/87; to H. Sutherland 29/9/53.

2. H. Grisewood ms note 17/3/76; *IN* 23; to J. H. Johnston 3/3/63; to H. Grisewood 29/6/58; to J. Knight 13/11/52; to J. Ede 17/12/52.

3. To H. Sutherland 8/10/52; P. du Sautoy to H. Read 22/7/70; Charles Monteith to Mr Crawley 16/4/70; to J. Knight 31/7/51.

4. To F. Morley unposted 1/53; G. Greene to DJ 23/2/53, permission to quote by Francis Greene.

5. To T. Stoneburner 20/11/64; to R. Hague 9–15/7/73.

6. To H. Grisewood 14/2/51; to J. Asquith 21/9/39; *DGC* 83; to H. Grisewood 3/6/40; to H. Sutherland 25/11/41.

7. DJ c. w. au. 24/8/72; to T. Burns 6/5/43; to H. Grisewood 13/4/40, 10/1/54; [Feast of] St Thomas 22/6/53.

8. R. Buhler int. 16/6/88; to N. Gray 16/12/52; to J. Ede 17/12/52; to N. Gray 14/4/61.

9. To H. Grisewood 16/10/52, 4/10/87; D. and N. Cleverdon int. 28/6/86.

10. To D. Tegetmeier 9/5/53; DJ c. w. au. 9/9/72.

11. *IN* 84; to H. Sutherland 26/5/53; to T. Stoneburner 8/9/65.

12. To E. Evans 22/5/53, 9/6/53; to J. Ede 20/5/53.

13. To M. Percival 15/10/67; DJ c. w. au. 24/8/72; to A. O. Davies 17/11/53; to V. Watkins 5/4/62, 24/7/57; to N. Sanders 9/11/72.

14. D. and N. Cleverdon int. 28/6/86; to N. Sanders 27/8/71; Dylan Thomas to H. Grisewood int. 4/10/87; to B. Dufort 20/11/53.

15. To H. Sutherland 29/9/53; to Mr Revel [1972].

16. D. Cleverdon int. 6/85; to E. Evans 23/5/53; E. Evans int. 20/8/86; to D. Pollen 6/9/61.

17. *IN* 84; to V. Wynne-Williams 27/9/73.

18. To H. Sutherland 4/1/54, 16/2/55.

19. To H. Grisewood 14/1/54; to J. Ede 2/4/54; T. S. Eliot to H. Grisewood 20/8/53; K. Clark to H. Grisewood 7/8/53; H. Grisewood int. 8/83.

20. J. Ede to DJ [1936], [1944]; D. Cleverdon int. 6/85; J. Ede int. 6/85.

21. P. Lowrey int. 20/6/88; to H. Read unposted 18/11/67; M. Hague int. 10/9/89; D. Cleverdon int. 6/85; M. Grisewood int. 24/6/89; N. Cleverdon int. 25/6/90; T. Hyne int. 6/90; A. Giardelli int. 8/6/86; V. Wynne-Williams int. 25/9/89; to W. Shewring draft n.d.

22. S. and M. Balme int. 24/6/88; to D. Travis 3/8/62; D. Cleverdon int. 6/85.

23. S. Lewis to DJ 26/6/54; to R. Hague 22/11/34; S. Lewis to DJ 12/9/37; C. Edwards to DJ 10/6/37; to H. Grisewood 8/8/54; S. Lewis to DJ 3/7/54; to S. Lewis 6/7/54, 13–14/11/59.

24. To S. Lewis 6/6/60; to C. Ivainer 13/6/61; to S. Lewis 2/9/70; to R. Hague 8/6/66; to A. T. Davies 7–8/9/70; to Anul Jones draft n.d.; S. Honeyman int. 1/9/87; H. Grisewood int. 8/83; to T. Stoneburner 7/10/68; Tate Gallery Catalogue 1955; S. Lewis to DJ 17/11/67; to N. Sanders 7/11/70; to V. Watkins 17/4/62.

25. Sir John Cecil Williams to DJ 1/3/56; H. Grisewood int. 5/10/87; to H. Grisewood 15/2/57; *LF* 32.

26. Morley Kennerley at Faber to DJ 16/1/53; S. Spender int. 5/12/88.

27. To H. Sutherland 3/6/54. The National Institute of Arts and Letters is the American Academy of Arts and Letters, and the Russell Loines Award has been discontinued.

28. To W. H. Auden 24/2/54; H. Grisewood int. 5/10/87; to H. Grisewood 12/8/57; to H. Sutherland 27/9/56; to H. Grisewood 18/5/56; S. Spender, *Journals 1939–1983* (New York: Random House, 1986), p. 153.

29. H. Grisewood int. 19/6/90; Natasha and S. Spender int. 5/12/88.

30. To J. Ede 16/9/63; to H. Sutherland 17/5/57; N. Spender int. 5/12/88.
31. To Anthony Steel draft 16/4/60; T. Hyne int. 2/5/93; to S. Lewis 22/3/65; to H. Grisewood 26/11/70; to N. Gray 4/4/61, 14/4/61.
32. To Wyn [surname unknown] 26/7/54; to Douglas Hall, Scottish National Gallery of Modern Art 27/1/68.
33. To D. Travis 25/12/54; to K. Raine draft frag. 21/12/54; to S. Lewis 19/11/54.
34. S. Honeyman int. 6/2009; to M. Percival 5/1/50; T. Burns int. 20/8/86; Barbara Wall int. 27/6/86.
35. To H. Grisewood 8/8/54.
36. To N. Gray 4/4/61; to P. du Sautoy 21/4/73.
37. To H. Sutherland 10/1/50.
38. To N. Gray 4/4/61, 14/4/61.
39. To H. Sutherland 22/8/61; to Ruan McLean draft 1/9/61; J. Miles and D. Shiel, *Maker Unmade*, p. 274.
40. DJ int. by P. Orr 1973.
41. To R. McLean draft 1/9/61; to H. Sutherland 9/7/56.
42. To N. Gray 4/4/61.
43. *LF* 42–3; to Mr Stephens [*c.* 1970]; to S. Lewis 19/12/60.
44. To Harry W.11/1/55.
45. H. Beyer int. 23/6/89; D. Kindersley int. 9/6/90; Michael Symmons Roberts, 'The Writing on the Wall', *Tablet* 17/9/2005, p. 28.
46. Geoffrey Treasure to au. 23/6/93; C. Wilcockson int. 22/6/88; C. Wilcockson to au. 12/9/88.
47. To C. Wilcockson 3/1/66; C. Wilcockson int. 22/6/88; to J. Stone 7/10/62; to S. Lewis 14/6/72; to B. Dufort 20/11/53.
48. To H. Sutherland 16/2/55; to R. Hague 2/6/55; DJ c. w. au. 9/9/72; John Pearson, *The Sitwells, A Family Biography* (New York and London: Harcourt Brace, 1978), p. 411.
49. To H. Grisewood 8/8/56.
50. To V. Watkins 6/6/55; to H. Grisewood 8/8/56, 17/9/57.
51. B. Moray int. 6/85; to R. Hague frag. 12/8/64.
52. To [Anna] Neuta Kallin 21/1/47; H. Grisewood int. 16/6/89.
53. H. Beyer int. 23/6/89; H. Beyer to au. 8/8/93.
54. To H. Grisewood 26/11/55; to H. Sutherland 22/11/55; W. Blissett, *Long*, pp 26–7; H. Grisewood int. 8/83.
55. To C. Eden 30/6/56; to H. Grisewood 24/8/56, 1/9/56; C. Eden int. 26/9/89.
56. C. Eden int. 26/9/89; to H. Grisewood Candlemas 1957, 15/2/57, 4/3/60.
57. *IN* 88, 89; to H. Sutherland 17/5/57; to W. Cookson, 24/1/65.

58. S. and M. Balme int. 17/6/90; to V. Wynne-Williams 23/2/61.

59. DJ int. by P. Orr 1972; to T. Stoneburner 28/9/67; C. Wilcockson int. 22/6/88; J. Shirley-Smith int. 21/6/90.

60. To C. Ivainer 13/9/60.

61. To R. Hague 9/4/60; A. Fraser. int. 5/8/87.

62. H. Grisewood int. 4/10/87; to H. Grisewood 15/2/57, Laetare Sunday 1957.

63. T. Stoneburner to DJ 2/8/61; S. Honeyman int. 20/6/86.

64. Neville Braybrook, 'David Jones: Painter and Poet', *Queens Quarterly* (Winter 1964), pp. 508–9; to J. Knight 20/7/57; to H. Sutherland 5/11/58; N. Braybrook to T. Stoneburner 18/9/75; to H. Sutherland 5/11/58.

65. J. Ede, *A Way of Life* (Cambridge: Cambridge University Press, 1984), p. 194; J. Ede to DJ 18/7/55.

66. To T. Stoneburner 24/6/61; *A* 15; to H. Sutherland 2/4/58.

67. J. Stone int. 2/10/87; J. Stone to DJ 11/6/63, 2/60.

68. M. Cochrane int. 20/6/88.

69. To Harold Rosenberg draft frag. 23/10/64; to J. Hooker 8/5/70; to A. Pollen 31/9/60; T. S. Eliot quoted by DJ c. w. au. 24/8/72; DJ quoted in A. Dorenkamp, *In the Order*, p. 21; P. Lowrey int. 20/6/88; Simmons at Faber to DJ 20/4/59.

70. To Edward Little 29/4/60.

71. To H. Rosenberg draft frag. 10/64; to H. Grisewood 4/5/70; M. Bulbrook int. 26/6/88; to K. Raine 20/6/59; to H. Read 7/3/65; H. Read 'David Jones, *Epoch and Artist*' (review), *Listener*, 14/5/59, p. 853.

72. J. Stone to DJ 26/7/59; K. Clark to DJ 28/9/59.

73. To H. Grisewood 18/2/60; to K. Clark 16/11/60; to J. Hooker 8/5/70.

74. *DGC* 177; V. Wynne-Williams int. 22/9/95.

75. V. Wynne-Williams int. 22/9/95, 25/9/89; to V. Wynne-Williams 9/6/59; *DGC* 178; to T. Stoneburner 29/6/65; to V. Wynne-Williams 4/2/59, 12/9/59, 5/6/59.

76. V. Wynne-Williams int. 25/9/89; to H. Grisewood 4/8/62; to J. Stone 7/10/62; to R. Hague 20/5/60.

77. To H. Grisewood 20/1/59; to V. Wynne-Williams 21/4/59; V. Wynne-Williams int. 25/9/89.

78. V. Wynne-Williams int. 25/9/89.

79. To V. Wynne-Williams 6/2/61.

80. T. Burns int. 25–27/6/89.

81. H. Grisewood int. 19/6/90; N. Cleverdon int. 25/6/90; S. Honeyman int. 20/8/86; to V. Wynne-Williams 7/2/60; to J. Stone 4/10/62; to V. Wynne-Williams 10/5/59.

82. To V. Wynne-Williams 5/6/59.

83. To V. Wynne-Williams 9/8/59.

84. J. Stone int. 2/10/87; to H. Grisewood 27/6/59; to J. Stone 13/10/59.

85. To J. Stone 1/12/61, 19/7/59.

86. To H. Grisewood 27/6/59, 9/10/61; P. Kelly int. 9/6/86.

87. H. Grisewood int. 4/10/87; V. Wynne-Williams int. 25/9/89.

88. To V. Wynne-Williams 11/9/59; to K. Raine 24/8/59; V. Wynne-Williams int. 25/9/89; Ray Howard-Jones int. 11/9/89; to V. Wynne-Williams 30/8/59, 12/8/59, 4/9/59.

89. To R. and J. Shirley-Smith 11/2/61; to R. Hague 9/4/60; V. Wynne-Williams int. 25/9/89.

90. To S. Lewis 13–14/11/59; S. Honeyman int. 20/8/86.

91. To J. Hooker 8/5/70; to V. Watkins 19/7/57.

92. W. Cookson to au. 12/2/90; W. Cookson int. 14/6/88; to J. H. Johnston 16/5/64.

93. To T. Stoneburner 30/8/63.

94. To T. Stoneburner 15/5/67; W. Blissett, *Long*, p. 25; to V. Wynne-Williams 30/8/59, 4/9/59.

95. S. and M. Balme int. 19/6/90; J. Scott int. 16/6/88; S. Balme int. 24/6/88; to R. Hague 27/4/64; S. Balme int. 7/5/93, 17/6/90.

96. S. Balme int. 17/6/90, 24/6/88; S. Dayras int. 9/89; C. Collins int. 25/6/89.

97. S. Balme int. 17/6/90.

98. To R. Shirley-Smith 16/12/60; to H. Grisewood 20/1/59; to J. Stone 13/10/59; S. Balme int. 17/6/90.

99. To T. Stoneburner 22/9/66; to V. Wynne-Williams 7/2/60, 10/6/60; to R. Hague 9/4/60.

100. To J. Stone 16/5/60; V. Wynne-Williams to DJ 8/11/61.

101. To A. Giardelli 9–11/8/73; M. Richey int. 18/6/89; DJ int. by P. Orr Summer 1972; J. Miles and D. Shiel, *Maker Unmade*, p. 225; P. Lowrey int. 20/6/88.

102. S. Balme int. 17/6/90; 24/6/88.

103. To A. Giardelli 9–11/8/73; Peter Campbell int. 23/6/86.

104. M. Cochrane int 26/6/88; M. Cochrane to DJ 12/12/65; K. Bell int. 12/6/86.

105. To V. Wynne-Williams 10/6/60; to R. Hague 29/2/60; to S. Lewis 6/7/60; to K. Clark 16/11 60.

106. To A. Giardelli 29/9/66, 9–11/8/73.

107. To A. Giardelli 8–9/3/[c. 1970].

108. To V. Wynne-Williams 6/8/62.

109. To S. Lewis 13–14/11/59; to V. Wynne-Williams 11/12/59; to J. Stone 16/4/60.

110. R. Shirley-Smith, 'An Outline of my contact with David Jones', TS; S. Honeyman 1/9/87.

111. S. Honeyman int. 6/86, 6/91, 4/93, 1/9/87.

112. S. Honeyman int. 20/6/86.

113. M. Cochrane int. 20/6/88.

114. To H. Grisewood 21/7/60; to C. Ivainer 13/9/60; to V. Wynne-Williams 26/12/64; to R. Hague 6/1/65; Peter Levi int. 19/2/90.

Chapter 14

1. To S. Honeyman frag. [1960]; to H. Grisewood draft 26/5/64; to Miss Selby 26/1/67.

2. To J. Stone 4/10/60.

3. To D. Travis 29/12/60; to V. Wynne-Williams 9/1/61.

4. To T. S. Eliot 7/4/61; T. S. Eliot to DJ 6/1/60; to K. Raine 23/4/61; *LF* 55; J. Scott int. 16/6/88.

5. To C. Ivainer unposted 6/2/61; to T. Stoneburner 20/11/64; to W. T. Noon 5/12/65, quoted in William T. Noon. SJ, *Poetry and Prayer* (Brunswick, NJ: Rutgers, 1967), pp. 342–3; DJ c. w. au. 9/9/72.

6. To J. Stone 6–7/9/60; to S. Lewis 6/4/61, 18/9/61, 20/11/61; to R. Hague 16/9/63; W. Blissett, *Long*, p. 35.

7. H. Grisewood int. 16/6/89; T. S. Eliot to H. Grisewood 29/3/61.

8. To L. W. Griffith 12/9/64; H. Boyers int. 23/6/89.

9. DJ to R. Wald, 'I Don't Think', p. 3; *LF* 72; to H. Grisewood 26/7/61; to Geoffrey Elborn 10/5/70.

10. To P. Donner 19/12/62; to J. Ede 3/2/63.

11. W. H. Auden, 'The Geste Says This', pp. 12, 13.

12. *Review of Politics*, 26:1 (January 1962), 62–87; to H. Grisewood 7/3/62; to Miss [J.] Carver 29–30/6/72.

13. L. Walton int. 13/6/88.

14. Ruth Simon to DJ 8/12/58; to H. Grisewood 26/7/61; to Donald Nichol 18/10/62.

15. Louis G. Cowan to P. du. Sautoy 4/4/62; to H. Grisewood 28/5/62.

16. To A. Giardelli 3/9/64; to H. Read 21/9/64.

17. To V. Wynne-Williams 24/11/62; to R. Hague 7/11/63; H. Grisewood int. 6/91.

18. To J. Stone 27/11/61, 1/12/61.

19. To H. Grisewood 28/3/61; to J. Stone 26/8/62.

20. V. Wynne-Williams int. 25/9/89.

21. Eglwys Dewi Sant, Paddington School to DJ 31/5/62; to S. Lewis 23/12/63, 24/4/62.

22. S. Honeyman int. by P. Orr, TS n.d.

23. S. Honeyman int. 9/10/87; V. Wynne-Williams int. 25/9/89.

24. To J. Stone 1/2/62; V. Wynne-Williams to au. 8/2005.

25. To W. Cookson 1/6/71.

26. To J. Stone 1/2/63; to H. Grisewood 1/1/63, 10/6/64; to S. Lewis 3/1/63; to S. Lewis 4/1/62, 18/1/62.

27. A. Giardelli int. 8/6/86; Robert Craft, *Stravinsky: Chronicle of Friendship 1948–1972* (New York: Knopf, 1972), pp. 227–8; to J. Ede 16/9/63; N. Cleverdon int. 25/6/90; F. Richards, *Remembering*, p. 4; A. Giardelli, 'David Jones Remembered', in James, *A Map of the Artist's Mind*, p. 58; M. Bulbrook int. 28/6/88; DJ c. w. T. and Pat Stoneburner 5/5/66; S. Spender, 'David Jones', *Man and Poet*, ed. J. Matthias, p. 53; N. Spender to E. Hodgkin 17/3/94; to K. Clark 9/7/63.

28. To H. Sutherland 26/11/63; S. Honeyman int. 9/10/87.

29. DJ c. w. T. and P. Stoneburner 5/5/66; to S. Lewis 2/7/73, 2/9/70.

30. H. Grisewood int. 8/83.

31. To H. Grisewood 29/8/63; D. Cleverdon's list of costs, TS.

32. D. and N. Cleverdon int. 28/6/86; N. Cleverdon int. 25/6/90, 18/5/93; N. Cleverdon, *Map*, p. 60.

33. To Andrew Mylett 9/10/65; L. Bonnerot int. 9/89.

34. To D. Blamires 6/11/66; to F. Kermode 12/7/66; to T. Stoneburner 18/6/75.

35. To S. Spender 6/5/63; W. Blissett, *Long*, p. 60; to K. Clark 9/7/63; H. Grisewood to J. F. Hewit 16/12/63, 14/12/63.

36. J. Stone to DJ 10/64, 11/64.

37. To R. Hague 27/4/64; S. Balme int. 7/5/93.

38. H. Grisewood int. 8/83, 19/6/90, 5/10/87; J. Stone int. 2/10/87; to K. Raine 23/4/61; to D. Travis 3/8/62; to C. Ivainer 17/10/61.

39. To M. Balme 14/4/64; H. Grisewood int. 6/5/93; to V. Wynne-Williams 16/9/64; to R. Hague 6/3/64.

40. To M. Balme 14/4/64; M. Bulbrook int. 28/6/88; to Theodore Bailly draft 2/65.

41. W. Blissett, *Long*, p. 34; S. and M. Balme int. 17/6/90; to C. Burns 17/4/64; to M. Balme 14/4/64.

42. M. Cochrane int. 20/6/88.

43. To A. Pollen 6/9/61; S. Honeyman int. 20/6/86.

44. S. Honeyman int. 6/86; J. Finzi to DJ 1/1/65.

45. M. Cochrane int. 20/6/88; S. Balme int. 17/6/90; W. Blissett, *Long*, p. 55.

46. M. Elkin int. 6/86; to H. Grisewood 31/12/71.

47. To V. Wynne-Williams 26/12/64; to R. Hague 2/4/74; to E. Hodgkin 29/11/65; to R. Hague 2/4/74.

48. S. Honeyman int. 1/9/87.

49. To H. Grisewood 17/7/64.

50. To P. Levi 27/8/64; S. Honeyman int. 1/9/87.

51. To H. Grisewood 28/3/61, 17/7/64.

52. N. Sanders int. 6/85; to P. Levi 27/8/64.

53. S. Piggot int. by T. Stoneburner 17/8/75; to R. Hague 19/6/67; to S. Honeyman 14/11/71; to N. Sanders 3/8/64.

54. To A. Giardelli 29/9/66; A. Giardelli int. 8/6/86.

55. A. Giardelli int. 8/6/86; A. Giardelli to au. 15/2/93.

56. A. Giardelli int. 8/6/86; S. Honeyman int. 20/6/86.

57. S. Balme int. 24/6/88, 17/6/90; F. Richards, *Remembering*, pp. 1–2, 4; to V. Watkins 26/6/60; to S. Lewis Med [9]/61; to C. Richards 25/10/64.

58. S. Dayras int. 9/89.

59. To H. Grisewood 7/2/56; to *Tablet* 7/4/56; to E. Hodgkin 29/11/65; Dominic Mellray int. 26/6/89.

60. To H. Grisewood 15–24/4/72; to T. Bailly draft 2/65.

61. DJ c. w. T. Stoneburner 5/5/66.

62. T. Powell to DJ 15/5/64.

63. To S. Lewis 22/3/65; S. and M. Balme int. 17/6/90; to R. Hague 8/6/66.

64. T. Powell int. 30/4/93.

65. W. Cookson int. 14/6/88; V. Wynne-Williams int. 25/9/89.

66. To N. Sanders 7/4/66; to P. Orr 25/9/65; S. Lewis to DJ Saturday before Easter 17/4/65; to V. Wynne-Williams 5/11/65. My thanks to Lewis's daughter, Mary Jones, for permission to quote from his letters.

67. To R. Hague 6/1/65; H. Grisewood int. 8/83.

68. To J. Stone 30/3/65; to R. Hague 18/5/65.

69. To A. Giardelli 21/5/65; to V. Wynne-Williams 4/6/65; to J. Stone 7/8/65; DJ c. w. T. and P. Stoneburner 26/5/69.

70. To D. Cleverdon frag. [1965]; to A. Giardelli 10/4/65, 21/5/65.

71. D. Cleverdon to L. Cowan 28/10/65; P. Orr, 'Mr Jones Your Legs are Crossed: A Memoir', *Agenda*, 15:2–3 (Summer–Autumn 1977), p. 115; to Will Carter 16/8/65.

72. D. and N. Cleverdons' visitors' book; N. Cleverdon int. 25/6/90.

73. To R. Hague 6/1/65.

74. To P. Levi 10/5/66; S. Honeyman int. by P. Orr, TS n.d.

75. P. Orr, 'Mr Jones', p. 117.

76. To J. Stone 30/3/65; to C. Rousseau 17/12/65; to H. Grisewood 23/12/65; *LF* 13.

77. To V. Wynne-Williams 5/2/61; to R. Hague 29/4/66; K. Raine int. 7/2/89; E. Hodgkin, 'Helen Sutherland', TS n.d.

78. N. Cleverdon c. w. T. Stoneburner 6/6/69; S. Honeyman int. 20/6/86.

79. S. Honeyman int. by P. Orr, TS n.d.; DJ c. w. T. and P. Stoneburner 7/6/69.

80. To J. Stone 18/4/65; S. Balme int. 24/6/88, 7/5/93, 17/6/90.

81. C. Hyne to M. Bradshaw int. by T. Stoneburner 1975; S. Wright int. 26/6/86; S. Williams to au. 13/2/2009.

82. R. and J. Shirley-Smith int. 21/6/90.

83. To A. Giardelli 29/9/66.

84. To H. Sutherland 14/11/39; to A. O. Davies 14/10/67; to T. Stoneburner Sat–Sun 2/67, 15/3/68; to Bernard Wall 1/7/67.

85. K. Bell int. 12/6/86; M. Elkin int. 1985.

86. A. T. Davies, 'A Note', *Agenda*, 5:1–3 (Spring–Summer 1967), p. 172; Anthony Powell to author 17/1/90.

87. DJ letter frag. n.d.; to J. Ede 21/2/70.

88. To H. Grisewood 15/8/71; C. Collins int. 25/6/89.

89. DJ c. w. T. Stoneburner 8/6/69; C. Collins int. 25/6/89; to H. Grisewood 14/7/71, 15/8/71.

90. To Mr Revell unposted n.d.; John Heath-Stubbs, 'Daughters of Memory', *Nine*, 4 (Winter 1953–4), p. 46; J. Heath-Stubbs to au. 28/7/86; G. Davenport to au. 10/2/92; W. Cookson int. 14/6/88; Basil Bunting to au. 18/4/79; J. Miles and D. Shiel, *Maker Unmade*, p. 9.

91. To T. Stoneburner 30/8/63.

92. J. Montague int. 9/9/89.

93. Anne Beresford, 'A Friendship with David Jones – a personal account,' TS n.d.

94. To P. Hagreen 19/10/72; to H. Grisewood 7/7/71, 4/8/71; to T. Stoneburner 8–9/1/70; to S. Lewis 10/72; to R. Hague 27/9/74; DJ letter frag. [*c.* 1972].

95. To S. Lewis 21/12/72.

96. To D. Travis 29/12/60; A. Malan int. 22/6/89; S. Honeyman int. 16/6/88; H. Grisewood int. 8/83; A. Bailley, 'The Front Line', TS 2/73; E. Hodgkin int. 5/8/87.

97. M. Bulbrook int. 28/6/88; to H. Grisewood 6/10/72; to S. Wright 26/2/73; J. Montague int. 9/9/89; W. Blissett, *Long*, p. 55; to D. Blamires 26/12/70.

98. S. Honeyman int. 20/6/86, 10/87.

99. S. Honeyman int. 1/9/87.

100. To R. Hague 16/4/70; E. Hodgkin to Mrs H. 5/4/70; to R. Hague 16/4/70.

101. K. Clark to H. Grisewood 13/4/70; to V. Wynne-Williams 27/8/70; to G. Elborn 10/5/70.

102. S. Honeyman int. 20/6/86; K. Clark to H. Grisewood 13/4/70, 7/4/70.

103. To T. Stoneburner 14/6/70; S. Honeyman to Sister Hugh 4/6/70; A. Beresford, 'A Friendship', TS n.d.

104. E. Hodgkin int. 5/8/87; to R. Hague 14/12/73; Sister Frances Rattigan int. 25/6/88.

105. R. Howard-Jones int. 11/9/89; P. Orr int. 2/6/86; D. Pollen to T. Stoneburner 21/10/75.

106. To A. Giardelli 9–11/8/73; to H. Grisewood 9/8/70; K. Clark to H. Grisewood 23/7/70; L. Jebb to au. 8/6/89.

107. R. Hague int. by P. Orr 15/2/77; to H. Grisewood 9/8/70; to R. Hague 2/5/70; V. Wynne-Williams to au. 2/2/2009.

108. S. Honeyman int. by P. Orr, TS n.d.; S. Honeyman to Ben Jones 1/6/70.

109. D. Cleverdon to H. Grisewood 26/4/70; S. Honeyman to DJ 7/12/70; S. Honeyman int. 10/87.

110. S. Lewis to DJ 20/12/70; S. Honeyman int. 9/10/87; G. O. Jones to A. O. Davies 10/3/72.

111. S. Honeyman int. 10/87; *Valuation for Probate* (1975); to S. Honeyman 16/7/71.

112. To V. Wynne-Williams frag. 1970; 'W. A. H. Stevenson', *British Medical Journal*, p. 472; to H. Grisewood 6/10/72; P. Orr, 'Mr Jones', p. 123.

113. H. Grisewood int. 7/5/93; S. Honeyman int. by P. Orr, TS n.d.

114. Melvyn Bragg, *Richard Burton* (Boston: Little Brown, 1988), pp. 55, 297; L. Cowan to P. du Sautoy 16/7/64; S. Honeyman int. 20/6/86.

115. S. Honeyman int. by P. Orr, TS n.d.

116. To K. Raine [1972]; D. and N. Cleverdon int. 28/6/86.

117. To H. Grisewood 24/8/70; DJ c. w. T. and P. Stoneburner 20/6/72; to H. Grisewood 5/4/73.

118. To A. Giardelli 29/9/66; N. Cleverdon int. 26/4/95.

119. To N. Sanders 11/7/72.

120. To W. Cookson 31/7/72; P. Orr to H. Grisewood 1/8/72, 8/8/72; C. Collins int. 25/6/89; P. Orr int. 2/6/86; P. Orr, 'Mr Jones', p. 120.

121. V. Wynne-Williams int. 25/9/89; S. Honeyman to H. Grisewood 13/4/70; B. Jones to H. Grisewood 7/4/70; to S. Lewis 6/7/70; H. Grisewood int. 16/6/89; S. Honeyman to B. Jones 13/9/73.

122. DJ c. w. T. Stoneburner 30/8/72; to H. Grisewood 11/9/72, 6/10/72; P. Orr to H. Grisewood 19/12/73.

123. W. Cookson to DJ 29/10/71; P. du Sautoy to DJ 27/7/71, 17/11/72, 27/9/72.

124. To H. Grisewood 29/12/72; A. Malan to au. 29/7/89; W. Blissett, *Long*, p. 131.

125. To P. du Sautoy 22/7/72.

126. DJ, 'Fragments of an Attempted Autobiographical Writing', p. 96.

127. To V. Wynne-Williams 27/1/74; S. Wright int. 27/6/86.

128. To W. Cookson 24/3/74; to R. Hague 26/2/74.

129. W. S. Merwin to au. 7/4/2008.

130. To R. Hague 27/9/74, 9–15/7/73.

131. To R. Hague 27/9/74.

132. To R. Hague 19/6/74, 2/5/74, 19/6/74.

133. To R. Hague 2/5/74, 9–11/6/74.

134. To S. Lewis 27/4/74; Bernard Wall c. w. T. Stoneburner 4/6/69.

135. To S. Honeyman 4/6/74; to R. Hague 19/6/74, 3/8/74.

136. To R. Hague 3/8/74, 11/8/74.

137. W. Blissett, *Long*, 146; George Johnston c. w. au. Summer/75; P. Hills int. 26/6/89.

138. T. Burns, 'David Jones', *Tablet* 2/11/74; S. Wright int. 27/6/86.

139. A. Beresford 'A Friendship', TS n.d.; H. Grisewood int. 6/5/93; M. Richey to R. Hague 5/11/74; M. Bulbrook int. 28/6/88.

140. M. Elkin int. 6/85.

141. H. Moore to P. Hills 21/4/80; H. Grisewood int. 8/83; M. Richey int. 18/6/89; T. Burns to D. Smith 10/74; T. Burns, *Use of Memory*, p. 163; T. Powell int. 30/4/93; C. Collins int. 25/6/89; B. Moray int. 6/85; P. Hagreen to T. Stoneburner 6/11/74.

142. S. Honeyman int. by P. Orr, TS n.d.; S. Honeyman int. 1/5/95.

NOTE: Works (literary and artistic) by David Jones (DJ) appear directly under title; works by others under author/artist's name

223 fact / false witness
151 modern spoons not metaxu
155 seeing what camera doesn't

the First Field Dressing is futile as frantic seamans shift
bunged to stoves ~~that~~ bulwark, so soon the darking
blood percolates and he dies in your arms, an get
back to that digging cantyer this aint a
bloodywake

      for these dead who soon have their
        burial.clots   heaped
dead for ~~busyoung flag~~ ~~this~~ ~~aued~~ ~~up~~ over
nor time for hassling.
    nor to cless green hounds   containing
    nor nuking Maries with their sealed ~~tinytul~~
    neither anyword spoken
    nor no decent nor ~~orderly~~ ritual sowing of this'e
    nor remembrance of the hardestring
    nor shaving of the head   each
   In these ~~virile's~~ under ~~any~~ tree.
    ~~no one~~ sings hullyhully   Jn XIX
     for the mate   39
    whos blood runs down.   shins
   but conversant his first flare. ~~sings~~
 hangs at ~~it~~ the ~~around~~ high.: top ~~the~~
             new   tuned trees
& white faces ~~to the~~ ~~stand with~~ tilts to ~~dy~~
like china ~~its~~ saucers for it was was almost al
when the trench was digged
and the bright lowR RE to
run out nine between the ~~methodicaly~~
peaced hidden.

2